Housing Disadvantaged People?

Social housing appears to offer a solution for the housing of poor and disadvantaged people. The French 'right to housing' offers this demographic priority in social housing allocation, and even a legal action against the State to obtain a social home. Despite this, France is suffering a long-lasting housing crisis with disadvantaged people having particular difficulties of access, often despite the efforts of local housing actors. This situation is affected by the European Court of Human Rights and EU decisions limiting diverse national housing and rental policies.

Between historic French revolutions and the modern riots, negotiated solutions to social dilemmas emerged. Despite progress in constitutional principles, complex local negotiations still ultimately determine who is housed. Local social landlords, mayors and employee and tenant representatives use their privileges to house their insiders: existing tenants, locals and employees, with rent insufficiently subsidized. 'Insider–outsider' theory is used for an economic analysis of exclusion in social housing allocation: its processes, institutional context and stigmatizing effects. This highlights the spatial effects of 'nimbyism', excluding disadvantaged outsiders, and concentrating them in deprived areas. Simultaneously, urban regeneration reduced affordable housing stock and the requirement for 'social mix' became an excuse to refuse a social home to a particular candidate.

History, comparative law, economic theory and local interviews with housing actors give a detailed picture of what happens in and around French social housing allocation for an interdisciplinary housing policy audience. Constitutional principles appear in an unfamiliar guise as negotiating positions, with the 'right to property' supporting landlords and the 'right to housing' supporting tenants. French debates about the function of social landlords are echoed across Europe and reflected in European policies concerning rights, and the exclusion of disadvantaged minorities.

Jane Ball was a lecturer in French law, property law and contract law at the University of Sheffield. After 14 years in English legal practice she spent another 14 years researching the French housing scene, using an applied mix of public and private law, economic theory and empirical study. She has been a lecturer at Newcastle University since 2011.

Housing and Society series

Edited by Ray Forrest,
School for Policy Studies, University of Bristol

This series aims to situate housing within its wider social, political and economic context at both national and international level. In doing so it will draw on the full range of social science disciplines and on mainstream debate on the nature of contemporary social change. The books are intended to appeal to an international academic audience as well as to practitioners and policymakers – to be theoretically informed and policy relevant.

Housing Disadvantaged People?
Jane Ball

Women and Housing
Patricia Kennett and Chan Kam Wah

Affluence, Mobility and Second Home Ownership
Chris Paris

Housing, Markets and Policy
Peter Malpass and Rob Rowlands

Housing and Health in Europe
Edited by David Ormandy

The Hidden Millions
Graham Tipple and Suzanne Speak

Housing, Care and Inheritance
Misa Izuhara

Housing and Social Transition in Japan
Edited by Yosuke Hirayama and Richard Ronald

Housing Transformations
Shaping the space of 21st century living
Bridget Franklin

Housing and Social Policy
Contemporary themes and critical perspectives
Edited by Peter Somerville with Nigel Sprigings

Housing and Social Change
East-West perspectives
Edited by Ray Forrest and James Lee

Urban Poverty, Housing and Social Change in China
Ya Ping Wang

Gentrification in a Global Context
Edited by Rowland Atkinson and Gary Bridge

Housing Disadvantaged People?
Insiders and outsiders in French social housing

Jane Ball

LONDON AND NEW YORK

First published 2012
by Routledge
2 Park Square, Milton Park, Abingdon, Oxon OX14 4RN

Simultaneously published in the USA and Canada
by Routledge
711 Third Avenue, New York, NY 10017

Routledge is an imprint of the Taylor & Francis Group, an informa business

© 2012 Jane Ball

The right of Jane Ball to be identified as author of this work has been asserted by her in accordance with sections 77 and 78 of the Copyright, Designs and Patents Act 1988.

All rights reserved. No part of this book may be reprinted or reproduced or utilised in any form or by any electronic, mechanical, or other means, now known or hereafter invented, including photocopying and recording, or in any information storage or retrieval system, without permission in writing from the publishers.

Trademark notice: Product or corporate names may be trademarks or registered trademarks, and are used only for identification and explanation without intent to infringe.

British Library Cataloguing in Publication Data
A catalogue record for this book is available from the British Library

Library of Congress Cataloging in Publication Data
Ball, Jane.
Housing disadvantaged people?: insiders and outsiders in French housing; Jane Ball.
  p. cm.
Includes bibliographical references and index.
1. Public housing–France. 2. Low-income housing–France. 3. NImBy syndrome–France. I. Title.
HD 7288.78.F8B35 2012
363.50944–dc22
2011012301

ISBN: 978-0-415-55444-2 (hbk)
ISBN: 978-0-415-55445-9 (pbk)
ISBN: 978-0-203-80324-0 (ebk)

Typeset in Times New Roman PS
by RefineCatch Limited, Bungay, Suffolk

Printed and bound in Great Britain by
CPI Antony Rowe, Chippenham, Wiltshire

Contents

List of tables	viii
List of figures	ix
Acknowledgements	x
Glossary of abbreviations	xi

Introduction		1
	0.1 Social housing and Europe	*2*
	0.2 A failing potential to house the disadvantaged	*3*
	0.3 French social housing in a history of conflict	*5*
	0.4 Insider–outsider theory	*6*
	0.5 Investigating exclusion and inclusion	*7*
1	Social landlords and insider–outsider theory	9
	1.1 Introducing French social housing actors	*10*
	1.2 Introducing social housing allocation	*16*
	1.3 Why insider–outsider theory is relevant	*18*
	1.4 Insider–outsider theory	*22*
	1.5 Conclusion	*33*
2	Exploring the function of social housing	35
	2.1 European social housing	*35*
	2.2 Disadvantage in French social housing	*46*
	2.3 Formulating this study	*50*
	2.4 Conclusion	*56*
3	The historical context: from revolution to rights	58
	3.1 From revolution to rights	*59*
	3.2 The opposition between property and social rights	*63*
	3.3 Social housing and its context	*72*
	3.4 Conclusion	*83*

Contents

4	The right to housing in context	84
	4.1 The legal effects of the right to housing	*85*
	4.2 The right to housing and social mix	*98*
	4.3 Contrasting approaches in France	*105*
	4.4 Conclusion	*110*
5	Complex institutions in the grip of change	112
	5.1 Housing actors in the context of decentralization	*113*
	5.2 Planning, construction and contractualization	*123*
	5.3 Contracting for divergence	*127*
	5.4 Conclusion	*134*
6	Social landlords and their financing problems	136
	6.1 HLM organizations	*137*
	6.2 Insider–outsider theory and rent	*143*
	6.3 Aids to the person and rents	*145*
	6.4 Construction funding and rents	*148*
	6.5 Taxation advantages	*155*
	6.6 Conclusion	*156*
7	The social housing allocation process	158
	7.1 Allocation criteria and demand	*159*
	7.2 Varying regional institutions	*166*
	7.3 The procedure	*171*
	7.4 The allocation commission	*178*
	7.5 Conclusion	*180*
8	'Insiderness' and local actors	183
	8.1 Applying insider–outsider theory	*184*
	8.2 Insiders	*191*
	8.3 Entrants' chances of success	*199*
	8.4 Conclusion	*202*
9	Stigmatization and outsiders	203
	9.1 Which groups tended to be excluded?	*204*
	9.2 Debt and eviction	*206*
	9.3 Household instability and domestic violence	*208*
	9.4 Ethnic minorities and young people	*210*
	9.5 Reviewing exclusionary processes	*221*
	9.6 Conclusion	*226*
10	Housing some of the disadvantaged	228
	10.1 An exclusionary legal process	*229*
	10.2 'Insiderness' in social housing	*235*

10.3 Transparency	*241*
10.4 Social housing and Europe	*244*
10.5 Reform	*251*
10.6 Conclusion	*253*
Appendix 1: methodological detail	257
A1.1 Legal considerations	*257*
A1.2 Survey method and questions	*259*
A1.3 Factors taken into account	*259*
A1.4 The questions asked	*260*
Appendix 2: allocation principles	279
Notes	**281**
Bibliography	**305**
Index	**322**

Tables

1.1	A snapshot of some French and UK housing statistics in 2005	20
2.1	The basic income ceiling for PLUS loans (in Euros) in 2007	47
2.2	The income of households by tenure in 2002	49
3.1	Some conditions of housing per 1,000 French people in 1906	74
5.1	The spread of inter-communality in France	121
6.1	Major features of social landlords during the study	142
6.2	The increase in level of effort to pay rent from 1988 to 2002	147
6.3	The percentage of social tenants receiving housing benefit (APL)	148
6.4	Average social rents per m^2 in 2004 (in Euros)	152
6.5	Government housing expenditure by tenure in 2004	156
9.1	Unemployment for immigrants in 1999	212
9.2	Poverty for immigrants in 1996	213

Figures

1.1	The income of social tenants 1972–2002	12
1.2	Housing tenures in France as a percentage of principal homes	13
1.3	The distribution of social housing in mainland France	14
1.4	The main levels of local governance in France	15
1.5	Typical streams of access to social housing in this study	18
3.1	A schematic view of the public and private courts	62
3.2	Housing construction starts 1954–2002 (in thousands)	82
3.3	Social housing stock by first year of rental 1950–2004	82
4.1	The main hierarchy of principle affecting social housing	90
4.2	The different levels of centrality of public law concepts in France	93
4.3	Barres in Nanterre	101
6.1	Social housing constructed by loan type 2003–5	150
8.1	The structure of households occupying social homes (percentage of tenants)	200
10.1	The perpetuation of the housing crisis	244

Acknowledgements

I would like to thank my supervisors, David Townend, Graham Battersby and David Hughes, together with additional help in Sheffield from Jeremy Scholes and Joanna Shapland, Tony Crook, Phillip Booth, Sue Bowden and Jonathon Perraton.

Many thanks to those who made my empirical study possible, particularly interviewees who took considerable time and trouble, and others who helped: Bernard Vorms, Emeline Baude and Hélène Roque of ANIL; Jean Bosvieux, and Frédérique LaHaye; Patricia Teulet, Dominique Perrot and Francis Chassard of the ADILs; and Jean-Philippe Brouant.

I am also grateful for the help, support, advice, information and materials from the following people: Denise Arbonville, Danielle Ballet, Michelle Bardin, John Bell, Francine Benguigui, Jean-Luc Berho, Sarah Blandy, Natalie Boccodoro, Alain Costa, Martin Davis, Patrick Doutreligne, DAL, all at FEANTSA, Benoit Filippi, Anne-Marie Fribourg, Laurent Ghékière, Barry Goodchild, Henri Jacquot, Jim Kemeny, Padraic Kenna, Jean-Luc Lemaire, Claire Lévy-Vroelant, J. Marie-Josette-Robert, Sarah Monks, V. Rougeot, Jean-Pierre Schaefer, Denis Snower, Christian Tutin and Françoise Zitouni.

Glossary of abbreviations

This contains abbreviations of common terms, including a section on legal sources below (treaties, legislation, codes) with some basic terminology for references.

ADIL	Agence départemental pour l'information sur le logement (Departmental Agency for Information for Housing)
AL	Allocation logement (housing benefit)
ANAH	Agence national de l'habitat (National Agency for the Improvement of Housing)
ANIL	Agence national pour l'information sur le logement (National Agency for Information for Housing)
ANRU	Agence national pour la rénovation urbaine (National Agency for Urban Renovation)
APL	Aide personalisée au logement (Personalized Aid for Housing)
Association	Voluntary body or NGO
CAF	Caisse d'allocations familiales (Family Benefits Office)
CIL	Comité interprofessionnel du logement (Inter-enterprise Housing Committee), collectors of contributions for the *un pourcent logement*
CIOD	Cellule interface offre-demande – the prefectural unit for inter-agency cooperation for allocation in Lyon
Conseil général	Democratic assembly for the *département*
Conseil constitutionnel	Constitutional Council, abbreviated in cases to C. cons.
DAL	Droit au logement – either the right to housing or the NGO of that name
DALO	Droit au logement *opposable* – the right to housing giving rise to a right of action against the State
DCFR	Draft Common Frame of Reference
DDASS	Direction départementale d'action sanitaire et sociale (Departmental Organization for Health and Social Action)

Glossary of abbreviations

DDE	Direction départementale d'équipement (Departmental Organization for Infrastructure), the prefectually controlled services concerned with general housing finance
ECSR	European Committee of Social Rights
ECtHR	European Court of Human Rights
ENHR	European Network for Housing Research
EPCI	Etablissement public de coopération intercommunale (Public Establishment for Inter-communal Cooperation), the corporate body for *communautés*
FEANTSA	Fédération européene des associations travaillant avec les sans-abri (European Federation of Associations Working with the Homeless)
FSL	Fonds de solidarité logement (Fund for Housing Solidarity)
GRIDAUH	Groupement de recherche sur les institutions et le droit de l'amenagement, de l'urbanisme et de l'habitat (Research Grouping for Research on the Institutions and the Law of Development, Urban Planning and Housing (and its environment))
Haut Comité	Haut Comité pour le logement des personnes dévaforisées (High Council for the Housing of Disadvantaged People)
HLM organizations	The largest group of social landlords in France. HLM means *habitations à loyer modéré* (homes at a moderate rent)
Logements intermédiaires	Housing for households with incomes below ceilings which are higher than normal (Table 2.1)
MIILOS	Mission interministérielle d'inspection du logement social (Interministerial Mission for Inspection of Social Housing)
OPAC	Office public d'aménagement concerté (Public Office for Concerted Development) – public HLM organization 1973–2007
OPH	Office public de l'habitat – the single public HLM organization since 2007
OPHBM	OPHLM prior to 1950
OPHLM	Office public d'HLM – public HLM organization 1950–2007
Opposable	A right where there is someone who can be sued (see DALO above)
PDLPD	Plan départemental pour le logement des personnes défavorisées (departmental plan for housing disadvantaged people)
PLA-I	Prêt locatif aidé-intégration (Assisted Rental Loan for Integration)
PLH	Programme local de l'habitat (Local Housing Programme)

Glossary of abbreviations

PLS	Prêt locatif social (Social Housing Loan)
PLUS	Prêt locatif à usage sociale (Rental Loan for Social Use)
Un pourcent logement	One percent housing (The housing funding scheme through which the CIL reserve homes)
RMI	Revenu minimum d'insertion (Minimum Income for Social Insertion), a non-contributory benefit
SAHBM	SAHLM prior to 1949
SAHLM	Société anonyme d'HLM – commercial HLM company
SCOT	Schéma de cohérence territoriale (Scheme for Territorial Coherence), a planning document
SEM	Société d'économie mixte – a public-private joint-venture company which includes social landlords in their number
SIAL	Service interadministratif du logement – the prefectoral service responsible for housing disadvantaged people in Lyon
UESL	Union d'économie sociale pour le logement (now Action logement), parent organization for the CIL. Since a 2009 re-organization, the acronym has been re-used with different wording to describe the organizing corporate body, the Union des entreprises et des salariés pour le logement (Union of Business and Employees for Housing)
USH	Union sociale pour l'habitat (Social Union for Housing), parent organization of HLM and related organizations
ZAC	Zone d'aménagement concerté (Zone for Concerted Development)
ZUS	Zone urbaine sensible (Sensitive Urban Zone)

Abbreviations of legal sources

Treaties

ECHR	European Convention for the Protection of Human Rights and Fundamental Freedoms
RESC	European Social Charter (Revised)
TEU	Treaty of the EU (consolidated treaty during my study)
TFEU	Treaty on the Functioning of the EU (current consolidated treaty)

Constitutions

The 1789 Declaration	Déclaration des droits de l'homme et du citoyen du 26 août 1789
The 1958 Constitution	La Constitution du 4 octobre 1958

Glossary of abbreviations

Legislation

Where sensible the popular names of these statutes are used.

The 1986 Statute	Loi n° 86-1290 du 24 juillet 1986. Rental statute amending the Quillot Act, still containing rules on tenant representation
The 1989 Statute	Loi n° 89-462 du 6 juillet 1989. The current residential rental statute
The Besson Act	Loi n° 90-449 du 31 mai 1990. Statute creating the current right to housing, as amended
La loi contre les exclusions	Loi n° 98-657 du 29 juillet 1998, reinforcing the Besson Act
The DALO Act	Loi n° 2007-290 du 5 mars 2007 (see abbreviations for DALO)
The Quillot Act	Loi n° 82-256 du 22 juin 1986 (repealed). Statute restoring security of tenure for residential tenants which first mentioned the right to housing

Codes

C.A.S.F	Code de l'action sociale et des familles
C. civ.	Code civil
C.C.H	Code de la construction et de l'habitation
C. com.	Code de commerce
C. consom.	Code de la consommation
C. communes	Code des communes
C.G.I.	Code général des impôts
C.G.C.T.	Code général des collectivités territoriales
C. pen.	Code pénal
C. rur.	Code rural
C.S.S.	Code de la sécurité sociale
C. Urb.	Code de l'urbanisme

Some basic legal reference terminology

al. (alinéa)	paragraph	J.O.	Official Journal
arrêt	a court decision	*livre*	book
arrêté	a government order	*loi*	statute
décret	decree	*titre*	title

Introduction

This book takes a long walk though the law, economics, history and practice of social housing allocation in France to discover how and why poor and socially disadvantaged people could be excluded from social housing, despite legislative priorities in their favour. It is a legal study based in economic theory to explain social processes of exclusion. This is supported by interview evidence from the main French local housing actors including: mayors, social landlords, civil servants and voluntary workers.

The necessarily broad and interdisciplinary accumulation of information means that it cannot be presented in a narrowly technical way, so this is a general account directed to a policy audience interested in housing those in housing difficulty. Social housing is often dealt with by lawyers as mainly a matter of the moral and legal principle that people in housing difficulty should be housed. French law is particularly concerned with the provision of a philosophical moral basis for action. It would be possible to fill several volumes with an abstract account of these principles, but this book is concerned with their application. Space requires that principles are only elaborated so far as necessary to show their effects, directed towards an understanding of the economic and legal processes of exclusion.

Social housing can be used anywhere to house the poor and other people having difficulty finding housing. For more than 20 years in France there has been a strongly expressed legislative priority in favour of disadvantaged people for access to social housing. This priority is articulated in statutory form as the 'right to housing' in a 1990 statute known as the 'loi Besson' (Besson Act).[1]

> Guaranteeing the right to housing is a duty of solidarity for the whole of the nation. Every person or family experiencing particular difficulties, notably by reason of insufficiency of financial resources or their conditions of existence, has the right to an aid from the State[2] on the conditions fixed by the present law to obtain access to a decent and independent home or to maintain themselves there…

Introduction

'Disadvantaged people' was a French legal category describing both people unable to afford homes and those having difficulty accessing a home for social or other reasons. This was worthy of study as a potential solution to the problem of housing disadvantaged people. Social housing was thus at the heart of social welfare provision, but many other sorts of people could quite properly access social homes.

In this study, the 'right to housing' could not be taken at face value, because of specific limitations, because of its use as a generic principle regulating several legal areas and because it was in conflict with other principles. The right to housing could also embody the political opposition between tenants and landlords, between capital and the oppressed, that had existed since the revolutionary French upheavals of the past. Legal systems change only slowly and this socialist–capitalist opposition still structured the French legal institutions concerned with allocation. For this reason, it must be shown how this history of struggle affected the law.

Disagreements were now resolved through an invigorating culture of opposition, negotiation and agreement. This history of oppositions and resolution of differences in the welfare system since the 1789 revolution is explained in Chapter 3, which uses a historical institutional approach to assist the understanding of modern law. The French law of allocation was marked by varied and protracted national and local oppositions in ways that the law of England is not.

French national debates about who should benefit from social housing have become important because of increasing European regulation. Amongst the different French models of allocation – housing workers, housing everyone, housing the poor or housing the disadvantaged – which worked best to relieve disadvantage in housing generally?[3] In fact, local housing actors were buffeted by the winds of political and economic practicality, by what could be done in this place, with this history and with this funding. Access of disadvantaged people to social housing in France was variable, limited and patchy. My field study took place in three French regions in 2005–6, underpinned by studying the French law relevant to housing from 1997 until 2011.

The use of insider–outsider theory for social housing requires introduction because it is usually applied to labour markets and demonstrated by quantitative evidence. Also introduced here are the background and context of French social housing and some major issues: the developing European regulation, the potential of French social landlords to house the disadvantaged, the conflicts in rights and how this study tried to make sense of varied local allocation practices using insider–outsider theory.

Social housing and Europe

European social landlords are very diverse, something looked at in Chapter 2, and increasingly affected by European developments. Modern housing rights are exercised within a framework of national, European and global rights. The 1948 Universal Declaration of Human Rights[4] sought to create a set of common values, ensure future peace and avoid the horrors of the Second World War. Article 25 included a reference to the right to housing:

> Everyone has the right to a standard of living adequate for the health and well-being of himself and of his family, including food, clothing, *housing*[5] and medical care and necessary social services, and the right to security in the event of unemployment, sickness, disability, widowhood, old age or other lack of livelihood in circumstances beyond his control. [My emphasis]

The Universal Declaration included both the older civil and political rights and the more recent social and economic rights, but in Europe these are found in separate treaties. The 1950 European Convention on Human Rights (ECHR)[6] and the 1996 European Social Charter (Revised)[7] (RESC) are the regional treaties implementing the Universal Declaration. France was a founding signatory to both those treaties.

There is a tension between these two groups of rights. De Búrca (2005: 4) said 'It seems that the very idea of social and economic rights raises deeply redistributive questions in such a direct and immediate way that it gives rise to sharper political and ideological opposition.' Social housing is affected by conflicts between rights. Some of these conflicts are inherent in the treaties. De Búrca's 'redistributive question' means that cheap rents and protection from eviction limit landlords' rights and profits, and thus the extent of their property rights.[8] As for equality, which finds stronger expression in the French Constitution than in the ECHR,[9] working citizens must shoulder the burden of housing for the poor in unequal ways and some disadvantaged citizens will obtain a social home and others will not.

Despite these conflicts, a European model of social landlord might be emerging, driven by EU policy and the social objectives of the RESC. A 2006 EU competition directive[10] limits state aid for social housing in major ways, but there is an exemption from competition control for housing directed to those in housing need, because this is a service in the general interest.[11] This means we are more likely to see European social landlords with an objective of housing the disadvantaged.

There is a danger that such objectives might effectively enable the housing of only a few needy candidates. Assessing achievement in housing disadvantaged people requires in-depth study of single countries such as this, to compare the reality of access for the disadvantaged to social housing with the national legislative objectives intended to achieve this.

A failing potential to house the disadvantaged

If a country can be judged on the extent of its rights texts and legislation favouring disadvantaged people, France was at the forefront in Europe. There were

Introduction

many mentions of the 'right to housing' in legislation concerning social aid, health, tenancies, planning, and throughout the law related to housing and the protection of residents,[12] because it functioned as a legal objective and as a legislative framework. This did not always give individuals rights to sue anyone. Nonetheless, a more specific objective to house disadvantaged people was compulsorily imposed on social landlords as part of their statutory organizational objectives,[13] and social housing rules gave express priority to these disadvantaged people, particularly vulnerable groups such as people in hostels.[14]

In *FEANTSA* v. *France*,[15] the Federation of European Organizations Working with the Homeless[16] made a collective complaint against France for breach of the European right to housing under Article 31 of the RESC. The European Committee of Social Rights (ECSR) is a quasi-judicial body of experts that hears these complaints and is gradually producing principles on housing standards.[17] Article 31 of the RESC says:

> With a view to ensuring the proper exercise of the right to housing, the parties undertake to take measures designed:
>
> 1. To encourage access to housing of an adequate standard;
> 2. To prevent and reduce the state of homelessness with a view to its gradual elimination;
> 3. To make the cost of housing accessible to people who do not have sufficient resources.

Despite the numerous French texts implementing the national right to housing, in 2007 the ECSR decided that French social housing allocation was malfunctioning. There was no effective recourse for applicants complaining about allocation decisions. There was an insufficient supply of social housing for low-income applicants. In addition, there was little progress in eradicating substandard housing, in protecting people from eviction or rehousing them when evicted, or in measures to assist the homeless.

There were clearly problems in social housing allocation for the disadvantaged. Early in 2007, the French government urgently produced a 2007 statute, known as the DALO (DALO Act).[18] DALO stands for *le droit au logement opposable*. *Droit au logement* means the right to housing and *opposable* means that there is someone to sue. Here the statute creates a right to sue the government for failure to obtain housing, in a new procedure allowing social landlords to be ordered to house them. The implementation of this right to housing[19] and other legislation giving access to social housing will be assessed in this book.

Social housing allocation mechanisms were and still are critical to fulfil the objective of housing disadvantaged people. Social landlords were not the only way disadvantaged people found housing, but the French social landlords described in

Introduction

the next chapter had an increasingly prominent role in policies to provide for them. There were practical reasons for this. French social rents were generally lower than private rents.[20] Social landlords received state subsidy, the classes of people they housed were regulated, and they made little or no profit. There was also a significant mass of social landlords who could provide housing, at 16 per cent of housing stock (USH 2009).

French social housing in a history of conflict

French housing rights for the disadvantaged were seen as conflicting with other constitutional rights and principles, a theme of Chapters 3 and 4. The right to property,[21] particularly, allowed social landlords to refuse applicants. Even the principle of equality[22] could be used to argue that disadvantaged people should not have special privileges, which should be available to all.

After 1990, there was another conflict of principle. French social landlords were obliged to allocate homes to create 'social mix'[23] in order to avoid concentrations of deprivation. This new principle could lead to rejection of the disadvantaged in deprived areas. Other social housing should be constructed elsewhere, but there were increasing tendencies to build this for the better-off. The 2005 riots on social housing estates gave political impetus to social mix policies, particularly directed to breaking up disadvantaged ethnic minority populations.

Disadvantaged people had express priority in social housing allocation, but many other sorts of applicant had lawful access to social housing and could effectively be housed instead of the disadvantaged.[24] These other applicants had to have an income below sometimes generous ceilings.[25] The reality of this broad access was that it could allow local choice in the principle applied to allocation and scope for negotiation between decision-makers about who should be housed.[26]

During the empirical study in 2005–6, there was no unanimity amongst the heterogeneous public and private French social landlord organizations about who should be housed, although they worked together as an effective political lobby. A French government policy of 'housing for all' (Lévy-Vroelant and Tutin 2007: 74) accommodated different local views rather than enforcing a uniform policy. Social housing in the UK, France, the Netherlands, Austria and probably other countries has its origins in the housing of workers, not housing the most disadvantaged (Hughes 2000; Reinprecht *et al.* 2008). It does not follow logically that all social housing will follow the same path from one to the other.

A short history of French social housing in Chapter 3[27] relates how the idea of social housing was originally conceived by socialist utopians but then promoted by conservative nineteenth-century industrialists and philanthropists. It was influenced by the garden cities movement and created by local initiative, predominantly in just a few regions. Social housing was still heterogeneous, including both high quality homes in desirable areas and the large system-built

Introduction

housing estates in ill-favoured out-of-town sites, the *banlieux*.[28] The largest housing estates tended to be in traditional strongholds of communist or socialist local government.

French debates around social housing were deeply marked by a history of revolution and street protest, right up to present day riots on social housing estates. These political debates took place in the context of a decades-long housing crisis.[29] If many people have difficulty obtaining housing, it is less clear that the most disadvantaged should be at the head of the housing queue.

Insider–outsider theory

Insider–outsider theory (Lindbeck and Snower 1988, 2002), with its account of favoured insiders and excluded outsiders, was a good fit for the evidence from interviews to explain the patterns of privileged access to social housing. French local actors involved in social housing allocation each tended to favour access by their own constituency, insiders in a broad sense: social landlords favoured existing tenants, mayors favoured local people and a percentage of vacancies were frequently reserved for employees with sufficient money to pay the rent.

Insider–outsider theory helps explain the economic drivers behind the protection of insiders and consequent exclusion of outsiders from labour markets. In the original theory (Lindbeck and Snower 2002) outsiders do not have a job and do not have the necessary skills or contacts to get employment. Similarly, outsiders excluded from housing are not existing tenants and do not have the necessary record or contacts to find a home.

The theory has many uses for labour markets, using a transaction costs analysis (Williamson 1979) to show how employee-insiders become protected by barriers to access to jobs and barriers to dismissal, generally preventing the hire of rival outsiders, who would work for less. This means an accumulation of rules in their favour.

Tenants can be protected in a similar way by barriers to eviction and to access to housing, directed to preventing insiders being replaced by outsiders who might pay more rent. This is highly desirable for welfare but, if taken to excess, the expense and financial risks of very strong security of tenure can mean that landlords withdraw from the market, a painful policy choice between protection from eviction and losing rental stock.

Exclusion of outsiders in both labour and housing markets causes social exclusion and a process of stigmatization. In the labour market, this is because insiders generally obtain and keep jobs to the detriment of outsiders. In the housing markets this is because insiders obtain and keep rented homes. The process of deterioration of someone who has no home, and its consequence of stigmatization, are clear – a vicious circle. This last application of insider–outsider theory is original, as are some of the modifications to the theory for housing markets, for

Introduction

social housing, for the process of allocation and for the spatial effects of favouring local insiders.[30] Ultimately, excessive protection of tenants or employees is probably not in the interests of insiders themselves, because of adverse effects on the housing market as a whole.

The theory is elaborated in Chapter 1, and throughout the book, in the light of the evidence, although it requires modification for housing markets and more modification for social rented housing. The special characteristics of rental markets include spatial effects by the rejection of non-locals, and the powerful focus of landlords on rent, where the tenant is not just a producer of profit but also the consumer. The application of this theory to housing has not received sufficient academic attention, given the strong linkages between housing, employment and the wider economy.

In social housing, there is an argument to make about the application of economics in an area apparently outside the market, and then there are extra varieties of local insiders in a wider sense – locals and workers. Analysing private rental markets is relatively simple because landlords alone could exclude disadvantaged outsiders. Despite their extra constraints, the French legal institutions involved in social housing allocation resembled those found in labour markets, because there was representation of insider-tenants and mayors in allocation processes, which facilitated this analysis.

The combined effect of local representatives' choices and current financial incentives was to exclude disadvantaged outsiders, particularly those who were not broadly defined insiders: existing tenants, workers and local people. Funding for the rents of disadvantaged people was inadequate and social landlords funding was strongly oriented to promoting construction or major improvement. The perverse effects of this construction culture to solve the housing crisis will be shown. Economic analysis can help with the adjustment of incentives, processes and representation for reform to assist the disadvantaged.

Investigating exclusion and inclusion

In my field study, it became clear that the social housing allocation process could seriously interfere with statutory objectives to house the disadvantaged, who were often excluded from social housing. Hostel-dwellers and the homeless enjoyed explicit priority in social housing allocation, but were the most stigmatized and least likely to easily access social housing, there being a series of other groups in difficulty.

French social housing has a role in housing the poor, but it was surprisingly difficult to work out the extent of this. The statistics were frequently far from clear and are explored in Chapter 2. Driant (2002) found that three-quarters of the people within the bottom 30 per cent of incomes did not live in social housing. Despite this generality, there was striking diversity in practices between the regions, and within

Introduction

regions. Some *communes* had housed disadvantaged people on an industrial scale but were often now excluding new disadvantaged applicants following regeneration projects.[31] This picture was complicated by an ongoing process of decentralization, which might empower local actors more and the outcome of which is still unclear. Will local actors become more altruistic or better organized and with more self-determination, or will the local tendencies to exclusion be reinforced?

Bourgeois (1996: 30) said that the allocation system was patterned by common institutions, financial incentives and law across France, although the results of the allocation processes varied, even between neighbouring *communes*. This was still true during my study, and Bourgeois's insight into procedure allowed the study of areas which produced dissimilar outcomes in social housing allocation. This also suggested the structuring importance of law and institutions for allocation, if not results. This study of a complex procedure and of local politics would not have been possible without her work in this politically sensitive and difficult-to-research area.

Bourgeois (1996: 8) raised serious criticisms of social housing allocation:

> The present functioning of the local system of social housing brings an inequality of access to housing according to the access routes used, as well as a different treatment of tenants according to the legal form of organization and according to the site. What is more it creates exclusion.

Her qualitative study provided a detailed account of local manoeuvring between interested parties around 1990. A different explanation of the exclusionary tendencies of French social housing allocation was found in insider–outsider theory. Lindbeck and Snower (2002) also raise questions about the unequal bargaining power between insiders and outsiders.

Housing problems are multifactorial but, on the face of it, this is a description of policy failure. France has a rich and innovative legal culture, both at national and local levels. This makes study of France rewarding, and makes it more likely that the right to housing can produce a more coherent scheme of assistance for disadvantaged people with time and new ideas, such as insider–outsider theory applied to housing.

1 Social landlords and insider–outsider theory

The extent to which social landlords can alleviate the problems of access to housing for poor and disadvantaged people depends primarily on social housing allocation – on who they house. Article L. 441-1 of the Code de la construction et de l'habitation (C.C.H.) provides priority for the disadvantaged in specific allocation rules. These rules will fix:

> the general criteria for priority for the allocation of homes, notably in favour of disabled people or families having a dependent in a situation of disability, in favour of people who are poorly housed, disadvantaged or suffering particular housing difficulties for financial reasons or relating to their conditions of existence as well as people in hostels or temporarily housed in transitional establishments and homes.

The major allocation rules and principles are translated in Appendix 1 (p. 257). These were the rules during my study in 2005–6,[32] and these rules still echo the right to housing, already quoted,[33] but the priority in favour of disadvantaged people was more limited than it first appeared: there were limitations and conflicts with other principles such as property, equality and social mix (more fully described in Chapters 3, 4 and 7), and there were other target populations. There were also conflicts with the interests of the representatives of insiders involved in the allocation process.[34] The allocation process itself was difficult and complicated to negotiate.[35]

Social landlords had strong objectives to construct housing, a policy which in practical terms reduced access to housing for the disadvantaged overall. The law had an accumulation of incentives from successive governments encouraging construction to solve the French housing crisis. Unfortunately, this had effects that included the handing over of control of allocation to local contributing parties, increasing rents, and reduction of cheap housing stock. This incentive structure forced landlords to consider rent returns first and foremost to service construction

Social landlords and insider-outsider theory

loans, adversely affecting the candidature of underfunded disadvantaged people, as explained in Chapter 6.

My field study, outlined in Chapter 2, found that many disadvantaged groups had difficulties accessing French social housing, such as single mothers, ethnic minorities, those in financial difficulty and particularly those in hostels. This was at odds with the sentiments expressed in the 'right to housing' and the apparent priority in allocation rules.

The institutional and allocation arrangements are explained in general outline in this chapter, introducing the *dramatis personnae* of local actors and the allocation process. Social housing had its roots in the aftermath of the eighteen and nineteenth century revolutions. French social landlords have a long and honourable record of construction to meet popular housing need, but have faced new challenges in recent years, not least the riots perpetrated by youths in the most deprived estates. The rest of this chapter sets out insider–outsider theory, adapting this labour market theory for housing markets.

This study takes the unambiguous viewpoint that the disadvantaged should be able to find housing somewhere. It does not matter if they are not accommodated in social housing, so long as there are other options, but several interviewees said that French private rented property was also socially exclusionary.

The success of French social landlords might be explained in terms of different purposes, but the objective of housing the disadvantaged attracts national funding and exemptions from EU competition policy, and this is explored in Chapter 2. European interest in social housing means the French debates about allocation policy are of wider interest for harmonization and regulation, including regulation within human rights. The relative effectiveness of the variable models of French social housing allocation thus has more widespread importance.

1.1 Introducing French social housing actors

The application of insider–outsider theory here cannot be properly understood without looking first at what it is applied to. Social landlords were founded in both the UK and France in the second half of the nineteenth century in a broadly similar history. French private social landlords first obtained funding privileges in 1894.[36] These social landlords were private limited-profit organizations, 'companies for good value housing' or Sociétés d'habitations à bon marché (SAHBMs). A public form of social landlord, the Office public d'HBM (OPHBM), followed from 1912.[37] Social landlords were influenced by the UK garden cities movement, which promoted green spaces and urban planning. French thinkers took this up at the beginning of the twentieth century and adapted these ideas to become part of France's movement for urban design and planning (Magri 1995).

HBM organizations were renamed HLM organizations (*habitations à loyer modéré* or houses at a moderate rent) in 1950. In 2002, HLM organizations

Social landlords and insider-outsider theory

were again rebranded as 'organismes de l'habitat social'[38] (social housing organizations), although they are still 'HLM organizations' in legislation. These changes might suggest a problem with their public image related to difficulties in problem estates.[39]

French HLM organizations have always had an important role as builders. They initially built homes primarily for purchase by workers, and still build homes for sale.[40] They had a major role in the post-war reconstruction of France and strategic urban development generally.[41] Construction is a strategy to meet housing need, but French construction incentives can impact adversely on the reception of disadvantaged people. An example is how new construction and improvement resulted in increased rents, which were not fully compensated by benefits.[42]

1.1.1 The organization of social landlords

L'Union sociale de l'habitat (USH) was the umbrella organization for the six main families of HLM organization.[43] Only three of these types of organization were important as social landlords in 2005–6, with others generally providing homes for sale. In this book, 'social landlord' generally means these three important types of HLM organization.[44] There are now 276 public and 281 private social landlords (USH 2010).

During my study, there were two kinds of public HLM organization: the 1912 Office public d'HLM (OPHLM) and the more modern Office public d'aménagement concerté (OPAC) created in 1971.[45] There is now only one type of public social landlord (p. 141).

The main private social landlords were the Sociétés anonyme d'HLM (SAHLMs). These were a specially adapted commercial form of company, with severely limited possibilities of distributing profits.[46] French housing is rather prone to acronyms, so there is a glossary (p. xi) for when these are used repeatedly. In many cases, acronyms are more commonly used than full names.

1.1.2 Social landlords' social mission

Despite different detailed rules, public and private social landlords had similar regulation in the C.C.H., and the same allocation principles,[47] with priority for disadvantaged people – a public policy orientation confirmed in government literature and research.[48]

Housing disadvantaged people was not the only objective of social housing, either historically or today. In 1954, social landlords' longstanding objective of housing workers was changed to add 'people of little fortune',[49] but the objective of housing workers was not removed until the early 1970s. There was no obligation on social landlords to house the most disadvantaged until relatively recently, when

Social landlords and insider-outsider theory

the Geindre report (1990) promoted reform in the loi Besson (Besson Act; see Introduction, p. 1).

French social housing candidates did not have to be poor or needy. Social landlords' mission at the time included: '... to improve the housing of people on a modest income or the disadvantaged.'[50] Those on a 'modest income' were generally defined as people within the three lowest income deciles, representing 37 per cent of the population (Ballain 2005). Even above this limit, anyone lawfully resident in France could apply for social housing anywhere in France, provided their income was below income ceilings.[51]

Amzallag and Taffin (2003: 110) said that social landlords housed the poor but did not succeed so well in housing the very poor. In 2002, 37 per cent of social tenants were poor (Figure 1.1). Nonetheless the distribution of social tenants' incomes shows a continuing presence of better-off households, and a minority of tenants under the bottom quartile of income.

The capacity of French social housing to house the poor also depended on the percentage of social housing stock, as shown in Figure 1.2. Social housing stock declined sharply up to 1995, but then maintained market share up to 2005, when social housing comprised 18.6 per cent of French principal homes. This declined again to 16 per cent of principal homes by 2008 (USH 2009). In practical terms, some of the poor are housed in private rented housing, 24.7 per cent of principal homes. From the 1990s, programmes of tax relief and subsidy encouraged private

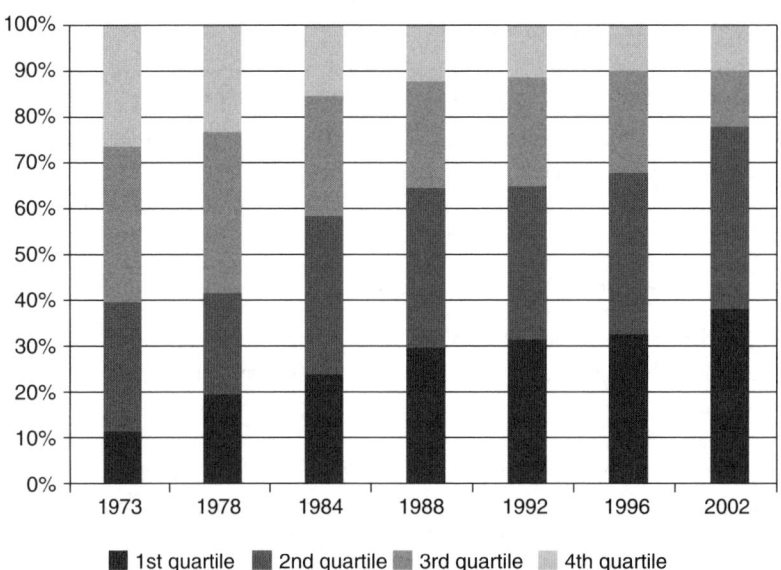

1.1 The income of social tenants 1972–2002. Source: INSEE (2002).

Social landlords and insider-outsider theory

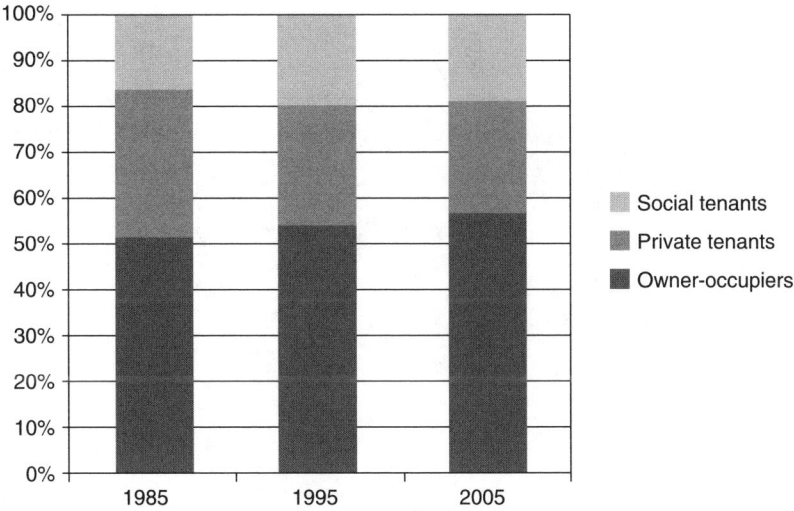

1.2 Housing tenures in France as a percentage of principal homes.
Source: EPLS (2005).

renting and in 2005–6 there were around two million small private landlords.[52] Owner occupancy had steadily increased to 56.6 per cent.

Social housing allocation was also inevitably affected by its uneven distribution across France. Figure 1.3 shows that French social housing was concentrated in particular regions, with more towards the north and east and much less towards the south, so social housing can be sometimes simply unavailable.

Generally statistics and law in this book cover the period of 2005–6, unless it is clear that another period is being discussed, because this is the period of the empirical study, to show how local decision-makers responded to the legislation then current. There will also be comment on later major legal developments. French law changes rapidly, but basic power structures and procedures change much more slowly, so the empirical study is still relevant.

1.1.3 Local government involvement

From 1911, local government bodies took the initiative in founding public social landlord companies[53] and were still involved in allocation. Consequently, the basic structure of local government should be explained, together with the role of other actors (see Chapter 5 for more detail). Figure 1.4 is a schematic representation of French local government. This has a double structure, being split between elected local bodies, shown on the right-hand side of the diagram, and the nominated local representatives of the central State, shown on the left.

13

Social landlords and insider-outsider theory

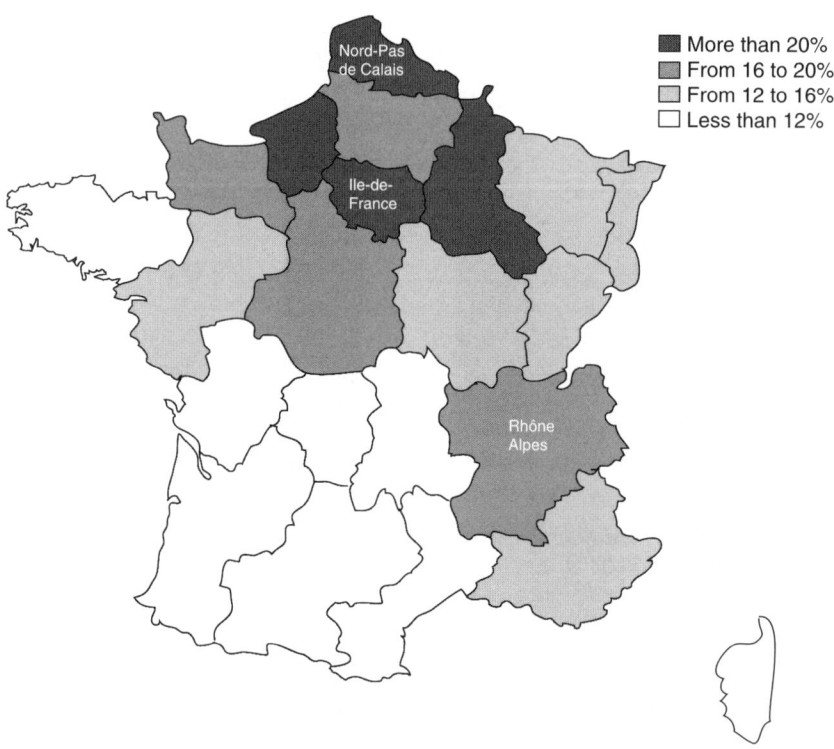

1.3 The distribution of social housing in mainland France. Adapted from Direction des Études Financières et Economiques (2005).

French local governance was characterized by a multiplicity of local government bodies, each possessing rights or powers affecting housing, although few had significant housing duties. There was fragmentation of powers and budgets, although local actors could act together. Public social landlords could be attached to any level of local government.[54] A social landlord might be controlled by one local authority, whilst another one financed its homes elsewhere. During the study, reduced central funding made local authority support indispensible.

The State was primarily responsible for guaranteeing the right to housing for the disadvantaged (see quote on p. 1). The State generally refers to the central state, which also had a local presence through departmental and regional prefects, an old and prestigious office. The prefect was nominated by government and charged with ensuring the legality of local decisions, although this power had reduced with decentralization.

The local prefects implemented State policies, including responsibility for housing. In theory, departmental prefects were entitled to access 25 per cent of all social housing vacancies for disadvantaged people, plus 5 per cent to house civil

Social landlords and insider-outsider theory

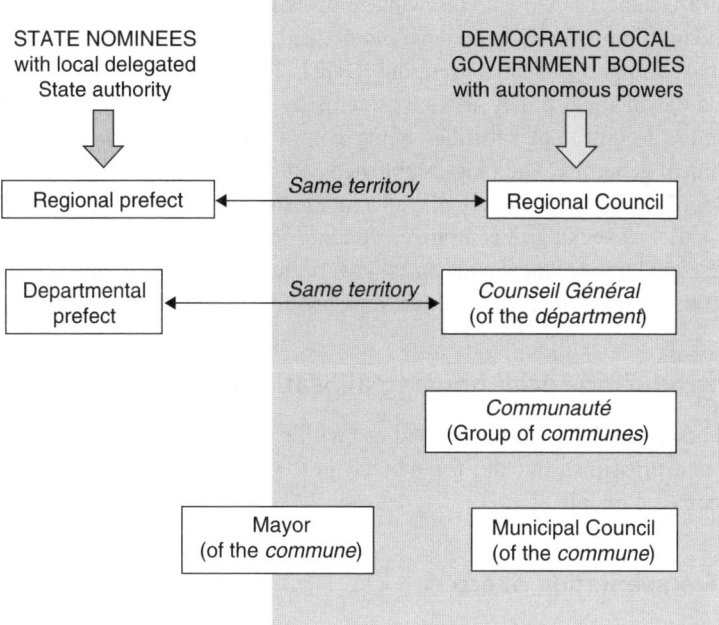

1.4 The main levels of local governance in France.

servants.[55] This 'prefectural contingent' had fallen into disuse in most areas,[56] although the new 2007 right of action against the government might have partly revived this.[57]

In Figure 1.4, the main democratic local councils are listed in descending order of size: region, *département*, *communauté*, and *commune*. The large cities of Paris, Marseilles and Lyon have yet another lower level, the *arrondissement*, and were given their own mayors (with limited powers) in 1982.[58] None of these councils were hierarchically inferior to each other and all could intervene in housing.[59]

The support of the mayor was essential for a successful local housing policy. Mayors were the executive officer of the *commune*, the smallest local government unit (unless subdivided into *arrondissements* in large cities). At the same time, they were also the local representative of the central State under the prefect. Mayors had multiple roles in social housing, including sitting on the committees which made local allocation decisions, and had influence through their power to grant planning permission or finance.[60] This could promote or inhibit access for the disadvantaged.

A new local government body had recently become important, the *communauté*, a group of *communes* encouraging mayors to work together. France had 36,000 *communes* but protracted urbanization and rural depopulation meant that around 28,000 had populations of less than 2,000, a major coordination problem

(Bernard-Gélabert 2004: 5). Following reforms in 1999, 87.3 per cent of people in mainland France lived in a *communauté*, and 93.1 per cent of *communes* had agreed to form part of such a grouping (DGCL 2009).

All areas of local policy will be affected by decentralization of power, with greater local control of subsidies being contracted to *communautés* and local government generally. The long-established *communauté urbaine* of Lyon, which includes 55 *communes*, already played a major role in coordinating local housing policy and was seeking decentralized funding in 2005. There was thus a multi-layered complexity of local and central government because so many actors could intervene. Central Lyon, for example, now had five layers of local government.[61]

1.2 Introducing social housing allocation

Social housing allocation was played out within the framework of constitutional rights and principles but the fragmented procedure itself caused difficulty for disadvantaged people.

1.2.1 Fragmentation of access

The organization of access to social housing differed between regions, but there were commonalities. My field study, explained in the next chapter, found that entry to the allocation process tended to be controlled by three actors: the prefect was entitled to process applications for 30 per cent of vacancies; local authorities processed up to 20 per cent; and up to 50 per cent of vacancies were reserved for employees by agreement. Application could be made to the prefecture, to any social landlord or to any actor reserving access rights.

The prefects obtained access for their 'contingent' as of right, but other local actors could reserve the right to propose candidates for social housing in return for subsidy, such as loans, cash gifts, the transfer or lease of building plots, help with interest rates or guarantees for construction loans.[62] Most social homes were constructed with loans from publicly owned banks and guarantees against non-payment were essential, usually from local government bodies. In return for guarantees, local government could negotiate to reserve a proportion of the homes constructed. Consequently, these local reservations were common.

Social housing vacancies were reserved for contributing employees through a national scheme. Post-war, a voluntary scheme to assist the housing effort allowed employers to deduct 1 per cent from their total salaries bill, still sometimes known as the '*un pourcent logement*'. This contribution, now compulsory, amounts to 0.95 per cent of the wages bill of private businesses with ten or more employees.[63] Around three million employees contributed (UESL undated). Employers also contributed, because the wages charged with the levy included employers' social contributions and payroll taxes.

This income was used for several causes. Although 0.50 per cent of funds automatically went to national welfare funds, some of the remainder was important for social housing, either through local housing assistance schemes or reservation of social housing places. The contributions were collected locally by organizations coordinated nationally by l'Union d'economie sociale pour le logement (UESL), which recorded an income of €3.7 billion in 2007.[64]

The most important collectors of contributions were the Comités interprofessionnels du logement (CIL). All collectors, including employers themselves, were allowed to use their collected funds locally. Local schemes included the reservation of up to 50 per cent of social homes for contributing employees; in such cases, the local CIL providing the funding had a right to receive housing applications.

1.2.2 The allocation process

The allocation process had both multiple access points and multiple stages. A two-stage process of allocation followed naturally from the autonomy of social landlords: one decision by people receiving applications, then another decision by the landlord. There might be a conflict of interests between these parties. The landlord needed the payment of rent, a well-behaved tenant to fit in with existing tenants, and to preserve the value of their assets. This tempered landlords' mission to house the disadvantaged. A public authority might seek housing for the most disadvantaged, perhaps with a record of debt or even a criminal record. This asked for a reversal of these normal landlord criteria.

In France, there was a third procedural stage. Typically, the applicant's written application passed through the hands of the receiving actor, then on to the social landlords for checking and, finally, went before the *commission d'attribution* (allocation commission). This seven-member committee made the final and, theoretically, the only allocation decision on behalf of the social landlord.[65] Allocation commissions were intended to make allocation more transparent. However, these were locally decentralized and included local interests such as mayors and tenant representatives.

An extra stage of the allocation process never increases applicants' chances, giving another opportunity for rejection or delay. Figure 1.5 illustrates a typical French allocation process, with three main streams of application progressing to the allocation commission. The social landlord does not appear in the diagram, because they were officially represented by the allocation commission. Despite this, social landlords still had an important role in processing applications, and a greater role where there were no reservations of vacancies or if the prefectural stream was inactive.

Disadvantaged people did not necessarily have the information or the literacy to apply in the right place, or in the correct written form in an unforgiving

Social landlords and insider-outsider theory

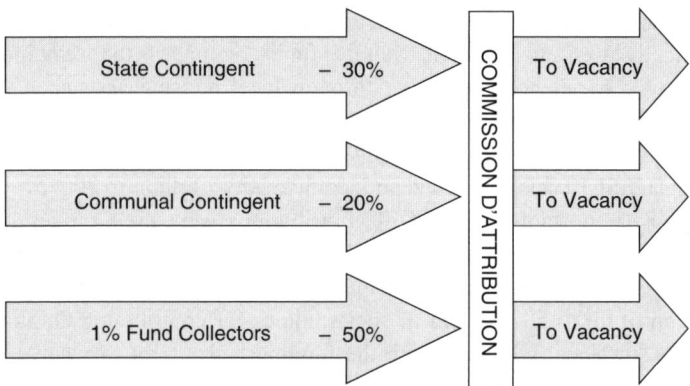

1.5 Typical streams of access to social housing in this study.

bureaucratic process. The complexity of the process could be mitigated by local initiatives, and efforts could be made to accommodate need by extra support.[66]

1.3 Why insider–outsider theory is relevant

Insider–outsider theory is a labour market theory drawing attention to an uncomfortable problem. It is clear that cheaper rents and strong security of tenure are desirable but can reduce the profits of landlords to the extent that they withdraw from letting or cannot repair their properties. This dilemma is not new and in France, differences between landlords and tenants concerning the level of rents and security are now played out within a legal framework oriented to resolving these conflicts by negotiation. Ideally, this study would have been preceded by a simpler general study of the application of insider–outsider theory in rental markets compared to labour markets. This was not possible but would reward study.

Both existing workers and tenants are insiders who have an economic advantage enabling them to negotiate privileges, although some of these negotiations can also benefit disadvantaged people. Negotiations can produce welfare benefits through social contributions to welfare, places in social housing and less likelihood of eviction. Unfortunately, the interests of socially comfortable insiders and disadvantaged outsiders do not always lie in the same direction. In limited housing stock in conditions of excess demand, favouring one group means excluding another.

Social progress in rights is assumed in French constitutional and administrative law in a ratchet effect (Dubois 2005: 335). The creation of the right to housing quoted above is an example of this progress. In the EU too, there are the *acquis communautaires* (the body of EU law), recording the progress of the union, such as in consumer rights, from which there should be no retreat. It is an

Social landlords and insider-outsider theory

attractive idea that everyone should advance socially together towards a peaceful and prosperous future. There is no doubt that the conditions of nearly everyone in France have improved through social provision of all kinds since the Second World War.[67]

Insider–outsider theory has two particular advantages for a legal account of social housing allocation. First, this is essentially a theory of economic and political power fitting well with both the housing policy literature and the national law. Kemeny (2006: 8) described the power relationship of landlords, tenants and the State as an 'iron triangle', which usefully described these power relationships in France. Second, insider–outsider theory describes the normal microeconomic process of social housing whereby insiders obtained advantages, but it can also suggest ways in which the adverse effect of this on the disadvantaged could be mitigated.

The accumulated privileges of both French tenants and workers included their representation rights within the social allocation process with other interested local groups.[68] This, in turn, could allow exclusion of outsiders or groups felt locally to be unattractive from access to social housing. This exclusion was not invariable, but merely a tendency.

1.3.1 A background of crisis and struggle

It was, and is, difficult to work out the extent of housing problems for the disadvantaged in France, with rival accounts, statistical difficulties and provision varying from area to area.[69] When the severity of the difficulties became clear; insider–outsider theory provided an explanation, particularly since the theory predicts general housing market difficulties.[70]

France had been suffering a housing crisis ever since this study began in 1997. There had been reports to Parliament[71] and news of housing inadequacy from the *associations*, non-governmental voluntary organizations. The Fondation Abbé Pierre[72] publishes annual reports on housing difficulty. Its 2005 report showed overflowing hostels which blocked any more access, young people unable to find homes, hidden homeless staying with relatives, adverse consequences for the disadvantaged from urban renewal, a lack of new social housing, inadequate aids and lack of coordinated decentralization in an 'implosion of policies in favour of the housing of disadvantaged people' (Fondation Abbé Pierre 2005: 217). In protest at the situation, the militant squatters' organization, DAL (Droit au logement), staged regular demonstrations and sit-ins (Batiactu 2005, 2006c).

This sense of crisis had a long history. France had substantial housing problems after the Second World War, following housing damage in both World Wars and inadequate construction between the wars.[73] Later, Castells (1977) argued that a satisfactory housing supply to resolve the crisis was not generally possible without State intervention. This Marxist analysis supported the French post-war tradition of subsidy for all housing.

Social landlords and insider-outsider theory

The scale of the modern crisis was difficult to judge, not because observers were wrong, but because information was harnessed to political opposition between left and right. This opposition was reflected in the legal mechanisms governing housing and within constitutional rights. France has a philosophical tradition perceiving conflict between the right to property for landlords and the right to housing supporting tenants and the disadvantaged, which is explained in Chapters 3 and 4.

French property owners have always relied on the absolute nature of their property rights in the French constitution to resist claims for increased tenants' rights.[74] Opposing this, DAL, campaigning against homelessness, proposed that eviction should not be allowed without rehousing, a powerfully redistributive position.[75] The situation of the disadvantaged was presented with particular force within this tradition of robust debate.

In England, in contrast, there had been no such extreme sense of crisis. The Barker Report (2004) argued that there was insufficient housing to meet future needs and raised the political profile of housing.[76] Nevertheless, the sense of crisis in France seemed more acute. However, France had a similar housing profile to the UK (see Table 1.1), with a similar population, lower population density, a similar number of people per home, larger new homes[77] and a much higher rate of construction. It puzzled French people, spoken to outside interviews,[78] why their crisis was so resistant to effort, and why there was then no such apparent crisis in the UK.

This raised a meta-question as to whether there was a distributional problem within French social housing that was contributing to the crisis. If social housing was distributed according to whether people were insiders, outsiders would not be sufficiently provided for. There might be insufficient cheap and accessible housing, rather than insufficient housing overall.

Table 1.1 A snapshot of some French and UK housing statistics in 2005

	France		The UK
Population (thousands)	60,561		60,035
Population per sq km²	110		246
Average useful floor space per occupied dwelling (m²)			
Dwellings completed in:			
1995	7.0		3.4
2000	6.4		3.1
2005	6.0	2003	3.2
Average no. of persons per occupied dwelling in 2000	2.4		2.3

Source: Ministry of Infrastructure of the Italian Republic and Federcasa (2006).

1.3.2 A late explanation for social exclusion

The importance of insider–outsider theory only became clear after the field study. A central objective of the study was to see if criticisms of allocation made by Bourgeois (1996) for the period 1988–90 were still true. She argued that opacity of process concealed the diversion of allocation legislation from its purpose: 'Opacity seems to be a condition for the autonomy and the profitability of management of most of the organizations.'(Bourgeois 1996: 223). There were improved statistics on the occupancy of social homes and more effective inspection by 2005, but the process was still opaque, often because of its complexity.

Although Bourgeois's procedural criticisms were often still true during my field study, her theoretical findings did not fit the data from the study. Bourgeois's central analysis was that public social landlords were motivated principally by profit and public social landlords principally by politics. This provided the overarching structure of her study but was problematic because most social landlords in 2005–6 had variable motives, not easily fitting this simple dichotomy. Both public and private social landlords now had mixed motives, including major concerns for both finance and politics, and there were other local factors (explored in the next chapter).

The theoretical dichotomy between public authorities acting in the general interest and private bodies' concern for profit is well-established. Hayek (1960) particularly placed altruistic motivations in non-market situations, whilst self-interest was suited to the market in the wider world. Discussion of the public–private divide is also found in the rental market literature concerning commodification of housing (Topalov 1987; Esping-Andersen 1990; Harloe, 1995; Kemeny 2006).

Decommodification is associated with the public sector, where the market is excluded. Esping-Andersen (1990: 21) said:

> If social rights are given the legal and practical status of property rights, if they are inviolable, and if they are granted on the basis of citizenship rather than performance, they will entail a decommodification of the status of the individual vis-à-vis the market.

This chapter will argue that the market does affect French social housing allocation because insider–outsider theory only concerns limited aspects of market behaviour.

Decommodification suggests clear distinctions between the public and private sectors. Social landlords were affected by these distinctions, but all were now bound by similar sets of rules based on type of activity.[79] All French social landlords were now part of a third sector with one foot in the market and the other in requirements of the State. Their financial and political motivations were more than usually tangled up, increasingly so in the face of financial constraints requiring economies.

Bourgeois (1996) complained about the commercialization of the organization of social landlords, as putatively involving a predominance of profit over public service. During my field study, a housing manager in either organization could be in a broadly similar position with similar training.[80] Public and private social landlords had similar financial and political limitations. No social landlord could either ignore the bottom line, or fail to pursue current government incentives and negotiate the sponsorship or permissions needed to construct.

A different theoretical basis for patterns of local social inclusion and exclusion was needed. Insider–outsider theory fitted the evidence of interviews and described a series of recognizable effects in my field study. The theory also provided an overarching structure to explain the general behaviour of actors in excluding socially disadvantaged outsiders by preferring insiders. This is not a technical account of economics but a qualitative framework, explaining major features of the social housing process. The theory is only a partial explanation for exclusion, because housing policy enjoyed some success.

1.4 Insider–outsider theory

Insider–outsider theory (Lindbeck and Snower 1988, 2002) can explain how French rented and social housing markets work. This section introduces the theory, showing:

- the ways landlords in general favoured existing insider-tenants who had a series of privileges
- how collective bargaining increased tenants' rights
- how outsiders became stigmatized
- the adverse effect of this on the market
- how this situation was reinforced by social norms supporting the housing of insiders.

It seems likely that there are special effects in housing markets compared to labour markets.

Insider–outsider theory does not distinguish between public and private markets in its account of power balances, although sufficient aspects of the market must survive public regulation for this economic theory to apply. There were multiple French groups effectively sharing the landlords' ownership rights. This complication of access and how local groups favoured their own insiders required explanation.

Insider–outsider theory has already been used to describe rental markets, although generally fairly briefly and dealt with by analogy. Berry and Hall (2005) used the theory as part of a conceptual framework re-organizing investment in low-cost housing in Australia, to take advantage of landlords' preferences for insiders. Malpezzi (1996) noted the exclusionary effects of local policies that favoured insiders on racial segregation, something also prominent in France. Dogge and Smeets (2007) found that favouring insider-tenants exacerbates housing shortage. Lux (2006) observed exclusionary housing practices by local mayors in Czechoslovakia, as in France. In a general metaphor, Grear (2003) described insiders and outsiders, concerning land, without reference to economic theory at all.

In this way, insider–outsider theory lends itself easily to an analogy between employment and rental markets, but it is rewarding to return to its basic features and to look at aspects peculiar to rental markets. The unusual combination of economics, law and sociological study in this book can identify the legal mechanisms which insiders can draw on to obtain privileges and how outsiders are consequently excluded.

An advantage of economic theory is that this is not a simple question of moral disapproval but describes a tendency produced by economic circumstances, which can be changed or displaced to an extent. This approach can be supported by quantitative economic data, not attempted here. In European labour markets, this empirical process has already led to some reform (OECD 1993, 1998).

1.4.1 The basic model and transaction costs

Karl Llewellyn observed in 1931 that a legalistic approach to transactions could obstruct the object of the transaction itself (Llewellyn 1931). The costs of transactions alter the economics of activities; this affects how people organize themselves – a theory developed by Williamson (1979, 1981). A transaction costs approach was applied to 'hiring and firing' in labour markets by Lindbeck and Snower in insider–outsider theory (1988, 2002). Transaction costs of any kind include not just the financial costs but search and information costs, negotiation costs, and the costs of implementing and enforcing the resulting agreements (Bergh and Camesasca 2006).

This account will show that these transaction costs were very high in the complex, negotiated French social housing allocation system. Williamson (1981: 574) commented that, 'the governance implications of transaction cost analysis will be incompletely realized in non-commercial enterprises, in which transaction cost economizing entails the sacrifice of other valued objectives'. It would be hoped that these valued objectives included housing disadvantaged people, although there were others, such as local consultation.[81]

Insider–outsider theory concerns employers' and landlords' profits. In labour markets, it is cheaper for employers to retain employees than suffer the transaction costs of 'hiring and firing'.[82] For tenants, it is cheaper for landlords to retain tenants than suffer the costs of eviction and recruitment of a new tenant (Lindbeck and Snower 2002: 6). In both cases, the costs and losses of removing them are a deduction from profit, a pure financial loss and to be avoided. Someone seeking employment will have to work for less to compensate for this loss, or someone seeking a tenancy will have to offer more money or be a better candidate. Existing employees and tenants are 'insiders'.

These costs of hiring and firing employees are 'transaction costs', which give workers bargaining power to negotiate for higher wages and better conditions, exploiting employers' reluctance to recruit outsiders on account of the financial losses this would involve (Lindbeck and Snower, 2002: 8). This toehold can allow employees to ratchet up their protection because it becomes increasingly expensive to remove them.

Employers will consider the known productivity of existing workers before hiring and firing them. The extra costs of taking on outsiders, who are not their employees, and 'entrants' are a risk to this productivity. Entrants are people well qualified to replace insiders, defined by Lindbeck and Snower (2002: 6) as people 'who hold jobs likely to lead to insider status'. This means they are more likely to be hired. Both outsiders and entrants also suffer from a relative lack of information about their productivity compared to insiders. This information asymmetry is a general problem (Oswald 1986), supporting employers' existing preferences for insiders.

Similarly, in rental markets, the landlord avoids the costs of 'hiring and firing' insider-tenants because the transaction costs of eviction and recruitment of an outsider (a prospective tenant) are an irrecoverable loss of profit. Like employers, landlords also will consider the rental productivity of existing tenants before recruiting or evicting and then weigh up the potential loss of profit for a bad choice of tenant. 'Entrants' are people who are already tenants elsewhere and likely to obtain a new tenancy, probably with a good record of payment and behaviour, to adapt Lindbeck and Snower's above definition. Again, both outsiders and entrants are a risk to the landlord's profits, due to a relative lack of information about them. Consequently, landlords prefer to retain existing tenants than seek new ones for practical financial reasons.

Lindbeck and Snower (2002: 8) said:

> To see why labor turnover costs are the ultimate source of insiders' market power, it is useful to recognize that a firm generally has two alternative partners in wage negotiations: the insiders and the outsiders. Labor turnover costs determine the degree of substitutability between these two alternative negotiations. The smaller are the firm's labor turnover costs …, the more profitable it is for the firm to stop bargaining with its insiders and start bargaining with the outsiders instead.

For rental markets the landlord has a choice between negotiating with the insider-tenant and the outsider. The individual insider always has some advantage over outsiders. If transaction costs are low then the landlord is more likely to choose

Social landlords and insider-outsider theory

the outsider. The balance between insiders and outsiders can thus be affected by outside factors, such as how government policy and subsidy affect the 'recruitment' of tenants by allocation, as considered in this study.

1.4.2 Collective bargaining

Lindbeck and Snower (2002: 11) suggested that unionization increases insider advantage:

> ... The greater is union density in an industry, the more leverage unions are able to give insiders in their threats of obstructive activity under bargaining disagreement, and thus the greater the bargaining surplus and the higher the resulting insider wages.

Trade unions are involved variously in harassment, obstruction and cooperation with employers to improve their position relative to outsiders who might work for less.

The collective representation of employees can thus increase their bargaining power over time (Sanfey 1993). Lindbeck and Snower (2002: 8) said: 'Firms are reluctant to replace their high-wage unionized employees by low-wage non-unionized employees because it is expensive to do so.' How do insiders secure their position? Employees might indulge in obstructive activity to protect themselves and so the employer might think about removing them. This is expensive, because of the loss of known productivity plus the costs of hiring and firing, particularly trying to fire all of them if on strike.

Lindbeck and Snower found privileges for insiders increased, whether only employees were unionized, or whether both employers and employees were represented for bargaining. Both sides were represented in France for both employment and housing bargaining, with 'unionization' of both landlords and tenants.[83] Esping-Andersen (1990) identified France as a corporatist social regime because there was a balance of power between the left and right and between employers and employees. Such countries were often conservative with a Christian background. They contrasted with countries where there was a hegemony of the left or hegemony of the right.

The formal organization of landlord and tenant representation in France echoed the collective representation of employers and employees.[84] The status of collective organizations in France was rooted in traditional political, cultural and economic movements in history, touched on in Chapter 3, rather than simply transaction costs. These collective movements provided the legal foundations for welfare, as well as creating political influence and legal privileges for workers and tenants.

Social movements in the twentieth century were mobilized for welfare to an extent never seen before, but the legal structures of the welfare state in France have

Social landlords and insider-outsider theory

a duality. The same representation of workers and tenants that fought for welfare benefits and access to social housing for the disadvantaged could locally support preferential access by workers and existing tenants to social housing. This tends to exclude the disadvantaged due to the inherent limitations of housing space.

1.4.3 Transaction costs and privileges for insiders

Lindbeck and Snower (2002) said that preferences for insider-employees mean that negotiation and effective collective representation will in time produce barriers to employment and barriers to dismissal to protect insiders. Barriers to exit from employment include job security, long notice periods to terminate employment, redundancy payments and negotiated procedures. Barriers to entering employment might be compulsory union membership or a licence or qualification. Another negotiated benefit is high wages that rise with seniority regardless of merit.

Lindbeck and Snower (2002: 34) described this situation, where there are high transaction costs and a high level of employee privileges, as 'insiderness'. They suggest that their theory might be used in any area where there are insiders and outsiders, and the parallels for tenancies are striking.

For French tenancies, there was a high level of insiderness, with barriers to both access and eviction. This insiderness seemed to be concentrated in practices within the rental environment rather than solely within tenancy law itself. An example was that eviction could be a long process and thus expensive for social landlords. No evictions were possible in winter without rehousing.[85] Problems could occur after the eviction order, including where execution was refused by the State,[86] often in towns where there was pressure on housing.[87]

Since it was difficult to evict, social landlords tended to be reluctant recruit new tenants who might have to be evicted.[88] Insiderness raises landlord requirements for high incomes and a respectable profile for tenants, and there were specific barriers to access, such as requirements for guarantees against rent arrears,[89] rental deposits and compulsory insurance against fire paid for by tenants.[90] This pursuit of apparently respectable tenants particularly adversely affected the disadvantaged.

French insider-tenants enjoyed rents falling with time.[91] In contrast, insider-employees enjoy rising wages, so the parallel is not quite the same. Wages are paid to employees but rent is paid from tenants, so there is a different direction of payment. In both cases, the insider enjoys benefits and the landlord or employer suffers profit reduction. Landlords could be discouraged from residential letting altogether. The best available security of tenure in a 1989 statute ('the 1989 statute')[92] was incentivized by subsidy in both public and private sectors,[93] halting a steady erosion in private rental stock in the 1980s, described by Euvrard (1992).

Insider–outsider theory is not normative and is empirical rather than anti-welfare in nature. Lindbeck and Snower also reported adverse market effects

Social landlords and insider-outsider theory

when there are insufficient barriers to hiring and firing. 'Churning' of employees happens where here are few such barriers and there is little mutual support or 'bonding' between employees. Here, because entrants will work for less than insiders, it is profitable to sack insiders (Lindbeck and Snower, 2002: 12, 34).

'Churning' of tenants could happen in an unregulated rental market with landlords constantly evicting to get higher rents. An interesting prospect is that the balance point between tenant security and insecurity in a particular well-functioning market might be empirically verifiable and should avoid landlords withdrawing from the market. Any market might include variable levels of security at different prices, for different mobility needs, for tenancies started at different times and other tenures, so this is not straightforward.

Insider–outsider theory particularly concerns tenants' security of tenure, but French tenants had additional advantages. Tenants had formal influence generally, but social housing tenants were represented on the allocation commission, deciding who should be housed.[94] Communication between landlords and tenants improves living conditions and fosters community involvement, but French social tenants' involvement in allocation, with other sorts of local insiders, seemed to inhibit reception of apparently less desirable outsiders.

Lindbeck and Snower (2002) proposed that benefits obtained by insiders may themselves constitute barriers to outsiders. French tenancy law has a principle that the reciprocal rights and obligations of landlords and tenants should be balanced.[95] This risked becoming a closed relationship bestowing mutual benefits which did not sufficiently take into account the needs of outsiders, an excluded third party from this negotiating relationship. Lindbeck and Snower (2002: 4) predicted that outsiders would be so excluded.

Because insider–outsider theory is based on economic influences, external financial factors could change the balance between insiders and outsiders, so that new entrants are preferred. In French social housing, outsider candidates could be assisted in places by extra finance, special vacancies and social care. However, the recent balance of incentives was such that the better-off had advantages everywhere.

1.4.4 Stigmatization and geography

Insiderness can have a devastating effect on outsiders. Favouring insiders has an indirect effect of stigmatization of outsiders, loss of social skills and their relegation to stigmatized residential areas. For labour markets, Lindbeck and Snower (2002: 24) described how the persistence of unemployment causes the stigmatization of outsiders: 'Since the outsiders' deterioration of human capital, stigmatization, and depressed job search become more pronounced as the duration of unemployment lengthens, the unemployed outsiders become less effective at competing for jobs with the passage of time.'

Social landlords and insider-outsider theory

Insiderness in housing markets produces similar persistence in housing difficulty for outsiders. Outsiders may lose social skills over time when they do not find a home and suffer deteriorating living conditions, lacking the information and contacts to become insiders. Lindbeck and Snower (2002: 3) described this stigmatization:

> Some individuals, families and other social groups are excluded from the mainstream networks of social relations within a society. They are typically unemployed or working at temporary, low-grade, or dead-end jobs. ... Some become long-term clients of various social assistance programs; others live on their parents' incomes, the black market, or even criminal activities. They often live in the underclass neighborhoods of large cities, with meager social services, poor schooling, and scant police protection. These are the real 'outsiders' in society.

Exclusion from employment and from housing are thus linked.

The geographical segregation of deprived neighbourhoods was a concern of French social mix policies, but insider–outsider theory could partly explain concentrations of particular types of tenant. Lindbeck and Snower (2002: 19) said that where there is insiderness, the type of entrant hired reflects the composition of the existing workforce. For tenancies, this could mean that better-off areas will continue to 'recruit' the same kind of tenant and the same goes for poor areas, staying poor. There were spatial and other effects of insiderness in housing markets to be considered, related to the unavoidably permanent and local nature of housing and other differences.[96]

Lindbeck and Snower (2002) also suggested that an indirect effect of insiderness was the persistence of unemployment, adversely affecting the whole employment market. A similar effect was found by Dogge and Smeets (2007) for housing markets, producing housing shortage. The persistence of the housing crisis in France could similarly be, at least in part, the product of insiderness in housing markets that are too rigid, although it would require quantitative work to show this definitively.

If correct, this persistence of housing shortage means that although public policy improves the position of insider-tenants, this has adverse effects on the housing market generally in France. Consequently, even insiders suffer a general sense of insecurity and seek greater protection. This in turn ratchets up insiderness again. A 2006 survey showed that 88 per cent of French people felt there was difficulty in finding a home (Batiactu 2006a).

1.4.5 Market effects and social norms

Lindbeck and Snower (2002: 22) said that social norms affect the opposition between insiders and entrants; for example, a norm that union members act together

Social landlords and insider-outsider theory

in a strike. This means people respond following the perceived value without thinking about it. Powerful groups generate social norms tending to reinforce the hegemony of the group (Hunter and Nixon 1998). In many situations, this creates insiders and outsiders within and outside different groups, without necessarily using the mechanism of transaction costs, a necessary societal tendency to form mutually supportive groups.

Other bargaining levers for groups that spring to mind are voting, fomenting revolution or using collective economic weight in the economy, some of which are shown in the history in Chapter 3. Regarding social housing, the lobby groups of tenants, landlords, social landlords, mayors and workers had a political effect on national and local government, not simply an effect of cooperating with, or obstructing, landlords. The economic and the political were thus closely linked.

Several social norms affecting French social housing allocation appear throughout this account, from legal texts and interviews. An example was that social mix was desirable in poor areas, justifying importing better-off tenants or building for owner occupancy there. Another norm affects this, a view expressed in interviews that dense ethnic communities were not a good thing and should be split up.[97] A third norm was the prevention of eviction in preference to promoting access to homes, consistent with the interests of tenant-insiders, already briefly described as part of the barriers to exit from housing.[98]

Social norms can support the political process of bargaining between landlords and tenants. The French creation of a national legislative norm in favour of the disadvantaged outsiders was not implemented in ways that overcame existing tendencies to favour insiders relative to outsiders. Insiderness was manifested by the difficulties of the allocation process itself for outsiders and the accumulation of rights and privileges for insiders already in positions of strength locally, and with other local insiders in a broad sense.

It would be tempting to apply group behavioural theory to this situation. This might be analysed in terms of group dynamics and their power relations (Stewart 1997; Shiller 2005). For a summary of recent work on group dynamics, see Forsyth (2006). This includes the idea of 'groupthink' expounded by Janis (1972), which has been widened to less extreme situations (Ahlfinger and Esser 2001). This model explains the inclination to follow social norms without thinking, reinforcing and interacting with Lindbeck and Shower's transaction costs mechanism.

This analysis of groups would not enhance this particular study, because there were variable local effects between French areas and multiple types of actor with different loyalties to different sorts of applicant. There were sometimes local economic impossibilities in housing the disadvantaged, originating in national financial arrangements (see Chapter 6). This was too small a study, with too many local variables, for analysis of group behaviour generally, particularly since part of the processing was by individuals, not groups. This study mainly identified the economic drivers behind preferences for different types of applicant

Social landlords and insider-outsider theory

and their effects, although a transactions costs analysis might help explain the circumstances under which actors worked together rather than separately.[99]

French local housing actors often had common economic or political motivations leading to local exclusion of the disadvantaged, but the difficult allocation process itself made a large contribution to exclusion. Insider–outsider theory gives insight into this analysis of both economic and legal processes.

1.4.6 Economic theory in a social market

French social landlords were profit-maximizing organizations because, as for private landlords, rent was their only profit. This factor is necessary to apply insider–outsider theory. It was still expensive for social landlords to evict and recruit new tenants. These transaction costs were still deducted from rent, making social landlords normally reluctant to change their tenant population, like any other landlords.

In order to cover their costs, French social landlords could increase their rents by constructing new homes or improving existing ones. Their financial regime, described in Chapter 6, forced social landlords to focus on rent recovery and construction. Social rents were controlled, but even ordinary re-letting often involved upgrading homes to new and higher statutory standards, which incidentally also allowed a higher rent. Public incentives in construction policy also encouraged such upgrading of housing or replacing cheap homes with new higher-rent homes. New construction for urban redevelopment allowed a choice of publics for whom homes could be built. Incentives for this construction could change the financial incentives and, in some places, could encourage social landlords to prefer better-off entrants to insider candidates.

Social landlords had to stay within a budget to provide services, even if altruistically inclined. Profits could not be generally distributed,[100] but could be used for better services for tenants, or the construction and improvement of homes. Recently, a financial penalty was imposed on social landlords who did not construct homes (OECD 2009: 52). Public and private social landlords with financial deficits could be merged or wound up and their stock transferred to other social landlords.[101] Bourgeois (1996) described social landlords who ran large deficits, believing the State would have to pay, but this was not now possible.[102] Social landlords thus had incentives to maximize profit and suffered sanctions if they did not, so the economic conditions to apply this economic theory existed.

The financial tensions inherent in rented markets apply to social housing, whether publicly or privately controlled. Elsinga *et al.* (2009) proposed a theory to evaluate competition between social landlords that concerns choice, risk and rivalry. The main rivalry relevant for insider–outsider theory is that between insiders and outsiders, not the normal market competition between landlords.

Social landlords and insider-outsider theory

Only a few aspects of social landlords' economic relations were relevant for insider–outsider theory, but risk and choice were primary factors.

Insider–outsider theory is based on landlords' choices between retaining existing tenants, who are insiders, and recruiting prospective tenants, who might pay more. Long waiting lists were prevalent in all areas studied,[103] giving real choice between candidates. Insider–outsider theory does not mainly concern the more limited choices of housing candidates. In fact, candidates did have choices in whether to apply for a particular area, or whether to withdraw after a home was offered. Massin *et al.* (2010) found that in central Paris around one-tenth of homes offered to the most disadvantaged by the prefecture were refused by candidates. For rehousing, 3,700 offers were made of homes reserved by the *commune* of central Paris, and 2,370 were refused by candidates. This was a distorted market but candidates could vote with their feet.

Risk was an important factor in social housing allocation. French social landlords had room to manoeuvre and social housing allocation was an important financial strategy. Even after the rent was set, recruiting the better-off or apparently more stable tenants and retaining those who were known to pay their rent increased social landlords prospects of making sufficient profit to cover their expenses. This aspect was immediately affected by the extent to which rent was covered by benefits or other tenant support.

The less financial support there is, the more social landlords are driven to recruit the better-off. The recent recession and debt crisis mean there is likely to be less financial support available, so that the French social landlords' dilemma is likely to become more common everywhere. French social landlords' choices between insiders and outsiders were strongly influenced by the economics.

1.4.7 A wider class of insiders

This book will show that each type of actor involved in allocation had a preference for particular kinds of candidate,[104] who were their insiders in a broad sense: Mayors tended to favour locals, the CIL always favoured employees, social landlords favoured existing tenants and between them these actors controlled or influenced access to most housing stock. Consequently, even without the intention to exclude, outsiders were excluded.

The use of insider–outsider theory in social housing is developed throughout the book. The theory is often explained within or after the legal or empirical evidence, which is perhaps academically unusual, but is a result of this development being the product of reflection and research after the empirical study, as permitted by grounded theory (Strauss and Corbin 1998).[105] This was a continuing process of discovery as to how well the theory fitted the evidence and thus it was important to present the evidence first, to avoid distortion.

Social landlords and insider-outsider theory

Even within local constraints, social landlords strongly influenced allocation. A recent French report on allocations (Massin *et al.* 2010: 6) found that social landlords generally 'fixed the rules of the game', so that emphasis on landlords in allocation is still appropriate. Normally, the application of insider–outsider theory to landlords in private renting would closely parallel the application of this labour market theory to employers. As property owners, landlords and employers control who is recruited into a tenancy or into employment. The results of this study show that social landlords' choices were restricted by allocation and public regulation and this made a difference, in variable ways, locally because of the influence of other actors.

Who shares the ownership rights for social housing with social landlords when choosing tenants? There was an extended French landlord grouping of local actors, who together shared the social landlords' rights of recruitment. Mayors or other local authorities, the CIL, the prefecture and the social landlords were all likely to have allocation rights and all shared the benefits and burdens of ownership. Each purchased rights in the allocation process: by actual ownership for social landlords themselves; by subsidy for the State, or by local government powers or purchasing a reservation for other actors.

Like joint landlords, each actor stood to gain or lose from the success of the social housing venture, both in populating homes with their target populations and in exposure to financial or political gain or loss. For social landlords this was clear, since they might lose rent from a poorer tenant. Mayors might also lose money under their guarantee of social housing construction loans. They sometimes also guaranteed rent arrears or bore financial support costs for deteriorating estates. Mayors might lose votes for failing to allocate as the community wished or if neighbours disliked incoming tenants. Tenants might also support allocation to known existing tenants for the same reason, because it was their function to represent tenants.

The CIL had financial interests in satisfying their clients, employers and employees. They should provide desirable housing by reservation, because they risked losing business to other collectors of housing funds.[106] They paid substantial sums for their reservations, the value of which appeared in their balance sheets, and this value could deteriorate in practical terms.[107] The CIL also guaranteed rent arrears through schemes helping individuals[108] and a deprived estate could mean heavy arrears.

The prefecture was primarily responsible for housing disadvantaged people. Bourgeois (1996) found that this was undermined, because they were obliged to negotiate with other actors to achieve all government policies. In placing an unpopular applicant they risked losing the cooperation of other local actors affected, particularly for construction. Prefects were thus reluctant to sanction failures to house disadvantaged people. With recent decentralization there was greater need than ever for the prefect to negotiate with other actors to achieve policies through contractualization.

In this way, all actors might have an economic interest in excluding disadvantaged people. Political motivations were closely linked to economic motivations: social landlords had to take account of local politics to obtain subsidy; the CIL needed to negotiate to obtain reservations, whilst pleasing contributing employers and employees; a mayor should satisfy local people to retain his or her office. This does not discount the practical necessity and importance of altruism, but people could not act alone. Everyone had to take account of the exigencies of their political and economic position, which often meant favouring insiders.

1.5 Conclusion

It is surprising how much had to be studied to obtain a picture of why and how disadvantaged people have difficulty in obtaining housing in France. There was considerable assistance and patience from interviewees and the many others who helped.[109] Many French people undoubtedly work constantly to improve the housing of disadvantaged people. The right to housing has been reinforced over a number of years, and this constant effort for improvement brings hope for the future, although early reports suggest it is not functioning well.

Insider–outsider theory raises criticisms of existing procedure. This is often not about criticizing the people, but is more a history of accumulated local rights which frustrate the efforts of those trying to house the disadvantaged. This rather bleak analysis in fact offers knowledge of process, which could lead to reform of the law and policy to house the disadvantaged. This could be done by creating a more level playing field in the allocation process between insiders and outsiders in a better functioning housing market, which consequently could meet better all housing needs.

Rueda (2005) noted that social democratic governments traditionally represent the interests of labour, of insiders, which could tempt them to implement inegalitarian policies. This happens because of an assumption that it is insiders in secure jobs who bear the brunt of unemployment, when in fact it is outsiders in insecure positions who act as a buffer in the labour market during recessions.

Accordingly, ignoring outsiders in these protective policies means ignoring the most vulnerable. Rueda suggested that social democratic governments are normally interested in full employment, but understanding the interaction of insider–outsider theory and working with the market can give governments more policy options, thus working practically towards higher employment and growth.

The housing equivalent to this would be the vulnerable position of outsiders in insecure and expensive private rented accommodation. Assisting the disadvantaged rather than insiders, who already have advantages, would increase policy options and improve the functioning of the market, thereby facilitating fuller provision of the sort of housing needed.

Insider–outsider theory provided a useful framework for analysis of the procedure, even though it was not contemplated in the study design. This analysis of the effects of the theory is found primarily in Chapters 6 to 10, although the institutional context illustrates this too, because of powers granted to insiders' representatives. There are multiple factors involved and general questions to be answered in the face of increasingly important European regulation. Applying insider–outsider theory to social housing:

- draws attention to important spatial effects, not present in employment markets, that intensify 'insiderness';
- can offer improved understanding of how an allocation process can fail to meet policy objectives.

Looking at the law and policy around French social housing is rather like cutting through a layer cake. To understand its complexities, it is necessary to start at the top with the influence of European debates about who should be housed, together with statistical information and information about the field study in Chapter 2. Then you can work downwards, through the French national history of constitutional rights, principles and institutions in Chapter 3 before looking at the regulatory detail and actors' views of the rights they apply in Chapter 4.

The detail of the social housing allocation process itself is in Chapter 7, but before this can be approached and understood, it is necessary to assimilate the information in Chapter 5 about the many local actors involved: local and central government, various special institutions and the social landlords themselves. All of this local governance is in the grip of change with decentralization. Social landlords' finance (see Chapter 6) is particularly important, because of the insufficient support for the costs of disadvantage.

It is then possible to look at what happens to exclude the disadvantaged, to consider why that is and what can be done about it. Those who obtain social housing are considered in Chapter 8, with more about the application of insider–outsider theory and about exclusion of disadvantaged outsiders in Chapter 9. Consideration of the effects of all this and proposals for reform mark the conclusion in Chapter 10.

2 Exploring the function of social housing

This chapter looks at three introductory elements of this study:

- the European context, debates and developing law
- the statistics on disadvantage
- how this study was formulated.

The first part of the chapter looks at the common threads in the European history of social housing, its current diversity and some key debates affecting its function. Various types of new European regulation could limit this diversity and close down prospects of innovation by limiting State intervention in housing.

The second part of the chapter briefly looks at the contradictory statistics available which might help to work out how far French social landlords are successful in housing disadvantaged people. The criticism by the European Committee of Social Rights (ECSR), mentioned in the Introduction, that French social housing does not satisfactorily house disadvantaged people[110] is not new, but this was not clear to a non-French observer during my study.

The third part of this chapter contains an account of how my investigation into French housing progressed. Bourgeois's (1996) detailed and critical account of social housing allocation was essential for formulating this study. Finally, the methodology for my legal and then empirical study must be briefly explained.

2.1 European social housing

Since my 2005–6 field study, scholarship about European social housing has accelerated. It is now possible to place French social housing in its European context, and to think in an informed way about the diversity and history of European social housing, about the different models of social housing allocation and about social rental markets. This also means looking in this section at the long-established interdisciplinary literature on the role of social housing rental markets. Kemeny (2006) divides European countries into 'unitary' and 'dualist' markets.

These different types of market have advantages and disadvantages, but it is now necessary to look at EU involvement in competition law and a recent decision by the European Court of Human Rights (ECtHR) which threatens the existence of unitary markets and this ECtHR decision contradicts a decision by the ECSR. Such cases could limit housing policy but also have the potential to change property rights across Europe in socially divisive ways.

2.1.1 Diversity and commonality in European social housing

Smith and Oxley (1997) said that European social housing was allocated with reference to need and not by price, although Oxley (2000) later felt it necessary to argue for the value of allocation based on need in Europe. It is questionable whether European social housing has a primary objective of meeting housing need. French social housing includes a small proportion of holiday homes[111] and Figure 1.1 (see p. 12) already shows that better-off French people can obtain social housing. Recently, much more has been learned about this and the nature and varieties of European social housing.

Although there was diversity in European social housing allocation, there were historical commonalities for some countries. Reinprecht *et al.* (2008) described social housing in Austria, France and the Netherlands as passing through several phases. From the nineteenth century, workers moved to large cities where they worked and lived in poor, overcrowded conditions. Industrialists and philanthropists constructed small amounts of housing for workers, but 'their aim was always to organise the relationship between workforce and capital in the most profitable way for the latter'.[112]

Reinprecht *et al.* said that municipal concern for social, economic and health conditions across Europe after 1900, and new legal frameworks, were to ultimately produce a high proportion of social housing in Paris,[113] Vienna (40 per cent of housing) and Amsterdam (52 per cent of housing). This social housing built before the Second World War across Europe was intended primarily for workers.

Not every country fits this template; for example Ireland and Spain have come late to the idea of rented social housing. In Germany, it is difficult to identify actual 'social housing' because this status expires or is personal to the person assisted. The German rental market as a whole enjoys secure tenancies and there are many private not-for-profit landlords who are not social landlords as such. In Sweden, in contrast, public housing companies have provided social housing. Private tenant cooperatives are common in Scandinavia and are difficult to classify because of control of ownership by occupants (Doling 1997; Donner 2000). It is thus difficult to define social housing in terms of public or private provision, particularly where there is broad housing subsidy. There have been long debates about this description.[114]

In the 1960s, Donnison (1967) started to look at the public and private provision of social housing comparatively as sufficiently similar to compare. Harloe (1995) described common European movements to mass housing, and a gradual retrenchment to residual provision for the poor. Reinprecht *et al.* (2008) also found a gradual withdrawal of the State from intervention in housing from the 1970s with policies increasingly earmarking social housing for social need.

2.1.2 Models of social housing allocation

European decisions from the EU, ECtHR or ECSR briefly described below could force more convergence of this pluralist housing provision. Social provision might be converging anyway towards a more residualized model, partly due to less available funding for general needs. Research into allocation of European social or below-market rentals has developed recently (CECODHAS 2006: 11; Fitzpatrick and Stephens 2007). Which model of allocation applies probably partly depends on when the social housing was provided or how far each country moved from common early models of housing workers.

Ghékière (2008) has provisionally suggested that amongst older EU members, social housing was provided: for workers (common in southern Europe), for everyone (a northern European model) and for the poor (in the UK and Ireland).[115] Ghékière then assumed the UK model was based on poverty, when need was the central criterion – a fourth model.[116] The advantage of this provisional scheme is its relationship to French types of allocation, although also common in Europe. Other countries might combine these four models. This is a simplified scheme because there might be different queues for different types of home or different social landlords, or particular percentages of homes earmarked for particular purposes.

All four models of allocation could be found in France in various combinations and were often in conflict there, but government policy during my study promoted general or universal housing allocation,[117] sometimes popularly referred to as 'housing for everyone'.[118] This policy was rather vague and allowed different strategies in different local areas. An example is that disadvantaged people might obtain social housing in priority but then others with less priority queued to fill remaining spaces.

Choice-based lettings in the UK and the Netherlands are another example of this, where people with more cumulative priority can have the first choice of available homes (Kullberg 1997; Pawson *et al.* 2006). This priority is determined by awarding points for particular disadvantages and other local criteria, so the person with the largest accumulation of points heads the queue. The effect of this is higher provision for the disadvantaged in those countries.

Exploring the function of social housing

Every government intends, at least officially, to house everyone, but French social housing catered for variable populations. Precisely which type should be favoured was not agreed, in practical terms, locally. The acquired rights of French workers survived quite strongly through reservations,[119] because legal structures promoting welfare also supported workers' and tenants' rights. This emerges from both the history, detailed in the next chapter, and the legal institutions.

'Universal' social housing allocation is associated with Scandinavian social housing systems. In Sweden or Denmark, social housing allocation has meant that applicants were accepted in the strict order of the waiting list, to ultimately accommodate everyone, whether rich or poor. More recently this has been breaking down. Lind (2007) found exclusive local allocation practices by Swedish mayors. In Denmark, Nielsen (2010) found new regulation excluding welfare recipients from certain areas and strong policies on eviction of criminal offenders' families.

The waiting list or queue, as a means of rationing social housing, can strongly represent equality and fairness. There are questions about who is allowed into the queue and whether queue-jumping is allowed. Urgent housing need is a common reason for queue-jumping. This theme is returned to in Chapter 10, to analyse the usefulness of the different models of allocation in the light of the evidence.

2.1.3 Social housing and rental markets

Kemeny (1995) analysed European theories for the management and function of social housing in 'unitary' or 'dualist' rental markets. Unitary rental systems were conceived by the Ordo-liberal movement in Germany between the world wars as a planned market to avoid the disruption of the Weimar Republic or the Nazi command economy.

In an integrated unitary market, publicly subsidized housing is deliberately in competition with the private sector, tending to reduce rents and improve conditions in the private sector. The initial public subsidy for construction to reduce the upfront cost of housing would be gradually withdrawn as finance was repaid and social housing became able to compete without subsidy. Kemeny (2006) found this approach in Germany, Sweden, Denmark, the Netherlands, Switzerland and Austria.

This contrasts with a 'dualist' system, where public or social housing is segregated from the market and is not allowed to compete with the private rental sector. Social housing then becomes residual, catering exclusively for the poor who are excluded from private rental markets. This residual housing typically becomes stigmatized.

A high percentage of home ownership is a common effect of dualist markets and is due to the general undesirability of renting. Dualist systems were found in the UK, Ireland, Finland and Norway (Kemeny 2006). Matznetter (2006) suggested that unitary rental markets were suffering increased residualization

Exploring the function of social housing

linked to the growth of owner-occupation, adversely affecting rental markets generally.

Kemeny (2006) was unable to identify whether France was unitary or dualist. The implicit idea of controlling the whole market with subsidy to housing for everyone fits with French traditions of *dirigisme* (interventionist approaches). Unitary markets linked to 'universal' social housing allocation, as in Sweden, appeal to France's traditional enthusiasm for equality, but France's allocation system was not straightforwardly universal in my study.

France probably does not have a unitary housing market. There was no systematic French national attempt to promote competition between social landlords or between social and private landlords. Competition between social landlords might or might not exist (Bourgeois 1996). This is because rents were not set locally for social and private sectors to relate to local rental markets. French private-sector rents were freely set on a first let, but social rents related to construction costs within regulatory limitations. Both types of rent were nationally increased annually according to different indexes.[120]

There might be local competition in particular localities, such as in the cheap rents in small provincial towns[121] or for new property in cities.[122] Whether such competition was possible also depended on there being a significant local presence of social landlords, but French social stock was unevenly distributed, with none in places.[123]

2.1.4 The challenge of European regulation

The next two sections review European policies affecting housing, but mainly concern legal action taken by European private landlords to improve their position. Such action has an impact on social housing and tends to increase European regulation of national housing policy. A common issue in all these areas was the extent of state intervention in the market, including intervention through social landlords. The Ordo-liberals used the competitive power of the state, intervening with below-market rents to produce more affordable housing; the EU approach limits this.

Landlords in France, Sweden and the Netherlands have complained to the EU Competition Commission[124] that they suffered unfair competition because of subsidies to social landlords. Nevertheless, the major rationale for unitary markets is that private landlords should suffer some disadvantage, owing to competition with social landlords, with a view to lowering rents and improving standards, as described above. Under this system competition should reduce landlords' profitability, but probably to a profit level viable to maintaining rental stock.

The profitability of private landlords was also raised in ECtHR and ECSR cases in Poland and Slovenia.[125] Eastern European EU members are in transition to a Western 'free' market for rented property. Kemeny (2006) suggested that the

Exploring the function of social housing

free market terminology tends to be associated with the dualist model of the rental market, but that model nonetheless still required heavy regulation to enforce segregation of social housing from the private market

2.1.5 EU regulation

Housing is not strictly an EU competence, although the Charter of Fundamental Rights of the EU[126] governs its institutions and has enhanced importance following the 2007 Treaty of Lisbon.[127] Article 34(3) of this charter echoes the right to housing in the revised European Social Charter (RESC): 'In order to combat social exclusion and poverty, the Union recognises and respects the right to social and housing assistance so as to ensure a decent existence for all those who lack sufficient resources.'

Despite this limited wording, EU policy affects housing in legislation concerning: discrimination,[128] mobility of labour[129] and the use of structural funds for construction. Tenancies have an importance for free movement of persons within the EU internal market,[130] and tenants can be consumers.[131] During my field study, EU social provisions were found in the Treaty on the European Union (TEU),[132] such as Article 136 (which stated social objectives), and reflected in the Lisbon strategy to promote the best social policies. This is known as the open coordination method. Article 136 was replaced by Article 151 of the Treaty on the Functioning of the European Union[133] (TFEU) of 9 May 2007, which replaced TEU after Lisbon.

French housing policies were also affected by the EU restriction of the national debt to 60 per cent of GDP by EU fiscal policies. Pébereau (2005) reported that French debt was 66 per cent of GDP and proposed remedial action. Since then other EU countries have also acquired high debts after supporting banks in difficulty, something affecting France less than most. Nevertheless, there was a persistent problem with French state debt. INSEE, the national statistical agency, found that the national debt was 84.5 per cent of GDP in March 2011. This budget-limited context strongly affects implementation of European and national welfare rights.

EU competition policy generally restricts subsidy to social landlords, where this benefits the better-off, because this distorts competition with private landlords in the internal market. Public and private social landlords[134] were not allowed to work together to prevent, restrict or distort competition within the EU internal market (Art. 81 TEU, now Art. 101 TFEU) or abuse a dominant position (Art. 82 TEU, now Art. 102 TFEU). This covered 'undertakings' (Art. 86 TEU, now Art. 106 TFEU) which included public organizations with special or exclusive rights. French social landlords received special funding privileges for construction and tax exemptions, and so are regulated.

During my study, state aid to social landlords was only allowed if it was in the 'general economic interest' (Art. 87 TEU), although there were various exemptions. The law has not substantially changed.[135] However, after strong lobbying, a new 2010 Protocol to the Lisbon Treaty is likely to affect the interpretation of future cases concerning services of general interest. The Protocol says that the European Court of Justice must consider the shared values of the union, including the importance of wide local discretion, the diversity of local situations and 'equal treatment and the promotion of universal access and of user rights'.[136]

Competition control does not in principle distinguish public and private undertakings, although the test for these differs (Fehling 2009). However, detailed regulation separates service providers into 'services of general interest' (SGI), 'social services of general interest' (SSGI), and 'services of general economic interest' (SGEI).[137] Most French social landlords probably fall into the latter category, which is one of the more controlled.[138]

The utilitarian test of the 'general interest' raises immediate and direct questions about the public usefulness of social landlords' activities. A 2005 decision defined social landlords as 'providing housing for disadvantaged citizens or socially less advantaged groups, which due to solvability constraints are unable to obtain housing at market conditions ...'.[139] This exempted these social landlords from notification requirements for their subsidies, a procedural advantage.[140]

This set the tone for Competition Commission approvals of subsidy for social housing. A 2006 directive followed, providing exemptions from competition control for SGI, based on the social provisions of Article 16 TEU (Krajewski *et al.* 2009). Consequently, social landlords were exempt from competition control if supporting those in housing need, on a low income, lacking independence or at risk of marginalization.[141]

The Competition Commission has negotiated with the Netherlands, Sweden and France following claims by private landlords of unfair competition, because of subsidies assisting the better off.[142] This limitation of housing subsidy makes it more difficult to run either a unitary rental market or universal social housing allocation. Both systems tend to allow allocation to the better off of subsidized housing alongside the disadvantaged, either by wide subsidy or by waiting lists not discriminating between rich and poor. This approach thus tends to support dualist and not unitary rental markets.

Both the Netherlands and Sweden have made changes to their social housing, in response to regulation (Lavrijssen and Vries 2009; Madell 2009). This focusing of social housing subsidy on the very poor may not currently be the geographical segregation typical of the dualist housing market. Poor and the less poor tenants remained where they were but with different landlords. Complaints about the French national action plan for social cohesion seem to have been resolved by negotiation, lobbying by interested parties and adjustment to both national plans and the rules.[143]

In the Netherlands, competition law was not thought to apply to social housing and no EU competition cases existed to provide a firm statement of the law for social housing (Lavrijssen and Vries 2009). The Netherlands complaint[144] concerned subsidized social housing construction schemes, with public guarantees, subsidy from central housing funds, special loans and transfers of land at below market rates, all features found in France.

The Commission decision said 'the offer of social housing should be adapted to the demand from disadvantaged citizens or socially less advantaged groups'.[145] Rents should be limited and 90 per cent of homes should be allocated to people with an income below €33,000, around 43 per cent of average income in the Netherlands, below poverty thresholds. If such rules were applied to France, most income ceilings would be very much lower.

A curious aspect of this is that, in France, competition can be thought of as red in tooth and claw, opposing welfare. Lechevalier (2002) said 'The Community competition law crashes more and more significantly into the national law of social protection.' It is ironic that the Competition Commission has effectively pushed for subsidy for those in housing difficulty, although possible problems can be envisaged.[146]

Another competition requirement is that state aid must satisfy conditions in the *Altmark* judgement concerning transparency.[147] For social landlords, this means: that public service obligations should be defined; that calculation of aid should be established in an objective and transparent way; aid should be fair and necessary; and the public service provider should be chosen by a particular procedure, such as by tender.[148]

Touvenin (2009) suggested that these criteria are not easy to satisfy but that this decision is a reasonable compromise allowing for public service burdens: given the potential risks and costs of housing disadvantaged people, exemption in their favour can be readily understood.

Transparency in general terms was an issue in French social housing.[149] EU competition law has not produced any decision against France, despite the opacity of social housing allocation and the subsidy for the better off. Is the subsidy of insiders fair and necessary? Opacity made it difficult to assess whether local allocation policies were in the general economic interest, as required.[150]

The Competition Commission applies economic theory to its decision-making, although in ways that are more traditionally *dirigiste* than in the US, including applying multiple values (Bergh and Camesasca 2006). This might yet mean these rapidly developing rules will change to accommodate unitary market approaches to rental markets, under the 2010 Protocol.[151] This book is not about EU competition rules, and cannot deal with these in depth, but their importance required comment and economic studies such as this have some bearing on social housing.

2.1.6 National constitutional rights, the ECHR, the RESC

National views of rights under the European Convention on Human Rights (ECHR) and the RESC are coloured by the way these echo national constitutional

Exploring the function of social housing

rights. Human dignity (below) has some promise as a common European approach to welfare, but national property rights can be very different. Recent cases in the ECtHR and ECSR emphasised the difference with England, and exposed conflicts between landlords and tenants and between the ECHR and the RESC. This difference between the English common law approach and the French civil law approach requires explanation.

National views of constitutional rights are a response to history. In Germany there was a concern to prevent a future rise of fascism. In England there had been historic battles for sovereignty between Parliament and monarchy, so the ECHR was incorporated into UK law in a way protective of this sovereignty.[152] In France there are iconic republican values from the revolutionary past.

Despite these differences, there has been some limited progress towards a common European basis for national housing rights based on human dignity. Post-war German social security rights have been based on human dignity from the beginning.[153] In England, the treatment of asylum seekers who did not obtain housing or sufficient benefits was found to breach Article 3 of the ECHR in 2005, sometimes known as the right to human dignity.[154] In France the right to housing has been based on human dignity since 1994.[155]

There is still considerable divergence around European property rights, English law being more different than most, lying outside the civil law family to which nearly all other EU members belong. Ireland and most of the UK have common law systems; Scotland has a mixed common law and civil law system.[156] Consequently, this book must often only refer to English law, for accuracy. It might surprise the English reader to see just how far, historically, property rights have influenced the institutions and practice of social housing allocation in France.

The French right to property only benefitted landlords.[157] French tenants did not and still do not generally possess any property rights in their tenancy, either in private law or under the Constitution, because the unitary and absolute nature of land ownership meant only one owner could have possession, which is the hallmark of ownership. Tenants only occupied land on behalf of the owner (Carbonnier 1973).[158]

From the nineteenth century, relations between landlord and tenant were seen as a struggle between capitalist landlords who had property rights and tenants who did not.[159] French tenancies were almost always defined by their lack of property rights, an important matter of principle going back to the 1789 revolution. Modern French writers still described the opposition between landlords and tenants as fundamental (Bourgeois 1993: 14; Radigon and Horvath 2002: 16).

Political, economic, social and philosophical thought promoting the benefits of absolute property goes back to the international movement that was the Enlightenment (or earlier) in a revival of Roman law. David Hume placed property centrally within his scheme of government.[160] Gonnard (1943) has suggested that the French notion of property was essentially the product of the Enlightenment

Exploring the function of social housing

and suited its purposes, rather than exactly being Roman. Certainly both English and French property concepts draw on Roman law, but these approaches have diverged over centuries. A common modern theme in England and France was a popular enthusiasm for property ownership and political pressure from labour movements for better housing and welfare provision.

Ideas about the nature of property differ when considered by the lawyer, by policmakers and by individuals (Blandy and Goodchild 1999), particularly in England where property law is very old, changing by evolution rather than revolution. Its structure does not easily lend itself to a Marxist–capitalist divide in the way that French law does. The post-war drive to protect tenants in England and France was the subject of substantial statutory intervention in both counties, but as a matter of principle English tenants' rights were not perceived as a social exception to absolute property rights in a different scheme of things (Ball 2003, 2010a).

Instead, English tenants are broadly conceived as having property rights,[161] a bundle of tenants' rights delimited by the terms of a lease and supported by a variety of statutes. People who in England consider themselves to be owners[162] have a similar kind of bundle of rights as tenants, only stronger and more permanent.[163] This could be seen as a species of equality between landlords and tenants, with the different economic values of these rights reflected in their price. A range of bundles of rights are available from the very secure to the insecure. In this way, neither the right to housing nor the social basis of property was necessary for legislation to support tenants' inherent property rights.

English property law, including tenancy law, has a dusty and uncontentious quality (McFarlane 2008). The debates in this book are played out at the political and policy level, rather than in the structure of property and contract law itself, although statutory protection of tenants varies with the political climate, as anywhere else (Schmid, undated). Presenting the English system in this rudimentary way is problematic, but necessary (see discussion in section 2.3, p. 30).

Spain, Germany and many other civil law countries have modified their constitutional right to property (COHRE 2000) so that unitary and absolute property ownership is mitigated by public or collective social rights. This represents the social basis for property allowing the protection of tenants by the imposition of security of tenure on landlords' right to property.

The European right to property in the ECHR, Article 1 of Protocol 1 – 'Every natural or legal person is entitled to the peaceful enjoyment of his possessions' – is more weakly stated than in the French constitution.[164] The French version refers to '*un bien*' (a good)[165] not 'possessions', but tenants' rights are not *un bien* in principle.

The ECHR decision below supports landlords, but this does not necessarily mean the ECHR does not support tenants.[166] A problem may be that tenants from most civil law legal traditions in Europe will not apply to the ECHR under

Article 1 of Protocol 1 because tenancies are not seen as property. Erp (2003) has suggested that for harmonization European rights should be either property rights or contract rights but not both, which is a civil law view. This calls into question the English scheme, where tenants have hybrid property and contractual rights, which should be supported under the ECHR.

Tenants in civil law countries may be more likely to file a collective complaint under the RESC when the right to housing in Article 31 corresponds to the national legal basis for tenant protection, as in France. The RESC contains collective social rights illustrating historic connections between social rights and collective bargaining by labour movements. The right to work is at Article 1 of the RESC, followed by employment and social rights, and, finally, the right to housing at Article 31.

The ECtHR recently strongly supported landlords in *Hutten-Czapska* v. *Poland*[167] by ruling against strong rent control, which might assist poor tenants, and insisting eviction should be possible. Strong rent control was a 'disproportionate burden ... which cannot be justified in terms of the legitimate aims pursued by the authorities in implementing the relevant remedial housing legislation'.[168] This decision was made in extreme circumstances of very strong security and low rents enjoyed by tenants,[169] imposed in the communist era. Most homes were sold cheaply to tenants, but people who remained tenants enjoyed strong security after restitution of homes to pre-communist owners. The ECtHR had previously approved more moderate rent control.[170]

Hutten-Czapska also decided that tenants' rights were a matter for State responsibility rather than excessive impositions on landlords.[171] This was in line with the derogation in favour of the State in Article 1 of Protocol 1, allowing restrictions on landlords' rights. This conceptualization corresponds to French legal thought.[172]

The decision even suggested that landlords should have a right to a profit, which should be guaranteed by the State.[173] Polish rents had already doubled since the end of Communism to reach a level of 60 per cent of the repair costs of the homes, but even this low level could still be unaffordable. Nine per cent of tenants were in arrears with rent in 2003,[174] but by 2007 this had risen to 45 per cent,[175] which might be a direct result of raising rents to satisfy this judgment.

In a similar situation in *FEANTSA* v. *Slovenia*[176] (*'FEANTSA'*), a collective complaint was made to the ECSR on behalf of tenants and people in housing difficulty after eviction. In the communist era Slovenian tenants had also been imposed on private owners, who had now recovered their property. These private secure tenants were charged rents designed to cover only the cost of repair.

The ECSR decided that Slovenia was in breach of the right to housing. This rent was unaffordable, the State should support those in difficulty and these private tenants should be compensated because they were unable to exercise their right to buy their homes, unlike public tenants. This failure was conceived as discrimination, not on the usual grounds of sex, race or religion, but seeming to imply that all tenants should be equal. How far is that consistent with a free market, where different tenants might have different bundles of rights for different qualities of premises at different prices?

It is a problem that the lowest rent permitted by the ECtHR in *Hutten-Czapska* was too high for the ECSR in *FEANTSA* because it was unaffordable for tenants. Could Polish tenants now apply to the ECSR because the rents proposed by the ECtHR are unaffordable? The problem is different provisions in the different treaties dealing with the same landlord–tenant relationship.

Many issues are raised by this (Ball 2010b). The decisions seem inconsistent in ways that cannot be explained by the different national circumstances and at worst show the ECHR supporting landlords and the RESC supporting tenants. In both cases, the International Union of Property Owners supported landlords and the International Union of Tenants supported tenants,[177] showing that these traditional oppositions are not purely French.

The second problem is that the combined effect of the two decisions is to impose heavy financial burdens of responsibility on the State, for compensation and support for both landlords and tenants. This also limits the policy tools by which these rights can be satisfied. Neither country had adequate housing benefit before these cases[178] and both decisions suggested a steep increase in spending in the current recession. This is difficult, when considered in conjunction with the EU decision, above, concerning the limiting of public subsidy for construction.

Hutten-Czapka seemed to assume a 'free' dualist housing market, because there is no mention of changes to the strong protection of public tenants, causing a schism in the market.[179] The *FEANTSA* case, on the other hand, suggested equality is necessary between the public and private sectors, suggesting an improvement in the security of tenure for Slovenian private tenants towards public sector standards, thereby supporting a unitary system. If *Hutten-Czapska* were applied to France, this could cause general rent increases because all French tenancies, whether for public or private landlords, are treated as private law,[180] although this is not necessarily an ECHR distinction. Disadvantaged tenants may depend on cheap historic-cost rents.

2.2 Disadvantage in French social housing

Disadvantage in this study is defined both by poverty and difficulty of access to housing in line with the Besson Act.[181] At the beginning of the study it was difficult to discover how far social housing catered for these needs because of difficulties with the statistics. There was also no systematic recording of needs met at the point of allocation. This part of the chapter looks at these statistics and introduces the patchy nature of French social housing allocation.

Exploring the function of social housing

2.2.1 How disadvantaged are French social tenants?

The mismatch between the law and its objectives was hard to predict before the study. Clearly, the right to housing was an objective rather than specifically binding, but there was substantial implementing legislation.[182] This difficulty was due partly to the locally variable nature of French social housing and partly to statistical problems.

Access to social housing by rich people was limited because applicants' income should be below income ceilings at the point of access, these varying between regions and increasing with household size. Single parents enjoyed slightly higher income ceilings. These ceilings were imposed by conditions attached to public construction loans.

The most common type of loan, the PLUS (Prêt locatif à usage sociale) had three different income ceilings.[183] The middle ceiling was the most common income limit for access to social homes and the 2007 figures are shown in Table 2.1. The 2005 ceilings were 2.9 per cent lower than that.[184] Higher ceilings for Paris reflected higher prices there, but the €57,819 ceiling for a single-parent family of five was not most people's idea of a modest income.

The three different PLUS ceilings were intended to produce social mix by having quotas for different tenant incomes within a single development.

Table 2.1 The basic income ceilings for PLUS loans (in Euros) in 2007

Category of household	Paris and neighbouring communes	Ile-de-France and neighbouring communes	Other regions
Single person	21,435	18,463	18,463
Two people not including any dependants, but excluding young households	27,593	27,593	21,435
Three people or a single person with one dependant or a young household	36,172	33,169	25,778
Four people or a single person with two dependants	43,187	39,169	31,119
Five people or a single person with three dependants	51,382	47,033	36,608
Six people or a single person with four dependants	57,819	52,926	41,246
For each additional person	6,442	5,897	4,602

Source: ANIL.

Exploring the function of social housing

Lévy-Vroelant and Tutin (2007) reported the approximate percentages of French households eligible for each quota of tenants:

- 60 per cent of new tenant households should have incomes below the basic ceiling (in Table 2.1), available to 71 per cent of French households.
- 10 per cent of the development should be higher-value homes, for tenants with incomes up to 120 per cent of the basic ceiling. These were theoretically available to 80.9 per cent of French households, if they could afford them.
- 30 per cent of new tenant households should have incomes below 60 per cent of the basic ceiling, available to 35 per cent of households. This was known as 'very social housing', although this ceiling was still above the poverty line.

If the objective of social housing was to house disadvantaged people, this was an expensive way to do it, because roughly two better-off tenants had to be subsidized for every tenant below the lowest ceiling. High levels of capital would not disqualify applicants for these classifications.[185]

National income statistics were not very informative about social tenants' real incomes. Income ceilings were based on taxable income, so the dominant national datasets did not show tenants' actual incomes before the deduction of tax and social security contributions. Exemptions included an automatic 20 per cent tax deduction for most employees, plus a large number of tax-deductible social insurance contributions.[186] French social insurance contributions tended to amount to more than the tax paid, including elective insurance add-ons. Social tenants' capital was not recorded.

An additional problem in assessing poverty was that household income statistics did not generally include non-contributory benefits. Benefits omitted from reported incomes include family, housing and disablement allowances, minimum pensions and the non-contributory benefit supporting a minimum income, the RMI (Revenue minimum d'insertion). The income ceilings thus start to look rather more generous.

Figure 1.1 (p. 12) shows not only the continuing presence of better-off households in social housing but also that poverty in social housing was increasing. Social housing stock housed proportionately more poor people and people on modest incomes[187] than other tenures. Nevertheless, the percentage of lower income groups in social housing was not large relative to private renting or even within owner-occupiers with a mortgage, as shown in Table 2.2.

As an English observer, the author's expectation that social housing would house more disadvantaged people arises because around 47 per cent of UK social housing is occupied by poor tenants, under more modern standards of 60 per cent of median income (EU Commission 2009). Other European countries studied housed between 24.5 and 27.4 per cent of poor people in social or below-market renting: Germany, Hungary, the Netherlands, Poland and Sweden. UK social

Table 2.2 The income of households by tenure in 2002

	Poor households	Households on a modest income	Other households	All households
Owners without a mortgage	27.9	35.0	37.4	35.8
Owners with a mortgage	7.2	13.5	25.9	21.5
Social tenants	32.1	24.7	13.2	17.5
Private tenants	24.3	19.6	19.1	19.8
Other tenures	8.5	7.2	4.4	5.4
Totals	100	100	100	100

Source: INSEE (2002): the most recent available figures in 2005.
Note: Poor was then defined as 50 per cent of median income and modest income as below the lowest three income deciles (for the definition of modest households see p. 12).

housing caters for more disadvantaged people than most. On another measure, the UK housed more than 40 per cent of its poor in this housing, although the Netherlands housed more than 60 per cent in a large social housing sector.

French social landlords housed more single parents and ethnic minorities (i.e. vulnerable groups) than were found in other sorts of housing.[188] Single parents comprised 16 per cent of social tenants as against 7 per cent in the population as a whole. For nationality, 10 per cent of social tenants were foreign as against 5 per cent overall.[189] Ethnicity could not be legally recorded in French statistics,[190] hence the reference to 'foreigners'. It cannot be assumed that the single parents or the ethnic minorities recorded were also those having housing difficulty. The figures recorded here show a mixed and unclear picture, where some poor people are housed, but not necessarily the disadvantaged poor.

2.2.2 Patchy reception

There were also strong local variations in the amounts of housing stock, incomes and allocation outcomes. The regions studied were Ile-de-France, the Nord-Pas-de-Calais and Rhône-Alpes (see Figure 1.3). These regional samples showed large differences in social tenants' incomes. Median incomes in central Paris were 60 per cent higher than in the rest of France, and 20 per cent higher in Ile-de-France (the Paris region).[191] Social tenants' incomes in Ile-de-France could be double those in the Nord-Pas-de Calais.[192]

Poverty could be very locally concentrated. More than half of the people below the poverty threshold in mainland France lived in 500 cantons, out of 3,653 such

Exploring the function of social housing

tax districts (Ministère d'Équipement, undated). Households receiving RMI were thus concentrated in the south of France and along the Belgian border, with sometimes 100 per cent of the tenants below the lowest income ceilings.[193] Some areas exclusively housed the poor.

There was also the uneven local availability of social housing across France, shown in Figure 1.3. Some areas had little or no social housing, whilst some had *communes* consisting almost entirely of large deprived social housing estates. Consequently, the exclusion of disadvantaged people from social housing was not the only French housing problem. Some social tenants also suffered social exclusion because of conditions in the worst housing (Deschamps 1998).

'Very social housing' described special loan provision for homes for low income tenants[194] but did really not help in describing poverty levels in social housing. Homes funded under these loans included some *foyers* and transitional social residences, not run by social landlords (Ballain and Benguigui 2004). The 'very social' income ceiling was not a proxy for poverty, allowing access to 35 per cent of French households, whilst only 6.3 per cent of French households were poor, when measured as below 50 per cent of median income in 2005, or 18 per cent of households below 60 per cent of median income (ONPES 2006: 29).

At a very local level, figures for the percentages of acceptance of people below the lowest PLUS income ceilings had been studied in Ile-de-France (Charlet and Laurent 2006). Acceptances were patchy and varied between 14 per cent and 100 per cent, with gaps in data. These figures were not fine-grained, measuring tax districts which are groups of *communes*, not individual *communes*. Social landlords interviewed suggested that neighbouring *communes* could vary radically in the types of people accepted. This study sought out reasons for these variations.

2.3 Formulating this study

Seeking French law about housing the poor was initially difficult. Sociological and economic information was easiest to trace, and, much later, sociological work provided the necessary information for empirical study. Both the legal and sociological method with its challenges should also be looked at.

2.3.1 More about Bourgeois's views

Bourgeois (1993, 1996) conducted more than 100 semi-structured interviews investigating social housing allocation by ten social landlords of the major types. French work on the practical detail of the allocation process is uncommon, partly because of difficult access to decision-makers in a politically sensitive area. Bourgeois had some similar concerns for process and poverty to my study and establishing whether her criticisms were still true was the basis for my field research about whether social landlords housed disadvantaged people, as well as how and why the results arose.

Exploring the function of social housing

Bourgeois found that allocation was often the product of bargaining in secret by local actors, often seeking not to house the most difficult candidates. Young professional tenants whose income was likely to rise above initial ceilings were preferred by the commercial social housing companies (SAHLMs). She found many irregularities, such as race discrimination and corruption. More commonly there was repeated failure of cooperation and the diversion of legislation from its purposes.

She also found that allocation was a bureaucratic and opaque process, used by local actors to their own advantage. This was facilitated by the fragmentation of the process between them and by private negotiations over individual cases. Existing tenants who paid rent and behaved well were actively favoured with better housing, a point supporting insider–outsider theory, because it privileges existing tenants. This variable treatment resulted in some urban areas being abandoned or relegated to undesirable candidates (Bourgeois 1996: 114, 130).

Were Bourgeois's criticisms still true after more than a decade of reforms? Corruption seemed less common and my study did not find any illegal allocation to applicants above income ceilings. From 1990, statute required a series of compulsory local contracts between actors to improve coordination.[195] Bourgeois's other criticisms were still true: opacity of process, bargained results and unequal treatment of applicants.

2.3.2 Updating Bourgeois

Bourgeois's study was helpful in drafting detailed topic guides, but she was vague about how her study was formulated. She initially explained how she interviewed social landlords and mayors, but other types of interviewees were only apparent from the labels on quotations. She concluded that the geographical site of organizations made no difference to her thesis (Bourgeois 1993, 1996: 32), but seven out of ten social landlords studied were in the Paris region, providing, perhaps, insufficient consideration of regional differences.

Although Bourgeois argued for the centrality of politics for public social landlords, she said little about the party politics of the people and organizations involved. This might have been to protect the identities of interviewees. Four of her ten organizations had left-oriented control, but she was silent about the other six, perhaps because this was unclear.

Chapter 1 explained how Bourgeois's main theoretical framework was that public social landlords (OPHLMs) were primarily oriented to political or electoral gain, whilst private ones (SAHLMs) were primarily profit-oriented. This view was complicated by the second, more commercial type of public HLM landlord, the OPAC.[196] This model had two boards – a political one for policy and a professional board for management. Bourgeois found a tension between these public policy and commercial elements.

51

Exploring the function of social housing

Even with this adaptation, it was difficult to conceive of a single predominant motivation for social landlord behaviour, and this study found that motivations were now mixed. There is some statistical evidence that public social landlords were not necessarily the most altruistic in accepting the poorest tenants. In 2003, a national inspection body (MIILOS 2003) investigated 78 social landlords and recorded the percentages of RMI benefit recipients accepted by the different types. RMI was received by around 8.1 per cent of French social tenants, as compared to 4.1 per cent for all households, and was thus a reasonable measure of poverty.

The report showed that all types of social landlord accepted a range of percentages of these poor people. The public OPACs did not have either very high or very low percentages of poor tenants, housing some poor people, but they were not in the forefront in housing high percentages of the poor. A few private SAHLMs housed close to 100 per cent of housing benefit recipients, contrary to Bourgeois's view of their profit motive, and the highest percentage of any HLM organization.

Although Bourgeois (1996: 95) said private social landlords were motivated primarily by profitability,[197] she also said they had to be profitable or viable by their own means, an important and slightly different formulation. This drive to avoid losses was still highly relevant for all social landlords.

Bourgeois's view of social landlords' political strategies could still partly explain the geographical patchiness of social housing stock, with large deprived estates in some *communes* and none in others. She said public social landlords were 'animated by "political" reasoning' (Bourgeois 1996: 16). *Politique* can mean either 'policy' or 'politics'. She was generally vague about what this meant, but the context repeatedly suggested this was about electoral gain for local mayors.

Bourgeois suggested that OPHLMs, the smallest public social landlords, could be seen as the political or policy instrument of the local *commune*, but that they were also very concerned to satisfy existing tenants, who were voters. Services to tenants were 'particularly marked by the delivery of free services and weak financial rigour' (Bourgeois 1996: 77). Bourgeois also recorded local allocation to party voters, and even corruption in allocating to political allies or for personal gain. This aspect of Bourgeois's study again supports insider–outsider theory that privileges are provided for insiders.

Politicians of any complexion might hope that grateful tenants will vote for them, but 'gerrymandering' is the improper manipulation of the local population for electoral gain. This English concept is roughly translated by *charcutage* in France, a responsibility of the Ministry of the Interior. In fact, social housing allocation can be prone to political manipulation without impropriety.

If poor people tend to vote socialist then an apparently altruistic local policy of allocating homes to poor people also increases the number of socialist voters. It is difficult to escape Bourgeois's political dimension of allocation. Even when the allocation process applied the rules with impeccable impartiality to house the disadvantaged, there could still be both political gain and altruism.

Exploring the function of social housing

The effects of the tendency for social housing to accumulate in particular French *communes* for political reasons could be seen in the riots of 2005. There were concentrations of social housing in Seine-Saint-Denis, a *département* north of Paris, which was traditionally communist or socialist. Those same areas and similar estates elsewhere suffered the worst riots. This was a particular combination of social housing with a tradition of radical political protest, although the elders of the rioting teenagers would not necessarily approve (Kokoreff 2006).

Traditional voting patterns, where poor people might be expected to vote for the left, might have changed since Bourgeois's study. The *département* of Seine-Saint-Denis and Nord in the Nord-pas-de-Calais were both traditional strongholds of the left, but Nicolas Sarkozy of the political right gained ground in the 2007 presidential elections,[198] obtaining 43.3 per cent of votes in Seine-Saint-Denis and 51.85 per cent in Nord.[199] This popularity might have been temporary or perhaps modern voting patterns are becoming less predictable.

Children of immigrants were also traditional supporters of the left, which could be a factor in political allocations. In 1988, 75 per cent of the children of immigrants were thought to vote for the left, but a 2007 survey found that around one third of these voters were interested in the positive discrimination policy proposed by Sarkozy in the presidential elections. Another 17 per cent of the children of immigrants voted for the National Front, though these were generally from earlier immigration from Europe (Simon 2007).

An interesting but unanswerable question is whether this electoral shift to the right resulted in left-leaning constituencies housing fewer poor people, because they no longer voted predictably. This was unclear because large social housing estates are not only found in left-leaning *communes*. It was also impossible to separate this question out from recent effects of government social mix policies encouraging the break-up of large deprived estates, and effects of insider–outsider policy, where existing tenants obtain privileged access, whatever the political complexion of the *commune*.

The political factor was not neutral in interviews, because if poor people were the target voters for the left, politically oriented landlords would tend to be more or less 'social' according to which political colour of tenant they wished to favour. This was shown in both of Bourgeois's municipal OPHLM within communist *communes* in Seine-Saint-Denis. These favoured low-income tenants by having 'social' policies avoiding eviction, charging very low rents and running large financial deficits – a species of 'insiderness'.

2.3.3 Legal difficulties in research and exposition

This section briefly concerns the problems in the legal study of this area. In England, 'housing law' collects a mix of relevant public and private law with associated sociological research, but this does not generally exist in France in that particular combination.

Generally, French similarities to England are striking, with common traditions of social housing, similar housing stock and multiple common influences and interactions. The French right to housing, with its priority for disadvantaged people in social housing, seemed initially to correspond to the 'reasonable preference' accorded to those in priority need in England regarding social housing allocation.[200] England has many similar problems to France.

This study still presented severe technical difficulties for research and explanation. Aside from the normal difficulties of mastering another legal system in another language, this study researched allocation in ways French lawyers would not do themselves. French lawyers generally specialize early in public or private law, and the combination of these is relatively uncommon (Richier 2002); French housing law research was concentrated in public law because of the increasing hegemony of this generally (Van Lang 1996). The absence of housing law was a disciplinary mismatch which required studying a large volume of law from different French subjects in order to examine context and equivalent law: property, special contracts, spatial planning, companies, public and administrative law, local government, tax, benefits, government aids, public agencies, banks and eviction to start with.

The generalizations of sociology and economics were useful. Economic theory provided an internationally common economic paradigm, even if used largely as a qualitative framework to explain human behaviour in a relatively non-judgemental way. Sociological empirical study radically improved an understanding of how the system worked. French law has a long and distinguished tradition of social theory, but empirical sociological studies by academic lawyers were uncommon.[201]

There was also mismatch within the important taxonomy of the law of property, tenancies and welfare provision, described in section 2.1.5 (see p. 40) and in the next two chapters. Taxonomy describes the extent and boundaries of legal areas such as contract and public law. The latter subjects are more important and extensive in France, covering areas dealt with by the law of property in England, so some areas fall within one set of principles and assumptions in France and a different set in England (Ball 2010b).

A later problem was the impact of European regulation. Every national lawyer now has to understand the impact of the EU, the ECHR and RESC on the local law studied. This also added to the difficulties of this study, and will probably also reduce the likelihood of empirical study by comparative lawyers, because of the volume of legal materials to be mastered first. Because of this volume of law, economics and sociology, this study offers the minimum legal references consistent with finding the sources,[202] facilitated by excellent French free public online resources.[203]

Exploring the function of social housing

The problems of exposition were, if anything, greater than the problems of research (explained in section A1.1, p. 257). This explains the comparative law debates generally, such as emphasis on difference rather than similarity, the way economists contribute to this debate, and other problems of this study.

This work falls within European housing studies, promoted across Europe by the European Network for Housing Research (ENHR) for 20 years, diffusing general interdisciplinary work to a wide policy audience, such as planners, sociologists, economists, geographers and lawyers. Academic work produced by this extended family of European housing researchers means that it is possible to find out general information on housing issues through periodicals like *Housing Studies*, *The International Journal of Housing Policy*, and *Housing Theory and Society*, for which the author is grateful.

The critical tone of this study at first sight seems uncharitable to my French hosts. This study relies on a long, happy and continuing collaboration with many of the French partners listed in the acknowledgements. Criticism reflects interview evidence and a quantity of similar French literature cited, and in some ways this book is less critical than many French studies. The use of economics generally avoids condemning actors who are doing their best in the circumstances and seeks to help by suggesting reform in an area of law frequently condemned in France. This is not a question of an outsider, alone, presuming to criticise a different culture, and the writer is often enthusiastic about other areas of French law, such as the coherence of the 1989 statute governing most residential tenancies (Ball 2003).

2.3.4 Designing the qualitative study

The study was to check whether Bourgeois's criticisms were still true, whether allocation actually housed disadvantaged people and then how and why this happened. French social housing applications were made in four principal places: town halls, social landlords' offices, prefect's offices and to the CIL (the organization that collects employers' and employees' housing contributions), so interviewees were sought there. Senior civil servants implementing national and local policy were also interviewed, as were administrators of voluntary bodies, the associations who worked with disadvantaged people and saw any problems. Interviewing social landlords was particularly important. Again, there is more information and the topic guides are in Appendix 2.

Anonymity for interviewees was important in a highly sensitive and political area. For example, a Marxist voluntary organization, SOS Racisme, threatened to prosecute particular social landlords for race discrimination after an apparently anonymous inspection report (Batiactu 2006b). Protecting anonymity in this study meant all direct quotes had to be specifically approved by interviewees. Vagueness was necessary about specific political parties, places and organizations, for fear senior interviewees would be identified.[204]

The regions of Ile-de-France, Rhône-Alpes and Nord-Pas-de-Calais together accounted for 44 per cent of all social housing in Bourgeois's (1996) study. These were chosen for study under the assumption that more social housing means fewer housing problems. In retrospect, this could be a wrong assumption, although, equally, existing difficulties could be alleviated by social stock.

These regions were economically different, geographically separate, illustrated different land prices and had very different average incomes.[205] Their location is shown in Figure 1.3. Within this, the *département* was the basic unit of study:

- The Hauts de Seine in Ile-de-France, immediately west of central Paris
- The Nord in Nord-Pas-de-Calais in the far north of France
- Rhône in Rhône-Alpes, towards the south-east (study was limited to 'Grand Lyon' [Greater Lyon] because this conurbation dominated the *département*, so studying the remaining handful of *communes* was impractical).

It quickly became clear that regional variation was very important. The Hauts de Seine had large *communes* that did not cooperate substantially, whilst the *communauté urbaine* in Grand Lyon included 55 *communes* working together, and five layers of local government. In the Nord, social landlords had a larger role in processing allocations. This meant adjusting the sample slightly to cover people with experience of these variations in allocation processes.

Other factors taken into account are dealt with in Appendix 1. The ubiquity of long waiting lists meant that areas of low demand were not covered, an important omission. After the study, Jean-Pierre Schaeffer[206] suggested that areas with low percentages of social housing also suffered low demand, because people did not know they could apply.

The interview questions also addressed various meta questions: whether there was a general distributional problem in France, causing the housing crisis, and whether this was to do with politics and money or other factors. New questions arose in interviews, such as the effects of the law of divorce, debt and race discrimination on social housing allocation. Interviewees spent up to three hours patiently answering questions.

2.4 Conclusion

This study started with some scepticism about whether there really was a housing crisis in France. The statistics were unclear about how far social landlords housed poor people, particularly those in difficulty. Detailed study of this would not have been possible without Bourgeois's criticisms.

The dilemmas faced by social landlords about who they should house reflected a European history common to several countries, rooted in the housing of workers but moving to modern diversity. This diversity is under threat by increasing

European regulation. The various types of French social housing have their origins in the historic social conflicts described in the next chapter.

The French view that landlords' and tenants rights' are perpetually opposed is just one possible national interpretation of rights in the ECHR and RESC, but might be widespread. *Hutten-Czapska* and *FEANTSA* seem to promote this opposition and limit housing policy, whilst EU competition policy also limits social housing subsidy.

This EU competition policy supports the idea that housing the most disadvantaged should be the main object of subsidy.[207] Although this focus is welcome, whether it actually results in more funding for the disadvantaged is unclear (see Chapter 10). Whether this is a coordinated European policy is also questionable, because of conflicts within these decisions.

EU law risks disrupting Kemeny's 'iron triangle'[208] of landlords, tenants and the State. The State must balance landlords' and tenants' rights, which is difficult where there is high insiderness or any state of tension finding expression in this political opposition. Outsiders can be left out of account (Rueda 2005). Political effort has to be made to these debates, which are settled in different ways in different countries. This chapter only reports a few cases but a legally supported tendency to re-open old quarrels is worrying.

3 The historical context: from revolution to rights

Rights were fundamental as a basis for French housing policy and for social housing allocations, and both were powerfully influenced by historical events. The revolution, from 1789, was both the dawn of human rights in France and a national trauma. It heralded new forms of private and public law, which have different meanings, weight and connotations than in England. This chapter looks at how these different perceptions of rights developed within a different institutional structure, to illustrate key aspects affecting social housing.

The 1789 revolution swept away a rigid hierarchical society. It reduced or removed forms of law that survived and developed in England to become the modern English law concerning discretion, trusts, equity, charity and heavy duties of good faith. Equity in particular is a large and important area of English law but is of relatively small importance in France (Ball 2006). Rather than being abolished, the UK feudal system adapted to modern requirements, and equity was part of the way it did this. The French can be hostile to English uses of all these terms because of their associations with the legal language of the *ancien régime* before the revolution, except for the relatively mild, general 'good faith'[209] in French contracts.

This short historical account shows how different types of French law developed as a framework for social housing allocation. As a preliminary, the first section defends the limited historical and legal approach which emphasises differences rather than similarities. This then shows the bare essential elements of the 1789 revolution as a background to the development of the public structures of governance, within which rights evolved. It also looks at problems for the poor in nineteenth-century slums.

Next, there is the development of important legal concepts, from the individualist and absolute right to property, used to resist imposition on landlords of any kind of duty, to the opposing development of social rights assisting the poor in solidarity. This oppositional legal debate, with its high degree of abstraction, has no precise English counterpart in the law. Social landlords were caught up in these protracted debates.

The historical context: from revolution to rights

Then follows the history of French social landlords, in the context of the housing, social and construction policies at the heart of the social state. This sets the scene for the following three chapters, explaining the institutional context, social landlords, their funding and then the allocation process itself.

3.1 From revolution to rights

The 1789 French revolution ended a period of absolute monarchy and led to the foundation of a new legal order. The king was God's representative on Earth and there had been no dilution of absolute royal power in France, unlike in England after settlements following the Glorious Revolution of 1688. When the French king was beheaded, this was awkward for property law, where all law and rights, including land rights, were conceived as descending from God through the king.

A new conception of property was needed, and this was provided by thinkers in the Enlightenment. New ideas of absolute and unitary property ownership spread across the whole of Europe, producing land reform. In France, new property ideas were to form the backbone of the new civil law after the revolution. This section briefly introduces the approach of this chapter and then describes major contextual features of French history, the revolution and how this impacted on: property, the development of administrative law and centralization of government.

3.1.1 A short history of difference

This chapter essentially uses a historical institutionalist approach. Lowe (2004: 19) said that 'institution':

> refers to a wide range of organizations, social groups and settings and value systems, encompassing relationships within and between agencies (government departments, central-local relations) elections and voters, political parties, the structure and organization of key economic groups (such as trade unions) as well as social structures (social classes) and social norms and values.

He added: 'The basis of this school is that history "matters" and that without a fundamental understanding of the long view of the factors that influence policy change, it is difficult to make sense of the present'. This history is limited to one chapter, but there is no better way to introduce the institutional differences for an English audience and others.

History is helpful in explaining how differences developed in the national legal taxonomy and in the differently configured disciplines.[210] Lawyers today specialize narrowly and the different national legal assumptions about property and welfare in France and England are not well known. The author has even encountered

The historical context: from revolution to rights

frank disbelief in both countries that the law of the other country is like it is, partly because familiar common legal words can have radically different legal significance and weight. This rather truncated account for illustrative purposes cannot do justice to this historical subject in general.

3.1.2 Leading up to the French Revolution

Feudalism was a system of property ownership, human relationships and government (Topalov 1987). All these elements were split and recast in the violent rupture with the past that was the French Revolution. Feudal land rights were very fragmented, with multiple complicated rights split between multiple owners in ways that varied between different parts of France. Selling land was thus difficult. The nobility was substantially exempt from land taxes, occupying a privileged position in a hierarchical and unequal society (Gonnard 1943; Doyle 1989; Bart 2009).

This inequality was reflected in the complex court system, with different courts for the church, the nobility and the people. Judges did not have a good reputation because they purchased their offices, took fees and could stop a trial to ask for more money (Doyle 1989: 25; Perrot 1995: 7). French government administration was complex, with different geographical divisions for judicial, administrative and fiscal purposes and different laws in former component territories. Wachsman (2005: 298) traced French attachment to equality (and thus hostility to positive discrimination in favour of disadvantaged people) back to these rigid and unfair social differences before the revolution.

Poverty and the social conditions for violent revolution were already in place. Doyle (1989: 16) described French poverty then as 'concentrated and eye-catching'. Bread normally made up three-quarters of a poor worker's diet and bread shortages were to be critical in the revolution. In the seventeenth century there had already been a general drift to the cities, with 'chronic endemic poverty and a soaring crime rate' (Kettering 2001: 127).

In France from 1622, syphilitic prostitutes, the mentally ill and others could be imprisoned in hospitals and beggars arrested. Workhouses appeared by the eighteenth century and, from 1808, beggars and vagabonds were criminalized as dangerous or marginal. Theoretically, the unemployed had to report to hospitals for work or be detained (Roman 2001).[211] Foucault described this imprisonment as 'the great confinement', exacerbating a French view that charity was paternalistic and contrary to human dignity, although Kettering (2001: 131) argued that he exaggerated.

In the crisis of 1789, the Estates General (comprising the three estates of nobles, clergy and the people) was called by Louis XVI, for the first time since 1612, to raise money. The Estates General then presented their *cahiers de doléances*, a list of complaints including demands for land reform, and feudal rights were

The historical context: from revolution to rights

effectively abolished by 1791. Prior to the revolution the people were represented in the Estates General by the bourgeoisie, but were outvoted by the other estates. However, these 'people' declared that they were a National Assembly and on 20 June at the Jeu de Paume, they took an oath not to part without creating a constitution (Price 1997). On 26 August 1789 the Declaration of the Rights of Man and the Citizen was read out to the crowd ('The 1789 Declaration').

Rights declared included equality, liberty, property and due process. The 1789 Declaration is still part of the current constitution of 4 October 1958 ('The 1958 Constitution'). This initial public law framework would later become increasingly important with the development of an administrative court system to support individual's rights, such as the right to housing.

3.1.3 The development of administrative law

Administrative law would expand and develop remedies supporting constitutional rights and freedoms, including the rights to property and, much more recently, the right to housing. During the revolution, a statute of 1790,[212] which is still in force, forbade the law courts from interfering with the administration. This gap in justice allowed free reign to a revolutionary government, but later was to lead to the development of separate courts for public law as a check on the State. Brown and Bell (1998: 25) said: 'The surprising feature of French administrative law is that, in spite of its totalitarian origins, it has survived to provide one of the most systematic guarantees of the liberties of the individual against the State known in today's world.'

By the 1870s, the Conseil d'État had started to provide remedies for individuals whose rights were infringed by the administration.[213] Napoleon I had resurrected the Conseil d'État, formerly the advisor to kings, to advise government. This Council expanded its powers, evolving to settle disputes between public organs and then as a general administrative court providing recourse for individuals.

The initial embargo on litigation against the government still means that this continually developing public law is different from private law and is still administered entirely separately. Before commencing action, litigants must decide whether their case concerns public or private law.[214] Figure 3.1 shows that the Conseil d'État is now the apex of the administrative court system, whilst the Cour de Cassation is the highest of the private and criminal courts.

Judges had generally lost respect prior to the revolution, and were then expected to be 'machines for judging' – simply interpreting statute – which represented the superiority of the will of the people within the Constitution (Bell 2001: vii). This theoretically denies the possibility of judge-made law.[215] Public law judges had extra flexibility, since they had some discretions concerning the law applied, not just the inherent leeway judges have in assessing the facts and their relevance to the law, *le pouvoir d'appreciation* (Whittaker 2008).[216]

The historical context: from revolution to rights

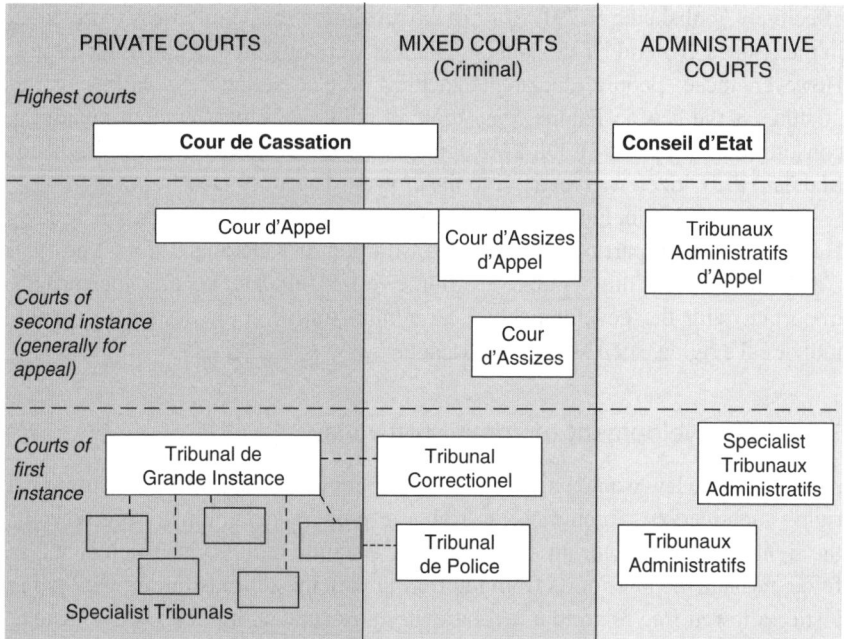

3.1 A schematic view of the public and private courts. (Note: Not all judicial institutions are included.)

Despite objections to judge-made law, public law was generally based on cases, or rather existing principles interpreted in cases, known as *jurisprudence*. This word has a common meaning in English and French legal philosophy but is a hypernym and has important extra meanings in French as the nearest translation for case law,[217] a linguistic overlap. This tends to conflate legal philosophy with the sharp end of *jurisprudence*: its compulsory application to individuals in particular cases. This applied aspect means that legal philosophy thus has greater practical importance than has been traditional in the UK.

France has a large volume all types of judgment to guide litigants, but the administrative courts always had advantages. Administrative court procedures have traditionally been more informal, flexible and pragmatic than private law courts and their caseloads have grown rapidly. Social landlords applied a daily mix of public and private law, which could be reviewed in either set of courts, complicating their administration.

After 1958, the new Constitutional Council, the Conseil constitutionnel, would have an important role in developing and consolidating constitutional principles, including the later right to housing.[218] This council of elder statesman can review the constitutionality of legislation prior to promulgation, with very recent expansion of their power to review cases from any court.[219]

The historical context: from revolution to rights

3.1.4 Historic centralization

Another important development was the considerable historic centralization of administration. From 1791 to 1793, *communes*[220] had been independent and not practically answerable to the national government (Brunelli 1998: 13). Centralization followed sharply in 1793, with mayors nominated by government. One of the plaques around Napoleon I's tomb declares that he had put an end to the chaos in the *communes*. The *département* was also created as a larger administrative area of fairly standard size, to make a clean break with the past, and administered by departmental prefects representing the central State.

After the revolution, there was continuing centralization and complexification of the law, with a corresponding increase in the number of civil servants in Paris. Dupuis *et al.* (2000: 11) described this administrative power: 'Its extension and its complexity, if not its obscurity, transform it in to a Kafkaesque universe. The users submit to it, but they do not know how it acts, or why it imposes on them this or that decision.'

Opacity in French administration thus had a long history, but since 1981 there has been greater administrative transparency and more decentralization, following national debates (Dupuis *et al.* 2000: 12). Housing-related powers were being decentralized during my study, but the responsibility of the State for the right to housing for the disadvantaged was not often decentralized.

3.2 The opposition between property and social rights

In the nineteenth century, the law supporting French individual constitutional rights developed in the context of the virulent opposition of conservative and socialist thought about property. French thinkers later formulated modifications to both contract and property law in tenancies in a process of settling debates through bargaining, a process still affecting social housing. This was the context for the development of welfare, social housing and also a growth of public law, which would much later provide a new legal basis for rights in human dignity.

Property was not the only right affecting social housing allocation, but had a particular role in aligning housing rights with workers' rights in opposition to capitalism. In English, 'property' in non-legal use tends to describe the thing owned rather than ownership itself, which has a slightly dated technical legal meaning of ownership. In French, *propriété* means ownership more clearly. To say '*Je suis propriétaire* (I am a land owner)' can still be a source of pride, although there is a popular drift to use 'property' to describe the thing owned in France too.

3.2.1 From property to social contract

The abolition of feudal property from 1879[221] was more divisive for farmers than for displaced country people arriving in towns to find no decent accommodation.

The historical context: from revolution to rights

Rural power relations were rapidly and sometimes violently renegotiated within this new framework (Bart 2009: from 409).

Revolutionary legal changes supported the ambitions of the burgeoning middle classes through a powerfully expressed right to property. Article 17 of the 1789 Declaration says: 'Property being an inviolable and sacred right, no one can be deprived of it, except when public necessity, legally stated, clearly demands it, and on condition of there being fair compensation in advance.' This is not a purely French idea and the legal principle of absolute property spread across Europe, with property rights differently implemented in the UK and Ireland.

The French concept of property ownership is unitary and absolute, theoretically derived from Roman law. Its unitary nature proposes a basic position that only one property owner is theoretically possible, which is why tenants are excluded from having any property rights.[222] Pauliat (1998: 11)[223] described this as 'a proud and egotistical absolutism', and that the history of housing was closely bound up with this right to property. To an English reader, the right to property might not seem directly relevant to social housing allocation, although its exclusionary nature can readily be appreciated.

The right to property was supported by the post-revolutionary reform of private law to fill the gap left by the abolition of feudal relations. Napoleon I sponsored the Code civil (C. civ.) in 1804, the first of five legal codes.[224] Article 544 of the Code civil still declares that property is the right to enjoy and dispose of things in the most absolute way possible, unless legally prohibited. The reference to 'legally prohibited' here means there is a derogation from the absolute right to property in favour of the State, also supported by Article 545, allowing intervention on the basis of public utility.

The right to property enabled private social landlords to reject social housing candidates. Public social landlords also did this, but their duty to balance their budgets played an important role. There was a practical correspondence between the right to property as a public constitutional right and the private law concept, although there were important differences. Unlike private property, public property was inalienable if required for a public function and so often could not be mortgaged (Jégouzo 1995: 114). This is why local authority guarantees for construction were essential.

The absolute approach to property was supported by the individualist conception of the contract, embedded in the Code civil. This replaced feudal bonds with contracts entered into by free consent. In Roman law, the contract had limited uses (Bell *et al.* 1996: 307). Using eighteenth-century writings by Pothier and Domat,[225] the contract was generalized and acquired new uses, such as regulating companies and matrimonial property regimes. Even today, this expansion of the contract continues with the use of contractualization as a mechanism for decentralization.

Another Enlightenment idea was Rousseau's notion of the social contract as a basis for the State's power. Men as autonomous individuals together formed a

The historical context: from revolution to rights

consensual civil society, and delegated part of their liberty to the State by contract.[226] This promotion of the individual led to nineteenth-century discouragement of organizations intervening between the individual and the State (Wachsman 2005: 24). This affected charities because, during the revolution, people stopped paying tithes to the Church, which supported voluntary work. Doyle (1989: 400) said: 'The old structure of charity was pulled apart and, for all the talk, nothing constructive put in its place.'

Nineteenth-century tenants theoretically obtained their homes by a mere hire contract and would later make common cause with workers to oppose property rights. Landlords housed workers and the poor in bad conditions; this also happened across the channel. DAL (1996: 20) described nineteenth-century French tenants as being at the mercy of owners who could evict them overnight.

3.2.2 Revolution and opposition

The 'right to insurrection' is the duty of the people to retake power, if good use is not made of it (Turpin 1994: 24). It is the French people who are sovereign,[227] not Parliament as in the UK, and the French people illustrated this fact by further revolutions in 1830 and 1848, when the Second Republic was founded. This only lasted until the coup d'Etat by Napoleon III in 1851.

France underwent later and quicker industrialisation than England, with the migration of agricultural workers to towns producing poor living conditions. From 1830 onwards, there were a series of critical State enquiries into housing conditions. Cholera outbreaks in 1832 and 1834 showed the consequences of overcrowding (Guerrand 1967). Some rather ineffective legislation was then passed in 1850 to address unhealthy living conditions.[228]

Poorer people were referred to as 'the dangerous class', not only because of their insanitary conditions and perceived moral deficiencies, but also on account of their inclination to revolt (Price 1997: 194). In a third revolution in 1870–71, the Paris Commune took over the capital, then under siege by the Prussians. This popular revolt, which was brutally put down, was notable for early housing legislation, such as rent relief and a limited delay before evictions. This was criticized as an attack on property, which was, and remains, a legal basis for resistance to State intervention (Guerrand 1967: 183–201).

These revolutions were not purely the result of agitation from the left, but were also due to difficult social, political and economic conditions. Until 1870, many clubs were banned and workers were obliged to have personal work passports, so troublemakers were blacklisted. Under the Paris Commune people freely formed associations, cooperatives and unions, the beginnings of social organizations (Sowerwine 2001).

Ten years after the Paris Commune, dissidents returned to Paris and there was a flowering of political thought of left and right, particularly concerning the unitary concept of property, which made few concessions to tenants. Nineteenth-century French socialist thought supported both tenants and workers, because they were exploited by property owners. Guesde (1882) proposed that the housing crisis would only disappear with the victory of the proletarian revolution. The well-known slogan that 'all property is theft' by the anarchist, Proudhon (1994, written in 1840), has to be seen as part of this revolutionary stream of thought.[229] French anarchy was essentially a species of small-scale radical socialism.[230]

After 1880, there was greater freedom of thought, allowing a number of revolutionary periodicals: *le Cri du peuple*, *l'Egalité*, *le Révolté* and *le Socialiste*. One popular song, published in *l'Anti concièrge*, to the tune of the national anthem, *la Marseillaise*, ran thus:

> Forward miserable tenants,
> The end of the tenancy has arrived,
> against us the landlords,
> The bloody standard is raised.
>
> (Quoted in Guerrand 1967: 234)

From 1880 to 1894, tenants campaigned with workers against capitalist employers and landlords. Both socialists and anarchists called for rent strikes, although the socialists were not significant electorally until the next century (Guerrand 1967; Shapiro 1985). Anarchists were active in tenant campaigns, forming the League against Property Owners. They were popular with poor Paris tenants, organizing removal of furniture by rope from first floor windows at night, because furniture could be forfeited to pay rent.[231] In 1878, in one night, 7,147 families decamped from their apartments (DAL 1996: 20).

For the political right, in contrast, property was an ideal with moralizing force and this was to become important as a reason to encourage social housing for purchase. Land had prestige (Doyle 1989: 24), and conservative thinkers ascribed virtue to property ownership. In 1792, Boissy d'Anglas said: 'A man without property needs a constant effort of virtue to interest himself in an order of things that holds nothing for him.'[232] Consequently, from the early 1850s acquisition of property by instalments was promoted in social housing through the concept of the *cité ouvrière* (workers' apartment block). Emile Cheysson enthused:

> With a little house and a garden, the workman is made a head of the family, really worthy of the title, that is, moral and planning ahead, feeling that he has roots and having authority over his family. Soon the house will take hold of him, will moralize him, stabilize him and transform him.
>
> (Quoted in Guerrand 1967: 267)

Frédéric le Play, the founder of the reformist Society for Social Economy, had similar views: 'The *classes dirigeantes* (managing classes) should encourage workers to save and to buy their homes' (also in Guerrand 1967: 261).

The historical context: from revolution to rights

Property ideals were also used to resist intrusions by public authorities for the purpose of public health. Paul Leroy-Beaulieu, a supporter of Le Play and fellow writer in *la Réforme sociale*, opposed financial impositions of all kinds: 'The principle of property has a wholeness, completely exclusive in nature, which rejects every sort of attack; it is something like virginity, which cannot be replaced when damaged.'[233] He opposed compulsory maintenance of property frontages and the social housing movement in 1894.

As late as 1885, a Paris judge ruled that water supply to a home was not a matter of public health but for the convenience and well-being of tenants. No effective mandatory national public health law was passed until 1902 (Shapiro 1985). A new class of experts, the hygienists, ultimately demonstrated the necessity of State intervention at the beginning of a period of political reconciliation.

3.2.3 Reconciling left and right in solidarity

At the end of the nineteenth century new ideas started to resolve disputes between left and right. Brousse ([1883] 1910) proposed an alternative to revolution by the gradual public absorption of monopolies, providing locally managed public services. Traces of this could still be seen in local political involvement of social housing. The Solidarists formed a party in 1881, and became a radical government from 1895 to 1896 and from 1902, the period when '*habitations à bon marché*' (HBM) organizations were developed.

Solidarism in France was a political movement distinct from solidarity, a pre-existing mechanism in contract law.[234] Since much of this book is about law, the English or common law reader needs to put out of their mind any national historical background to solidarity, to try to think of this as just a piece of law like any other. It does have great political importance, as explained in this section and the next, but its use in this book is in describing the way the institutions and procedures around social housing allocation were structured. This affects social housing allocation both in the diffuse form of regulation and in the extended social–contractual forms of process.

Léon Bourgeois was a politician, who became Minister of the Interior in 1890. He conceived modern solidarity as a third way between socialism and conservatism, based on social duty towards others, for which he obtained the Nobel Prize in 1920. Bourgeois built on much earlier philosophical foundations[235] and on the French socialist cooperative movement, which played an important role in social housing (Fourrier 1829) and was taken up by Charles Gide and Emile Durkheim. Shapiro (1985: 145) said:

> Solidarism was designed to defuse social conflict by replacing competitive individualism with associationism, mutualism, and cooperation. It stressed social interdependence, claiming in essence that man was born the debtor of society and that this debt to past generations was to be paid to future

The historical context: from revolution to rights

generations through the mutual guarantee or insurance of each other against life's risks. Specifically, solidarism sought to revise liberal contract theory, which had allegedly failed to take into account the inequality of bargaining positions among the parties.

Solidarism addressed a legal problem that rights provided benefits to individuals, but lacked a principle to impose duties on citizens to achieve them. This was particularly so for social and economic rights, or even for greater imposition of taxes on the rich,[236] faced with a principle of equality. This is how the legal aspects of existing law on solidarity were adapted and extended.

Léon Bourgeois was inspired by French contract law, which has greater associations with freedom and autonomy in France than in England (Bell *et al.* 1996). Solidarity in the 1804 Code civil was and is an often uncontentious device, described below. Bourgeois attached a social welfare dimension to this contractual device, at the same time providing a basis for settling, by agreement, the violent nineteenth-century disputes between left and right. Bourgeois saw that rights and responsibilities could be implemented by collective contracts.

Solidarity, as a private contractual legal mechanism is an almost boring part of the Code civil. *Responsabilité solidaire*[237] is frequently uncontentious. 'Solidary' responsibility means that a group of people agree to pay the whole of a collective debt, including each others' share of that debt. This contrasts with *conjointe* liability, where people only pay their proportionate part of this collective debt, used particularly for non-business people.[238]

Terré *et al.* (1996: 920) describe this contractual solidary obligation[239] as 'interdependence and community of interest'. At its heart is an agreement to pay more than an equal share by consent within a contract. In England, a similar private-contractual effect is created by 'joint and several liability'. At the simple level of language, you could not base a political movement on joint and several liability. It would never catch on, nor does it have strong philosophical or social associations.

'Passive' contractual solidary responsibility imposes mutual burdens on more than one debtor whilst 'active' solidarity distributes benefits to more than one creditor in ways that are not necessarily either equal or limited to contracting parties.[240] The debt or credit does not have to be monetary.[241] Legislation might be needed to extend benefits under a contract to people not a party to the contract.[242] Today, this solidarity is still an everyday and normal part of private-law collective contracting arrangements, such as when extra benefits are purchased by the various French social security funds for scheme members and their families, above compulsory state benefits.

Courvoisier (2005) dates the idea of solidarity back to Roman times, where it was associated with mutual support in family law. In modern France, solidary responsibility in the old family values sense still arises in several family

The historical context: from revolution to rights

situations; when benefits are enjoyed or responsibility imposed: on spouses; in civil partnerships (*pactes civils de solidarité* or PACS, but not automatically[243] or at all between cohabitants;[244] and between parents.[245] This does not arise by default or at all between beneficiaries on death).[246] It is sometimes hard to say where the dividing line is between contract and solidarity in public law as a value. There are also very important commercial uses.[247]

In private law, Terré *et al.*'s 'community of interest'[248] in matrimonial special contracts (*régimes*) binds married couples by contractual solidarity towards third parties. The matrimonial regime alters property relationships during the marriage and provides for an agreed later split of their matrimonial assets by consent, whilst public law can adjust these obligations for social reasons. The latter is a public law imposition by the State, which could be seen as notionally based on the divorcees' consent through their elected representatives, within Rousseau's collective contract of government, or as more ancient mutual bonds of support. Public law family obligations for mutual support are not defined as solidary in the Code civil (distinguishing them from contractual obligations) but as *obligations alimentaires*.[249] These family responsibilities can be seen without any individual contractual consent in compulsory inheritance regimes (Dyson 2005) and in obligations towards relatives.[250]

In social welfare law there is a clear connection between solidary responsibility in private law and solidarity in the public law with its values of collective mutual support. This might be an obvious connection for a civil lawyer, but is less obvious to a common lawyer. French welfare started as private provision imposing private collective contractual insurance burdens and providing the benefits of social protection, worked out in negotiation with employers. This gradually became a formal system of negotiation over social rights.[251] Wieacker (2003: 436) describes this as, 'The progress of law from self-help towards public order.'

With increasing State intervention and contribution after the Second World War, the social security system steadily moved out of the private law to find its public law basis in social rights, but aspects of the institutional structure of collective employer–employee negotiation remained. The result of these negotiations bind a union or tenants' organization by solidary responsibility in private law for purchased benefits, or by statute, to extend and generalize the effect of the agreements to other people or other situations, whether in private or public law.

There are, however, serious problems of extent of solidary responsibility, and of imposition on people against their will of such collective contracts. This happens to a limited extent through binding collective negotiations, but much more through the public law within Rousseau's social contract of government, as amended by Bourgeois. Dubois (2005: 336) distinguished the '*choisi*', a mutual support which is chosen, and '*subi*', mutual support which is imposed.

One person's private contractual benefit through solidarity is another person's burden. Today, private solidary obligations cannot theoretically be imposed on

The historical context: from revolution to rights

individuals without consent or the imposition of statute.[252] However, the default nature of some private solidary obligations means the ill-advised, and individuals who change their mind or suffer changed circumstances, will later be bound by them, such as within matrimonial regimes on divorce.

David (2005) and Courvoisier (2005) traced the juridification of solidarity in public law in successive French constitutions, from a first mention in the draft constitution of 1848, which ultimately referred to mutual aid or brotherly assistance, connected to *fraternité*, in the motto of the French Republic: 'liberty, equality and brotherhood'.[253] The terminology of solidarity could be elusive in the twentieth century, perhaps because of its connectedness to Russian communism (Beguin *et al.* 2005).

Proudhon (1994) suggested that universal solidarity regulated property law, an early statement of the social nature of that law, which implied property owners' solidary responsibility towards everyone. This is an early statement of the goodwill to all mankind expressed much later in the Universal Declaration of Human Rights, although there, responsibility was undertaken by States.[254]

Alternative expressions to solidarity, such as social cohesion, can be used, but recently the use of the word solidarity has tended to re-emerge. Even when solidarity as a public-law value faded in public law because of its connection to communism, the mechanism of solidarity in the private law still remained as the everyday workhorse in contract, commercial, and family law and in welfare. Arguments about solidarity in France thus concern its extent rather than its existence, and no doubt European national experiences of solidarity will differ with different political histories.

Prosser (2006) argued that the value of solidarity for European public regulation was qualitative, allowing the implementation of public service, and 'balancing competing values, setting out the sort of society we want to live in'. This would qualify economic regulatory approaches and is an attractive vision. Unfortunately, in French social housing allocation, the 'competing values' are not balanced in any consistent way, with different actors seeking to house their own candidates. This also underestimates the role of solidarity as a coercive mechanism exercised over individuals by the State. Without State intervention by legislation, allocation would not happen quite like this.

3.2.4 Solidarity and the social basis of property

Solidarism required rethinking the role of property. Duguit (1912: 15) reconciled absolute property rights with social obligations in his argument: 'Ownership is no longer a right attaching to the owner; it is the social function of the holder of wealth.' This 'social function' of ownership was a theoretical basis for collective limitation by society of property rights, such as by requirements for planning permission, compulsory purchase, tenants' rights, requisition of

The historical context: from revolution to rights

unoccupied homes and a basis for housing the disadvantaged, through the right to housing.

French thought had an important role in developing the idea of the 'social' basis of property, and the mechanism for enforcing social rights through the contractual notion of solidarity. This 'social basis' of property rights now forms part of the constitutions of a large number of states globally (COHRE 2000). Despite this, in France, a 1946 draft constitution which mentioned solidarity was rejected by referendum.

Solidarity still represented a legal basis for social rights: a value and justification for imposition on individuals for public utility.[255] The modification of French property rights for social reasons was found in several ways through the intercession of the State.[256] An example was the idea of abuse of rights,[257] a creation of the judges, whereby principles of morality and fairness were used as sanctions against actions causing serious damage to another (Steiner 2010: 185). Statutory limitations to property were also required by planning permission, rights of way (*servitudes*) and other functions of land regulation (Pauliat 1998). Importantly for this account, tenants' statutory rights limited landlords' property rights.

Solidarity was thus a key mechanism in imposing and creating social obligations towards other people. In private contract law, the substantive content of solidarity depends on what solidary contractual liability is being consented to. In public law, its application must depend effectively on public morality or solidarity as a value, based on *jurisprudence* or statute, although this still seems morally indeterminate and flexible.[258] The role of solidarity as a mechanism can mean it might not appear in books on constitutional rights such as Wachsman (2005). It is not a right, as such, although it enables the performance of state duties to provide rights.

3.2.5 Welfare and increased public law hegemony

Voluntary collective contracts between workers and employers or with mutual assurance companies were the foundation of the French welfare state between the Wars (Dutton 2002). The expression 'welfare' is generally used in this book to suggest the care of those in difficulty, to distinguish this from the sort of contributory social security that could provide generous contributory benefits.

The post-war French State increasingly sponsored, funded and organized social welfare funds, but with the continuing participation of union, employer and other representatives in negotiations. Durkheim (1986: 32) said that intermediaries between state and individuals were necessary: 'Collective activity is always too complex to be able to be expressed by the sole and unique organ of the State; moreover, the State is too far from individuals...'

French social rights gradually became public law, because the State enjoyed a derogation from property law, enabling impositions on individuals for public

The historical context: from revolution to rights

utility.[259] Also important was increased administrative involvement in every aspect of life. Social progress in France also involved the elaboration of a detailed public structure of rights, including wider and different philosophies of human rights and the nature of State power as a basis for public regulation. The right to housing in public law was recent – it was only formalized in 1994.[260]

Although solidarity is not an English legal device, English authors working on solidarity for an English audience include Prosser (2006), who emphasised its moral qualities, Ross and Borgmann-Prebil (2010) and Bell (2010). This focus on public law and philosophical aspects of solidarity understated its background in contract law, also understating the uses of solidarity for coercion. This philosophical approach also paradoxically underestimates the basis of solidarity in contractual consent, at least in private law, to preserve individual liberty, autonomy and democracy.

This book concerns the local effects of these principles, which might not correspond to the international philosophical literature. Legrand (1996) said that even if there were a common European legal system, the application of law would differ locally, given different national cultures, institutions and languages.

Collective contractual approaches were found everywhere in French organizations of any kind, supplemented by public-law solidarity to facilitate and enforce collective responsibility and collective generosity. Altruism arises naturally in the hearts of individuals, but organized altruism is channelled through national organizational devices. Associations, not-for-profit and often political organizations were collective contractual organizations connected to the 'right of association'.[261] Companies, *sociétés*, were also conceived as collective contracts.[262]

Actors interviewed tended to think that individuals acting collectively were moral, altruistic or at least keeping an eye on each other.[263] This contrasts with Lindbeck and Snower's (2002) observation that employment markets, where employees are unionized, do not tend to act altruistically. The results of this study tend to support Lindbeck and Snower for most social housing allocation. Altruism has to be judged by outcomes. For a lawyer, those outcomes were in part the result of particular legal mechanisms, although understanding the economic interests of participants is also essential.

3.3 Social housing and its context

French social landlords were hybrid institutions influenced by the political thought of both left and right. They had always been builders with an objective of alleviating the social conditions of workers, a reaction to nineteenth-century housing conditions (introduced later in this section). From the original ideas of the socialist utopians, social landlords had evolved through the adaption of utopian ideas by conservative philanthropists, crystallizing into essentially their current form from 1894. Their primary objective has never effectively been to

The historical context: from revolution to rights

house the most disadvantaged. In the past, the poorest people primarily found homes in private rented housing.

From these hybrid beginnings, social landlords were still affected by 'social' and collective movements, and still assist with construction in continuing housing crises. Social landlords became government policy instruments after 1945, part of a major national effort towards reconstruction and a better planned environment. Even the shift in policy towards housing benefits did not displace this culture of construction as a solution to housing problems.

3.3.1 Housing conditions in the nineteenth century

Nineteenth-century housing conditions were desperate. In Paris, a mother might be evicted after giving birth, because tenants with children were unwelcome (Shapiro 1985: 66). Lodging conditions did not give individuals sufficient light and space, causing epidemics such as cholera. Others lived in makeshift constructions of plaster and board, without sanitation, at the edge of the city. In 1838, Victor Considérant described Paris as:

> A great manufactory of putrefaction in which poverty, plague, and disease labour in concert, and air and sunlight barely enter. Paris is a foul hole where plants wilt and perish and four out of seven children die within the year.
> (Quoted in Shapiro 1985: 37)

In response, Baron Haussmann's city improvements under Napoleon III after 1850 were notable for a holistic approach to planning. This included hygienist ideas: the construction of housing with light and air for the middle classes and large, straight boulevards with drains and street lighting. However, landlords whose property was expropriated were handsomely compensated, whilst tenants were evicted and driven to the periphery of town. Flamand (2001: 57) said:

> There, where the pickaxe of the demolition men has not yet passed, in the old buildings inherited from history, yet, in all the interstices still left free by the advances of the modern town, the poorest and the most deprived, still found their base.

Haussmann's work increased house prices and rents, and left Paris with a large debt (Guerrand 1967).

Substantial problems remained across France in 1906. The first national housing enquiry by Bertillon found unsatisfactory conditions for 620 of out 1,000 French people (Guerrand 1967: 307–8), shown in Table 3.1. Social landlords provided islands of decent homes in a sea of difficulty, pioneering security of tenure and sickness insurance for tenants around 1900 (Laë 2002).

The historical context: from revolution to rights

Table 3.1 Some conditions of housing per 1,000 French people in 1906

260	Occupying overcrowded housing (more than two people per room: the kitchen being counted as a room)
360	Occupying inadequate homes
168	Occupying adequate homes (one person per room)
212	Occupying big or very big homes

Source: adapted from Guerrand (1967: 307–8).

3.3.2 The origins of social landlords

Probably the first French social housing was conceived by Fourrier (1829). A socialist utopian, he proposed an ideal workers' community, the Phalansterie or *cité ouvrière* (workers' housing): a central building with homes, community work areas, rest rooms, exchanges and a library and study room, built around a green court. In the 1850s several private *cités ouvrières* were built, mainly by employers, with homes primarily for purchase by instalments.

Napoleon III subscribed 50,000 francs to the Cité Napoleon, in Paris, which had some communal facilities. This communal concept offended liberal philanthropists who thought a concentration of people would incubate revolution, disease and moral degeneracy, whilst the working classes regarded these as barracks and an attempt at social control (Moret 1998: 23).

A more recognisably modern private social landlord, la Société d'HBM, appeared in 1884 and in 1889, Jules Siegfried founded the Société française des HBM (Magri 1995: 9–11). Siegfried worked with Picot and Cheysson, supporters of Le Play,[264] a philanthropic, conservative group of men, supporting both social housing and an organization promoting hygienist, social and urbanist ideas, the Section d'hygiène urbaine et rurale du Musée social. English ideas of garden cities, providing 'green lungs' were influential[265] (Magri 1995).

Homes for salaried workers were provided without common areas, such as the *cité ouvrière* of 800 homes built at Mulhouse by the industrialist Jean Dolfus, one of several influential employer philanthropists. Picot voiced a strong opinion:

> The big *cités ouvrières* have failed almost everywhere, in Paris, in Lille and elsewhere, and everywhere for the same reason: People have thought it possible to make a portion of the life of the tenant communal. That is a capital error. People succeed when they find the means to achieve the absolute independence of each family to the profit of the tenant.
>
> (Quoted in Magri 1995: 25)

The new Sociétés d'HBM were limited-profit, private companies enjoying tax exemptions[266] from the Siegfried Act of 30 November 1894. They could now

The historical context: from revolution to rights

borrow from a State bank, the Caisse des dépôts et de consignations (CDC),[267] and departmental committees could be formed to promote them.

This legislation became the template for State intervention in social housing: a package of tax relief and assisted loans, with income limits for applicants and State regulated governance. By 1905, there were 25 active local departmental organizing committees, but only 1,360 houses had been constructed (Stébé 1998: 50). Acts of 12 April 1906 and 10 April 1908 extended the number organizations that could invest in or give land to HBM companies and founded credit companies for special loans.[268]

Pressure by the municipalists, supporters of more local governance and Paul Brousse's ideas,[269] led to a statute of 12 December 1912 creating a publicly controlled social landlord organization. Bonnevay, the statute's promoter, thought central State construction was inefficient, and that *communes* were best placed to supplement private initiative. However, the debts of Haussmanization[270] were a recent memory.

The prospect of debts encumbering *communes* was a concern because of: 'some indisputable dangers which it would present in certain regions and at certain times for the good management of public affairs and the healthy administration of finances' (Jégouzo-Viénot 2002: 11). French local authorities are still not generally[271] allowed to hold social housing directly.

The new Offices publics d'HBM (OPHBMs) were public corporations allowing local authorities to get involved and feel responsible whilst retaining central government control. *Communes* and *départements*[272] could request the formation of OPHBMs for the construction, sale, improvement and management of homes, with sports fields, crèches, public baths and even garden cities. From this stems the modern social landlords' importance for urban development – so much so that they provide services and skilled personnel to private developers (Keck 1995).

These forms of social landlord have remained essentially similar, with the addition of the more modern OPAC from 1970.[273] Local initiative has thus always been important, and is becoming even more so because from 2007 a new single form of public social landlord removes representatives of the central State from public management boards and requires a majority of local government representatives.[274]

Progress in constructing any French housing was slow between the wars. France was weak after great wartime loss of life and property damage. There were manpower shortages, an inefficient agricultural sector and the need for re-construction, which increased the large national debt. Many French people faced unpleasant housing conditions, food shortages and prices increasing faster than inflation.

There were 42 governments in the inter-war period, reducing the possibility of intervention (Price 1997). Material and labour costs were three or four times their pre-war level, so the 35 existing HBM organizations could not act without State

The historical context: from revolution to rights

aid, particularly since rents had been frozen from 1919 (Jégouzo-Viénot 2002: 11). Low rents discouraged investment (Stébé 1998: 63).

After considerable delay, the Loucheur Act of 13 July 1928 required an HBM organization in every *département* and financed 260,000 homes for rent and purchase, including 60,000 HBMs.[275] These were directed towards the middle classes, with more than 150,000 people on Paris waiting lists by 1936. France constructed 1.8 million homes between the wars, including 170,000 HBMs and 300,000 homes constructed by employers. This compared to 3.66 million homes constructed in the UK, which included 1.1 million council homes. Germany constructed around 4 million homes (Holmans 1987; Stébé 1998: 72–77; Jégouzo-Viénot 2002: 12). There was thus relatively little French social housing before 1945.

3.3.3 'Social' movements and collective advantages

French social housing was tied up with collective 'social' movements. In the French social model, the social State was the product of negotiation and representation, sometimes simply organized lobbying. This collectivist approach was not purely about trade unionism, as illustrated by the many consultative and representative bodies involved in housing.

What does '*social*' mean in French? '*Faire du social*' is to do good work, as one would expect. However, if a train is delayed due to a strike, notices announce a delay '*suite à un movement social*' (literally, 'following a social movement' [here a strike])', a strong connectedness to labour and protest movements. Also '*droit social*' means company law, not social law, referring to the status of companies as collective contracts (*sociétés*).[276] It is small wonder that there is difficulty defining social landlords at European level, with such a multi-facetted label.

The French welfare state and widespread social benefits did not really get off the ground until after 1945 (Damon 2006). Trade union membership fell steeply in the economic crisis of 1932. Nonetheless, a bill for compulsory sickness insurance was introduced by Poincaré and continued by Tardieu and Laval, becoming law in 1928. Some employers experimented with paying extra wages to workers with families, or family allowances (Dupeyroux 1998: 42).

Since charities no longer existed, associations now carried out voluntary work using a simple collective-contractual corporate form, created by a statute of 1 July 1901. The purposes of associations were not limited, provided they had non-profit objectives which were neither immoral nor to overthrow the republican form of government.[277] French voluntary bodies could thus be much more political than English charities, which must have only specified 'charitable' objectives, including relieving poverty.[278]

French tenants joined in collective action. Between 1911 and 1913 Cochon, a carpet maker and anarchist, organized demonstrations and mass squats protesting

The historical context: from revolution to rights

against evictions. He founded a national tenants' union in 1919 which had 100,000 members,[279] when a rent strike produced a long rent freeze effectively until 1948. This worked with the Confédération général du travail, a major revolutionary trade union, and then with the communists. This tenants' union ultimately became the modern Confédération nationale du logement or CNL (DAL 1996: 20–23).

There are now five major organizations all representing tenants in negotiations, each with between 17,000 and 100,000 members.[280] These are registered as consumers' associations, giving them powers of legal advice and to represent individuals or groups[281] before the courts. Landlords' organizations were also important, particularly the Union nationale des propriétaires immobiliers.[282]

Collective action can affect tenancy terms. The long rent freeze from 1919 meant that, by 1948, rents were 1.5 per cent of the average family budget (Duclaud-Williams 1978: 34). A statute of 1 September 1948[283] allowed increased rents every six months by decree (*décret*). Today, it is mainly social tenants who still benefit from the security of tenure in this act, strongly limiting grounds for eviction, *le maintien dans les lieux*.[284]

The slow post-war dismantlement of the 1948 Statute followed, by gradual decontrol, area by area, and reducing the types of home covered. This provoked a rent strike of 20,000 people from 1975 to 1980 (Galano 2002). By 1982, this protest had produced agreements between landlord and tenant organizations, which in turn formed the basis for the Quillot Act,[285] a statute improving tenant security and the first statute to mention the right to housing. In this way collective bargaining can underpin law.

Later statutes adjusted the balance between landlords and tenants. Many tenants' rights to representation were recent, from the 1986 Statute[286] which also slightly reduced security of tenure. This security became a relatively settled compromise in the 1989 Statute, with three- or six-year fixed-term tenancies for unfurnished private tenancies,[287] or monthly periodic tenancies for social housing, supplemented by security of tenure (*le maintien dans les lieux*).[288] The negotiating power of the tenants thus predates the modern formal embodiment of this. It would be possible to write a good deal more about tenancies, but since the focus of this book is social housing allocation, regrettably it can only show sufficient to illustrate transaction costs, although there is a general account in Ball (2003).[289]

Collective contracts between landlords' and tenants' organizations on minor aspects of tenancy law were binding on all members of those organizations *erga omnes*. This means that these contracts bind individual members to the agreement made by their representatives, whether the individual agrees or not, as for collective contracts between unions and employers.[290] Agreements could then be extended with regulatory force to all or part of the rental market.

This was a logical development of the fact that in the Code civil all contracts of any kind were defined as having the effect of legislation between the parties.[291] This 'legislative' effect of contracts has a series of probably connected effects:

increasing the weight of the contract, reducing the availability of self-help remedies for breach and as a reason to attach further legislation regulating contracts. Article 1135, Code civil, allows for contracts to be binding on non-contracting parties as a consequence of equity, custom or statute, according to the nature of the particular obligation. This is the hook by which public morality is attached to contracts, whether imposing solidary responsibility by collective agreements, or other modern modifications of contract law.

Negotiations between landlord and tenant organizations were co-ordinated by the Commission nationale de la concertation, a government-funded body of representatives of landlords, tenants and property managers.[292] As in labour legislation, there were procedures for recognition of tenants' organizations by landlords.[293] Social tenants' rights were generally noticeably stronger than those for private tenants.[294]

The combined power of social landlords and tenants, and loose alliances with trade unions, gave them post-war welfare advantages, despite losses of security of tenure between 1948 and 1982 (Duclaud-Williams 1978). These collective arrangements are a kind of democracy between people with shared interests, such as landlord and tenants. Unfortunately, the fundamental problem raised by insider–outsider theory was that negotiations about these shared interests exclude outsiders, except through the intervention of the State, which is ineffective in social housing allocation.

Political influence through tenants voting in alliances with workers was probably more important than the collective negotiations on minor aspects of tenancy legislation, a double economic and political force. Nonetheless, insider–outsider theory was relatively easy to apply in France because this collective organization of tenants reflected the unionization of workers.

Ultimately, it is the legislature that settles both the extent of both job security and tenants' security of tenure, something not figuring strongly in Lindbeck and Snower's (2002) account. There could consequently be 'insiderness' in countries where the formal bargaining procedures do not exist. The voting and economic power of employees and tenants ran in parallel, so that rental markets theories based on an implacable division between the state and the private sector were difficult to apply here.

3.3.4 Post-war action and continuing housing crisis

The Constitution of 27 October 1946 was distinctly of the left[295] and its preamble was still part of the 1958 Constitution. Rights in the 1946 preamble included rights to education, work and social security and its social tone contrasts with the individualist 1789 Declaration.

The immediate post-war years saw the founding of the modern social security system, extending pre-existing mutual support and provision within employer-

The historical context: from revolution to rights

employee agreements and increasing non-contributory family allowances, housing benefit and tax relief for families, all relevant to this study. A contraction in the population from 42 million in 1936 to 40.5 million post-war, led to natalist family policies to encourage an increase in births (Damon 2006).

French housing need was then acute, a serious shortage contrasting with the situation during my study, when insiderness affected housing access. Sixty thousand houses had been destroyed, 1.65 million had been seriously damaged, with the complete destruction of some towns. Between 2.5 and 2.8 million homes were old and in poor condition. Only 1.2 million out of 13.4 million homes possessed a water supply, interior WC, bath or shower, electricity and central heating (Stébé 1998: 86).

In 1950, Henry (1949) reported that 9 million more houses would be needed over the next 30 years. Further housing needs were generated by 1.5 million immigrants in the 1950s and by 1.2 million people fleeing after the Algerian war in 1958. With longer life expectancy and reduced infant mortality, the population increased from 42.5 million in 1954 to 52.6 million in 1972. Further urban migration also meant greater housing needs in towns (Bosvieux 1998).

Stébé (1998: 95) described the lack of effective government intervention in housing until 1953 as 'the shame of the French'. However, France faced the costs of war with Indo-China between 1946 and 1954 and in Algeria from 1954. The compensation scheme for repair of existing property was expensive, obstructing proper planning. The construction industry was unsuitable for mass construction, owing to manpower shortages and technical deficits, and the government's first priority was to reconstruct the severely damaged economy.

In 1945, about 2.4 million people flooded back from Germany: prisoners of war, deportees, and former forced labourers (Stébé 1998). To facilitate requisition of empty homes for the crisis, an order of 11 October 1945 created an optional local communal housing service to review local housing, list under-occupied houses for requisition, manage priority housing applications and recruit controllers. One Mme. Stock made the mistake of going away to Toussaint for four days, and returned to find her home requisitioned (DAL 1996: 86).

Today a French municipal housing service may process social housing applications, but they never acquired the formal accumulation of housing responsibilities imposed on UK councils. A national housing service was created at the same time, to facilitate State intervention in all housing through planning, compulsory purchase and involvement in construction. Central government action rather than local action dominated. The National Agency for the Improvement of Housing (ANAH) was set up to finance repair of existing housing and is still active. Lefèbvre *et al.* (1991: 9) suggested that the repair of existing buildings absorbed most housing funding in 1945–7 without assisting others in need.

With no equivalent of English building societies, there was no market for long-term private credit. The Treasury made loans to social landlords at two per cent

The historical context: from revolution to rights

for 60 years. Other loans were available from public banks, the Caisses d'épargne, a state-owned network of mutual savings offices, and the Caisse des dépôts et de consignations (CDC), a huge State bank, created in 1816, which still makes long-term loans to social landlords. In addition, grants were paid by instalments for the construction, reconstruction or extension of any principal home, by a decree of 2 August 1950 (Lefèbvre et al. 1991).

Claudius-Petit was Minister for Reconstruction and Urban Planning from 1948 until 1954 and was committed to modern construction methods, quality improvement and mass construction for practically everyone. He created the first national plan for regional development, which contemplated holistic planning of the housing environment (Flamand 2001: 197–8).

Legislation to facilitate construction accelerated in the period 1952–4 and HLM organizations (renamed in 1950) were important partners for housing redevelopment. Their funding steadily improved. From 1953, assisted savings schemes were created (and were still providing funding from deposits during my study). These schemes could offer loans to social landlords at special rates, and deposit accounts included the Livret A, which paid low tax-free interest, and special savings accounts that also gave borrowers access to a housing loan. The *un pourcent logement*, introduced in Chapter 1, became compulsory to provide housing funding, also from 1953. The CIL (see Glossary) still used collected funds locally to build or buy land, to lend to employees of participating companies, to buy shares in social landlords and construction companies, to lend for construction and to reserve housing vacancies for contributing employees.[296]

A statute of 6 August 1953 radically increased State powers of intervention and expropriation of land, allowing quicker planning procedures and boosting housing construction, shown in Figure 3.2. Nonetheless, working-class housing was only built on a large scale in the 1960s, when homes became smaller and used industrial production methods. Mass construction of social homes was predominantly undertaken in *communes* of the far left, producing the 'red suburbs', including large housing estates known as the *grands ensembles* (Flamand 2001: 188).

The State had been obliged to intervene post-war through a lack of other capable agencies. In 1960, three-quarters of all housing was subsidized, but then State funding gradually retreated (Lefèbvre et al. 1991: 6, 23). Now, following the creation of a private mortgage market in the 1960s, private mortgage funding dominated the housing market. Government policy was increasingly realized by incentives and regulation of other housing providers. Lefèbvre et al. (1991: 280) complained: 'To place social housing within the mentality of the market is perhaps to forget it.'

Early post-war reforms increased housing starts, but did not have rapid enough effect. On 1 Feburary 1954, the Abbé Pierre, a respected cleric, made a radio appeal beginning: 'My friends, help. A woman has just died frozen this night

The historical context: from revolution to rights

at 3 o'clock, on the pavement of the Boulevard Sébastopol, clutching to her the paper by which she had been evicted the day before yesterday...' (DAL 1996: 30). He spoke of the urgent needs of people sleeping rough in winter, appealing for blankets, mattresses, soup, tents and stoves, and 500 million francs were donated. There were protests and demonstrations, yet more housing funding was provided and metro stations were opened for the homeless. Housing became and remains a subject of hot debate. Post-war housing conditions gradually improved, but a sense of housing crisis remained. *Insiderness* in protection from eviction could in part be a response to living memories of such extreme conditions.

3.3.5 Benefits and construction

By the 1970s, the emphasis on construction funding had started to produce problems. In 1958, specially funded zones were created – the ZUP, Priority Urban Development Zones[297] – the first of many special planning zones. These resulted in the construction of the *grands ensembles* on greenfield sites around towns.[298] These large mono-functional estates included tower blocks and *barres*, large and long uniform flat blocks.

Many such areas became stigmatized, without services such as shops or adequate public transport for out-of-town sites (Flamand 2001: 280–83). Today, the ZUS (*zones urbaines sensibles*) have been set up to provide special funding and other assistance for these deprived areas,[299] but they have become a marker for troubled areas with poor living conditions. Their predecessors, the ZUP were abandoned in 1969 because of bad connotations of the name, but such massive housing projects had produced 803,000 homes in 195 zones.[300]

Initially such large suburbs received an enthusiastic welcome from their new occupants, used to poor dwelling conditions. However, reports in the period 1975–7 showed 15 million people still poorly accommodated in old housing, and expressed disapproval of new HLM housing because of inadequate soundproofing and waterproofing. Design and amenities were poor and by 1975 some buildings, after only 15 years, were already showing signs of physical deterioration (Stébé 1998; Flamand 2001), confirmed by influential enquiries and reports.[301] Everywhere in my study areas in 2005, these large estates were undergoing major rehabilitation work, with remodelling or demolition, and there are relatively few tower blocks and *barres* left.

The Barre Report (1976) proposed radical change: a shift of funding from construction to housing benefits so people could choose their home funded by benefits. The first housing benefit was introduced in 1948; it was non-contributory, and initially only for families but it gradually expanded into other categories. By 1976 there were a similar number of houses as people seeking them, and 75 per cent of houses had bathrooms and sanitary fittings. Despite this change, the Barre Report recommended continued support for construction.

The historical context: from revolution to rights

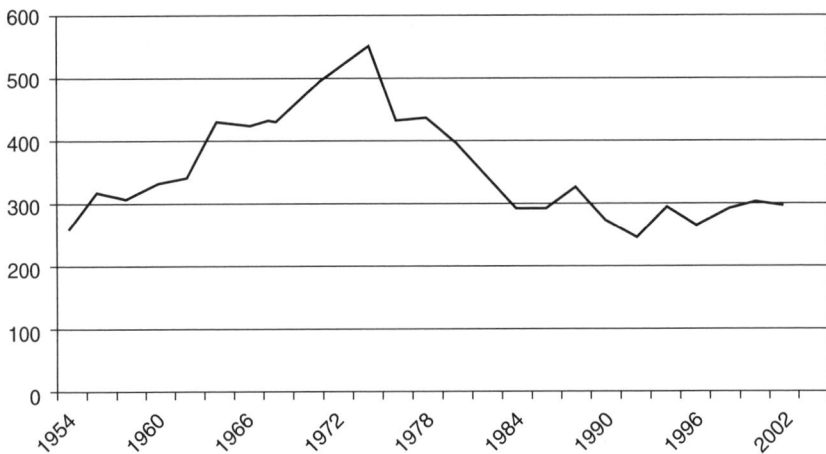

3.2 Housing construction starts 1954–2002 (in thousands). Source: Lefèbvre, Mouillart and Occhipinti (1991) and Ministère du Logement.

Overall, French policy had considerable success in generating housing construction, rising to more than half a million annual building starts for every year between 1971 and 1975 (Figure 3.2). Social housing construction also enjoyed a peak between the 1960s and 1980s, shown in Figure 3.3. Recently there

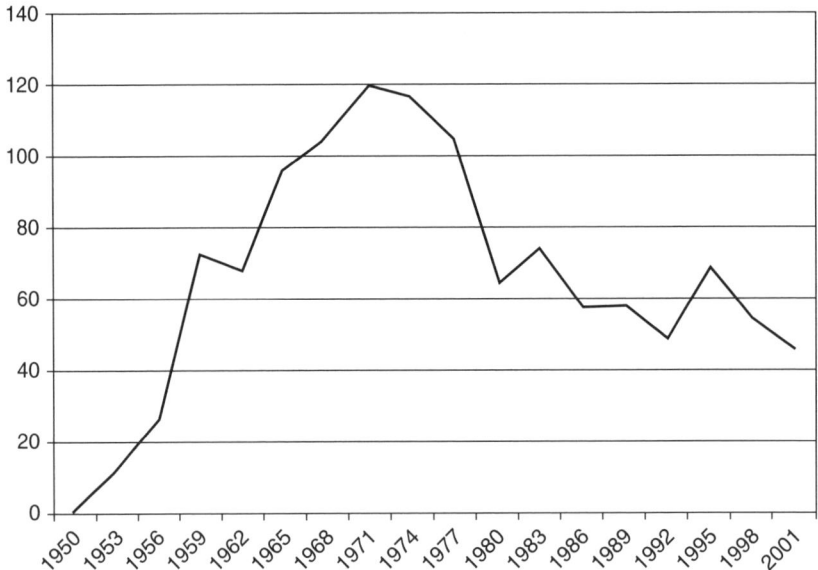

3.3 Social housing stock by first year of rental 1950–2004 (in thousands). Source: Direction des Études Economiques (2005).

has been an increase in private social housing construction by the commercial landlords organizations (SAHLMs), but not by public social landlords.

3.4 Conclusion

French national views of rights and, later, welfare were heavily affected by the upheavals after the revolution, and social landlords were founded at a time of resolution of those struggles. This history introduces a series of French ways of doing things relevant to social housing: the tradition of collective protest in informal alliances of interests; the opposition between tenants and landlords; the history of solidarity; the collectivization of policy consultation; the rigid division between public and private law; the rise of administrative law; the high level of state subsidy and intervention; the development of strong construction and planning policies; and the historic privations suffered by many French people since the revolution.

Some French legal ideas around property are also prevalent in Europe: the unitary conception of property in civil law property systems; the consequent theoretical reduction in tenants' positions; and strong twentieth-century statutory tenant protection across Europe. Equally common is a civil law notion that tenants' rights are social and collective rights, also found in the revised European Social Charter (RESC). It is dangerous, however, to assume that national approaches are similar in practice, given the variability of national institutional history and statutory detail (Schmid, undated).

The inherently slow penetration of change into legal systems means French legal structures reflecting the struggle of collective rights against capital are still with us, together with the mechanisms for resolving these disputes. Different concepts of property and solidarity have many consequences in French national institutions, including a proliferation of representative organizations and oppositional approaches within a history of violent revolution and street protest.

It does not follow that the disadvantaged will always find limited access to French social housing. In fact, there are important trends to pauperization of social tenants and EU competition policy during the study would tend to reinforce this.[302] However, the question is not solely about poverty but about how to house those in cumulative need, who might be unpopular locally. To achieve this, the law implementing public policy should take into account insider–outsider theory: in this case the effects of the headwind of local insider opinion protecting very local positions against stigmatized groups. This means adjusting the allocation process to take account of such behaviour.

4 The right to housing in context

Social housing allocation in France was governed by a normative framework of rights that governed all public activity, and breach of these rights could lead to action before the administrative courts. The right to housing in the Besson Act was a general principle of law which suggested in strong terms that disadvantaged people should be housed.[303] Although this authorized preference for the disadvantaged could be considered to be contrary to equality, the same outcome could have been achieved by other principles in the past.

This chapter will introduce the right to housing and social mix, and also includes, briefly, the technical effect of treaties in France, particularly European treaties. France has a constitutional tradition long predating the European Convention on Human Rights (ECHR), and the Conseil constitutionnel can act as a protective buffer against outside intrusion into the coherence of French law.

This section on the right to housing reflects a characteristic common law preoccupation with legal remedies. Rights in this section are primarily important for what they do in practice in allocation, not what they are. The various rights and rules can be used as mechanisms to support outsiders or insiders by people in power. This might be a small implementing detail or a wider conflict of principle, so the force of the right to housing must be particularly explored.

For this reason, the major constitutional rights of equality and property were primarily dealt with by the history in the last chapter, which is sufficient to introduce their rather diffuse role in allocation. Equality, for example, was a primordial principle of the French Republic, within a profuse number of judicial decisions, but its strongest effect here was a continuing attachment to apparently universal housing allocation and universal subsidy, a background effect with strong cultural elements. There were additional issues around equal treatment of social housing applicants, also related to legality and the idea of equality of opportunity. Equality of opportunity is grouped with social and economic rights and was not generally prominent in the evidence. Equal treatment is important because of the different treatment of different social housing applicants, although not often explicitly referred to by interviewees.

Next, the context and nature of the right to housing has to be explored with a typology of implementing statutes, then the possible remedies available to a disappointed applicant, including an outline of new legal action for disadvantaged people under the 2007 DALO Act. Then local actors' views of the right to housing are also reported, because these affect the implementation of this for the disadvantaged. Social mix must also be introduced as an important new qualification to the right to housing.

Finally, there are broad contextual matters. The form of the law still bears strong traces of the corporatist balance between capital and labour, between landlord and tenant and between left and right, and other oppositions. These are not generally consumer approaches, and some effects of these traditional oppositions are looked at, initially considering whether landlords and tenants' economic interests are always opposed.

4.1 The legal effects of the right to housing

Priority in French social housing allocation for disadvantaged people today depends on the right to housing. This raises a number of questions affecting the implementation of this right. How do relevant European treaty provisions penetrate French law? What is meant by 'right'? What does the right to housing do as a principle? How do the courts regulate the necessary discretion of local actors? Did individuals in 2005 have a remedy for a refused social housing application or for delay? How does the new court action to obtain social housing work?

4.1.1 The hierarchy of norms and treaties

Some laws are more important than others. France has a hierarchy of legal norms, superior legal rules and principles, so any other elements of law must comply with these superior norms, a process supported by review in the Conseil constitutionnel and the administrative courts. The highest French norm is still the Constitution. This affects both the implementation of international treaties, including obligations under the revised European Social Charter (RESC), and the national ranking of the right to housing in the hierarchy of importance of laws, the hierarchy of norms. Whether the right to housing is inferior to the right to property is important for the treatment of housing cases and is disputed.

France was a monist country, meaning that, in principle, all treaties had immediate internal effect provided they had been ratified or approved[304] but, despite that, international treaties have a lower ranking in the internal normative legal order than the Constitution itself. This does not mean that European treaties are ineffective, but it does leave them open to reference to the Conseil constitutionnel.

The Conseil constitutionnel rules on whether statutes conformed to the higher norm of the Constitution.[305] Article 55 of the 1958 Constitution said that treaties have an authority superior to that of statute,[306] but treaties did not necessarily have this higher authority in practice, and there was a complicated *jurisprudence*. An example is that the Conseil constitutionnel would not usually declare that a statute did not conform to a treaty, but only that it did not conform to the Constitution.[307] When taken with the fact that the Constitution is the highest norm, this limited the effect of treaties in the internal French normative order, because stipulations contrary to the Constitution could not be incorporated into French law.[308]

Many treaty provisions could be taken into account directly by the administrative courts as norms within the hierarchy, but at the same hierarchical level as ordinary statutes,[309] below the Constitution and the structural *lois organiques* (statutes with constitutional importance). Despite this, some treaties can have strong direct effects, particularly EU law. This was implemented by *Nicolo* in 1989,[310] a decision of the Conseil d'État. An administrative judge can assess the conformity of a statute with the Treaty on the Functioning of the EU (TFEU), within limits.

Law from the ECHR is treated similarly to EU law, so the ECHR can also be taken into account by the administrative courts. This is important because the French right to housing also takes effect at this lower level, as a basis for action by housing applicants, not giving rise to the possibility of reference to the Conseil constitutionnel during my study. This rather rudimentary account is necessary to show how the European provisions already described fit in the French scheme of things. France has a view of its own sovereignty which means it can still be rather late in implementing directives or taking community law into account (Dupuis *et al.* 2000: 105). The content of national constitutional rights differs between countries, and the vocabulary is not common.

4.1.2 Rights and law

Different understandings of basic terminology between England and France were a problem, particularly the word 'right'. English lawyers are traditionally prone to conflate a right with a 'remedy', because of the strongly procedural nature of their legal system (Gordley 2006). It is difficult to translate the English word 'remedy' into a single French word because it implies that an aggrieved possessor of a right will succeed in their legal action – both in recourse before the courts and in effective execution of the law. An 'effective recourse' is probably the best overall translation for 'remedy'.

The right to housing under the 2007 DALO Act[311] ('the *opposable* right') creates a right for a disadvantaged person to sue the State for failure to access a home. Part of the 2007 European Committee of Social Rights (ECSR) decision against France[312] found there was no effective recourse for breach of Article 31, the European right to housing under the RESC. The DALO Act amended the

Besson Act[313] and could meet this criticism. The idea of this was already looked forward to by actors in my 2005 study, and institutions now administering this were already in place.[314]

The nature of the right to housing is strongly affected and limited by its context. 'Right' and 'law' are the same word in French (*droit*) and in German (*Recht*). French rights can be distinguished from law by speaking in the plural: *les droits* (rights) as against *le droit* (law). Another way is to refer to established justiciable rights as *le droit du logement* (the law of the home) as opposed to *le droit au logement* (the right to housing). *Le droit du* ... is more precise and less contentious. Similarly, *le droit du travail* is simply employment law and *le droit au travail* is the right to work and is more political.

Many types of rights are referred to as *le droit à* ... (the right to ...), including civil, political, social and economic rights and general principles of law not necessarily enforceable by individuals. Some rights supported traditional political campaigns, such as the right to work, or campaigns, such as *le droit au vélo* (the right to cycle). Some referred to individual statutory entitlements, such as housing benefit, whilst others represented collections of laws or legal frameworks, such as *le droit à la ville* (the right to the town)[315] or *le droit á l'environnement* (the right to the environment).[316]

Le droit au logement was claimed by housing campaigners. In 2006, for example, more than 300 squatters were evicted from buildings at Cachan and went on hunger strike claiming their right to housing, which was closely followed by the media (FR avec AFP 2006). Lafore (2004: 42–3) suggested that the creation of the right to housing represented a failure after a century of French housing policies that had not been based on any such principle. He said that the right to housing was not necessarily instantly effective, and represented a complex and relative position in the face of existing liberal rights and basic economic and property requirements.

In this way, rights cannot be seen as standing alone, but are in a relationship with other rights, balanced by the courts. The right to housing and other rights for the disadvantaged can be seen as being in opposition to equality. Equality is central to the principles developed by the Conseil constitutionnel, with redistributive justice generally being justified only by different specific factual circumstances (Brown and Bell 1998). As a consequence, Roman (2001:451) concluded that all assistance was a species of gift granted through the right to human dignity, with a tension between human dignity and equality because of the selectivity of assistance.

4.1.3 The right to housing

The right to housing was first mentioned in the 1982 Quillot Act, but such an ordinary statute was insufficient to grant constitutional status. Different formulations of the right to housing were scattered across several types of statute by 1994. Then, in their decision in a planning law case ('the 1994 decision'), the Conseil constitutionnel effectively endowed the generic right to housing with the status '*de valeur constitutionnel*' (of constitutional value).[317]

The terminology of 'constitutional value' identified the right to housing as a general principle of law, a lower norm than the right to property, which was a full constitutional right within the hierarchy of norms. Other general principles included equality before the law,[318] and the autonomy of local authorities.[319]

In a different kind of legal basis, the 1994 decision[320] found that the right to housing was derived from the right to human dignity, from the preamble to the 1946 Constitution. This was probably influenced by the longstanding German basis for social rights.[321] Seeking an equivalent in the ECHR, the right to human dignity in Article 3 of the ECHR only says 'No one shall be subjected to torture or to inhuman or degrading treatment or punishment', the wording of which does not immediately suggest a basis for anything but very limited welfare provision. However, Article 3 has no derogation from these duties in favour of the State, as there is with many other rights,[322] which perhaps makes it easier to argue for its use in welfare. There are thus arguments about the active extent of such duties.[323]

This new legal basis, created some time after the statutory the right to housing, made little difference to the existing mechanisms of negotiation concerning tenancies and social housing allocation, which even now continue to use formal and informal negotiations between insiders. The use of human dignity was still limited in France[324] and still underdeveloped by *jurisprudence* for application of the right to housing for social housing allocation.

Probably the importance of the 1994 case was that it bolstered the right to housing by attaching it firmly to a constitutional right, to assist against arguments based on equality and property. Both solidarity and human dignity can provide a basis for protection of vulnerable outsiders. Human dignity still requires definition. In just how undignified a position do you have to be to qualify? Human dignity also requires mechanisms for its enforcement, such as the coercive power of solidarity as a value and existing mechanisms of the social state in collective contracts, supplemented by statute.

As a private collective contractual device, the content of the support supplied in solidarity is defined by the contracting parties but inevitably subject to moral arguments about whether the parties should help others, such as to support human dignity, and the question of consent. Solidarity was thus double-sided, primarily providing social cohesion, community, autonomy and protection for defined insiders (not necessarily limited to contracting parties[325]), but inevitably excluding outsiders, unless the benefits provided were truly universal. This will never be possible in social housing allocation, simply due to limitations of stock while demand exceeds supply locally.

The right to housing in context

French constitutional rights and general principles regulated the administration and could allow action through the administrative courts, but only full constitutional rights, such as the right to property, gave rise to applications to the highest jurisdiction, the Conseil constitutionnel.[326] Not everyone agreed that the right to housing was inferior in this way. Radigon and Horvath (2002: 16) argued that the right to housing for tenants was equal to the right to property, owing to the way it limited property rights within tenancy law.[327] However, recent reform means lower courts might now refer cases to the Conseil constitutionnel where a legislative disposition attacks rights and liberties.[328] The limitation of the right to housing to the lower courts might change.

The right to housing had several uses in statute, both implementing and limiting the right. Article 1 of the Besson Act,[329] for example, expressed the current right to housing in favour of the disadvantaged, based within the constitutional order as described above. The right to housing in turn provided a legal basis for the more specific and concrete allocation rules. The original principle was important, even essential, as the legal basis for the implementation. These statutory principles were often implicitly or expressly connected to constitutional rights and values. This is unsurprising, after more than a century of legislators and administrators looking over their shoulders at regulation by public law judicial bodies.

A second example of the generic right to housing was Article 1 of the 1989 Statute, concerning unfurnished tenancies (see p. 77). This asserted the importance of the right to housing, but also formally recorded that relations between landlord and tenant should be balanced at both the individual and the collective level, a reference to the differences between landlords and tenants. The reference to balance between individuals contemplates that individual landlords might be vulnerable facing particular tenants, but the collective bargaining power of tenants backed by unions was not so easy to regulate politically.

Article 1 of the 1989 Statute also included statements protecting the general interest, such as the right of everyone to access rented and owned housing without discrimination. Such qualifications in the general interest are found elsewhere in derogations from French property rights,[330] and in a number of European human rights, particularly the right to property in Article 1 of Protocol 1 of the ECHR.[331]

It is also found in the Competition provisions as a basis for exemption for State aid already described.[332] The French right to housing, as a principle which allowed protection of the general interest, could defeat the 'insiderness' caused by exclusive negotiations between landlords and tenants, by statutory imposition.

In tenancy law, conflicts between landlords and tenants were only resolved by imposing responsibility for the right to housing on the State. The 1994 decision recognising the right to housing[333] found a balance between the right to property and the right to housing by a statement that the constitutional value of the right to housing was on condition that the right to property did not become devoid of its nature and purpose.[334]

The right to housing in context

Despite the way that the right to housing practically limited the right to property for landlords, another case in 1995 said that the right to housing did not conflict with the right to property. This was because the duty of solidarity implicit in the right to housing was imposed on the State and local authorities.[335] Consequently, this duty could not be imposed on individuals except in exceptional circumstances within a statutory framework.

This was a similar view to that taken by the ECtHR in the *Hutten-Czapka* case.[336] In France the central State was also responsible because the President of the Republic was the guardian of respect for the Constitution[337] and the government was the guarantor of solidarity within the nation (Brouant and Jégouzo 1998: 14).

This was a rather awkward solution to the conflict between property and tenants' rights. Private law disputes could be resolved by individual and collective contracting, but State support for these solutions should be based on the derogation in favour of the State. The gaze of the landlord or tenant was dragged away from their negotiating partners, upward to the State to impose tenant security.

This State-centred view means any normally negotiated tenancy conditions could be seen, not as the product of an economic bargain in return for payment, but as an imposition on the inviolable and sacred rights of property owners. This requirement of State intervention of itself tended to wind up the importance of politics and political group organization. The twentieth-century solution of heavily State-imposed tenants' rights did not really reflect the negotiated interdependency of landlords and tenants both in insider–outsider theory and in reality.

A general typology of these three main types of statute implementing the right to housing is shown in Figure 4.1. The right to housing provided a framework for administrative action in: tenants' rights, housing action to assist the disadvantaged

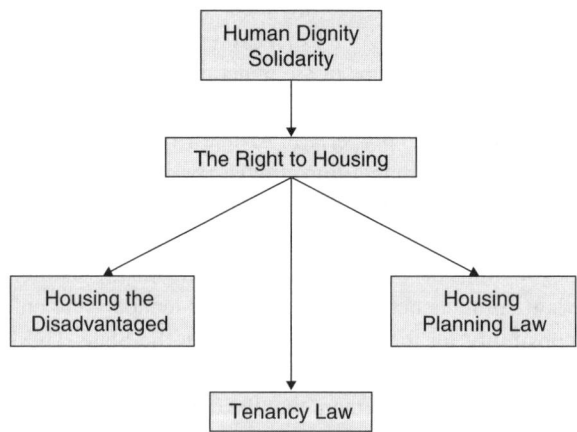

4.1 The main hierarchy of principles affecting social housing.

and the law of planning and construction (not including social security statutes). Another relevant general principle, which was more than usually vague, was the 'right to the town' created by a 1991 framework statute, the 'Loi d'orientation pour la ville'. This was a principle for urban planning and concerns the quality of life in the built environment.[338]

Article 1 of each statute is tailored to the purpose of the statute in wording related to higher norms. This also provides a basis for interpretation of the provisions that follow by the administrators and the courts. The tenants' right to housing supporting security of tenure has been argued by some to be more like a full constitutional right, rather than a purely administrative principle. This is because tenants' rights did not involve positive State action, rather like the civil and political rights which are more strongly and directly enforced by individuals than many social rights (Goodchild 2003). This favourable treatment of tenants' rights would be predicted by insider–outsider theory.

The version of the right to housing in the Besson Act combats social exclusion and was accompanied by mentions in a range of other statutes. This provides the detailed mechanics of its implementation, including in allocation principles. The *opposable* right to housing amended the Besson Act, strengthening the statement by adding the right to sue and to implement regulation. Brouant (2011) said that this created an obligation of result imposed on the State to create access to housing for individuals; thus it is far from being simply an objective.

The third type of right to housing was found within planning objectives. An example is Article L. 302-5 of the Code de la construction et de l'habitation (C.C.H.), obliging larger *communes* to have at least 20 per cent social housing[339] or pay a fine. Deschamps (2005) suggested this imposition is based on solidarity.[340]

Solidarity was both a public-law value and a pervasive basis for imposition of duties on the State and on housing actors in all three types of statute. First, it was explicitly mentioned in Article 1 of the Besson Act. Second, it was a mechanism for the imposition of obligations on *communes* to construct social housing, and as a private law mechanism for imposition within social agreements. Third, the precise form of tenancies in the 1989 statute was affected by formal solidarity-type negotiations between landlords and tenants.

4.1.4 The regulation of rights by the courts

The right to housing might support individual recourse in administrative law, as for any rights and general principles. Bell *et al.* (1996: 33) said: 'The category of the general principles of law is a creation of the courts. … Principles were necessary in order to create a backbone for the development of rules governing the actions of the administration.' Any judge might base a judgment on such principles (Bell 2001: 248). Individuals can apply to the courts to quash a public law decision as *ultra vires* or in breach of any these principles.[341]

Recourse to administrative law depended on the public law status of activities affecting an individual. Public and private social landlords' allocation decisions were always public law decisions. Nevertheless, the split between the courts meant that the public law was applied to private social landlords' allocation decisions in private courts. This recourse was rather ineffective during the empirical study,[342] but the usual recourse was substantially displaced by the *opposable* right. This public law status of a legal act enabled both old and new forms of complaint.

The core functions of the French State were the *fonction publique*. In the UK, the idea of public function has developed to identify activities subject to rights and obligations under the Human Rights Act 1998.[343] Public function means something rather different in France, describing a much narrower part of essential State activity, which is only part of the public law subject to control by the administrative courts.

The wider concept of *service publi*c was more important for housing. French public service was defined in legislation or case law, placing activities in the public or private law sphere. Criteria for this were initially determined by an 1873 administrative court decision, *Blanco*.[344] First, the public service must be carried out either by or on behalf of a public organ. This means private bodies, such as private social landlords, can carry out a public service on behalf of the State. Second, the service must meet public need or utility, a marker for public service. Third, the service provider must have particular special prerogatives in providing the service or suffer special burdens (Brown and Bell 1998: 129–135; Dreyfus 2009).

Figure 4.2 shows the different levels of centrality of public function, public service and public utility for the State. The public function concerns the central activities of the State, whilst the other vocabulary is to some extent interchangeable: public service, public utility and the general interest, the European term. Additional criteria were applied concerning who provided the service or the terms of that service, to determine public law status. Consequently, simply providing a service of public utility, such as the activities of many associations, was not sufficient by itself for the service to be regulated by public law.

To apply the criteria for public law, all public or private French HLM organizations (see Glossary) were said to provide a public service in French law[345] and had a mission of general interest. They had special advantages, such as tax privileges, and were subject to public supervision (Jégouzo-Viénot 2002: 236). *Service public* was thus the foundation of social landlords' funding and other privileges and duties.

There is some pragmatism about these distinctions based on particular activities. All social landlords were governed by the public law for allocations, but all were governed by private contract law for tenancies, an equal treatment of public and private social landlords. This meant that evictions were private law for both. Despite this simplification, the necessity of applying the different public or private law to different areas of activity was complex.

The right to housing in context

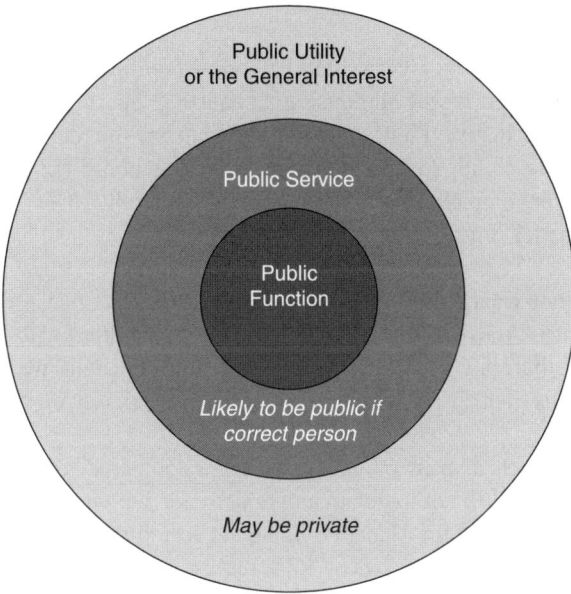

4.2 The different levels of centrality of public law concepts in France.

In recent years, the European 'general economic interest', permitting subsidy under EU competition law[346] has often been substituted for public utility or public service. This EU concept did not correspond precisely to French conceptions, although they have much in common (Prosser 2005; Dreyfus 2009). An example was that the Conseil d'État decreed in 1992 that French social landlords' public service mission towards people on a modest income was in the general interest under Article 86(2), TEU (Treaty of the EU).[347] This, also, does not correspond to more recent Competition Commission approaches favouring the disadvantaged.

If disadvantaged people are not housed, does public law regulation give them an effective right to complain? In French terminology, rights that are justiciable can be taken into account in court, whilst the 2007 *droit opposable* was much stronger (introduced in section 4.1.6, p. 95). Nonetheless, the new *opposable* right works through the same 2005 institutions described here, with surprisingly slight later adjustment.

4.1.5 Remedies for refusal to allocate

Those seeking a remedy based on the right to housing faced a variety of problems in 2005, many of which have not been overcome, including evidential problems,

The right to housing in context

problems of the status of the right to housing, procedural problems and problems of execution.

Social landlords must give written reasons for refusal to allocate a social home, to assist review by the administrative courts,[348] but the reasons commonly given were uninformative. First, someone unable to pay the rent could be refused, tending to interfere with social landlords' mission to house the poor. Second, a voluntary worker complained of '*excuses bâteaux*', literally 'boat excuses', vague generic reasons for refusal such as social mix. She said:

> They do not want to say that they refuse a candidate because he is black, because he is Arab or I don't know what, thus the landlord will say it verbally, 'Well no, there are too many people of colour and thus we have rejected these' – thus there are never elements which you can rely on.

There was a French distrust of oral evidence[349] compared to written evidence which here made it difficult to obtain any remedy for such treatment.

Most interviewees in the Hauts de Seine suggested that applicants unable to afford the rent would be refused by allocation commissions. In the Nord and Lyon this could also be true, but applications were often postponed to seek a cheaper property. Despite this difference, on limited information, levels of refusal were not apparently any lower than in the Hauts de Seine. Refusal by allocation commissions was generally 1–5 per cent everywhere in my study, occasionally rising to 20 per cent, although this was not a representative sample.

There were inherent difficulties and delays in both allocation and in administrative review, but despite this, there were some court decisions supporting disadvantaged applicants. In 2001, the Administrative Tribunal of Marseilles[350] suspended a social landlord's allocation regulations which imposed minimum income limits. This was contrary to its mission to house disadvantaged people.[351]

Another decision led some social landlords to seek reasons for refusal additional to inadequate income. In 2001, the Administrative Tribunal of Versailles[352] quashed a refusal to house Taga Fosso, who lived with his pregnant wife and five children in an overcrowded, unfit building. Refusal was an error in law, as it was based solely on ability to afford rent. Most landlords interviewed did not seem constrained by this, but a social report could provide an additional reason for refusal, if an applicant is thought to be in need of 'rehabilitation' before housing (a common expression).

These were isolated instances, and not binding on other courts. In 2005, the Conseil d'État had refused to recognize the right to housing as a fundamental liberty[353] and higher courts had not yet based relief on the right to housing. There were few decisions concerning housing refusal compared to abundant court decisions on urban planning refusal. The latter similarly concerns the right to property, because the right to develop was attached to ownership (Gill *et al.* 1996).

The right to housing in context

As for execution, in 1999, Actualité HLM (HLM News) advised social landlords that the consequences of such court action could be small damages for the loss of a chance or, rarely, criminal responsibility (UNFOHLM 1999). A successful litigant would not necessarily obtain extra priority and a court cannot directly impose a tenant. Section 9.5.2 (p. 222) shows that a tenant still cannot easily be imposed, even though the new *opposable* right allows the prefect to impose a tenant on social landlords.

Normal administrative tribunal hearings could mean delays of two to four years and even then public bodies could be reluctant to implement tribunal decisions (Bobasch 2003). Taga Fosso, whose refusal decision (above) was quashed, did not find social housing for another two years after yet another refusal.[354]

All actors interviewed showed independent-mindedness in allocation, perhaps partly because French public legal personalities have full constitutional rights. Weis (1995), describing Germany, said public bodies should not have such rights because this would lead to quarrels between public bodies, rather than assisting the individual against the State, although this view may have changed since then.

French actors in allocation did not automatically follow central government policy. At the time of the study, those making allocation decisions might avoid judicial review by postponing decisions. A difference from the UK is that *politique* in French means both 'policy' and 'politics'. '*Mener une politique*' means to carry out a policy firmly attached to the politician or body conducting this, without quite the extended English meaning found in 'public policy'.[355]

Instead, social landlords often spoke of *légalité*, an obligation to act within the law, in accordance with *l'État de droit* (literally the State of law). *Légalité*, loosely translated as the 'rule of law', meant acting within administrative principles and rules. This constraining cage could nonetheless give a certain amount of administrative autonomy arising from the choice of which principle to apply, particularly when taken with the vagueness of the principles (Whittaker 2008) and other practical reasons.

4.1.6 Remedies for delayed allocation

Delays in a decision could have the same effect as refusal to allocate social housing. Massin *et al.* (2010) studied 17,320 allocation decisions in the Paris Commune and found that the most important reason for refusal of candidates by social landlords was insufficient income, and refusals overall were roughly 10–14 per cent. This was only part of the story, because there were 115,000 people on waiting lists. The people waiting went through a process reducing their number to the three applicants presented to the allocation commission, probably mainly by delay inherent in waiting lists.

Delayed applicants could complain to the mediation commission, a tortuous route to justice and mostly staffed by the kinds of people who failed to house

The right to housing in context

disadvantaged people in the first place, although these volunteers may perhaps have fewer very local loyalties. This departmental body was compulsory from 1998 and comprised representatives of the Conseil général (the democratic departmental body), *communautés*, social landlords, tenants and approved voluntary bodies concerned with disadvantaged people.[356] This commission did at least include a small minority of representatives of disadvantaged outsiders through the voluntary bodies, and the Conseil général might assist because it had social responsibilities.

It seems possible that, because this body covers the larger area of a whole *département*, it might mean less local reluctance to house outsiders, who could become neighbours in a smaller local authority. Increased influence on allocation by the larger *communautés* could have a similar effect. This might make it easier to consider the general interest, as slightly removed from the local context.

Individuals who could apply to the mediation commission in 2005–6 included two groups: specified disadvantaged groups and applicants beyond the regulatory 'abnormal delay' in waiting for social housing.[357] The eligible disadvantaged people were those threatened with eviction or those living in temporary shelters, slums or unfit housing. The abnormal delay was then a period decreed by departmental prefects, then varying from 12 months to four years (Brouant 2008).[358]

The mediation commission reviewed written evidence and referred priority cases to the prefect, who consulted the local mayor and took into account social mix. The prefect could request that a social landlord house the applicant. This procedure was later reinforced in 2006[359] and again by the 2007 DALO Act, boosting the role of the mediation commission.

During my study, there was no functioning mediation commission in the Hauts de Seine. In both Lyon and the Nord,[360] a commission existed and local actors had found funding for someone to review old applications that were becoming urgent. Even then, some actors regarded this as a step towards an *opposable* right to housing, which many supported or promoted.

An overall view in 2007 on the situation before the *opposable* right was expressed by the ECSR in *FEANTSA*: 'It is particularly difficult for disadvantaged, homeless people to obtain access to these courts and the chances of having a decision refusing to allocate them housing set aside are virtually nil.'[361]

4.1.7 The *opposable* right to housing

The 2007 procedure extended the 1990 right to housing for disadvantaged people. A new Article L. 300-1, C.C.H. states: 'The right to a decent and independent home, mentioned in the first Article of the Besson Act ... is guaranteed by the State to anyone, lawfully residing on French territory, ... who cannot access this by their own means or maintain themselves there.'[362] This right is exercised through a two-stage procedure for complainants:[363] by the initial compulsory mediation procedure already described (on page 96), and the State can be sued for failure to access any home.

The new right has neither changed social housing funding nor its basic allocation mechanisms. The new procedure is not significantly different from the mediation procedure already described. The reader still needs to be aware that the historic sources of the mediation procedure cited above have changed, principally with greater detail. One of the joys of codification is that new law can usually be found with a similar Article number to the old law.

The procedure for the *opposable* right did not displace existing allocation arrangements protecting the rights of locally influential groups. Places available to disadvantaged people by this new route are limited to the prefectural contingent. In Lyon, with its active and oversubscribed contingent, a court order could remove a place from another deprived applicant, or elsewhere this might simply mean a longer application procedure than previously.

Again there are two classes of applicant. The first includes limited classes in housing difficulty: the roofless, those in unfit or manifestly overcrowded housing with a dependent child,[364] those under an eviction order without rehousing; hostel residents after six months[365] and certain disabled people or carers.[366] The *opposable* right should be good news for the disadvantaged, although there is obvious procedural difficulty in accessing this. Neither the mediation procedure nor the court action affords any interim accommodation to the homeless, who are not the best litigants.

The second class of applicant consists of people suffering abnormal delay in their applications, but these actions have been deferred until 2012. Applicants suffering abnormal delay can apply for mediation but not for the court procedure. This measure seemed to imply that delay is caused by maladministration, because 'housing for all' suggests that everyone will ultimately be housed. This also illustrated the conflict between the queue for universal allocation and priorities for the disadvantaged. Some delayed applicants might have been waiting for years, because of stigmatization or discrimination, but the process risks being swamped.

The mediation commission enjoys the same broad discretion as for normal allocation decisions. All applicants must act in good faith, which is not defined.[367] All current applicants need housing, but there was no objective mechanism to prioritize between needs or particular groups, either in 2005 or currently.

Before applying to the mediation commission, the claimant must first apply for social housing, which is difficult for some. The applicant does not attend the hearing, so preparation of a good file favours those with greater literacy or greater support. The mediation commission must decide the application within three months, or six months in larger towns. If not dealt with in time, this is treated as a refusal of the application and any such administrative refusal allows action to be taken in the administrative courts – not an easy alternative (Brouant 2008).

A social home is only allocated exceptionally by this procedure. After considering the applicant and their circumstances, the mediation commission can direct that the applicant should be housed by their family. Articles 2005–2011 of the Code civil can oblige individuals to maintain their lineal blood relatives such as parents, children and sons-and daughters-in-law. Alternatively, the applicant can be placed in a hostel to meet their needs,[368] which has a certain circularity if the applicant came from a hostel.

Finally, the mediation commission can decide the applicant is in urgent need of social housing. As before 2007, a list of urgent cases is then sent to the prefect who consults with local mayors, and considers local agreements and the principle of social mix, which could exclude applicants from cheap areas.

Prefects will then identify available vacancies and propose applicants to a social landlord. This means cases passing through the mediation commission or the courts usually have to be considered by the social landlords' allocation commission at the end of the procedure (Brouant 2011). This process is thus a complicated addition to the normal problematic procedure, not a substitute for it.

If the social landlord refuses, the prefect can exercise a new power to allocate the social home directly.[369] Prefects have had the power to allocate all of a social landlord's homes since 1998,[370] but this was uncommon. The weakness of the prefecture in enforcement is a consistent theme of this book. Recent difficulties in execution are reviewed in section 9.5.2 (p. 222).

When successful applicants under the *opposable* right come before the social landlords' allocation commission, the commission now faces two sets of criteria: for normal allocation and under the *opposable* right. This could be a problem because Brouant (2011) found that mediation commissions were not interpreting allocation priorities in the broad way that the Besson Act contemplated, instead treating them as competing categories.

Support for applicants from an *association* was essential for accommodation, providing an address and assistance with procedure within a more general bureaucratization of voluntary support. Hostels obtained state benefits for bed spaces by contract, a justification for increased regulation. Associations were already accustomed to searching their databases for applicants acceptable to social landlords.[371]

Individuals without temporary accommodation can now sue under the 2007 Act to obtain a hostel place. This belies their temporary nature, although places in popular rehabilitation centres might be contested.[372] Associations risked becoming an arm of government policy with regulated access, a sub-class of social housing (Uhry 2007).

4.2 The right to housing and social mix

The views of individual local actors on the right to housing must be introduced here because these are critical for its implementation. Even before the 2007 *opposable* right, most actors interviewed spoke about individuals possessing a right to housing, rather than treating this as the kind of generic objective found in urban planning statutes.

The right to housing was effectively limited by other principles, including social mix, but the meaning of this was particularly unclear. The law of social mix should also be introduced in its legal context in general, particularly its possible application to ethnic minority groups. Actors' views on the practical application of social mix are in section 7.1.3 on process (p. 163).

4.2.1 Actors' views of the right to housing

When asked what they understood by the right to housing, most actors proposed an abstract principle but then qualified this. The practicalities of finance and housing stock were a major qualification, looked at in Chapter 6. A state actor[373] said: 'It is not sufficient to vote to pass legal texts if you do not have the practical possibility to house people. That serves absolutely no purpose.' This was easily the most common view.

The principles suggested were often quite practical. Four actors[374] suggested an obligation to offer people a home. A social landlord said: 'What I understand by the right to housing is that everyone should be offered a home.' This was because some people refused homes. Others suggested a home should be offered within a reasonable time. Some descriptions were closer to legislative statements. One mayor of the left regretted that the right to housing was not equal to the right to property.

The value of the right to housing could be forcibly expressed by social landlords, for example:[375] 'The right to housing is a fundamental tool in the life of a person. That means that without it he cannot build a life[376] or reconstruct his life', and,' We are in the land of the rights of man and today it is inconceivable that a person should find themselves without a roof over their head. That is the right to housing.' This contradicts Bourgeois's view of their selfish motivation, but does not necessarily mean that this was achieved in practice locally.

Seven actors expressed the right to housing as an obligation for the State to provide a home. This might be seen as confining responsibility for the disadvantaged to central State through the prefect and their contingent of vacancies.[377] This is difficult to judge. One actor described the right to housing as a State guarantee.

Five actors expressed this principle as only the grant of an opportunity to obtain a home; one social landlord, with some cynicism, said:

> Some people would like for it to be as for work. It must be the State[378] which must give a guarantee or give you work, a job, or a home – why not marry your children for you? For me it must be an obligation for the public authorities to organize things so that everyone has their opportunity, thus

The right to housing in context

to give the financial means and legally to have a system which allows more equal treatment of the files, but it is not a duty for me.

Four other actors tied the right to housing to the means of the applicant. Even a voluntary worker qualified the right to housing:

For me the right to housing, I would say that it is that everyone should have access to a home, but, I don't know. I would refuse anyone coming from a squat, anything like that, but in addition I will say [the right would] give a chance to people who have the financial means, who can, who are ready.

Affordability was thus a problem, but this also illustrates the stigmatization of squatters. Another actor would exclude applicants not in good faith.

Six actors expressed severe concern that the right to housing was enacted without the financial means to provide homes. One state actor said that this meant the right for each person to have a home but the legislator had not explained how it would provide finance for the necessary number of roofs. These financial drivers were a pervasive theme of interviews. A voluntary worker said:

It is a vast programme. The right to housing at the end of the day is the right to a decent home for everyone. It is a beautiful theory, isn't it? After that, what are the financial means that they are using to put it into effect? For me the right to housing is a quality which corresponds to the income of the occupants. ... Otherwise how are you going to put it into effect?

There were thus divergences in views about the extent of the right to housing and concern about means to implement it. There was goodwill towards an objective of housing everyone.

4.2.2 Introducing social mix

The principle of 'social mix' was an obligation imposed on social landlords effectively qualifying the right to housing[379] to avoid urban segregation, or *ghéttoisation*.

The term *banlieu* or suburb (an inadequate translation) was synonymous with such segregation, poor living conditions, lack of repair and difficult populations. Social landlords had constructed large housing estates, the *grands ensembles*.[380] The long, uniform flat blocks or *barres*, such as the one shown in Figure 4.3, were becoming less common with urban renovation accompanied by social mix principles.

As a legal principle, social mix found its legal basis in solidarity to spread the burden of disadvantaged people in social housing between *communes*,

The right to housing in context

4.3 Barres in Nanterre.

an imposition on some and a benefit for others. This might create equality of opportunity for those no longer stigmatized by their neighbourhood, with its lack of facilities, or provide other advantages (Deschamps 1998, 2005).

Steiner (2010) explained how French judgments traditionally contain little concerning the social and other policies in succinct decisions focusing on legal principle. There is a trend against this and judges in fact give considerable consideration to policy factors in deliberations with other judges. Deschamps (1998) argued for social mix, citing sociological evidence and government reports concerning the benefits of this mix and the social problems of deprived areas. The usefulness of social mix thus rested implicitly on sociological evidence of its benefits, or on more recent literature about problems created by its implementation, such as Lelévrier (2008) and Blanc (2010).

Peillon (2005: 325) describes the problems of inhabitants of deprived areas:

> The rejection of cheques by shopkeepers in the shopping centre, with the refusal of employment or an apprenticeship – the address being eventually connected to the surname – constitute so many manifestations of the disqualification which afflicts the residents of these areas of social housing, guilty of a sort of crime of address and collective stigmatization.

Deschamps (1998) considered such urban segregation of disadvantaged areas as a failure of planning law because of the specialist zoning of poor locations. The problem was identified by a circular of 1973[381] but not legislated on until 1990. Account had not been taken of spatial effects of social housing allocation to create concentrations of poverty.

Article 1 of the 1991 statute, the Loi d'orientation pour la ville,[382] established a statutory principle of social mix, stated as favouring social cohesion and intended to avoid or remove the phenomena of segregation. Amongst the many legislative statements of the right to housing, even the 1990 Besson Act, Article 28, originally spoke of a 'necessary diversity', and of spreading this burden of housing the disadvantaged between *communes*.

Michel Delebarre, president of the HLM movement, expressed the value of social mix thus:

> What do people expect today from social housing? Do they want us to create a closed-in camp for the reception of the poorest people or to conserve for it a wider vocation and to make it play a role as a 'regulator of the markets'? In the first case, this would reject the objective of social mix and in the end recreate the conditions of urban disorder that everyone denounces today, but in the second case the allocation of public money should be in coherence with the objective made public.
>
> (quoted by Buttin 2006)

Social mix was thus seen as reducing *ghéttoisation* of disadvantaged people. Buttin refers to the idea that cheaper public housing could 'regulate' markets, to produce cheaper housing generally in unitary markets (Kemeny 2006).[383]

There is a large and growing international literature on the benefits and disadvantages of social mix (Bolt *et al.* 2010). In the UK, there has not been a generally enthusiastic reception for ideas of social mix (Tunstall 2003; Turkington and Sangster 2006). Galster (2007) reviewed social mix generally, finding benefits for the disadvantaged and no disbenefits for others. There was, for example, a fall in local social problems when poverty fell below 20 per cent in a neighbourhood and less stigma in the job market, but there might be loss of social capital, loss of bonding relationships and of institutions.

Galster expressed a caveat about creating social mix by policy, describing this as a slippery concept, with imprecision about the composition of populations, the level of concentration of poverty that was undesirable and about the scale of neighbourhood studied. Goetz (2010: 154) illustrated this implementation difficulty in the demolition and dispersal of public housing in the US, which he described as having limited and inconsistent economic benefits.

Blanc (2010) suggested that the benefits of implementation of social mix in France were less than the rhetoric surrounding it. These policies strengthened

The right to housing in context

ghettos and hindered the right to housing for the very poor. Lelévrier (2008) confirmed that the most disadvantaged people in Ile-de-France tended to either stay where they were on urban redevelopment or to move to other sensitive urban zones (ZUS)[384] or be re-concentrated in fragmented enclaves, whilst the better-off obtained homes in more attractive localities outside the ZUS.

The primary concern with social mix in this book is with perverse effects of this implementation for disadvantaged people: about the use of social mix as a motive for refusal of social housing, for demolition of housing for the disadvantaged, for their exclusion from cheap areas and for increased rents for improved homes. This is not exactly gentrification, but something with similar effects for *communes* successful in attracting middle-class tenants – a permanent state-assisted reduction in the availability of housing for the disadvantaged there.

Social mix as a legal principle had not been defined in any concrete detail in any authoritative source, even though refusal to allocate could be based on it. In 2002, a tribunal supported a refusal to allocate a social home to a widow with four children with social problems in a difficult area, because this would not support their social inclusion (Bissuel 2002).[385]

In a similar reasoning, but using a different principle, the Conseil d'État has used the principle of social cohesion to buttress social mix in resisting the creation of dense ethnic communities. Social cohesion is closely related to solidarity[386] and thus used to support assistance for the weak. In contrast, this was used to give the *commune* of Grenevilliers sufficient legal standing to refuse the creation of a foyer to house foreign employees of the neighbouring *commune* of Puteaux. This was because this would: 'aggravate the social and urban imbalances that it has by reason of the large number of immigrant workers already settled in its area and also increase its financial burden'.[387]

In fact the court held that the foyer did not offend social cohesion in these circumstances, partly because it was very small. Brouant[388] questioned whether a density of foreigners would necessarily cause trouble, or be a financial burden, since the intruding immigrants were employees. He said judges had difficulty assessing this kind of problem and that social landlords have a certain expertise.[389]

This decision came perilously close to supporting the idea that there could be too many foreigners. Social mix could thus act in opposition to the right to housing, with actors having a choice whether to accept candidates on the basis of disadvantage or to reject them on the basis of social mix.

4.2.3 Social mix and ethnicity

Interviewees generally thought disadvantaged people were not helped by living with others in social difficulties, thus supporting social mix. Deschamps (1998) said a development of large homes would also concentrate large families. Several interviewees said that 'large families' was a euphemism for ethnic minorities.

The right to housing in context

France has had waves of immigration, sometimes because of war, such as in Algeria from 1954 to 1962, but frequently due to imported labour, with a relatively generous law on nationality for children of immigrants. The Second Empire was predominantly African, with a particularly close relationship with North African countries, and Algerians were the largest group of foreign residents (Tchibindat 2005: 56).

Another constitutional principle, *laïcité*, is seen as preventing the collection of statistics on ethnicity. *Laïcité* requires secularity, state neutrality and impartiality, including impartiality towards ethnic minorities. The 1958 Constitution says: 'France shall ... ensure the equality of all citizens before the law, without distinction of origin, race or religion. It shall respect all beliefs.'[390] This impartiality means statistics for religion or ethnicity generally cannot be obtained, except concerning 'foreigners'. This makes informed treatment of problems difficult.

The redoubling of efforts for urban renovation and social mix should be seen in the context of the 2005 riots and similar riots in 1980 and 1990–91 (Deschamps 1998: 12). 'Urban segregation' often referred to an ethnic concentration in social housing. It was implicit in effecting social mix that these would be broken up (Laval-Reviglio 2005: 307; Peillon 2005: 321). Riots were frequently centred in the *grands ensembles* and in ZUS, the zones with special funding status intended to help residents.[391] *The Economist* (2005b) reported:

> The bleak high-rise estates that encircle the French capital have long been neglected in more ways than one. Physically removed from the elegant tree-lined boulevards of central Paris, they house a population that is poor, jobless, angry and, mostly, of North African or West African origin.

During the autumn 2005 riots, it was noted that 1,500 people were arrested and 21,000 cars were burned by rioters (*The Economist* 2005b).

A week after the end of the riots in November 2005, the author was interviewing in Paris, and television news channels all week debated housing and the children of immigrants. It seemed strange that the author saw no TV interviews of rioters themselves. One interviewee calls this: 'this prudishness with regard to nationality'. Some other interviewees were reluctant to discuss ethnicity.

Nicolas Sarkozy, then Interior Minister, initially referred to rioting youths as '*racailles*' (scum).[392] However, within French participative democracy, any perceived injustice might produce mass protest. Informal alliances of sympathetic organizations might obtain concessions or even destabilize a government, as in 1968, something with resonance in the 2010 protests about increasing the pension age.

After heavy-handed policing of the 2005 riots, the government recognized these riots as a legitimate display of social protest, a *mouvement social*, proposing a package of measures on unemployment and schooling. *The Economist* (2005b)

The right to housing in context

quoted youths as saying that they were of the wrong colour and constantly stopped by the police.[393] A concern to break up ethnic communities was one of the causes of race discrimination in social housing allocation.[394] Not all principles were thus benign for the disadvantaged within principled French approaches to allocation.

4.3 Contrasting approaches in France

There were important differences from England in the conceptual environment of social housing allocation. The allocation decision itself was not generally conceived of as allowing discretion for decision-makers but more as a 'power of appreciation' (discussed in the next subsection), which was not the same thing. Only a brief French–English comparison can explain this, and the overall effect was to give French actors room to manoeuvre and negotiate.

The allocation process was also affected by corporatist approaches to social housing, involving various kinds of traditional oppositions and political alliances. Consumer approaches were not prevalent in social housing and these oppositions affected local negotiated allocation processes. On an economic analysis, the rights of the landlords and tenants are not always opposed. Outsiders do not necessarily benefit from their alliances with tenants.

4.3.1 Room to manoeuvre

This section considers the different way room to manoeuvre is conceived in England and France to explain French allocation decisions. In France, because hierarchy was constitutionally repugnant for reasons of equality, this meant each government body had a bundle of attributed powers under the Constitution, so no central or local government organ was theoretically inferior to another.

In contrast, in England, the UK statutory delegation of housing action for those in need often means imposing duties on local authorities, rather than bestowing rights on individuals, although allocation processes include recourse for disappointed applicants.[395] Gradually increasing tendencies towards central control of policy (Sharland 1979: 6) mean allocations take place within strong constraints, and more detailed constraints in legislation and cases.

The judicial review of UK discretion recognizes that an administrator necessarily has a choice which, although limited by the legal framework, allows sufficient flexibility for the policies to be creative and effective (Davis 1977: 27). The similar French word *discrétion* has strong associations with arbitrary and unchecked freedom, but the English 'discretion' of the housing officer is relatively narrow and limited by a large legal framework. This is very specific on concrete detail (Whittaker 2008)[396] and not as obviously conflictual as the opposing principles faced by French decision-makers.

The right to housing in context

To implement local rules determined within national local rules, English local authority housing officers act mainly alone to investigate and assess applicants' cases and then to allocate homes (for directly owned homes) or to nominate a tenant for a vacancy with private social landlords. English housing officers traditionally acted 'quasi-judicially', since their decision has a strong effect on an individual and decisions could ultimately be quashed by the courts.[397] More rarely, a social tenant could be imposed by court order.[398] UK housing officers must be impartial and thus have no personal interest in the matter (Galligan 1986), so the French representative process of allocation would be improper in England.

French administrative decisions should also be impartial[399] but this impartiality could be differently produced, such as by balanced representation of local actors. The author did not immediately realize that French social housing allocation was not quasi-judicial, because some specialist tribunals (such as those concerning agricultural tenancies and benefits[400]) comprise equal numbers of representatives of landlords and tenants or employers and employees, respectively.

It does not necessarily follow that the problems in this book apply to those tribunals. Social housing has a peculiar combination of local situation, permanence, limited supply and the sheer local expense of one home. Allocation decision-makers were broadly defined insider representatives, where insiders could benefit from particular allocations. Thus they were not disinterested, and outsiders were not generally represented.

The French terminology of *actes discrétionnaires* could not be used for interviews, now only describing exceptional acts (Brown and Bell 1998: 253–7).[401] Instead, *pouvoir d'appréciation* (power of appreciation), describes the necessary room to manoeuvre to assess a situation in relation to the facts. This legal power of appreciation primarily concerns judicial room to manoeuvre,[402] not fully describing the law imposed on a bureaucrat.

Apart from leeway in assessing facts, different types of public law decisions were subject to differing levels of supervision by the courts, including consideration of the level of decision-makers' expertise. Experts were more lightly supervised[403] and social landlords' perceived expertise[404] was important for this reason. If higher expertise leads to less judicial supervision then this practically increases discretion (in English terms).

In the courts, Whittaker (2008) found that private-law judges in both England and France had room to manoeuvre in more freely assessing facts,[405] in contrast with settled law. In France, a much larger category of situations were classified as 'fact' (and not law) than in England. This gave French judges effectively more room to manoeuvre when assessing these 'facts' within broadly expressed principles. In contrast, English judges create law by effectively prescribing rules for a large number of detailed fact-situations, limiting freedom of assessment. Wider principles give more room to manoeuvre.

The right to housing in context

The position in administrative law was rather different, with a different amount of judicial room to manoeuvre depending on the powers of the assessor and situation concerned.[406] There were usually still facts to be assessed,[407] and assessing facts using broad principles, described by Whittaker (2008), was to an extent a common skill.

Actors assessing applications also had practical freedom of action, within the limits of legality, which facilitated negotiation over who should be housed. Decision-makers were not disinterested and allocation commission members represented people who might prefer not to house the disadvantaged.[408]

4.3.2 Corporatism rather than consumer approaches

This section records a certain reluctance in France to see social housing as regulated by consumer approaches associated with the market. Solidarity links employers and employees in the common effort towards social progress, including assistance for disadvantaged people. In France social objectives were realized through a modern corporatism (Esping-Andersen 1990) in labour relations, welfare, social security and social housing, the heartlands of collective social approaches.

Kemeny (2006: 9) suggested that Esping-Andersen's classification of welfare states might differ from one sector to another within one country. In France, some legal institutions within housing and employment markets reflected corporatist opposition between capital and labour or owners and tenants but this was not necessarily so in every part of the economy, particularly commercial areas.

In England, all tenants are now seen as consumers. Adams and Brownsword (2000) classified English judicial approaches as market-individualist or consumer-welfarist. Market-individualists apply the law strictly in the interests of certainty, whilst consumer-welfarists seek legal devices supporting the weak in society. Within this protective tradition and with strong consumer law, it was natural to apply consumer protection to all English tenancies (Ball 2003).

This link between consumerism and welfare was not so obvious for French tenancies. Consumer law concerns relations between consumers and registered businessmen (*commerçants*)[409] but many small French landlords were not classed as businessmen (Ball 2003). One interviewee had a 'users' committee' for housing clients, not a consumers' committee. He said: 'We don't have too many "consumers",' which was thus not the usual terminology.

Baudrillard (1990: 86), writing in 1970, described the workplace as a place of solidarity where people could not be exploited, whilst consumerism isolated people in their homes. This was now less true in France because of effective collective protest[410] and tenants' newer collective rights.[411] Powers bestowed on tenants' organizations as consumer organizations were spliced on top of longstanding forms of collective representation.

The right to housing in context

A survey by Globescan found that 71 per cent of Americans agreed that the free-market economy was the best system. In France only 36 per cent agreed (*The Economist* 2006c). For some, consumer rights could be an intrusion into a traditional sphere of collective influence, where social housing is 'outside the market'.

This has a direct bearing on current EU debates about allowable forms of social housing subsidy. The 'general interest' delimits a specially protected or decommodified sphere of public service excluding the market.[412] Dreyfus (2009) said that this allowed management of some areas to be retained within the jurisdiction of the administrative courts. This could be seen as useful, as it makes it possible to review allocation decisions. Dreyfus (2009: 288) also said:

> In France, behind the debate on public services lies a political or even ideological vision of the State. The notion of *service public* was promoted to legitimise the intervention of the State in the lives of the citizens, in order to ensure the common good. In this context, supporters of a strong welfare state believe that many social activities should remain in the hands of public authorities and outside of market rules.

Despite this, consumers and welfare are firmly linked in economic models, particularly those concerning Pareto efficiency, measuring the advisability of pursuing particular policy objectives (Stiglitz 2000; Bergh and Camesasca 2006). However, pursuing an economics explanation for social housing allocation might be unwelcome in France for some.

For EU competition policy, this non-market sphere amounts to a limited exemption from the legal rules, rather than proposing that housing stands outside this economic paradigm. The French State itself constantly used economic subsidy to incentivize currently socially desirable action within the market, some shown in Chapter 6. The extent of subsidy and its effects was an issue here.

4.3.3 Effects of opposition and transaction costs

The oppositions apparent in the French legal structures of representation had national and local effects on the governance of social housing. Human rights lawyers are accustomed to balancing rights conflicts, but in France there were many entrenched oppositions: the political and the economic opposition between capital and labour (and owners and tenants); the right to housing versus the right to property; social mix versus equality; and disputes about the extent of State intervention.

This account can do no justice to the subtlety of French legal doctrinal thought, and Turpin (1994: 27) said the old Marxist/liberal opposition had some obsolescence because the French were more concerned with the quality of State

The right to housing in context

management. However, if the grand narratives of socialism against liberalism and property are embodied in debates on legal principle and perpetuated by these representative institutions within welfare, then they can not be entirely dead.

Another opposition was between supporters of decentralization and a strong central State. Some French communists might support central control, since the party abandoned a policy of revolution in favour of extending social and welfare rights (Bell 2003: 29). Some members of the political right, sometimes still known as Jacobins,[413] also supported central *dirigiste* policies promoting equality. Decentralization was traditionally supported by anarchists representing small-scale socialism in the nineteenth century. More recently, the right saw the advantage of local contribution to State costs in decentralization (Sauvez 2006: 15).

The multiple possible combinations of these political elements have meant coalition government and historic tendencies for parties to fragment. There were political power blocs, and alliances of the left and right, with politics centred on personalities, particularly in local politics (Evans 2003: 165). This study cannot accurately convey this diversity, particularly when anonymity of the mayors interviewed is required.

Alliances between campaigning groups were also important. Campaigns for tenants' rights often had strong support from disadvantaged people, even when not tenants. DAL, the militant squatters' organization, was a strong campaigner for housing rights. The 1970s rent strike was led by immigrants staying in *foyers*,[414] but the strikers did not gain much. This was because *foyers* are still a form of collective housing with little security of tenure. The support for tenants was in part aspirational, a hope for something better, but also moral support about sufficiently decent living conditions.

Insider–outsider theory offers a slightly bleak view of this, because the rights of existing tenants can block access by aspirant disadvantaged housing applicants. Doling (1997) suggested that the degree of decommodification of housing could be judged by the rules of access to housing and the rules for exit. This seems to imagine unlimited housing stock. Unfortunately, insider–outsider theory suggests that high security of tenure enjoyed by tenants, in the form of barriers to entry and exit from rental property, is a transaction cost, making landlords reluctant to let and reducing available vacancies.

If the logic of transaction costs is followed, there is no permanent opposition between landlords and tenants. As long as the level of transaction costs means it is not economically worthwhile to evict existing tenants, the interests of landlords and tenants lie together in supporting each other to keep the tenant in place.

If transaction costs are reduced, or financial incentives to accept outsiders are increased, or if the tenant cannot pay, then the interests of the landlord in re-letting are increased. At that point, the interests of the landlord and the insider-tenant are opposed, and the alliance between the dispossessed and tenants becomes directed to reasserting the status quo of reasonably secure and attractive tenancies. This does not necessarily help the outsider, unless lucky enough to become a tenant. If you regard insiders, entrants and outsiders as competitors for housing places, as required by insider–outsider theory, insiders tend to win.

Traditional French oppositions and negotiations directed to resolving them have local effects on allocation, because national decisions allow large room for manoeuvre and thus scope for local bargaining and *ad hoc* alliances. This approach is also formally reflected in the compulsory representative legal structures around social housing allocation.

4.4 Conclusion

This chapter has shown the legal nature of the strongly stated right to housing in its context, ways the right can be promoted or constrained and the room to manoeuvre of local decision-makers. The short references to England were mainly to illustrate differences in institutions and processes, and some rather diffuse cultural differences, difficult to document for a lawyer.

The right to housing in the Besson Act represented an objective of constitutional value and was necessary as a legal basis for action, but vagueness of principle, local room to manoeuvre, local representation of insiders and conflicts with other rights, including social mix, equality and property, could obstruct its implementation. If the right to housing represented something in the future, it was likely to sound better than its actual benefits, which must tempt some politicians to express such statements forcefully. Then there is a practical problem in the transition from futurity to implementing such strong, even impossible, statements.

A long history of conflict, including the way nineteenth-century debates had crystallized around the right to property, led actors to take an oppositional position on rights. Neither the strongly stated right to property, whereby the landlords could dispose of their property absolutely,[415] nor the right to housing, whereby all disadvantaged people were helped to obtain access to a home, could be entirely effective in their stated form. This was particularly so when French housing campaigners demanded that there should be no eviction without rehousing.[416] The real state of the right to housing was a locally variable compromise, not what texts proposed.[417] The rest of the book will show how these various rights were played out in the allocation process.

The system then contemplated a series of possible court actions, none of which appeared to deliver a reliable remedy for the most disadvantaged people, who are often passed over in favour of better-off insiders. This raises questions about the nature of conflict in European equivalents of these constitutional rights and principles, about the nature and function of social landlords' allocation processes and about how to avoid exclusionary tendencies within allocation.

Control of the heterogeneous process of social housing allocation by public authorities was split between local and central government with different interests. All were caught up in a process of change with decentralization, but local government and other housing actors were more affected by the economic realities of the situation than central government. These institutions are described next.

5 Complex institutions in the grip of change

Power and influence over social housing allocation was fragmented between many local actors, none of whom had complete control over the process. The various access points to social housing had different criteria and an application could be handled by several actors successively. Consequently, the characteristics of local actors were important. Chapter 1 introduced these and this chapter explains more about them and how they interacted in other areas.

France has a culture of representation in social housing allocation, allowing local voices to be heard not just in setting local priorities but in the allocation process itself, and the powers of these representatives and other actors are explored here. Where local insiders were represented in this way, their economic interests become political interests, alongside other concerns. A democratic government representing everyone can legitimately legislate as to who should be housed, but the much more limited representation of very local interests in the allocation process itself was problematic.

The spatial aspects of insider–outsider theory start to become apparent, including 'nimby' attitudes ('not in my back yard') or nimbyism, particularly the exclusion of non-locals by mayors. The peculiarities of social housing affect this: limitation of stock, its expense and permanence, the slowness of housing construction to meet demand and the geographical specificity of its location. A single home cannot be split between applicants and there has always been a choice between known local insiders and outsiders. Housing locals would help solve local housing problems. Unlike distributing money, allocation brings the disadvantaged person, with their financial risks, physically closer to home, particularly in a small *commune*. Given the stigma attached to unknown outsiders, particularly when associated with antisocial behaviour in the *banlieuex*, local nimbyism became likely.

There were national difficulties in pushing through housing reform, and decentralization was a solution to some local problems such as fragmentation of powers between *communes*. Often the pace of French change was not as fast as it might appear from the copious legislation, but the local government framework

Complex institutions in the grip of change

for housing powers was still changing rapidly with decentralization. Central government responsibilities for disadvantaged people were rarely successfully imposed locally. Social landlords were particularly important and so are separately described in the next chapter.

Central implementation of local policy was frequently by contractualization. This was particularly so for construction and planning, which had a major influence on social housing allocation. There were compulsory contracts intended to link local actors to coordinate policy. These were not seen to be particularly successful in this study, and contracting increased complexity. At the same time, decentralization increased existing local divergences. Finally, it is possible to theorize about why actors expend such effort on negotiations.

5.1 Housing actors in the context of decentralization

There were national difficulties in implementing housing policies against this backdrop of decentralization. More information about the roles of local actors is needed, since they were often expected to act together for all local policies: the prefect, the mayors, the *communautés*, the Conseil général for the *département* and the regions. All actors in the extended landlord grouping might receive social housing applicants, although sometimes their other powers were more important.

Tenants sit on the boards of social landlords or on the allocation commissions (see p. 179), but they are mostly absent from this chapter about housing powers. No tenants were interviewed, as insider–outsider theory was applied after the field study. Nevertheless, tenants appeared in the evidence intermittently as making their local demands strongly felt,[418] and were implicated in the high percentage of vacancies awarded to insiders, particularly to existing tenants.[419] Many might act altruistically but the evidence suggested that their actions were governed by similar local interests to mayors. Tenants had many representative positions[420] but those in allocation were the most important.[421]

There were undoubtedly some tenant representatives dedicated to housing the disadvantaged, but the powers of others acting on their behalf, particularly mayors, were important – perhaps more important. In these fora, Mayors acted in allocation commissions in front of an audience of voting tenants, who report back to other voting tenants. Social landlords also took care to look after insider-tenants, including in social housing applications.[422]

The associations were important local actors, but were excluded from allocation and were often excluded from important negotiations. Their inclusion here was as commentators, because of their care for the disadvantaged.

5.1.1 Decentralizing power

Prior to 1981, theoretically, the central State alone was responsible for housing, partly because housing and construction were important both as a fiscal tool and economic factor. The State guarantee of rights was also important[423] in that the right to housing assisted in combating social exclusion, which Article L. 115-2 of the Code de l'action sociale et des familles (C.A.S.F.) described as 'a national imperative based on human dignity'. Local government and social agencies 'participated' in this imperative but were not necessarily responsible, although contractualization could bring more local duties by agreement.[424]

The first wave of decentralization was in 1982–3 and a second wave of decentralization was underway. The first wave generally gave *communes* the power to grant planning and building permits, an important source of influence with other actors. However, there was a fear that more decentralization might threaten equal treatment of citizens (Jégouzo-Viénot 2000: 296–305), that variability in local welfare provision could mean people obtaining different help in different places – a postcode lottery.

In the second wave, the preferred form of decentralization was by time-limited local contracts. There were also compulsory local agreements, organized by the prefect and intended to settle local implementation of particular policies. Compulsory contracts are a contradiction in terms, but some are described in section 5.3 (p. 127).

From 1982, management of most social work and some important benefits for the disadvantaged were also progressively decentralized to the democratic organ of the *département*, the Conseil général, and this is a continuing process.

Within a gradual withdrawal of State funding, local actors frequently called for more State involvement:

> We find that it is totally abnormal for the State not to make a greater effort, taking into the account the crisis that we have, to permit the production of social homes in sufficient numbers and at a price permitting the financial equilibrium of operations.
>
> (Mayor)

Some recognized it was difficult for the State to pay more. There were concerns about land prices and the precarious nature of tenants' finances which meant that local financial effort was also necessary.

5.1.2 Problems with national politics

French housing regulation could be impressively coordinated across ministries; for example the 'Loi contre les exclusions'[425] was the product of 14 different ministries. Nonetheless, reform tended to have a scattergun approach, responsive to lobbying, demonstrations and parliamentary amendments to bills.

The right to housing was supported in principle by both the political left and right. The coalition government of the left from 1997 to 2002 promoted rights

Complex institutions in the grip of change

texts, such as in the Loi contre les exclusions, reinforcing the Besson Act. The right to housing under the political right was then much more concerned with construction, but the Sarkozy government also passed the statute creating the *opposable* right to housing, the DALO Act (see section 4.1.7, p. 96).

In Parliament there could be difficulty passing statutes. From 2004 to 2006, two private members bills from the left proposed 'housing for everyone'.[426] In response, a 2006 statute[427] contained a package of aids to housing. This bill initially had 10 Articles but increased in size by amendment and parliamentary negotiation to 112. Even when promulgated, one statute in two was not ultimately brought into force (Goze 2005: 8). Political disagreement over housing at all levels made consistent application of government policy difficult. Then there could be conflict over funding between the ministry promoting housing[428] and the Treasury.

Political personalities often accumulated national and local influence. There were examples of this in the areas studied: Jean-Louis Borloo, Minister for the Town in 2005 (Mayor of Valenciennes) promoted le Plan Borloo – 250,000 new homes were to be built, 500,000 rehabilitated and 250,000 demolished between 2004 and 2009.[429] There was also: Sarkozy, then Minister of the Interior and departmental president, the Hauts de Seine; Martine Aubry, former Finance Minister, and Mayor of Lille, now Socialist leader; and the late Raymond Barre, author of the Barre report (2006), former Socialist prime minister and regional councillor in Rhône-Alpes. Local politics could thus have national importance, particularly around Paris, and national policies could be tested or showcased locally.

In this interleaving of local and national power, mayors had an important local influence on allocation. They could also be members of parliament. A social landlord said: 'This is a sort of schizophrenia, because it is difficult for a MP who is a mayor, where half of MPs are mayors, to say: "I shall take away from you the right to allocate places".'

5.1.3 The prefect: applying national policy locally

The office of prefect was created under Napoleon I. They were responsible for informing the government of local concerns, implementing national policies and representing the central State locally. In the late nineteenth century the prefect's powers were increased to reduce the congestion in Paris caused by centralization.

Local government until the early 1980s was under the *tutelle* of the prefect, requiring advance approval of regulatory acts. *Tutelle*, a word also used for guardianship of a child, was abolished in favour of *contrôle de légalité* (supervision of legality). Prefectural offices then checked local regulatory acts after they were made, increasing local authorities' autonomy. In 1997–8 around 5.5 million regulatory acts were supervised by prefects and 140,000 letters with observations were sent out (Brunelli 1998: 26).

Social landlords were still under the *tutelle* of prefects, but their other forms of supervision are described in the next chapter. The prefect refers any problem cases to the administrative judges, who take action against incorrect decisions.

This supervision and coordination between many local government bodies occupied much civil service time. There were 5 million civil servants in France, compared to 1 million more than 20 years ago (*The Economist* 2006c). Brown and Bell (1998: 26) commented: 'French civil servants have always had a great deal of responsibility and it is sometimes said in France that "we are not governed but administered".' Today, civil servants generally obtained their posts by competitive exam, ensuring high qualification. The author found them intelligent, pragmatic and well-informed, but there is a question about the high cost of these complicated administrative arrangements.

The 'prefectural contingent', allowing the prefect access to 25 per cent of social housing vacancies for disadvantaged people, was not much used nationally. The extra 5 per cent destined for civil servants[430] could be useful for providing public services, but within my study areas the prefecture was generally only active in directly housing the disadvantaged in Lyon, a striking local divergence. Bourgeois (1996: 77) found the prefecture weak, because they proposed unwelcome social housing candidates who were poor or might have behavioural difficulties. The prefecture still took on the most difficult cases, which could be politically sensitive, such as mass squatting.

One actor recalled 103 immigrant families squatting in camps by the site of the new national library in 1991. African workers had been imported under a labour scheme and many were polygamous. Polygamous families were not allowed residence permits or access to social housing, so divorces were arranged. The State services found social housing for the divorced families all over Ile-de-France.

Prefects' powers over allocations included rights to information and then to take over all allocations in the case of default,[431] but the use of such compulsory powers was thought unlikely. A state actor said past prefects had been proactive in housing but now: 'The prefects are led more and more to use their powers of influence and negotiation, rather than means of enforcement.' Two state actors said that the public policy push for construction weakened the prefecture. Formerly prefects could withhold State funding or impose fines for letting anomalies, but today local contribution was needed to build. Imposing penalties could decrease available contributions to construction or local actors could withhold finance.

Prefects had multiple tasks, acting as local agents for all national ministries, and they still provided some local public services. The prefect also had powers in local distribution of national finance. They were consulted in technical matters and were party to the negotiation of contracts to deliver local services with the various local partners concerned.[432]

Prefects and the Conseils généraux (the democratic assembly for the *département*) were assisted by both their own civil services and by two central

Complex institutions in the grip of change

government agencies – the Direction départementale d'équipement (DDE) and the Direction départementale d'action sociale et sanitaire (DDASS).[433] The latter had provided social and related healthcare. services[434] including the care of the homeless, and social workers to liaise with the DDE concerning housing and hostels. Most, but not all, DDASS services had been decentralized to the Conseil général, including social workers (see p. 121).

The DDE were in a position of power in approving technical aspects of construction schemes and advising on the granting of many types of finance. They also advised on enforcement measures against actors in breach of legal obligations. The DDE were thus a source of technical expertise, advising the prefect on all housing problems, including housing condition and local need.

The DDE also negotiated, or facilitated negotiations, with other organizations to implement housing policy. This included an important local housing plan, the Plan départemental pour le logement de personnes défavorisées (PDLPD),[435] and the Programme local de l'habitat (PLH)[436] a local housing programme concerned with spatial planning. Since 2003, the DDE also negotiated contractual decentralization of important central government powers to local government.

One state actor said the DDE had acquired extra responsibilities:

> In the last year [we are responsible] more strongly for everything to do with the housing of disadvantaged populations; all the regulatory investigation and supervision of HLM organizations in terms of financial and social management; everything concerning pursuing rent arrears; concerning the departmental section on APL [housing benefit]; and then for liaising with DDASS;[437] for everything that is to do with the financing of specific structures; for emergency shelter, social residences, and *maisons relais* [intermediate housing between hostels and normal housing] and thus this is a service which covers every area of State power.

She felt decentralization would mean more work by practical assistance and supervision after formulation of local policies. Mayors and their *communautés* were beneficiaries of this greater decentralized power.

5.1.4 The mayor: acting for locals

Although the 36,000 mostly small *communes* in mainland France represented a coordination problem, 103 *communes* had more than 50,000 inhabitants and the single central Paris *commune* had around 2 million (Bernard-Gélabert 2004: 5).

Communal boundaries had hardly changed in centuries of urban migration. A state actor said that she did not know of one *commune*, even one with 50 inhabitants, which would agree to abandon its identity or associate itself with the next *commune*. Goze (2005: 10) said people feared that the larger *communautés* would cause a dilution of the *communes*, in which they celebrated the values of closeness, conviviality and solidarity. A social landlord in the Nord said:

> In greater Lille, families are very attached to their *communes* ... and when these families look for a home they look in priority within their communal boundaries. They do not go out to Greater Lille. We do this very rarely even for existing tenants, and ... to succeed in moving a family from Roubaix to Villeneuve d'Asq, ... that doesn't happen. It is very difficult.

Mayors can help disadvantaged people, but a majority in my study also refused access to social housing by non-locals, despite the fact the law is clear that candidates could apply to be housed in any *commune*.[438] This evidence came both from mayors themselves and most other actors. Allocation rules allowed consideration of applicants' proximity to work and local facilities,[439] but two social landlords said *communes* liked applicants to have a local name. Local descent seemed more important here than local employment, which in practice could discriminate against incoming ethnic minorities.

The extent of mayors' practical importance for allocation was not immediately apparent from the legal texts. They were members of any allocation commission concerning homes in their area, with a casting vote.[440] They could reserve access to up to 20 per cent of a social housing development. One mayor estimated this cost €50,000 of loan guarantees for each home reserved, and social landlords could not borrow without such a local guarantee.[441] This would vary locally. Local construction also required gifts or leases of land,[442] or cash assistance for local bodies, giving rise to more reservation. Mayors' influence could also arise from founding OPHLMs or OPACs (see Glossary), each of which was attached to a particular local authority. That local government body nominated the company president and one third of the board.[443]

Mayors' power to grant planning consent was of primary importance and mayors used it to exclude some types of housing or to bargain. A social landlord said:

> When I go to see a mayor and I propose an old person's home to him or her, I am received with open arms. It is not a problem. I go to the same mayor and on the same plot I propose to do a programme of emergency housing. I would not say that I was received by the same person. Everyone agrees we should house people with behavioural problems ... but in the *commune* next door, not in my home.

This nimbyism was very prevalent in French social housing allocation. It helped to produce some very localized spatial effects of social housing, such as concentration or exclusion of disadvantaged people.

Actors often spoke as if planning consent was within the mayor's personal gift. Morlet (1999) studied mayors in Ile-de-France:

> In the small *communes*, the administrative personnel only comprise a few tens of people; planning is only one file amongst others and nobody is a specialist in the area. Most often it is the general secretary, an elected councillor, even the mayor in person who is concerned with it.

Larger *communes* had sufficient civil servants to recruit specialists, but mayors in small rural *communes* could be personally involved. Mayors generally have a very personal style of governance, with their *adjoints* (deputies) in their cabinet.

Planning permission and allocations were bargaining chips in negotiations not confined to housing questions, because local actors were in a continuing relationship. A decision in one forum affected a decision in another. One mayor tried to be impartial by neither attending allocation commissions nor personally handling files. He was still obliged to attend one commission, because he said a social landlord was making difficulties in revenge for the mayor's objections to a construction project.

Mayors' had some personal responsibilities in the front line for tackling homelessness, because they had delegated duties for *la police administrative*. This describes mayors' policy and enforcement powers and duties for public order. The latter is a wide concept, defined in the Code des communes (C. communes), Article L. 131–2 as corresponding to peace, security and public health; that is, avoiding individual or collective damage caused by disorder, accidents and the undermining of health and public hygiene.

For a family with children to be on the street was a breach of public order, thus mayors' submitted housing requests to the prefect. They might find hostel or hotel spaces temporarily in an emergency. One mayor said that when he woke up in the morning, he would ask himself whether the population in his area had something to eat and a roof over their heads.

5.1.5 The potentially powerful communautés

The rapid movement to create groups of *communes*, the *communautés*, is likely to change the landscape of French housing policy, but this was in its infancy. Intercommunal cooperation was radically extended by two 1999 statutes. These replaced seven forms of cooperation by three types of *communauté*. Each had corporate legal personality and a council comprising councillors from its constituent *communes*. There were financial incentives to form *communautés*; for example, contractual decentralization partly allowed *communautés* themselves to carry out the State processes of investigation, advice and approval required for public loans[444] and to obtain increased grants, a popular incentive.[445]

The three types of *communauté* were:

- the *communauté urbaine* for large conurbations,
- the *communauté d'agglomération* for groups of medium-sized *communes*, and
- the *communauté de communes* for groups of small *communes*.

Larger *communautés* had greater integration of competences than smaller ones. Some were long established, predating current reforms. From 1966, a *communauté urbaine* was imposed on Strasbourg, Bordeaux, Lyon and Lille.[446] The areas studied were at different stages of this rationalization. The established *communautés urbaines* dominated local housing policy in my sample. There were medium-sized *communautés d'agglomeration* in the Nord, the most rural *département*. The few small *communautés de communes* had no compulsory common competences at all.

The Hauts de Seine was unusual. Sarkozy, then departmental president, favoured channelling national construction funding through the *département* to *communes*, not to *communautés*, although legislation favoured *communautés* (Houard 2009). Houard recorded how the prefect responsible for enforcing this policy suddenly moved to Corsica, during the time when Sarkozy was also Minister of the Interior, responsible for appointing prefects.[447] Houard implies, but does not prove, impropriety.

The contract delegating housing funding was finally made with the *département*. *Communes* in the Hauts de Seine had been slow to form *communautés*, partly because they were already large enough to support services alone.[448] Six *communautés d'agglomération* had been created by 2005,[449] but housing policy was still strongly based in individual *communes*.

Communautés were generally successful, not only because of funding incentives but also because they did not call into question the autonomy of *communes*, providing a larger voice in politics and coordinated technical services.[450] For this reason, one mayor said that his *communauté* president had agreed to assemble all political parties together for its administration.

Each *communauté* was proposed by mayors[451] and tailor-made. *Communes* agreed the precise boundaries of cooperation and settled institutional control. All *communautés* could choose to have common local tax-raising powers. Other common powers might be housing, refuse, tourism, équipement (infrastructure), roads, water and public health, culture, social action and transport. Housing was the most popular competence, taken up by 80 per cent of *communautés* (ANIL 2005).

With incentives, *communautés* were becoming the vehicle for decentralization, and for construction and housing policy. Their rapid spread is shown in Table 5.1. In Lyon particularly, the *communauté urbaine* contributed strongly to make up shortfalls in construction funding. The 2004 decentralization legislation[452]

Table 5.1 The spread of inter-communality in France

	1999	2006
Number of communes forming part of *communautés*	19,140	32,913
Population living in *communautés* (millions)	34.0	53.3
Percentage of population living in *communautés*	52.2	90

Source: Direction générale des collectivités territoriales.

allowed *communautés* to take over communal allocations, which could allow inter-communal mobility, but this had not yet happened anywhere in my sample, except, for special purposes in Lyon, particularly to rehouse people displaced by urban reconstruction.

5.1.6 The Conseil général and the region

The departmental Conseil général had increased powers after the first wave of decentralization but was not generally as popular as the *commune* (Goze 2005: 10). One social landlord predicted their disappearance within 15 years. *Conseils généraux* managed several important social policies. They were responsible for social workers, who provided support for disadvantaged individuals and prepared reports for social landlords, although there was a shortage of social workers.[453] They administered the minimum non-contributory benefit, RMI, and the PDLPD, the plan for housing the disadvantaged described on p. 128.[454]

Several actors commented that *conseils généraux* had trouble raising funds through local taxation. Nonetheless, a study by ANIL (Agence national pour l'information sur le logement)[455] in 2005 found that housing was felt to be an important strategy for 90 per cent of *départements*, with 40 per cent having a housing policy beyond their strict competencies and 65 per cent having a housing service.

The *conseils généraux* and the regions could then also propose the creation of public social landlords and reserve social housing. Regions cannot now create social landlords. For both, reservations were often to house their civil servants, although departmental social landlords were instruments of social policy. Democratic regional councils were created in the 1960s to provide larger-scale economic and social planning, leadership, funding and information. They were omitted from the study due to limitations to interview time and their relatively minor importance for housing allocation.

5.1.7 The CIL and housing policy

The CIL (see Glosssary) and other collectors for the *un pourcent logement* scheme provided very cheap loan funding for construction and improvement, and 50 per cent of the social stock in my sample was reserved in this way for contributing workers. For one municipal landlord this was only 30 per cent and for one commercial HLM company (SAHLM) 60 per cent.[456] CIL involvement in allocation arose from this.

The scheme could be attractive to employers and employees because letting was not tied to the employment.[457] Bourgeois (1996: 248) found employers disliked committing funds to employees who might either leave or reject stigmatized homes, but there was now renewed interest because of increasing private rents. Only in the Nord, where the *un pourcent logement* was invented, did actors refer to candidates from the CIL as 'subscribers', as for an insurance scheme.

The CIL could also invest in and control SAHLMs, but these were overall the least socially minded social landlords in my sample, tending to economize on service provision and to prefer better-off tenants (see Chapter 7). In contrast, some SAHLMs, owned by workers and employees, were the most socially minded social landlords, avoiding eviction and giving access to disadvantaged candidates.

Most actors in my study mentioned the impartiality and speed of response of the CIL in processing applications generally. The fund had a variety of other benefits. The scheme provided guarantees against rent arrears for contributing employees, plus guarantees for many non-contributing young people.[458] After the study, the national organization UESL created a universal rent guarantee, available to all landlords for a small fee, although the fee could limit its use.

Despite this, the CIL were criticized in 2008 by the national audit body, the Cour des comptes, for financial deficits, lack of transparency and the high pay for some directors (one earned €900,000). As part of reform, the number of CIL organizations will be reduced by merger from 110 to between 20 and 25. Their future is in doubt, because they are increasingly asked to make grants rather than loans, diminishing their longer-term funding (Le Figaro 2009, Bissuel 2010). The effect of larger CIL organizations on local relationships is hard to predict.

5.1.8 Associations representing outsiders

Associations were generally non-profit non-governmental organizations, carrying out voluntary work.[459] Some associations described themselves as 'militant'[460] and were highly political.[461] A state actor said they could be political, religious or philanthropic. Some developed diverse specialisms to assist people in housing difficulty, some helping clients with their housing applications and making social reports about their clients for social landlords.

These associations could comment on the consequences of housing policy, but one voluntary worker observed that the other local housing actors acted like 'a closed club'. This would be predicted by insider–outsider theory, because they assisted homeless outsiders. Associations were frequently used by government to assist the homeless, obtaining tax relief. This has changed so that many associations depended on tightly defined government contracts; for example, limiting the number of days a homeless person could be sheltered. They received intermittent construction assistance, and a housing benefit, the Allocation à titre temporaire, paid per bed space.[462] Associations also received gifts from the public.

A government policy of delivering services through associations was intended to create more bottom-up policies, improve targeting of aid, democratize service delivery and strengthen the associations. In fact implementation of this through a large bureaucratic infrastructure reduced their autonomy because of a need to obtain local patronage (Nicholls 2006).

Uhry (2007: 397–9) observed that funding associations enabled the State to house people in insecure conditions, which were illegal for normal renting. The associations often acted as intermediaries to manage and improve inferior property, renting two-and-a-half per cent of social stock for this (Fitzpatrick and Stephens 2007: 45). Associations might also be obliged to use any available space for emergencies. An example of possible problems was that a 2005 fire in an overcrowded Paris building used as a hostel killed 22 of the occupants (N. C-M avec AFP 2005).

5.2 Planning, construction and contractualization

Construction was important for allocations, first because it was financed in exchange for reservation of places, second because the size and type of homes constructed governed the type of families housed and third because the push to construct homes or conduct large-scale renovation had many consequences, such as increased rents. Construction and planning were frequently seen as the solution to housing shortages, with a series of perverse effects on housing for the disadvantaged.

This section concerns the institutional context where enthusiasm for construction as a solution for housing problems was channelled through multiple local compulsory negotiations concerning multiple objectives (Renard 2003: 9). The principle of social mix was implemented in ways not sufficiently taking into account the needs of the disadvantaged.

5.2.1 Construction and housing problems

In many ways French enthusiasm for construction was successful, producing substantial amounts of housing since the last war.[463] A strong view amongst most interviewees was that if only enough houses could be built this would solve the housing crisis. A state actor said:

> We need to produce more private rented homes because there are households that will go into the private rented sector, who will not find housing in HLM

stock. The problem of the offer of housing is a global problem which is not solely limited to HLM housing. In fact, we have a problem of insufficient housing stock.

All actors who commented, except one, felt land was too expensive, making it difficult to make rents affordable within statutory limits. A state actor commented: 'What is lacking today is building plots.'

The view that more housing would improve cheapness and availability of homes is a respectable economic position. Nevertheless, French housing provision of cheap housing was affected by the steady demolition or major upgrading of existing cheap stock, particularly the large homes occupied by ethnic minorities. To pay for the cost of construction, the new and improved homes had more expensive rents. These tended to be directed to the better-off. When taken with the 'insiderness' of the French rental market, this meant an increasing lack of availability of affordable housing stock – a distributional problem.

A common view across all regions was that access to homes was blocked, causing difficulty in getting into hostels, into social or private rented housing, or affording home purchase: A voluntary worker said: 'In fact the system is blocked and at the same time there are people who need social support, poor people who are like anyone, except that they are in a shelter and they have problems.'

Actors identified different reasons for access difficulties: unwillingness by some mayors to grant planning permission; competition for building land with private promoters; insufficient homes; family break-up creating housing need; single old people occupying family-sized homes; poor families unable to afford rent because of reducing benefits; and increases in private rents. Private homes could be unaffordable or were unavailable for large families, whilst large social homes were demolished and not all replaced.

5.2.2 Planning and regeneration of deprived areas

Alongside construction, breaking up areas of social deprivation was an important concern of planning policy, as well as the integration of ethnic minorities.[464] There had been major reforms of competitive tendering and planning. Each *département* should have a SCOT (Schéma de cohérence territoriale), a holistic development plan combining plans for housing, transport and commercial activity, and later a plan for social cohesion under a 2000 statute (the SRU Act).[465]

The new, better coordinated planning schemes assisted regeneration by using transport links to connect deprived areas, which was not a new idea. The RER line A, a generally useful rapid transit line, was built from east to west across Paris in 1970, passing through Nanterre and Champigny, incidentally two areas which had the largest shanty towns and large ethnic minorities (Tchibindat 2005: 27). In the Nord, the former mining towns of Roubaix and Tourcoing had been connected to

Complex institutions in the grip of change

Lille by underground. During the study there was a planned new line in the Hauts de Seine and extension of existing lines to deprived communities in la Tête d'Or in the Nord and to Vaulx-en-Vélin in Lyon, the scene of particularly bad riots from 1980.[466]

New, attractive homes were more spacious, although more expensive, and there was landscaping. The plans also included facilities, bringing in businesses and associations, said by one social landlord to create a town (*ville*) in the suburbs (*banlieues*), many of which suffered a lack of such infrastructure. There were many types of redevelopment plan and zones such as the *grand plan urbain* and the *zone d'aménagement concerté*.[467]

One special zone, the deprived ZUS, was important for this study.[468] Average incomes within the ZUS were half those elsewhere and unemployment levels were double (DEEF 2005). Seventy-four per cent of social housing in the ZUS was built between 1956 and 1975 and was in need of renovation (Filippi and Tutin 2006). The ZUS were often the public face of social housing, but only around a quarter of social housing was in these areas and the rest could be very pleasant. A social landlord said: 'People live well in our estates. What I want to know is, do people live well in your estates?'

5.2.3 Local effects of social mix and planning

In all three regions, social mix, as a planning principle, was involved in wholesale restructuring of disadvantaged areas and constructing social housing elsewhere. The SRU Act extended requirements for larger *communes* to have 20 per cent social housing,[469] or pay a levy towards a fund for local social housing construction.[470] Simultaneously, social stock was being reduced in *communes* with existing dense social housing: by introducing owner-occupancy, by demolishing or upgrading existing homes and by introducing better-off tenants.

Social mix policy was a major distortion to social housing allocation, by reducing the intake of disadvantaged people in poor areas. A voluntary worker said: 'The homes that are demolished are homes built before 1977. These are not expensive homes. What they are building are expensive homes and not well assisted if you do not have any money.' In areas where housing should be built to replace stock removed elsewhere, Filippi and Tutin (2006) also found a preponderance of new *logements intermédiares* for the better off. These could be constructed by *communes* to meet their obligatory 20 per cent. Only four of the 55 *communes* of Grand Lyon had not completed their obligatory construction of 20 per cent of stock as social housing.

Reductions of cheap stock were not generally matched by new cheap housing elsewhere. A state actor said many poor people could not get access to social homes in traditionally cheap areas where mayors said they wanted no more, but mayors with few social homes did not want to build, because, they would

Complex institutions in the grip of change

say: 'There are no services – there is not the necessary social support for these populations and that cannot work.'

A voluntary worker complained that demolition of social stock was a certainty whilst construction of new stock was optional: 'Where are they, the 20 per cent of social housing for 70 per cent of the population? Who are they for? They are intermediate social homes that people are producing. They do not produce social housing. That is finished.' The 70 per cent here was the percentage of French people under general income ceilings.

Lyon had the most coordinated housing policy, where social housing was particularly segregated. In 2002, la Duchère had had 100 per cent social homes, LePlateau 90 per cent and other areas such as Mermoz, Vaulx-en-Velin and Vénissieux between 65 and 78 per cent. This level was being rapidly reduced. A local actor said: 'These are areas that are devalued, and rather stigmatized, so that even candidates in a difficult situation refuse homes that we can offer them in these neighbourhoods.'

There was no suggestion anywhere that social tenants were not rehoused on redevelopment. Unfortunately construction blocks up new allocations because of rehousing requirements. There were also increased rents on improved property. In Lyon, 11 per cent of displaced tenants wanted homes in favoured western *communes* and 8 per cent obtained them, thanks to joint working arrangements.

For urban regeneration, the next step could be to change the population. In Lyon, there was a system to improve management of blocks of flats, with a view to importing a different type of person:

> You must work on the management of the flat block before working on occupancy. Thus the lift must work. There must be a *gardien* who takes out the bins. You must tell the children not to clutter up the stairwells, so people do not have to get through a human mass to go upstairs. From that moment you can try to ... take someone with a similar profile but who would not pose problems.
>
> (Local actor)

Regenerated areas everywhere formerly had high tenant turnover of up to 10 per cent annually, but began to have a low turnover, so waiting lists developed as a result of the reduction in vacancies. In the Nord there was a process of re-education for tenants, offering workshops on hygiene, decoration or managing a budget, and there was activity to reconstruct ageing social housing stock, particularly in Valenciennes. There was no talk of changing the population of difficult estates there.

Reconstruction was also common in areas of private housing, particularly those occupied predominantly by ethnic minorities, such as in south Lille and in Clichy in the Hauts de Seine, reducing the amount of cheap stock there. In

Complex institutions in the grip of change

the Hauts de Seine, social housing stock was also being reduced in areas with large social housing estates, as in Colombes, Asnières, Genevilliers, Villeneuve-la-Garenne, Nanterre and Boulogne-Billancourt.

Two actors said richer towns there could afford to pay fines rather than build social homes. Neuilly-sur-Seine, where Sarkozy was mayor until 2002, had one of the lowest percentages of social homes in France. Areas with insufficient social housing were often the better-off areas such as leafy western parts of the Grand Lyon. Social mix could be met by building intermediate homes, partly because such schemes were expensive in better-off areas where higher land prices made it practically difficult to produce low rents.

Even in poor areas, Friggit (2006: 7) said local authorities tried to attract better-off tenants by discounted rents. Areas with the greatest density of high-incomes relative to rent were also those obtaining the largest discount on market rents. Consequently, public subsidy could be channelled to create cheaper homes to attract the better-off. Construction can thus cause as many problems for the disadvantaged as it purports to solve.

5.3 Contracting for divergence

Construction and allocation took place within a web of locally negotiated agreements. Bourgeois (1996) complained about lack of transparency in allocation; compulsory local contractualization might have improved this. Local actors did not necessarily view compulsory contracts kindly. In Lyon and the Nord many felt they were in advance of national requirements and did not need them. One social landlord said an agreement supposed a space for negotiation, and there was none with the many standard agreements, described below.

The first section below describes the failure of a number of unfunded agreements, but also the success of one funded agreement. Next, there is the highly successful contractual delegation of central government powers, which carried incentives. Finally, it is possible to raise two hypotheses about why actors' informal agreements were so useful and why local actors organized themselves in a fragmented way around allocation.

5.3.1 Local standard contractualization

As a generality, compulsory and other contracts unsupported by incentives were not very successful but involved considerable bureaucratic effort. There were unique local arrangements, which tended to lead to divergence in treatment of allocations between areas, described in section 7.2, p. 166. This section looks at the importance of some agreements, including plans to house the disadvantaged and the new contractual decentralization.

The *conférence intercommunale de logement*[471] was a potentially useful agreement to adapt national allocation criteria and coordinate allocations between *communes*, but this existed hardly anywhere. In the Hauts de Seine, the agreement should be regional and was compulsory,[472] but political disagreement with socialist Paris meant this was always unlikely. Driant (2004) observed that there was a split between the Paris region and *départements*, with divergent interests of *communes* and *communautés* and relatively low funding from decentralization.

In Lyon, a different new contract caused the prefecture to switch resources before this *conférence* was complete. In the Nord, this had also failed and another contract, the *chârte de prévention de l'expulsion* (charter to prevent eviction),[473] existed only through a locally invented spin-off, the *commission d'ultime recours* (commission of last resort). This assembled all local parties, including mayors, police, landlords and social workers, to together meet tenants threatened with eviction in a last-ditch attempt to prevent this.

Similarly, the *réglement départemental d'attribution* (departmental regulation of allocation,[474] now abolished), was a compulsory, negotiated compromise between national and local allocation criteria. This had been generally unsuccessful and had been little used anywhere.

The PDLPD, the local plan to house the disadvantaged, was a significant funding device. This compulsory local agreement under Article 4 of the Besson Act was specifically intended to facilitate reception of disadvantaged people. The State and the Conseil général were obliged to set up a fund, le Fonds de solidarité logement (FSL), to assist those in housing difficulty. *Communes* and other actors could be partners and local funding was matched by State funding. The fund was important in all regions and one state actor described it as 'a precious tool'. The agreement could provide social work to help applicants manage money[475] and encourage them to pay. It also provided rent guarantees, loans or subsidies for the first month's rent, until housing benefit arrived, and could prevent eviction by paying arrears. Forty-five per cent of such FSL funds were paid to young people as part of the Loca-pass scheme, administered by the CIL to give rent guarantees (Fondation Abbé Pierre 2006: 131). FSL funding had increased from €53 million in 1991 to €252 million in 2004.[476] The number of people assisted rose from 232,904 in 1998 to 273,930 in 2002.[477]

Another voluntary worker complained that applications were 15 pages long and bureaucratic, and that the FSL was 'a big machine'. There were complaints of delay and bureaucracy in all regions. Another voluntary worker complained that the FSL was intended to help small private landlords, but they were still not accepting these guarantees so the money from this fund was going to large social landlords instead.

There was inequality in benefits received between regions and FSL funds were budget-limited. An actor from the Hauts de Seine said some towns had more funds than others, so some ran out. In the Nord, grants were sometimes provided instead of the loans dominant elsewhere. Only one accommodation deposit per household was available there every five years, so one applicant, who had to move twice, had

Complex institutions in the grip of change

to be provided with a private loan for this[478] to be paid off over two years. In Lyon, people with debts above €3,000 were not aided. Consequently local landlords reacted very quickly to arrears and there was a problem with large debtors.

Such discretionary benefits limit expenditure because many people will not apply, partly because of the uncertainty of success, and particularly because some have difficulty completing forms or lack information, although they might need the benefits most. The discretion can be used to tailor benefits to need, but also to keep the fund within the budget, causing inequality and unmet need for those who get nothing when the fund runs out.

In Lyon local actors generally worked well together, but the *département* was politically controlled by the right, whilst other local organs[479] were controlled by the left. Consequently, the local PDLPD was negotiated but never signed, although civil servants worked as if it were in place. Other actors tended to learn about departmental policies from the newspapers.

A related compulsory agreement was between the prefect and social landlords,[480] who each agreed to accept a particular percentage of disadvantaged people. A voluntary worker dismissed these: 'The objective of the landlords was that the collective agreements should commit them to less than they do already... This is not a very limiting commitment.' He said this was a masquerade. One Lyon landlord committed to housing eight per cent of disadvantaged entrants,[481] less than even the prefectural entitlement. Social landlords in the Nord housed a high proportion of low income applicants, much more than expected by compulsory agreements, which were thus not useful. A local actor said: 'Listen, in this region we manage penury.'

5.3.2 Contractual delegation of housing powers

Temporary State delegation of housing powers by contract was new. This required amendment of the 1958 Constitution because it concerned the unity of France. A new Article 72–2 provided that duties assumed by local authorities would be compensated by the State, to meet local worries about imposed costs.

State construction funding or housing powers could now be delegated by the contract for the local three or six year local housing programme (PLH).[482] There was enthusiasm for delegation of construction funding in all three regions. A social landlord looked forward to negotiating only with the mayor, rather than the mayor and prefect. However, a voluntary worker was concerned about having to seek funding from many scattered *communes* instead of just the prefect.

There was less enthusiasm for the delegation of social housing allocation powers. Nevertheless, in the Hauts de Seine, the administration of the prefectural contingent was delegated to individual mayors, who agreed to take around 5–10 per cent of non-local candidates, a very low proportion. Only 30 single *communes* nationally had taken allocation powers (Costa 2007: 35) and around half of these would be in the Hauts de Seine. A local actor commented:

> I don't know many mayors in the Hauts de Seine who sign an agreement with the prefect in the area of housing who respect all the obligations in the agreement. Thus afterwards there will be a negotiation. The prefect can withdraw the delegation of his contingent.

This new contractual delegation to local authorities, compared to permanent decentralization, could give leverage to a committed prefect, even though prefects' existing powers were not frequently used. The *communautés* in the study often took decentralized construction powers, but not often allocation powers.

Communautés might obtain delegation of allocation privileges, both upwards from *communes* and downwards from prefects, but even large, established *communautés urbaines* such as Lille and Lyon had not taken over the prefectural contingent. These *communautés* obtained social housing places by negotiating social housing reservations in return for financing and guarantees. These reservations were used for limited purposes such as relocation for regeneration, but the remaining allocations were passed back to mayors.

Much decentralization was underway, particularly by contracts between the State and various local government bodies. A contract was about to be signed with Grand Lyon[483] and one with the Conseil général of the Hauts de Seine.[484] Taken overall, these agreements increased the powers of mayors collectively, but they were already increasing institutional divergence.

5.3.3 Possible economic analyses of organization

Actors expended much time and effort, which are transaction costs, negotiating about who should access social housing and considering policy in surrounding areas. A transaction cost analysis could be undertaken concerning the organization of the local actors. This section about collective asset management and asset specificity arises from the author's puzzlement at the complexity and large effort in allocation. This effort seemed to go beyond what was necessary to protect insiders, although it did have that function. These are simply hypotheses, not specifically proved, but could perhaps help explain this situation.

Such a market-based analysis is less commonly applied to the public sector even though the French State itself used market methods of incentive by using subsidy to achieve public policy ends. The effects of incentives on people's behaviour were not always as the administration intended. Even though social housing was decreed to be in the general interest by the Conseil d'État, allowing subsidy, and was thus outside the market for regulatory purposes,[485] the transaction cost of time and effort of housing actors was still relevant. People put extra effort into relationships and negotiation for a reason, even outside the market.

Complex institutions in the grip of change

There are two arguments concerning transaction costs in local public contracting generally. It was clear that local actors did not take up compulsory collective contracts where it did not pay them to do so, and enforcement of these was not strong. Limited budgets here have similar effects to profit requirements. That much is clear without economics.

First there is an argument about the benefits of local flexibility as against detailed imposition. Schlager and Ostrom (1992) found that the collective management of an asset, in this case fisheries, could be efficient. In contrast, Heller (1998) based his condemnation of collective ownership and praise of individual ownership on the transaction costs of interaction between owners.

Social housing was a species of collectively owned asset, in real terms, between the extended landlord grouping. Schlager and Ostrom (1992) identified the importance of particular rules on management to create long-term investment: exclusion and access to space, and alienation or transfer of rights. Certainly the extended landlord grouping were encouraged to invest in social housing in return for access rights. Schlager and Ostrom also argued that flexible collective-choice rules allow groups to avoid inefficient economic outcomes and to produce rules closely matched to the physical and economic conditions of a particular site, and that these rules can accommodate change.

For Schlager and Ostrom's collectively managed fisheries, it was the informal collective-choice rules produced by fishermen themselves that made this work, but new government regulation could undo existing successful efforts to solve very difficult problems. For this reason, when managing social housing, the innovative local agreements produced by housing actors between themselves could work better than the crushingly detailed and prescriptive compulsory local agreements that characterized this area, which gave little real choice. These local informal arrangements were vulnerable to changes in national legislation.

It does not follow that such more efficient agreements would benefit disadvantaged people, nor particularly that they would not. This is more a question of the form of national intervention in rigidly regulated 'agreements'. Instead, the cheaper transaction costs of local informally settled agreements described in this chapter could mean more time and effort directed to the housing itself, whatever was agreed.

Actors were not working for their own benefit, which might qualify this, but had multiple motivations such as: political or altruistic motives; seeking power; construction; obtaining benefits in other projects; and because they were employed to negotiate. It would consequently be difficult to measure economic benefit to prove this hypothesis for social housing, except by changing the rules and seeing what happened.

The second argument concerns Williamson's (1981) views regarding both asset specificity and organization, developing ideas from Coase (1960), about why businessmen sometimes work in firms or groups and sometimes separately. In a market this would depend on which arrangements carried the lower transaction costs. Time and effort are also currency in the voluntary sector. In allocation, the transaction costs of social housing allocation were very high, entailing a considerable amount of effort not just in money but in high investment in maintaining relationships, in an environment of proliferating formal contractualization.

In social housing allocation some social landlords conflicted constantly and others sometimes worked together as a group or collectively delegated allocation to one actor, as happened in the Nord. Why? Different political persuasions and interests were an important part of this fragmentation, but in contrast, different political parties could work well together within *communautés* on common tasks.[486]

Social housing was a physical asset so that dealings with this were 'asset-specific',[487] because a transaction such as the purchase of reservations locked people into a long-term relationship of exchange, the effects of which Williamson (1981: 555) described as economically 'idiosyncratic', also adding: 'The issue is less whether there are large fixed investments, though this is important, than whether such investments are specialized to a particular transaction. Nonmarketability problems arise when the specific identity of the parties has important cost-bearing consequences.'

The reservations purchased by the CIL and local authorities were generally non-marketable and specific to a particular physical asset, and the actors involved were constant and locked into a long-term relationship after the initial reservation transaction. This argument is still not easy to make for social housing allocation because of the variable motivations of actors.[488] This contractual imperfection is a feature of asset-specificity, affected by human factors.

So why did actors negotiate in this time-consuming way, within the already complicated legal requirements? A feature of asset-specificity is that contracting parties can obtain a quasi-rent from this situation. The quasi-rents or return that local actors obtained for maintaining these expensive relationships was higher than the transaction costs.

For each home, the quasi-rent here was the benefit that each actor obtained for the normally very expensive objective of housing their target insider in one home, fulfilling their political and economic objectives more cheaply than the cost of the whole home. This was because a wide class of social housing applicants meant that each actor could obtain a social tenant to meet their political or financial objectives. The mayor, the CIL and the social landlord could ideally obtain a single tenant who combined all these desirable attributes, – someone who was a local, a worker and who could pay the rent. Consequently, a single actor such as the mayor obtained the whole benefit of housing a local, but did not pay the whole of the cost of the asset, the home.

If it was not possible to satisfy all three objectives, they might take turns in meeting objectives in an ongoing negotiating process for subsidized benefits.

Social housing allocation is essentially a process of distribution of subsidy, and it is desirable that as much subsidy as possible goes to the applicants for allocative efficiency. Unfortunately, the allocation process can diffuse the benefits of such subsidy in order to achieve locally important objectives, which can displace housing the disadvantaged.

Each actor thus obtains a quasi-rent, or profit, from the investment of public effort and money. These were Williamson's 'cost-bearing consequences'[489] that meant human exchanges around social housing were more high-cost than they needed to be. Asset specificity is characterized by a number of theoretical consequences, including uncertainty (due to lack of knowledge of outcomes) and 'bounded rationality' (lack of knowledge of what was happening, owing to complexity). Where small numbers are involved, this is also prone to opportunism, where the quasi- rents can be disputed after the original transaction or advantage taken of the situation. Opportunism can include disguising intentions, distorting data and obscuring or otherwise confusing the issues (Williamson 1981: 554). These behaviours were evident in social housing allocation where small numbers of actors who had rights to process candidates were locked into a long-term relationship and continually re-negotiated who should be housed after the initial bargain. An example of opportunism would be when mayors or others allocated for personal gain.[490]

Actors had multiple values and objectives which could distort negotiations (Williamson 1981). Local consultation was a value in itself, although the large number of repeat occasions on which mayors in particular were consulted[491] seemed to get in the way of housing disadvantaged outsiders. It would also be wrong to assume French social housing was solely about housing disadvantaged people. From the point of view of creating construction, it was and is successful.

The process does not have allocative efficiency, and aspects of the process could be improved without displacing its non-market objectives, for example in improving data, simplifying the process and greater certainty of outcomes. The question is whether the values which justify removing social housing from the market also justify such high costs; that is, it is a question of proportionality.

Bergh and Camesasca (2006) said: 'Price theory analyses stating how allocative efficiency can be realized lose their validity when high transaction costs have to be incurred in order to achieve an efficient outcome.' Although this is not a market transaction, are these particular costs required to achieve these particular results? There might be a direct link between high transaction costs and tendencies to exclude disadvantaged people in hard times, the means displacing the end. However, the usefulness of this in allowing social landlords to survive economically can be appreciated.

These two hypotheses are ancillary to the central thesis in this book about the effects of insiderness in excluding disadvantaged people, and so are not fully argued here. If the first argument regarding procedural flexibility were correct, allowing local people to work out the best way to assist the disadvantaged within the priority rules would help, rather than detailed intervention in every aspect of procedure and entitlements, some of which regulation was ignored anyway.

If the second organizational analysis were correct, an enforced narrowing of the allocation criteria, or simply enforcement of existing priorities, would reduce the possibilities both of quasi-rents being gained by particular actors obtaining candidates for their own purposes and of opportunism generally. Choice might also be narrowed by local political agreement or availability of only poor candidates in some areas, such as in parts of the Nord, where actors delegated allocation to social landlords. This reduction in time and effort could be because the value of the quasi-rent from the high-transaction costs negotiation was reduced by lack of choice in candidate type. This theoretical analysis was developed late and is thus after the description of the contracting environment.

5.4 Conclusion

Despite the weakness of local representation of disadvantaged outsiders, innovative local working arrangements might improve the lot of the disadvantaged. Some non-standard, locally coordinated housing partnerships are discussed in section 7.2 (p. 166). These were not achieved through imposed compulsory contracts, which took much effort and often failed unless accompanied by incentives. These successful local arrangements succeeded despite the complexity of local institutions but still were unable to overcome all the problems of social allocation processes (detailed in Chapter 7, p. 158).

This chapter has described the local actors involved in allocation, but also starts to show the importance of geography and politics, reinforced by decentralization. Allocation takes place in a complex negotiated context with actors described in this chapter constantly interacting across a range of policies, sometimes as a 'closed club'.[492] This contractualized representative democracy had drawbacks as well as advantages. A particular drawback was the large amount of effort required to get anything done, which added regulatory transaction costs, including the high transaction costs of the allocation process itself.

Decentralization will certainly have a strong effect on this environment, although there is no let-up in central government production of regulation. Decentralization had already produced important changes with increased local control of construction funding and the FSL to assist the disadvantaged, but a social landlord commented on complexity: 'We are right at the beginning and what there is to fear is that it will be an extra layer to the *mille feuilles* that exist already. Thus if that is the case, then there will be a catastrophe.'

Differing regional institutions made common regulation difficult, which meant local treatment for allocation would differ. In an environment where many unfunded compulsory contracts failed, a state actor commented on the need for

Complex institutions in the grip of change

leadership: 'The functioning of groups of partners together is not easy, thus we need a strong political pilot. We also need an equally strong *animateur* for the group.'

It is to be feared that these contractual processes could encourage the taking of adversarial positions for bargaining and political purposes. This could take politicization, fragile temporary results with changes of central government policy, and local fragmentation of policy by competing local bodies even further into the heart of the administrative process. Civil servants, who should be impartial, continually negotiate with representatives of insider groups for conflicting objectives. All types of actor in this chapter would have been members of national representative lobby groups, so also negotiating at national level, meaning there was a constant interaction between local and national bargaining.

6 Social landlords and their financing problems

Social landlords are central to allocation, but must act within funding constraints, the major concern of this chapter. Different social landlords had different views of their mission. Some supplied *logements intermédiaires* for the better-off, whilst others struggled to house the disadvantaged with similar funding directed to construction. Social landlords were affected by the local conditions, as discussed in the last chapter, but more information and statistics are also needed, particularly about their legal form.

This chapter first describes the institutional form of different sorts of social landlord (see also section 1.1, p. 10). Bourgeois (1996: 20) found different strategic approaches by different types of social landlord. Today, these tendencies could partly be explained by their rules of governance, together with other local factors and their size.

Social landlords these days have more in common than dividing them in their regulatory framework, but differences in regulation can be scrutinized for possible effects. All social landlords were obliged to house people below prescribed income ceilings. Bourgeois (1996: 23, 80 and 113) found some social landlords took tenants above ceilings, but a national inspection report more recently found this was no longer true for a majority (MIILOS 2004). Those landlords interviewed emphasized their compliance with ceilings.

Social landlords' only profit was the rent, which funds tenant services and repairs and pays for the predominant loan funding, so social landlords will be concerned to preserve this income. This paramount importance of rent to social landlords leads to the many expected effects of insider–outsider theory, and this is considered in section 6.2.

Then social landlords' funding is explained including benefits, construction funding, rent control and tax relief, to illustrate and explain the situation. The landlords' behaviour in seeking to protect their rents was reinforced because of shortfalls in the funding of rents by benefits.This had a particularly adverse affect on the disadvantaged, making it risky for social landlords to house them, so reliable and solvent tenants were important. This central concern with rent tended also to exclude people who might be seen as creating neighbourhood expenses and social problems. Finally, social landlords' funding structure (including their tax regime) was primarily concerned with construction, which had direct effects on allocation.

6.1 HLM organizations

Social landlords' common organization, described below, affected their behaviour. Nevertheless, social landlords' different sizes and different detailed rules could help explain differences between them. The larger organizations tended to be SAHLMs (see Glossary), with greater possibility of detaching themselves from local policies and achieving economies of scale, although there were some small SAHLMs.

This greater scope for landlords to choose where and how they operated could partly explain why they were both the least social and most social HLM organizations. These rules are looked at more closely, first for private SAHLMs and then for public social landlords.

The governance of all social landlords was heavily weighted to the representation of local insiders, some of whom might wish to exclude disadvantaged people, often for financial reasons. For public social landlords, local politicians were important, something increased by their reform since my study.[493] Private social landlords had greater freedom to consider their own policies and economic needs, although they still operated in a political environment.

All social landlords had tenant representatives on their boards, and sometimes trade union representatives, despite the low French membership of unions or tenants' organizations. France's trade union membership is about eight per cent, although unions can still lead large general protests, with support substantially above their membership (DARES 2008). In 1999, the level of voting for the nationwide elections of tenant representatives was 26.81 per cent, which was rather low (Batiactu 2002).

Between them, all of the heterogeneous HLM organizations housed close to 10 million people, and employed 69,000 people with 13,000 volunteers (USH 2010). The movement also included 160 cooperative HLM organizations, mainly constructing for purchase, 59 credit organizations providing loans to individuals and regional HLM associations. A rare form, the HLM foundation slightly resembled a UK charity. The HLM landlords described here owned or managed 4.1 million social rented homes.

There were other social landlords: the nearly 250 publicly dominated joint-venture companies, SEMs (sociétés d'economie mixte), managing another 520,000 social homes. There were 140,000 homes owned in 2003 by a subsidiary of a State bank, CDC,[494] and 210,000 places in *foyers* for young people, workers,

Social landlords and their financing problems

immigrants and the elderly, often not managed by HLM organizations. Public bodies owned some social homes directly – around 50,000 in Paris and the Hauts de Seine.[495]

The definition of social housing was disputed even within France, and could turn around the type of organization, such as HLM landlords, around the type of funding or because they housed poor and disadvantaged people.[496] The latter fits with EU competition policy, but in France cheap, private rented housing could be known as *logement social de fait*, or *de facto* social housing.[497]

6.1.1 Profit and loss within a common regulatory regime

HLM organizations had common types of loan and tax reliefs, with many common powers, regulated by Book VI of the C.C.H. All social landlords were obliged to have an allocation commission for allocation decisions.[498] Directors of HLM organizations received no remuneration, although they could claim their expenses.[499]

HLM organizations had non-profit objectives, except that SAHLMs could distribute a very small profit.[500] Capital gains could not be distributed and no organization interviewed paid dividends, one SAHLM describing its work as 'a citizen's contribution'. Another said the allowed profit was hardly worth distributing. This works against Bourgeois's comments that SAHLMs were primarily interested in profitability. Nevertheless, if a concern for not running a financial deficit was a concern for profit or *rentabilité*,[501] Bourgeois's findings were still correct for all social landlords studied.

It might perhaps be possible for employees of large social landlords to be highly paid, like the €900,000 per annum paid to a director of the CIL (Interprofessional Housing Committee),[502] or to make themselves very comfortable. There may thus be some qualification to the not-for-profit motivation of social landlords.[503]

Profits made were generally ploughed back into maintenance or construction, which is difficult to criticize, even though some SAHLMs housed mainly better-off tenants. Economizing on services could be a problem. Some actors in Lyon complained that SAHLMs subcontracted cleaning, which produced clean estates, but tenants complained they had no social support or human contact point.

The independence and autonomy of social landlords within a strict financial regulatory regime meant they could not exceed their budgets to house candidates unable to pay rent or who needed social support. For SAHLMs, French private company law required that fixed capital should not be disposed of, so it would be available to creditors on liquidation. This limited the use of that capital (Foster and Ball 2006: 99). Public social landlords were closely financially controlled

Social landlords and their financing problems

and public land could not be mortgaged if it was required for their public function (Jégouzo 1995: 114). This meant a dependency on guarantees to raise loans, usually from the local authority.

Deficits were less common during the study than in Bourgeois's day,[504] with social landlords interviewed reporting financial health. Municipal OPHLMs (see Glossary) could still run a small deficit funded by their *commune*. Regulation by the prefect was supplemented by reporting and inspection procedures for accounts, by regulation of loans and by the MIILOS (Mission interministérielle d'inspection du logement social). Founded in 1993,[505] this national inspection body was a major and effective innovation, perhaps because inspectors were not part of the local web of contractualization. The MIILOS (2002) complained about social landlords' weak financial position and accounting anomalies.

Later MIILOS reports showed increased supervision of allocations. The MIILOS (2005) concluded that a majority of social landlords had allocation anomalies, although more than half complied with the law generally. Its reports initiated prosecutions, describing specific anomalies and poor practices, but did not name those responsible.[506] Reports did not deal with who was housed in principle or with allocation priorities. The conflict between financial limits and objectives to house the poor was never addressed.

Four social landlords talked about the thoroughness of the MIILOS inspections and how they were keen to comply with any MIILOS requirements. One said: 'They absolutely do not give away any presents.' Only a police investigation was to be feared more than the MIILOS. Another social landlord said the MIILOS looked at all records and talked to tenants, and a mayor said they could require resignations for improper practices.

The opinions of the MIILOS on proper practice might have no legal force; for example, insisting that three candidates' files should be presented to the allocation commission for each vacancy.[507] A state actor suggested there should be a code of deontology for this procedure. Such codes set detailed procedural professional standards, such as for architects and the police.

6.1.2 The public social landlords

Jégouzo-Viénot (2002) argued that there should be a single type of public social landlord and that the local organizational type of the public social landlord was not adapted to their task of managing a national social housing service.[508] Despite this last criticism, recent reforms have emphasized local control, where government was actively seeking local contribution to public policies.

By definition, OPHLMs were administrative public corporations[509] and OPACs were public corporations that were industrial and commercial in nature.[510] The latter form was used, not because it was commercial but because it was more modern, less cumbrous and saved money (Jégouzo-Viénot 2002).

Social landlords and their financing problems

Public social landlords were created on the initiative of a local authority.[511] This local authority location limited where public organization could operate. All OPHLMs were generally limited to operating within a *département* or part of a *département*[512] whilst OPACs could operate within a region and neighbouring *départements*.[513] In contrast, SAHLMs could operate over a region without this attachment to a local authority, and neighbouring départements or beyond with authority.[514] OPACs and SAHLMs might act in groups, extending their reach.

The public status of social landlords has a number of effects, including greater competencies than SAHLMs. OPHLMs could compulsorily purchase land, and both public forms could initiate some development schemes.[515] People working for OPHLMs were civil servants with strong statutory employment conditions, whilst new OPAC staff were employees with normal contractual employee status.[516] OPACs could also opt for commercial rather than public accounting practices.[517]

The OPHLMs, which were usually municipal, had a board comprising 15 members balancing power between three groups: one-third nominated by the local authority, one-third nominated by the prefect and one-third comprising various other local representatives: one from the CIL (see Glossary), one from the local family benefit office, CAF (Caisse d'allocations familiales), often to help with administration, and three elected tenant representatives.

It sounds slightly odd to say the OPACs larger supervisory board with 21 members was less cumbrous, but this separated the political supervisory board from the professional management. The supervisory board was similarly divided into three: local authority nominees; prefectural nominees and various representatives – two trade union representatives and three elected tenant representatives, one from the CAF.[518]

This apparently balanced governance in both public forms did not show the leadership of mayors as founders and directors, nor mayors' influences on planning, funding and allocation and the certain imponderable prestige attaching to mayors. This local control contributed to strong tendencies to limit allocation to local residents.[519]

The OPAC was used mainly for *départements* and *communautés*. The larger board allowed representation by mayors of left and right, working together. The presence of trade union members on boards supported access by employees, reflecting the long-standing alliances of tenants and workers.[520]

Bourgeois (1996: 133–8) had suggested that separating supervisory and management boards of OPACs produced conflict between the political and commercial approaches of the respective boards. This would not be surprising if supervisory boards wanted to support poor tenants and funding was insufficient. Nevertheless, the author interviewed directors and managers in all types of social landlord and saw no such tension, although the study had strong limitations in this respect, compared to Bourgeois's study. However, it was hard to tell, in my

Social landlords and their financing problems

interviews, who was an employee, civil servant or director, if you did not know already.

The new single public social landlord from 2007, the Office public de l'habitat[521] (OPH), seems a modernized version of the OPAC. There is a large board of 17–27 members, but with a more flexible size and composition.[522] Prefectural nominees were removed and a majority of voting members are always local elected representatives, which is significant in view of local nimbyism. There are still between three and five elected tenant representatives, and a new vote for the CIL.[523]

The reformed supervisory board elects a smaller more manageable *bureau*[524] comprising only four members and including a tenant representative. These tenant members are now in a powerful position and with increased real influence.

The *bureau* appoints a paid director-general, who is solely responsible for management.[525] This is closer to the commercial arrangement of the French *société anonyme*, where the president and director-general are often a single person (Cozian *et al.* 2008). It remains to be seen whether Bourgeois's complaint about increasing commercial approaches to social housing and tension between commerce and public service is still relevant. With local political will, this could work more efficiently with more focused management.

This new arrangement does not generally bode well for improved access for disadvantaged outsiders, given the new primacy of local politicians and continuing influence for insider-tenants. However, the new board must have at least one representative of an association concerned with the insertion of disadvantaged people, with one or two votes,[526] which is a small step towards balanced representation.

6.1.3 The private SAHLM

The private SAHLM was the oldest form of social landlord and they are now an adapted form of commercial company.[527] There were then no special limitations concerning who could found a SAHLM, but the prescribed form company rules[528] had to be approved and registered by the minister responsible for housing after local consultation.

SAHLM had varied types of shareholder. In 2003, 34 per cent were controlled by the CIL, chambers of commerce and industry, private enterprises or employee unions. Other HLM organizations controlled 26 per cent, whilst local authorities or SEM controlled 13 per cent and banks 14 per cent (Amzallag and Taffin 2003: 21).

Despite heavy and complex regulation, which changed constantly, SAHLMs had more autonomous governance than public social landlords. This was particularly true in their allocation processes described in the next chapter. Nonetheless, there were three elected tenant representatives on the board of all social landlords during my study, with local authorities, public bodies and tenants

Social landlords and their financing problems

Table 6.1 Major features of social landlords during the study

	OPHLM	OPAC	SAHLM
Public or private status	Public	Public, but a choice of public of private accounting regimes and new employees not civil servants	Private
Privileges	Could expropriate land and initiate certain developments	Could initiate certain developments	None of the powers in this row
Board size	15 members	21 members with separate managing board	Variable
Board composition	5 representatives of the local authority	7 representatives of local authority	Variable according to adapted law of commercial companies
	5 of the State and	7 of the State and	
	5 others	7 others	
Tenant or union representative board members	3 tenants	3 tenants and 2 union representatives	3 tenants
Geographical limitations	Within *département* or part of a *département* and neighbouring communes	Within region and neighbouring *départements*	Within a region and neighbouring *départements*, see p. 140

sharing one-third of the votes[529] in the general assembly. Now, this is still similar but there should be three board members nominated by local authorities or other public organizations.[530] Political power thus seems more entrenched.

Table 6.1 summarizes the major features of the different types of social landlord. Although my study could not observe any conflict between politics and profit, there were distinct corporate cultures, from limited observation within their offices[531] and from comments from others.

Some social landlords were more socially minded than others. Unsurprisingly, SAHLMs run by the CIL were most concerned with workers. Generally, the locally dominant type of corporate culture often seemed to correspond roughly to the dominant local political culture, for example, tending to favour poorer applicants in traditional areas of the left. One actor said her local social landlords were all communists.

Social landlords and their financing problems

Mayors might be able to favour particular social landlords for political purposes. Twenty years ago, even estates of fifty homes would include individual houses built and managed by each of all fifteen or so local social landlords. Several interviewees said there had been rationalization of ownership, so mayors might work with a small number of preferred social landlords.

This could indicate politicization of social landlords, with mayors as clients, but this was not clearly demonstrated. In fact, several social landlords mentioned conflicting with mayors' geographically restrictive allocation policies or trying to balance them.[532] Lack of tenant mobility was contrary to the interests of social landlords. Even municipal social landlords interviewed had some autonomy in allocation. This might not be typical.

Perhaps the main factor to retain from this section is the constant representation of insider representatives in social landlords' governance, whether workers, existing tenants, or local authorities.

6.2 Insider–outsider theory and rent

French social landlords' financial environment forced them to focus on rent recovery. They needed this rental profit to function, accentuating the importance of transaction costs as a deduction from this profit in 'hiring and firing' tenants, in eviction and social housing allocation. This section considers adaptations to insider–outsider theory arising from the importance of rent, whilst the following three sections explain the funding itself.

Wages in employment markets and rent in housing markets are not precisely equivalent. In legal terms employment is a contract for the hire of a person, and renting is a contract for the hire of a thing.[533] A difference is that for employment markets, wages are a deduction from profit, whilst for renting the rent *is* the profit. The direction of payment is different: tenants pay, whilst employees are paid, but in both cases transactions costs of 'hiring and firing' reduce landlords' profit.

This means the market power of the insider could more strongly affect landlords than employers. The connection between the tenant and the profit is closer than between a worker and profit. The worker produces the goods which are sold to produce the profit, but the tenant directly pays the profit, as a paying customer as well as insider. Within this funding regime, landlords could be expected to act strongly to protect rent as profit, and social landlords will prefer to retain insiders to avoid the expense of eviction and allocation. Because tenants are also customers, this probably means that, like a hotel owner, a landlord will ensure guests are very welcome during their stay, but must ultimately show them the door if they can no longer pay.

In France, the bargaining power of tenant-insiders was supplemented by local and national contracting and representation arrangements, already described in the last chapter, creating pressure to improve the conditions of tenants and other

Social landlords and their financing problems

locally influential groups. Social tenants could combine the roles of insider-tenants, voting insider-locals and perhaps insider-workers as well, an economically and politically strong position.

In France, to some extent this was an overflow of economic power from employees to tenants, although tenants used the same methodology to secure insider status as employees. French tenants, like French employees, have conducted strikes, such as the rent strikes which gave rise to increased tenant security in 1919 and 1982.[534] Like strikes by employees, this cuts off the 'economic rents', the profit on which landlords rely.

The associations had very effective campaigns,[535] but they do not have similar representation in social housing to local insiders. Representation of the disadvantaged has improved slightly, but they have neither the basic economic power nor the series of alliances that could produce the political movements to endanger government. The 2005 riots in social housing estates might have posed such a threat to Sarkozy's government, but there was little response by sympathetic demonstrations or strikes from other collective organizations.

Insider–outsider theory is used here as a qualitative tool to show how social housing applicants were divided into privileged insider-tenants and outsiders who were unlikely to obtain any housing and who suffered stigmatization as a result. This analysis is taken further in section 8.1 (p. 184). The significant aspect of the theory at this point is the importance of rent.

According to two social landlords, the French funding regime was constructed so that rent was the social landlords' only income. This funding was also primarily directed to construction using assisted loans, so that landlords had a debt to service, the cost of which had to come out of rent. This made it even more important that prospective tenants should afford the rent, particularly since tenants were not necessarily easy to evict under French rules, and allocation to a new tenant was an expensive process. There was assistance to social landlords by tax reliefs, but receipt of rent was still important because they had to receive rent in order to get tax relief on it.

It was also in the interests of the public authorities and other funders that social landlords should balance their books, reducing public cost. This duty of financial prudence[536] might conflict with their duty to house disadvantaged people, when benefits were insufficient. For this reason, the adequacy of housing benefits to pay rent became very important. Insider-customers were supported so long as they could pay sufficient rent. When support failed, tenants might be evicted despite the costs of replacing them, because of the serious loss of profit, resulting from the failure to receive this income.

During my study, the balance of the important construction funding for the disadvantaged and social mix policies shifted to favour the better-off, arising from the available choice by social landlords to take up funding for higher-rent housing, explained in section 6.4.1 (p. 148). Funding shortfalls could mean social

Social landlords and their financing problems

landlords were obliged to go upmarket or to prefer better-off entrants over insiders to obtain subsidy. Long waiting lists also meant plenty of choice of broadly defined insiders, so disadvantaged insiders might also not find a place.

6.3 Aids to the person and rents

The difficulty in housing poor tenants was exacerbated because benefits neither covered the whole rent nor the whole of increased rents from construction improvements. There was a general insufficiency of non-contributory benefits and support for some poor workers. Some historical information about the partial shift to housing benefits from construction funding is also needed and about shortfalls in housing benefits.

The French benefit system was reasonably generous to the insured unemployed compared to England (Stephens *et al.* 2002) but increasing numbers of people had difficulty paying rent. Article 111-1 of the Code de la sécurité sociale (C.S.S.) described solidarity as guaranteeing workers and their families against risks of any kind that could reduce or curtail their earning capacity.

Social security had grown organically since the War with nine *régimes* and nine different benefit funds for different professional groupings. Management of these funds often included representatives of employers and unions, although with increasing public control. There was supplementary negotiated provision from mutual funds with optional extras (Dupeyroux 1998).

There was also a system of non-contributory benefits, including RMI, family allowances and housing benefit, and strong benefits for children. These benefits were important for helping disadvantaged tenants pay rent. RMI was intended to provide the minimum revenue for social 'insertion' (as its name suggests), funded by contributions from the government, social security funds and local taxes. Payments were linked to a percentage of average incomes, rather than based on purchasing power, to provide a necessary minimum for living.

This benefit system was generalized to all French citizens in 1988, but there were still surprising gaps. There was not one but nine different benefits and 1.2 million unemployed people received neither unemployment benefit nor even RMI (ONPES 2006: 62). The difficulty experienced by the *départements* in raising extra local taxes (see p. 121) also applied to the RMI, which they administered.

There was also no benefit to systematically support poor workers to produce an overall minimum income, despite the minimum hourly wage (Dupeyroux 1998).[537] Two interviewees said part-time workers suffered particularly, because they were working fewer hours. This absence of a real minimum income for workers was important where housing benefits did not pay a high proportion of the rent. Several social landlords thought poor workers were in particular difficulty.

The ADIL (Departmental Agency for Information on Housing) in the Val-de-Marne found that local employees suffered particular difficulties with rent and that

Social landlords and their financing problems

70 per cent of people locally threatened with eviction were social tenants (Martin and le Jouan 2006). Most eviction procedures resulted in a repayment plan of €100–€150 per month over two years, which would cause further difficulties. However, the ADIL also found that private tenants were more affected by actual eviction than social tenants. Social landlords in this small study thus seemed more inclined to threaten than carry this out.

After the Second World War, non-contributory housing benefit was continually expanded and then generalized in 2002. This formed the majority of public housing expenditure with €13.9 billion paid to 6.05 million beneficiaries in 2004.[538] There were still three surviving types of housing benefit, although all now used a single benefit scale.[539] The rules differed slightly between schemes; for example, students and young people were usually attributed a fixed income. People under 25 commonly received neither housing benefit nor RMI, despite being the age group most likely to be unemployed (Paugam 2002: xxvi).

The Barre report (1976) caused a shift of public funding towards housing benefits, a common European trend (Kemp 2007). Barre saw this as allowing tenants to afford a better quality home, rather than paying existing rent. The benefit calculations thus took into account rent below a local ceiling, income and household size but did not pay the whole rent.

Kemp (2007: 7) in a study of ten developed countries across the globe, said that housing benefits were still usually below 100 per cent, most often so that tenants will contribute, avoiding the moral hazard of tenants in expensive homes by giving incentives to seek lower rents. My interviewees generally said the French tenants' contribution to rent meant they would behave more responsibly. However, others said many candidates could not afford the social rent on the available benefit.

From 1977, a new French housing benefit, the APL (Aide personalisée au logement),[540] was introduced, primarily for social landlords contracting with the State. This had the advantage that it was always paid directly to landlords, reducing the possibility of arrears. Social landlords thus had a strategic advantage.

A method for calculating housing benefit rates was the 'level of effort', which was used in 1997 by all the then EU members, except the UK. This expressed rents as a percentage of average incomes; that is, the effort from a tenants' budget. This calculation linked average incomes, benefits and average housing costs, but this was not a direct connection enabling affordability of particular rents by particular tenants (Bégassat 1997).[541]

This could mean rents were not affordable by poor individuals in expensive localities, in newly constructed homes or necessarily on property improvement. Bourgeois (1993, 1996: 120 and 141) found that after building works for home improvement, net rent after benefit increased on average by 50 per cent for tenants not receiving benefit and by 10 per cent for tenants receiving benefit. Interviews confirmed that this increased rent was still not fully compensated by benefits for tenants.

Social landlords and their financing problems

Another difficulty for many poorer tenants was the cost of *charges* (service charges that included both payment for repairs[542] and energy supply). Housing benefit paid a fixed sum for all *charges*, unrelated to actual cost. For poorer tenants in older, cheaper flat blocks, the *charges* would be high, because of high maintenance and energy costs. They consequently suffered the biggest benefit shortfall, and 87 per cent social housing was in apartment blocks.[543]

Two studies in 2005[544] showed that between 1990 and 2002 the highest rent increases were suffered by tenants in the bottom decile of income (Bissuel 2002). There were both increased levels of rent and 'levels of effort' by tenants (the percentage of their income required to pay rent) between 1998 and 2002, although private sector tenants paid more, as shown in Table 6.2.

The Fondation Abbé Pierre (2006: 67) said the figures in Table 6.2 were underestimated because they assumed that rents did not exceed the maximum supported by benefits. They also did not include *charges*. It said the real level of effort was around 48–49 per cent for a private tenant and 22–28 per cent for a social tenant. The percentage of income spent on rent was thus higher for private tenants than for social tenants.

For the poorest 10 per cent of all tenants, housing benefit paid only 60 per cent of the rent (Lévy-Vroelant and Tutin 2007: 79). This confirmed Rueda's view (2005) that the most securely protected insiders were not those most affected by an economic downturn. He was referring to employment, but social tenants were also insiders enjoying generally lower rents and more security than private tenants.

The annual housing benefits increase was frozen in 2006, as part of a process known as *bouclage* to limit State budgets. The loss of benefit relative to the cost of living was not fully reinstated, within a general erosion of aids (Lévy-Vroelant and Tutin 2007). Percentages of people receiving APL in social housing had then fallen, as shown in Table 6.3. This was when the incomes of social tenants was generally falling, not rising (see Figure 1.1, p. 12).

Table 6.2 The increase in level of effort to pay rent from 1988 to 2002

	Gross level of effort			Level of effort net (of benefits)		
	1988 %	2002 %	Change (in points)	1988 %	2002 %	Change (in points)
All low income households	29.0	40.1	11.1	12.9	16.1	3.2
Social sector	26.6	33.4	6.8	7.6	10.0	2.4
Private sector	31.3	50.8	19.1	19.0	25.7	6.7
All tenants	15.3	20.2	4.9	12.8	16.4	3.6

Source: Adapted from Fondation Abbé Pierre (2006: 65).
Notes: Low income here is a 'standard of living' below the central median.

Social landlords and their financing problems

Table 6.3 The percentage of social tenants receiving housing benefit (APL)

	Per cent
1997	50.5
2000	52.2
2003	50.6
2006	48.3

Source: Ministère du Logement (2007).
Note: The housing concerned is HLM and SEM (p. 137).

Generally, many actors complained that poor tenants could not afford rents or that benefits were insufficient, although many social landlords were fairly satisfied with current construction subsidies. The French benefit system seemed to cause real affordability problems in accessing housing for the poorest.

6.4 Construction funding and rents

Kemp (2007: 282) suggested that supply-side subsidies were reducing in most countries, although this was not necessarily so much the case in France, with its enthusiasm for construction. He also said that housing benefit had to be taken into account alongside the general benefits package, which in France has problems for housing disadvantaged people. EU competition policy was limiting state aid to construction,[545] tending to increase the trend observed by Kemp.

Construction aids do not necessarily lead to historic-cost rents, as in France, but these reduced rents for insider-tenants. This benefit was not based on need, raising an issue of fairness of use of public subsidy. The nature of French construction funding should thus be explored with other problems this might cause, and how the all-important rents are set. There was also some limited gap funding.

6.4.1 Loans for construction

Social landlords' funding by public loans was not just a construction incentive but also the main mechanism for imposing allocation requirements, within detailed standard loan agreements. Other effects such as reservation of vacancies and the uses of social mix have been introduced, and this section shows how the loans worked and how they provided for better-off groups.

Since 1894, the main funding for social housing construction had been special loans from State banks, now the CDC or the Crédit foncier de France. Early postwar loans were for terms of up to 60 years, and at low rates, even at one per cent (Lefèbvre et al.1990).[546] Most social landlords at the time of this study used CDC loans because of preferential variable rates, some at 2.5–2.75 per cent, which

Social landlords and their financing problems

were low, but less favourable than historically. Many felt the CDC looked after its client group of social landlords and was unlikely to create general financial difficulties. Some social landlords used private loans for renovation because of more advantageous fixed rates.

These public loans were earmarked for different income groups, specifying which income groups they must house, although social landlords could choose which loan-type they used. There were three main types of loan:[547]

- The mixed income ceilings for tenants under PLUS loans (described on p. 48).
- The PLA-I (Prêt locatifaidé-intégration), exclusively for less well-off tenants below the bottom PLUS ceiling, with lower, more affordable rents.
- The PLS (Prêt locatif social) with a higher income ceiling of 140 per cent of the middle PLUS ceiling.

The PLS loan commanded up to 150 per cent of normal rents. These were thus directed at better-off tenants. PLA-I and the 30 per cent PLUS housing were intended for 'very social housing', directed at poorer tenants. The home quality had to be generally similar to normal housing, but rents were required to be low. Consequently, despite a favourable interest rate and some grant assistance,[548] any funding shortfall had to be found by the social landlord or from local actors. This made it much less likely that very social housing would be built. Social landlords choose to take loans or not, and these will not be used if uneconomic.

Filippi and Tutin (2006) looked overall at housing funded historically by the different loan types and their fairly similar older version from 1977 to 2006:

- 73.3 per cent of new housing was funded by PLUS-type loans.[549]
- 8.6 per cent was directed to the poor by PLA-I type loans.
- 16.6 per cent was for the better off, funded by PLS-type loans.

By 2003–5, the percentage of housing built for the better-off had increased. Figure 6.1, shows the grant of these three different loan types during my study. The Fondation Abbé Pierre (2006) complained that PLS for the better off should not be considered social housing, but it constituted 29 per cent of production.[550] At the same time, a mere 30 per cent of homes under PLUS schemes were being made accessible for poorer tenants; this was an inadequate response whilst rents were increasing, housing benefits reducing and incomes under pressure (Fondation Abbé Pierre 2006: 48, 149). Figure 6.1 shows percentages of homes built under the different schemes. In total, social housing constructed in 2005 under PLUS and PLA-I loans was only 28 per cent of homes constructed.

It was difficult to reconcile the gradually increasing levels of poorer people in social housing[551] with the new loan finance figures. This was partly because of

Social landlords and their financing problems

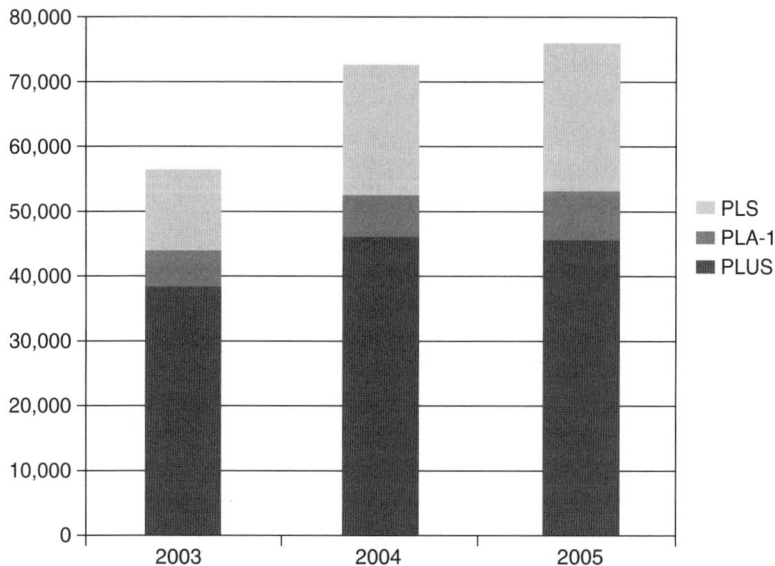

6.1 Social housing constructed by loan type 2003–5. Source: Ministère du Logement. Not including homes financed by ANRU, around 20,000 in 2006.

spaces in older stock. Loans since 1977 accounted for nearly 1.4 million newer homes but approaching 2.4 million homes were constructed prior to 1977 (Filippi and Tutin 2006). These were a reservoir of cheaper places for the poor, until construction or improvement.

Reasons why social landlords might house poor tenants, apart from special finance, included the reducing incomes of existing social tenants (shown in Figure.1.1, p. 12) and the views of some social landlords that it was their mission to house the poor.[552] Social landlords in the Nord departed from PLUS requirements to rent to more poor tenants after a first let.[553] In some areas only poor tenants were available, particularly in the 'sensitive urban zones' (ZUS) where better-off applicants might refuse housing. Social landlords' willingness to house the poor did not extend to new applicants too poor to pay rent with benefits.[554]

One social landlord said that building intermediate homes freed up social homes when better-off tenants moved up from cheaper housing. It is hard to see how building expensive homes could help with the structural shortage of homes for the poor in France. On city sites, new loans and social mix requirements could in practical terms shift the balance of funding to favour an influx of the better-off into poor areas, with low-rent homes being demolished or substantially improved. Apart from social landlords' requirement for higher rental income, other possible reasons included the high value of urban land, political pressure from better-off city residents, and a tradition, since Haussman, of decanting poorer people out

Social landlords and their financing problems

from the town centres.[555] This raised important distributional issues about the beneficiaries of this policy. This idea of 'filtering down' was rejected in the UK in the 1930s as not working (Cowan and Marsh 2005: 28).

After 1977, many conditions governing rent, housing quality and tenants' incomes were imposed by various standard agreements between social landlords and the State.[556] Most social housing was subject to these agreements, which brought special loans for construction or large improvement works and allowed social landlords to receive housing benefit directly. Five years after the loan term, restrictions on letting also expired.[557] Thus government policies in the form of loans could strongly influence types of tenants taken.

Reservations by local actors could also expire if homes were reserved for only one letting. There were a few social landlords in Paris with expired agreements and no reservations. A local actor said these homes were often useful to house the poor. In my sample, nearly all housing was reserved, thus situations with no reservations were not researched. It is interesting that those social landlords did not choose to take richer tenants, when free to do so, although there would no longer be loan payments to service from rents, making it easier to house poor people.

Cheap loans were also available from the CIL at 0.5 per cent or 1 per cent.[558] These loans amounted to €820 million in 2006. One social landlord expressed the view that it was 'almost free money'. Loan repayments here replenished CIL funding, to be lent again,[559] but this was an important vehicle for reservations for workers affecting allocation.

Under European competition policy rules, State construction subsidy should be for those in need, but many tenants housed under PLUS and PLS were not poor. In addition to the measurement problems from section 2.2.1 (p. 47), a new tenant's income was calculated from the previous year's tax assessment, favouring those on rising incomes.[560] An existing tenant might become comfortably off, despite paying a minor rent supplement.[561] *La Tribune* (Batiactu 2010) reported 53,000 HLM tenants with monthly incomes above €11,000. This is not the general situation, but it does raise questions about the extent of subsidy of insiders relative to outsiders who might need this more.

6.4.2 Construction, rent setting and competition

This section shows the variability of rents based on construction costs and how this was affected by land prices. High and variable land prices make access to new property for the poor both complex and more expensive. They also raise questions about competition and the advantages and disadvantages of this funding.

In 2004, HLM rents nationally averaged €5.02 per square metre per month, although 16.1 per cent of rents were below €4 and 27 per cent were above €5.5. This was quite variable but the geographical variation of average rents between zones shown in Table 6.4 was not large.

Social landlords and their financing problems

Table 6.4 Average social rents per m² in 2004 (in Euros)

Zone		Average rent
1*bis*	Paris city centre and neighbouring communes	6.32
1	The Paris conurbation, new towns and particular planning zones	5.97
2	The rest of Ile-de-France and conurbations of more than 100,000 with other exceptions	5.05
3	The rest of mainland France	4.83

Source: Direction des Etudes Financières et Economiques (2007).

Although unfurnished private and HLM rented housing were both governed by the 1989 statute, rents were differently regulated, with HLM homes exempted by Article 40. Private rents were set freely on a first let and there was more opportunity to increase rents.[562] Private rents generally increased annually following a consumer prices index.[563]

Older, unimproved social homes generally had lower rents because these were based on historic construction costs. Rents were increased nationally per square metre by ministerial order,[564] differing slightly between zones and between loan types. Rents on new homes were higher but varied more, with differing land prices and local financial contribution to reduce construction costs. New construction required higher quality standards for new lets,[565] contributing to higher rents.

This land price variability meant that social tenants in urban areas, particularly in Ile-de-France, obtained a much bigger discount on local private rents than in rural areas. Land prices were more variable than rents. Acosta and Renard (1993) observed considerable variability between land prices in different regions of France. Filippi and Tutin (2006) still found prices in central Paris could be ten times more than in other parts of the region. Even in Lyon, land prices could be three times higher in some areas than others. The different rent-setting mechanisms meant that private rents reflected these variable land prices more than social rents.

Central rent control did not allow rent to vary as much as land prices. It was thus harder to bring social rents within allowable limits in expensive areas. An important concept for new homes was the '*loyer d'équilibre*' (the balancing rent). The permitted statutory rent had to cover loan payments, but these payments could be reduced by local capital contributions. These contributions needed to be much higher in expensive areas, requiring cash, guarantees and land from local actors.

Social landlords might refuse to build if they were unable to produce a sufficiently low rent, particularly for very social housing. A mayor explained: 'The gap between the price needed to balance the books of a housing project and the market price is such that when we propose a project to social landlords, the landlords say, "well, no, we cannot do it".'

Social landlords and their financing problems

Social housing is strongly affected by any funding shortfall, particularly because of the desirable but expensive quality standards for very social housing. A shortage of such stock limited its usefulness in relieving disadvantage. At national level, a special budget for such housing loans might lead the public to believe politicians were taking care of the problem of poverty, even when loan budgets were unused.[566] The poor might practically be confined to such special housing, because other new stock was unaffordable.

Despite this, providing aid by lower rents rather than benefits was popular with interviewees. Six interviewees representing all three regions (not including mayors) thought reform should enable lower rents. A social landlord said: 'For construction aids, I think that the dignity of the poorest people is also for them to obtain access to a home which they can pay for out of their own resources.'

The older, large housing estates and other unimproved older property often had low and reducing rents, which were an important factor in creating concentrations of poor people there. A social landlord in the Nord pointed out: 'If you accept a family into your housing, which cannot pay you a rent to balance the books, you transfer them to old stock, to allow you to balance the books. You have no more problems with arrears.'

In Lyon, where there were larger deprived estates, this was seen by several actors as causing difficulties. A state actor talked about older housing:

> It is a problem because we have an enormous amount of social housing in the big neighbourhoods where there are already lots of people in difficulty. Nearly 40 per cent of social housing in the Lyon conurbation is in these neighbourhoods – that is a lot. On top of that, they are the cheapest homes. ... Thus on a purely economic reasoning it is logical to concentrate people with the lowest incomes and with social difficulties, because these go together in those neighbourhoods. The result – the riots of a month ago, then the riots of 10 years ago and then those of 10 years before that.[567] It is to fight against this that the *politique de la ville* [urban renovation policy] has been put into effect.

This illustrated some reasons to break up areas of disadvantage.

Another problem with historic-cost rents was the difficulty in persuading older tenants to leave large, cheap family homes for retirement flats. A state actor said: 'If you are an old person, it is necessary to move to a new home which is smaller and the rent is dearer, and they say, "Well no. I shall stay where I am," and there is a big problem in that.'

Did historic-cost rents have advantages? Lower rents could mean less need constantly to turn to taxpayers for support. Poorer tenants could afford to live in social housing because of them, even if those same rents meant they could not afford to move out. The low annual social rent increases protected vulnerable tenants but also benefitted the better off.

Social landlords and their financing problems

The Ordo-liberale[568] believed a sufficient mass of low social rents would lower private rents by competition, as discussed in Chapter 2. Testing competition levels was not an object of my study, but French social rents could be so low that there was no competition with the private sector. This was the product of greater 'insiderness' in social housing, but one which did not always benefit disadvantaged social tenants trapped in poor quality housing.

France had a diverse mixed system, so it is small wonder that Kemeny (2002) was unable to classify this as unitary or dualist. Two-thirds of French housing was in the pre-1977, cheap category, some of which was residualized as in a unitary market. However, this lack of competition was not universal: sometimes, a local policy could promote competition between social landlords (Bourgeois 1996). For new housing, social landlords could compete with the private sector for better-off tenants, perhaps as in dualist markets, but not systematically.[569]

Lux (2006) said Czech social tenants were insiders obtaining benefits unavailable to those outside social stock. Using insider–outsider theory, he questioned why better-off insiders in social housing should be subsidized by people in the private sector. The same applied in France.

One social landlord wondered whether a solution to the crisis would be to decrease housing quality standards, which is a difficult question. HLM housing was of generally higher quality than private rented housing, and more spacious, although private sector quality standards had also improved. A voluntary worker believed that: 'A social home is a home of good quality.' Nevertheless, he was initially shocked when social tenants complained of damp walls and insect infestations in some older stock in need of renovation.

In 1894, French social homes were a beacon of quality in a sea of awful housing. This could justify helping 'insider' workers rather than bringing their housing standards down to the poor conditions elsewhere, and protect workers' productivity. By 2005 this housing shortage was now much less acute, yet a pervasive sense of crisis remained, which was still used to justify housing the relatively well-off.

The quality and price of social housing meant increased demand for it, and this did not help disadvantaged people with no choice but social housing. Some actors felt workers were more deserving than the poor and unemployed. No French equivalent of the English expression 'the deserving poor' was used by any of the actors, but it well described the type of tenant often pursued and favoured by social landlords.

6.4.3 Grants and gap funding

Gap funding provides grants bridging the gap between loan finance and construction costs. This became more common during my study of the period between 1997 and 2005. PLUS and PLA-I loans could be accompanied by larger

Social landlords and their financing problems

State grants.[570] There were 20 per cent grants for demolition associated with urban renovation[571] and also for schemes initiated by *communautés*.[572]

ANAH[573] still provided grants and loans for large improvement works in all housing sectors. Grants could be higher for special needs, such as dealing with lead poisoning in older property.[574] Their PALULOS scheme provided grants linked to extra loans.[575] A new national urban renovation agency, ANRU, was founded to advance the Borloo plan, already described,[576] with grants for construction and renovation. These national agencies incidentally meant continuing central control of some public funding, despite decentralization.

Central government funding might be used to reduce the rents of poor tenants, and construction subsidies were reinforced by tax reliefs, but these were still not the most significant form of funding.

6.5 Taxation advantages

Tax incentives tended to favour social landlords more than other market sectors, and particularly incentivized construction or large improvement works. The author did substantial work on the taxation of land and landlords detailed in the General Tax Code, the Code général des impôts (C.G.I.), but only some reliefs clearly affecting the allocation process are reported here.

French tax reliefs were set against a background of high marginal rates of tax and many compulsory social levies. This burden was offset by many special tax reliefs, which had some tenure neutrality. Assistance was also available for both home purchase and private renting. Jean-Pierre Schaefer of the CDC said, 'Everybody gets something'.[577] Social landlords had extensive tax reliefs from income and capital taxes, including reliefs from local taxes and a reduced VAT rate at 5.5 per cent.[578] These increased the probability of large improvement works which would increase rents.

The ubiquity of tax reliefs for social landlords in the C.G.I. was striking. The tax and aid system was shot through with incentives for construction and large-scale improvement, and disincentives for inactivity. An example is that, for tax, social landlords were exempt from one of the major local land taxes for 15–20 years after construction,[579] but after that the tax increased on unimproved homes. This meant higher taxes were payable on older homes likely to be occupied by poorer tenants. The tax thus penalized unimproved property at the same time that historic-cost rents decreased rent returns.

Two actors suggested that private sector construction incentives also increased pressure on land prices. An important example of this was that, since 1996, private landlords had enjoyed several different tax incentive packages providing capital allowances for newly rented property, sometimes with income limits for tenants but usually with construction or improvement requirements. One of these schemes accounted for a quarter of all new homes in 2002.[580]

Social landlords and their financing problems

Table 6.5 Government housing expenditure by tenure in 2004

Tenure	Grants, subsidies and tax expenditure		Construction subsidies	
	Billions of Euros	*%*	*Billions of Euros*	*%*
Private rented	3.1	28	0.4	8.7
Social rented	2.8	26	1.9	41.3
Owner-occupied	4.9	45	2.3	50.0
Total	10.9		4.6	

Source: INSEE (2004) adapted from Lévy-Vroélant and Tutin (2007: 83).

Social landlords generally received more subsidy than private landlords, particularly when taking into account the larger size of the private rental sector. Table 6.5 shows government subsidies to the different sectors, including tax reliefs, but does not show the many small, complex reliefs enjoyed by social landlords. An example of an unquantifiable benefit is the payment of housing benefit direct to social landlords (but not to most other landlords).

6.6 Conclusion

The financial environment and variability of landlord cultures and local governance produced some very different types and qualities of homes, and varying initial rents. Low social rents for insiders were produced by subsidy and historic-cost rents, not generally by competition.

Social landlords' funding both encouraged construction of more expensive homes and focused social landlords' attention firmly on the recovery of rent, an essential precondition for the application of insider–outsider theory. A social landlord said: 'We are landlords, thus we seek to find good tenants for social homes.' Bourgeois (1996: 76, 124, 195) also found this attitude in several different social landlords. Social landlords might thus pursue the 'better' kind of tenant.

Two social landlords commented that their only income was rent. At the same time benefits and social support for the most disadvantaged applicants was inadequate. When poor people could not pay rents, as seemed increasingly the case, there was a direct conflict between social landlords' duties to balance their books and their mission to house the most disadvantaged applicants.

Loan funding for construction was necessarily paid before occupation of a home, so people were selected later; this is a problem when extra social costs, relating to disadvantaged tenants, arise later and are not directly funded (Czischke 2005). This could also be an incentive to select the limited number of low-income tenants required amongst those perceived as stable, rather than those feared to have social difficulties and expensive needs who might trouble neighbours.

Social landlords and their financing problems

Social landlords had to provide social care, fund higher maintenance costs and provide sufficient *gardiens* (caretakers); they were not paid either by construction funding or the regulated rent, for the unpredictable costs of disadvantage or of tenants falling on hard times. In particular localities and within tightening budgets, social landlords might actually be unable to help the disadvantaged.

Interviews suggested that mayors, similarly, did not seem adequately compensated for the extra costs of the most disadvantaged by payment transfers from other *communes*. Rowdy tenants or tenants with children required play areas, schooling, extra policing and perhaps special healthcare or social work. It was asking a great deal for mayors to contribute money to receive people who were unknown and might upset neighbours who were voters.

Insider–outsider theory particularly concerns landlord's choices as to whether to retain or replace existing tenants.[581] This replacement could take place through expensive reconstruction, which affected new social housing applicants, particularly disadvantaged outsiders, more than it did insiders who must be rehoused, even if struggling with new increased rent for improvements.

Disadvantaged people could be housed despite this funding regime, but the funding regime tended to militate against housing outsiders in many places. Most social landlords expressed concern for both existing tenants and the disadvantaged. Since they also had pride in their financial prudence, it was often hard to tell how far they in fact allocated homes to disadvantaged people, something sometimes learned from other actors.

Results of this study about allocation, described in the next three chapters, underline insider-centred concerns that tenants should pay rent and not cause problems to other tenants. Concern for tenants is an attractive landlord trait, but this is a question of degree. The inherent limitations to space in housing means that this concern with insiders can result in exclusion of disadvantaged people, particularly when taken with concerns about rents. Both social landlords' funding and institutional arrangements focusing on rent recovery were set up in such a way as to intensify the disadvantage of outsiders. Movements to house the disadvantaged at national level could also be frustrated by complex contractual arrangements between the extended landlord grouping and the detailed allocation procedure.

7 The social housing allocation process

The complexity of the French allocation process is well illustrated by the amount of information required in this book to reach the point where the social housing allocation process can be described and understood. This process had a personality of its own, with its split entry points with different allocation priorities, and its several stages. Often the process itself seemed the problem. The compulsory insider representation was the product of the law. Decision-makers had to allocate homes in this way and perhaps the difficulty of this imposed process, with the financial limitations of the environment, can defeat individuals' altruism.

Insider–outsider theory suggests a different analysis. The system tends to exclude outsiders because of the economic and political interests of decision-makers, who can be expected to act to protect the insiders they represent. Landlords are driven to reject people they cannot afford to house, whatever the system. The French system exhibited substantial 'insiderness' in the high transaction costs of the allocation process and the accumulated privileges of insiders; thus the extended landlord grouping could be expected to either protect insiders, or take incentives which currently made it worthwhile to house better-off entrants.

This chapter first describes the high demand everywhere, which was a necessary condition for processing actors to have a choice of candidates, as required by insider–outsider theory. Next, there were the detailed applicable principles, including limitations of the duty towards the disadvantaged and significant lack of clarity. Then, the principle of social mix particularly limited intake of the disadvantaged in variable ways, so actors' understanding of what this meant in practice should be explored. The very different regional institutions, which changed the basic procedures and might help the disadvantaged, were also important.

The remainder of this chapter concerns the social housing allocation procedure itself, from reception to the final decision of the allocation commission. In theory, nobody could reject an applicant in advance of the allocation commission making its decision. This account, of course, focuses on the mechanics of how outsiders tended to be excluded.

The social housing allocation process

7.1 Allocation criteria and demand

This section explains some basic conditions for allocation. In a context of high demand, there was a long process of filtration of applicants, or rationing, often simply because waiting lists were so long. There were important preliminary issues about the process: who exactly should be housed, what social mix meant to decision-makers, and the effect of reservations. If reserving actors decided who should be put forward for allocation, how could social landlords hope to manage their populations to produce social mix?

7.1.1 High demand

There was high demand for social housing in all regions studied. In the Nord, one in ten applicants per annum were housed, and in the other two regions, one in four. All social landlords had generally low vacancy rates, as low as 1 to 2 per cent in places, compared to ten per cent for unimproved estates prior to regeneration in the sample of landlords.

The Nord was similar to northern England in the historic loss of coal and steel industries and in the tradition of social housing. More low-demand or vacant homes were expected in the Nord because of this similarity to northern England, which had a problem with empty homes in places (Cole *et al.* 1999). The French policy of renovation had advantages in avoiding such deterioration. Nevertheless, one local actor mentioned the high level of social transfers to the Nord, so this policy was not cheap.

Social landlords found statistics from waiting lists unhelpful. The lists included people needing homes, people not qualifying for homes, people already housed but looking elsewhere and people seeking 'improved comfort', a phrase used by several social landlords. Despite this mix of need and possibility, the figures were frequently used to argue for more construction locally and nationally.

Every *département* was required to have an observatory of housing demand,[582] but implementation was patchy. Local actors generally talked about demand rather than need, except in Lyon. Social landlords were obliged to furnish allocation information to the prefect, but in Lyon they sometimes had trouble obtaining this. Local statistics generally helped formulate policy, but in the Nord a social landlord said: 'However well you identify the 200 to 300 or more families who don't get into emergency shelters ... They still don't get in.'

It has to be asked whether more social housing solves the problem of long waiting lists, where there are such genuinely broad allocation criteria. The regions studied all had high levels of social housing[583] but also high demand far beyond supply. All those eligible would still not get in. High demand meant they had a range of candidates to choose from, and conflicting allocation principles meant actors had a choice of which principle to apply. This did not work in favour of disadvantaged people.

The social housing allocation process

7.1.2 Allocation criteria

The statutory allocation principles were an expression of the right to housing, but this was effectively qualified. Chapters 2 and 3 have already discussed how principles of equality and the right to property and good public management could interfere with objectives to house the disadvantaged. These principles were not in the allocation rules but could not be excluded, because any public action was capable of review in the administrative courts under those other principles.

The principles and the mechanics of allocation were in the French building and housing code, the C.C.H., L. 441 to L. 441-2-6, and implemented by the government in acts. R. 441 to R. 441-12. The allocation principles are translated in Appendix 2. These principles were both very important and not as important as one might think. Their importance was shown by the continual process of parliamentary and other amendment of these rules, Articles L.441–1 and L.441–1-1 having been amended approximately ten times between 2000 and 2010.[584] However, there were constant elements in these articles to be discussed.

It was the broadest allocation criteria that were enforced in determining intake. Unlike in England, the only principles that classed as 'criteria'[585] were the generous income ceilings and the statutory requirements for size and type of house relative to household composition and income, enforced by inspection by the MIILOS (see Glossary).

The statutory 'priorities' had a lesser practical significance than the enforced 'criteria' to do with fitting the correct size of family into the correct size home, supplemented by income ceilings tied to loan funding.[586] Brouant (2007: 413) commented that even priority social housing applicants (described below) still might not qualify under the stricter technical criteria for particular homes, such as income and family size.

Social housing applicants also had to be lawfully residing on French territory, with a residence permit of more than one month.[587] This was quite generous, and useful for labour schemes, but meant asylum seekers were excluded from social housing.

Other principles in the allocation rules were reduced in importance for several reasons. The national priorities could be amended by the current local agreements, for example the charters and *conférences intercommunales* in Article L. 441-1-4, the *règlement départemental* in R. *441-3, and by the departmental agreement between social landlords and prefects to accept a quota of disadvantaged people, all described in section 5.3.1 (p. 127). These agreements were not really a process of imposition by actors, often being little respected or not even existing. On top of that, the basis for allocation was continually being re-opened by actors within the allocation process itself. One social landlord said that allocation had not changed in the more than 12 years that he had supervised the process, a practical view.

Some elements of the rules were present in all versions. The first principle

The social housing allocation process

in Article L. 441 said that allocation implemented the right ... to housing, a reference to the Besson Act. However, the section continued: ... 'to satisfy the needs of people of modest financial resources and disadvantaged people'. There was already a conflict with the slightly better-off.

In this 2005 version of the rules, groups with priority were:[588]

- people in a situation of disability or families having a dependent in a situation of disability
- people who are poorly housed, disadvantaged or suffering particular housing difficulties for financial reasons or relating to their conditions of existence
- people sheltered or temporarily housed in transitional establishments and homes.

The inclusion of those in hostels and in severe housing difficulties, as well as people suffering financial and social difficulties, reflecting the Besson Act, were generally found in every version of these rules.

An important qualification was the requirement of 'social mix' and diversity in the second paragraph of Article L. 441, which tended to limit the priorities. Where the right to housing was found in legislation, the principle of social mix was usually close by. This limitation was also found in various agreements intended to apply the principles locally.[589] Social mix was not defined but had the highly practical effect in negotiations of varying national priorities. Local actors, particularly social landlords, could limit the number of disadvantaged people that they planned to house, either to attract the better off or limit disadvantage. On contractual delegation of construction funding, income ceilings could be increased, such as to attract the better-off to the deprived ZUS.[590]

There were other circumstances to be taken into account in L. 441, including equality of opportunity (*égalité des chances*), diversity (representing *mixité sociale*). Equality of opportunity was not frequently mentioned by any actors interviewed, and was not particularly common in the literature cited,[591] hence its low profile in this book. There were various non-priority considerations for example, consideration for mothers' assistants, consideration of the applicant's current housing condition, local facilities available to meet needs, and distance from places of work.[592]

People with children were not a statutory priority, although actors interviewed often in fact prioritized them when homeless. In 1986, large families, single parents and young people became priorities, but this was later repealed (Bourgeois 1996: 35). Priority applicants under the 2007 *opposable* right included some children.[593]

Actors also said that applicants obtained priority after a period of 'abnormal delay', something not mentioned in these central allocation priorities. This was considered a priority because delayed applicants could apply to the new mediation commission.[594] The length of this abnormal delay was decreed by the prefect[595] and was originally three years for the Hauts de Seine and 18 months or two years for the other regions, but has since tended to lengthen.[596] Two interviewees who sat on allocation commissions described this as a new priority for those subjected to abnormal delay, essentially anticipating the intervention of the mediation commission[597] and using this alongside the principles already described. They also told of an increasing inclination for their commissions to use the queue as a default mechanism for fairness. This would tend to crowd out applications based on need.

There was thus a confusion of principles and no formal way to decide between priorities. In the implementing regulations, Article R. *441-3 added cumulative social and economic need and urgency as priority, but cumulative need did not seem in fact to increase priority. There was no points system, as common in England, whereby each need factor had a points score credited to the individual,[598] objectively increasing their priority and favouring cumulative need. This has its faults but it does leave an audit trail for transparency.[599] Three interviewees were interested in these UK practices, but found it mechanical and lacking the human touch.

Many French decision-makers avoided accumulated disadvantage. Rent was not the only problem. A state actor described social landlords' attitudes:

> Above all, it is ... a problem for them to house the sort of family which might have relationship problems because of their behaviour and as a result the good tenants around them do not want to stay there any longer. Often their fear is more to do with that.

Consequently, multiplying categories of need was problematic, because categories of disadvantage were in competition rather than cumulative.

This problem was not new. The 1990 right to housing, with its broad statement of housing difficulty, was an innovation. There were already multiple special categories of people to be assisted, and the new law was intended to help those not falling within existing categories (Ballain and Benguigui 2004). If cumulative need did not have real priority, multiple categories increased decision-makers' discretion, without helping the most disadvantaged.

Obligations to disadvantaged applicants were thus limited. There was a common view that responsibility for the disadvantaged lay with the central State, a duty not generally delegated to mayors,[600] who could pass disadvantaged candidates to the prefecture. The Geindre report (1990: 11) on social housing allocation said it was: 'contrary to good local management that only the fraction of homes reserved by the State should be concerned with the reception of people excluded from social housing' (Deschamps 1998: 184).

All actors were bound by these rules. Article L. 441 applied the rules to social landlords and their allocation commissions[601] expanded in the rules, and supervised by the State. Local authorities' involvement was to 'work towards' the realization of the right to housing and social mix[602] within the framework of local agreements. However, mayors would be bound by other allocation rules in activities such as processing candidates (through agreements) or sitting on allocation commissions.

7.1.3 Actors' application of social mix

Social mix was not defined by statute, so how actors applied this has practical interest. This was not a new practice. Bourgeois (1996: 36–7) described 1985–90 as a period of constantly changing authoritarian 'scientific' practices on social mix, with thresholds limiting acceptance of particular groups. She said that one commercial social landlord (SAHLM) informally limited immigrants to 20–25 per cent in each block (Bourgeois 1996: 114). In my study actors generally spoke of balance in the population, although several still talked of limiting thresholds for disadvantaged categories.

Social mix was thus an attempted manipulation of particular types of population. This had strong support amongst interviewees, particularly to avoid creating 'ghettos': Deschamps (1998: 213) said that prefects were accused of: 'blindly "parachuting" disadvantaged people into *communes* already in difficulty', which showed that accepting the disadvantaged there was seen as a problem. A state actor said: 'To play the devil's advocate – you cannot ask the HLM organization to house all the misery in the world and nothing but the misery of the world …'

The majority of actors' definitions of social mix concerned getting on with neighbours. A social landlord explained: 'When an apartment comes free, I would like our collaborators to look amongst the applicants and see whether they don't risk creating a problem with the neighbours afterwards.' This also showed a concern for existing tenants, for insiders.

Definitions were very diverse. One mayor thought that mixing types and sizes of home was important. Other definitions involved mixing different population types. A common criterion, particularly in poor areas, was a preference for employees as new tenants. One mayor in a ZUS said:

> We realized in the past that amongst our tenants, many only lived on minimum benefits, thus one of the principles which has been put forward is that at least … one of them [in the applicant household] should have a steady job and an income from work and they are not living on non-contributory benefits, and thus this element is taken into account.

Here the economic power of the employee-insider was shown in comparison to outsiders, something not depending on their local representation or existing tenant status. This is a question of purchasing power, along with inherent perceived virtues of this type of candidate – a question of social norms.

The social housing allocation process

A social landlord in the Nord said that balance in their housing developments of age, job, level of resources and family composition should be respected. Others proposed a mix of rents, or types of activity by tenants, for example, so someone would be around in the daytime. Concentrations of vulnerable women were to be avoided because drug dealers and pimps could exploit them.[603] Two social landlords concluded that their estates were peaceful and so tried to maintain this good balance, something Bourgeois (1996: 114) also observed.

The most contentious interpretation of social mix was that of avoiding ethnic concentrations. One actor suggested that you would not necessarily house a Kurd next to a Turk. A voluntary worker said (in a way tending to conflate poverty with ethnicity): 'Social mix is legitimized discrimination – it permits the refusal of access to cheap homes for poor people without allowing them access to bourgeois homes, thus social mix ... is an obstacle to the exercise of the right to housing.'

A state actor was blunter:

> If social mix ... means to say that in a neighbourhood there are already too many North Africans or too many poor people, too many etc., in this case I think that is not a good definition of social mix. But at the same time if, in a large-sized block of flats, the majority of inhabitants are North African or unemployed, you do not give good conditions for the social and economic inclusion of those people.

Most actors thought social mix conflicted with the right to housing, although two regarded social mix as an ideal which occurred naturally with sufficient housing choice, just as different sorts of people congregate in a public park. He said it was thus synonymous with the right to housing. This argument is consistent with universal housing allocations.

> In some ways it is through policies directed to managing the population, to balance, and to the necessity for having the best harmony possible, because we must imagine that all those people must live together, with each other, with a certain promiscuity.
>
> (Social landlord)

Finally, one social landlord said social mix was nonsense.

Whether people agreed with social mix and how they applied it depended on how they defined it, which was very variable. It has to be questioned whether this can produce fair or equal treatment of applicants, particularly when the principle was used to refuse housing.[604] It almost always limited access for particular categories of people, particularly the disadvantaged in poor areas, so less housing was available to them than is apparent from the percentages of social stock.

The social housing allocation process

7.1.4 Reservations and contingents

Reservations and contingents had important effects on outcomes and interfered with landlords' ability to control their intake for social mix. Two actors spoke of proposal rights as if the proposer owned the homes. Reservation was a vested interest in allocation, appearing as assets in the accounts of UESL (Union d'économie sociale pour le logement), umbrella organization for the CIL (see Glossary).

These rights were not like nominations under the Housing Act 1996 in England, where local authorities received and selected applicants and then nominated them to registered social landlords for housing.[605] Formal French public deliberation theoretically happens at the end of the process, not at the beginning. France was different because '*le tri en amont*', the filtering out of applicants upstream by reserving actors, was not generally thought proper. Social landlords' must consider proposed candidates within agreed time limits, but the allocation commission could still refuse them.

There was something of a fiction that the allocation commission made the allocation decision and all relevant applications would proceed before them, in situations where demand radically exceeded supply. A social landlord said:

> They say that it is the responsibility for the landlord to allocate a home. That's true, except that the landlord does not see all the files. Thus it is easy to say that the HLM organization filters the applicants, but ... the mayors do not want to lose people that they want within their contingent.

Several social landlords said they limited their interpretation of allocation criteria to conditions of nationality, home size and ability to pay rent (the firmest of the above requirements) for their own processing.

Despite the apparent hegemony of social landlords, applicants in my study were effectively refused or held up earlier in the allocation procedure. Organizations with proposal rights were allowed to make general policy concerning proposals, provided they did not contravene the rules (Jégouzo-Viénot 2002: 148). The importance of proposal rights did not seem sufficiently recognized in the regulation and inspection of social landlords, although they had the effect of fragmenting the process, creating extra criteria, and increasing opacity due to their complexity.

7.1.5 Can social landlords manage populations?

Theoretically, social landlords were responsible for social housing allocation[606] and thus whether housing the disadvantaged or social mix could be attained. A state actor said: 'Allocation is the responsibility of the HLM organization. It is the owner. It is the organization that carries financial and social responsibility. Thus it is normally, effectively, and logically, from this that the power of decision comes.'

The social housing allocation process

Despite this, reservations limited the choices of most social landlords. One social landlord said that, when an apartment fell vacant, they sent a letter to the actor entitled to propose applicants, who then sent an application *dossier*. This was studied by the allocation commission, which said yes or no. Another social landlord commented on their duty of social mix: 'It is not easy, to the extent that we are not masters of the proposal of tenants. I am obliged to take the candidates sent by the proposers.'

One municipal social landlord found room to manoeuvre through their relationship with the town hall:

> The civil servants of the town are a little bit our cousins. We discuss with them. ... Thus people keep an eye on certain addresses so as to be careful when they want to put forward someone or a file. In difficult neighbourhoods, it is also necessary to put people there who are a little less in difficulty so that people can help each other.'

In the Nord, where the prefectural contingent was not functioning, social landlords controlled that free percentage of allocations.

Despite the limitation of reservations, social landlords' ability to say no was a source of influence, either when conditions were not met (particularly concerning rent) or when the allocation commission refused an application.

SAHLMs controlled their own commissions, which were composed of a majority of SAHLM employees or directors.[607] One SAHLM interviewee was asked if he approved of the allocation criteria. He replied that they were not the authors of the criteria, but it was he that applied them. This illustrates their significant room to manoeuvre. Social landlords' local ability to control allocations also depended on local cooperation, and their view of what social mix meant.

7.2 Varying regional institutions

The three regions had different institutions affecting allocation, which are described in this section. Local culture amongst interviewees in Lyon tended to favour the disadvantaged, and in the Nord this favoured poor workers, although all attitudes (particularly in favour of workers) were found in all regions. The Hauts de Seine was very mixed.

7.2.1 The Hauts de Seine

In the Hauts de Seine, housing policy substantially depended on individual mayors and there was little inter-communal cooperation for allocation. There were few locally cooperative procedures, due to slow take-up of inter-communality, few special local institutions and the effective failure of compulsory local contracts without incentives. There was no functioning departmental observatory of demand although there were important regional observatories.[608]

It has been seen how Sarkozy favoured delegation of State powers to *communes*, bypassing the *communautés* (p. 120). In 2005, the departmental prefect was beginning to delegate his contingent of vacancies to individual mayors. This delegation of state power was unusual, particularly to single *communes*.

The prefectural housing office was still functioning at a low level to receive applications from mayors not yet managing the prefectural contingent. Prefectural housing receptions had recently been closed to the public nationwide, when funding was withdrawn. A social landlord said:

> Since the State is sick of managing people's difficulty, you know what they have done? They have shut the reception for registering applications at the prefecture because every two years there is nervous depression amongst the personnel, with increasing violence at the prefectural level.

At least half the 35 *communes* in the Hauts de Seine had contracted for delegation of the prefectural contingent. The agreement provided that 5–10 per cent of non-locals should be housed, which was not a large commitment, and not necessarily honoured.[609] Large urban *communes* were likely to have a specialized housing service (*service logement*) or communal centre for social action to handle this.

A few local *communes* had a communal housing charter to assist coordination.[610] This set out policy and was signed by the multiple social landlords present in most urban *communes*, who agreed to house a percentage of disadvantaged people. A voluntary worker supported local policies, saying local mayors had to be persuaded to support social housing but: 'When they do social housing they do real social housing.'

Houard (2009) said that *communes* taking delegation of State construction powers were allowed to derogate from requirements to construct social housing up to 20 per cent of their stock. The prefectural contingent was also used to house people who were not disadvantaged, using communal housing charters. This might create social mix in the disadvantaged *communes*, which still exist in this rich *département*. This was a local innovation, but one causing loss of housing vacancies for the disadvantaged.

7.2.2 Lyon

Lyon had many unusual innovations. A local actor said local people had tried for years or even centuries to ensure things went well, sitting round a table to pool their respective competencies.

The social housing allocation process

There was an unusually active and autonomous prefectural housing allocation unit for Rhône-Alpes, the SIAL (Service inter-administratif du logement). This worked closely with other actors and was housed within the Conseil général offices. The SIAL's website (SIAL 2006) explained that it had 8,211 applicants and housed 1,359 people annually, and pragmatically suggested making multiple applications. Theoretically, the SIAL was able to have access to 25 per cent of all vacancies for the disadvantaged, but the figure was actually 18 per cent.[611] The institution enjoyed local confidence, so no local actor interviewed wanted the prefectural contingent delegated. One said this was because the State should be responsible for the disadvantaged.

The SIAL suffered huge pressure. Recent amendments to statutory criteria had made people from shelters a priority, which a state actor said did not help them. She said this might have given pleasure to the person making the amendment but that was about all. There were three times more urgent situations than vacancies and they had to seek the priority of priorities. The longest wait was for large homes, which were in short supply.

The state actor said that people in shelters were at least accommodated, and were passed over if there was suddenly a battered woman with children on the streets. National funding withdrawal meant SIAL receptions allowed only postal applications. The SIAL was trying to persuade the Conseil général to open a reception. Other local actors were shocked at closure of the reception and were working on a single access point for all applicants, as in Nantes, but this has not yet happened.

The SIAL and others had created the CIOD (Cellule interface offre-demande), with four agents funded by the social landlords, the State, Grand Lyon (the Greater Lyon *communauté urbaine*) and the Conseil général. The latter had later withdrawn. The CIOD dealt with families with difficult behavioural problems, in partnership with other actors, often moving people from conflict situations across town and providing packages of support. Its impartial status was useful for negotiations.

Grand Lyon was an important local housing actor, even though this large *communauté urbaine* had no compulsory housing powers. The Lyon area had many estates needing renovation following historic activism in constructing large estates, and some had become stigmatized. All 55 *communes* had delegated their planning powers upwards to the *communauté*, increasing its influence. The *communauté* provided finance and guaranteed all social housing loans, and so became entitled to many reservations.

Grand Lyon housed its personnel first, then made places available to the CIOD and to rehouse victims of lead poisoning, also pressurizing mayors to allow inter-communal transfer. The remaining reservations were passed to local mayors. The local *communes* collaborated primarily to rehouse tenants displaced by redevelopment. Sometimes all actors would cease construction activity for a year

The social housing allocation process

because they recognized that rehousing blocks access to social housing for those in need.

Despite this cooperation, a majority of mayors excluded non-locals in their allocations, particularly in more rural areas. In the city of Lyon itself, *arrondissements* had observatories of demand, twinned with a commission presided over by a councillor. This worked with social landlords to agree who had greatest housing priority and to arrange social support.

A state actor described the value of local knowledge:

> Compared to what happens in Paris, where I imagine nobody knows if the person is living in a hole in Arras – here everyone knows it. Thus it is not that these are ignored, relatively speaking, nor that there are no abominable situations [here]. There are, but these are known, thus the problem will be dealt with afterwards.

He reflected that observatories were generally found in difficult *communes*, not in outlying ones where the social landlords and mayors kept information to themselves.

7.2.3 The Nord

In the Nord actors also traditionally worked well together, but without so many unusual institutions. A strong regional social landlords' organization produced statistics and facilitated tenant transfers between members.[612] Some larger towns had observatories. Local *communautés*, such as Dunkirk, were amongst the first to sign construction decentralization agreements.

The prefectural stream was not formally functioning in the Nord, although the prefect sometimes asked social landlords to house particular families. This did not adversely affect the poor, because very many were housed, many more than the 25 per cent prefectural contingent. This formed a sort of 'virtual' prefectural contingent reflecting generally low local incomes.

The local CIL did not process social housing applications for their reservations. Applications were instead made directly to social landlords. After housing people, the landlord counted the number of qualifying employees and asked the CIL for funding accordingly. Recently, the CIL had started to want more control over reservations.

Many mayors also allowed social landlords to process applications, some sending incomplete files. Generally, however, mayors and *communautés* were pressing for greater control, sometimes because of tenant relocation for urban regeneration, as in Lille. A social landlord said the *communauté urbaine*: 'plays a very strong housing role, and this *communauté* has also started to give us lists of families that have priority in their eyes, for reservations and for allocation.'

169

The social housing allocation process

Some mayors simply wanted homes reserved for locals. One social landlord said:

> If we house a family from Ose in Emberça or from Emberça in Ose or from Barolles in Madelaine, whatever – this is a great moment ... We have an open and tough fight with certain *communes* which consider these properties to belong to them, and thus they will even ask for homes way beyond that, from [homes for the] *un Pourcent logement* which are normally devolved to us.

The *communes* wanted new tenants to originate in the *commune* or have family there. The Nord was the most rural region and where mayors were most exclusionary.

Another informal local practice was that actors with reservations would not take reserved vacancies after the first letting, even for perpetual reservations. A relaxed attitude to income after the first PLUS (see section 2.2.1, p. 47) letting also made collective assessment of tenants' incomes less complicated and enabled landlords to house predominantly poor people.

In this way, social landlords in the Nord had greater control over allocations than elsewhere and possibly the most uniform treatment of files, because all were generally processed by social landlords themselves. However, this local consensus was breaking down with more active policies by other actors and some social landlords were more 'social' than others.

Each region had different institutions and practices set up locally, although these were politically fragile and thus vulnerable to local and national change. These could help the disadvantaged but this local assistance was variable. Geography was thus a major factor affecting allocation but, everywhere, the allocation procedure could still obstruct housing the disadvantaged.

This variability means that it cannot be assumed that the creation of a *communauté* will assist housing the disadvantaged elsewhere in France. There is a new *communauté urbaine* in the Toulouse conurbation, a large, historic industrial town in the south west, where the political left has a majority. The *communauté* includes 25 *communes*, 20 of which have obligations to have 20 per cent of stock as social housing.[613] Only one of those *communes* currently satisfies this requirement and there is a problem of visible street homelessness in this generally prosperous town. The Toulouse *communauté* was created in 2009, so it is early days.

That area of the south west has no tradition of social housing and one of the fastest growing populations in France. The new *communauté* has embarked on a catch-up plan but the slow nature of housing construction means they are likely to have to pay financial penalties for a long time. It does not follow, necessarily, that this process of construction will solve the problems of the very disadvantaged.[614] Much depends on how this is done.

The social housing allocation process

Local political culture, different institutions and different amounts of housing stock make it difficult to generalize about whether decentralization will produce better housing for the disadvantaged, particularly in areas with no social housing tradition.

7.3 The procedure

Applying for social housing in France was a tortuous and bureaucratic process that depended heavily on correct documentation. This section describes the procedure, and then the important allocation commission decision is detailed in the next section.

7.3.1 The application

The written application file or *dossier* was important for candidates' chances of success. This gave reasons for applying and was accompanied by supporting documents. The law prescribed some documents, such as proof of income, and prohibited others, such as bank statements. Written evidence was strongly preferred to oral evidence, a 'distrust of orality' (Bell *et al.* 1996: 84). A state actor expressed their opinion: 'I think that to enter social housing in France, it is necessary to have a certain form of integration, taking account of the necessary elements and the conditions to be respected. You have to submit to a certain procedure.'

The form had to be correctly completed. A social landlord said:

> Sometimes there are signs – a poorly completed file is dirty. You have trouble finding the accompanying documents. The file is incomplete. You would say to yourself that this is a file that is not good. There are little indicators. Often when you try to find what is behind this, you see that they are very bad tenants. There are eviction proceedings for antisocial behaviour and things like that and one discovers this sort of thing.

This actor would then order a social report.

A file would not be registered if incomplete or incorrect, which would not be recorded as a refusal in statistics. A mayor said: 'In reality, if you give an incomplete file to the head of the [housing] service he cannot give it a number.' These were unforgiving requirements, with few alternative means of documentation, within a risk-averse rental market.

A voluntary worker described a young English immigrant with a good job staying temporarily with friends. He was unable to find any rented home without the necessary three months' rent receipts until the *association* helped. Some private landlords required evidence of membership of one of the major

The social housing allocation process

contributory benefit schemes, ensuring payment but excluding people on RMI (the Minimum Income for Social Insertion).

Social landlords' requirements disadvantaged the less literate and immigrants. A birth certificate no more than three months old had to be produced, which might be difficult or expensive for poor immigrants. All documents had to be renewed and resubmitted each year whilst waiting.

Some mayors in the Hauts de Seine were said to improperly refuse to register a complete file or require a 10-year residence permit for foreign applicants, when a permit of one month was sufficient.[615] Some mayors in Lyon required a certificate of residence in the *commune* for three years. These were unlawful practices. It was legal, however, to refuse to house a large family if there were no large homes locally.[616] This was discriminatory when coupled with reluctance to build large homes.[617]

The author was slightly concerned at how personal information was passed around. She was kindly given two sample applications to look at, but personal details had not been deleted, although of course no harm was done. The collective processes in the Nord and Lyon also involved substantial information sharing for the benign purpose of helping applicants, but improper access to information could be possible. Bourgeois (1996) said that candidates' ethnicity was known even if not recorded.

Receptionists and agents processing claims helped applicants to a variable extent. Bourgeois (1996: 114, 156, 200) found filtering or rejection by receptionists, which could still happen, but it is hard to say how far this was on instructions or because of incomplete or non-qualifying files. A study of race discrimination in Lyon found this happened most frequently at receptions.[618]

Unassisted postal applications to the prefecture would be difficult for the disadvantaged. Associations everywhere helped clients to assemble a *dossier* but, nonetheless, this bureaucratic obstacle course of inflexible legal requirements could obstruct disadvantaged applicants.

7.3.2 Registration and file transfer

To assist with transparency and file management, all applications should initially be granted a centrally recorded single departmental number; in compliance with the Besson Act. In Lyon, some actors did not give departmental numbers because statutory information was thought inadequate, and some social landlords adopted a double numbering system. Theoretically the departmental number made applications valid everywhere locally, but each actor struggled to house their own applications without considering others.

Information from the applications accumulated in the databases of receiving actors until passed to social landlords, where this accumulated until the allocation commission decision. Bourgeois's study (1996) found that applications were not computerized, but during my study computerization was ubiquitous. Even associations recorded and searched for applicants like other actors. All actors searched their database for a household matching the size and type of vacant home. Since there were multiple eligible applicants, choices must be made at this point.

Probably the town hall was the most popular application point. A mayor explained: 'When people want a social home, they naturally turn to the town. Thus it is the town where they live or within which the applicant has family or their parents.' In some ways, a French sense of belonging in a particular place is admirable, but it favours local insiders.

Bourgeois (1996: 338) reported particular mayors sending the prefecture their most undesirable candidates whilst at the same time assuring the candidates the application had their personal attention. She said one mayor informed applicants personally of their success, but the social landlord would handle any rejections. Such devious practice was facilitated by the fragmentation and opacity of the process.

Where social landlords' entire stock was reserved, theoretically they had no vacancies for their own direct applicants, such as their own tenants. Presumably this meant direct applicants to social landlords would be transferred to other actors entitled to receive applicants. Nobody mentioned this and it was a puzzle. This probably involved variants of local cooperation, real influence or only a few applications going directly to landlords' receptions, except in the Nord.

7.3.3 Enquiries and social reports

After application, further enquiries could be made. Town halls might make enquiries, such as checking the existence of children with a school. One mayor described this process as pulling together information which the *commune* already had. This raises questions of confidentiality of data held for different purposes, which is difficult in a small *commune*.

A social landlord said they phoned previous landlords for a reference. Another in the Nord might offer a home visit to help applicants, but also to observe them in their home setting. Procedures used by the CIL are not known.

Traditionally, the anonymous standardized *dossier* was thought to lead to bureaucratic *neutralité* (impartiality) even though from 1990 individualized files could be kept for RMI applicants (Paugam 2002: XIX). For social housing allocation, further enquires might be needed to establish extent of need, to distinguish between multiple similar applicants and to avoid a tendency, explored in Chapters 8 and 9, to base allocation on stereotypes. Critically, however, further enquiries were often used to find out who would pay the rent and behave well rather than to seek out need.

Social reports were used for difficult cases. Bourgeois (1996: 115) described social reports as stigmatizing and making a candidate less desirable. This was

The social housing allocation process

still true during the study and mentioned by Paugam (2002: 44). When asked if everyone had a social report, a social landlord said: 'No, fortunately, eh? We would have to say that all applicants have social problems. Thank God that this is not the case.'

The MIILOS (2005: 40) described a social report commissioned without good reason as an attack on private life, showing the high value placed on privacy. Some reported that social inquiries made by social landlords or receiving actors seemed improper. Some looked at household maintenance, perhaps a cultural matter. Others observed whether couples quarrelled, to avoid households likely to split up. A voluntary worker complained that applicants were asked why their marriage broke up or why a child failed their exams. Reports could thus be used to reject tenants.

Alternatively, a social report could allow social landlords to accept difficult cases, assessing the applicant's capacity for independent living and permitting tailored support. One social landlord said that two-thirds of people with social reports obtained a home. There was a shortage of social workers, so reports were commissioned from associations in Lyon and the Nord. These were paid for by the social landlords in the Nord, part of a generally higher level of support for poorer applicants that was reported. Nonetheless, two voluntary workers expressed concern about unregulated conflicts of interests when disclosing clients' characteristics.

The system lacked some standard way of collecting necessary further information that was not stigmatizing. Social reports had a tendency to be an instrument of exclusion rather than inclusion, without other legal means for enquiry. Applications could be investigated twice: by proposing actors and social landlords.

7.3.4 Proposing candidates

Three applications should be placed before the allocation commission, to permit a choice of applicant, but in fact these were proposed in strict order of priority. The commission was expected to allocate to the first person listed. A social landlord described this:

> It is not us who decides. It is the person entitled to the place that sends us a candidate ... Very rarely, we receive two candidates and when we receive two candidates there is an order of preference – first candidate, second candidate. If the first candidate is good he gets the home. If the first candidate is not good ... we move on to the second candidate.

Grand Lyon would insist on good reasons for refusal of its first candidate to avoid discrimination. Sometimes three candidates could not be found for the worst homes.

The social housing allocation process

The proposers generally had to send a successful candidate within three months or lose their entitlement under reservation agreements. The first-ranked candidate was allowed to inspect the home to avoid losing time by refusal after allocation. These time constraints also meant that proposers tended to send candidates likely to succeed or unlikely to refuse the home. Middle-class candidates might not be sent to a ZUS at all for fear they might refuse to go there. This situation was worse where local agreements provided that proposers should pay rent on empty property.

One social landlord would agree a candidate with local mayors in advance and put forward just one file to the commission. This had produced only one rejection in five years, to save a mayor the embarrassment of personally rejecting a candidate. No rule required the presentation of three files. He said: 'I abide by the law. I do not abide to the spirit of the law. Anyway, if I wanted to abide to the spirit of the law ... I would have an allocation commission every day.' Recently, Massin *et al.* (2010) reported an average of 1.5 dossiers being put forward for social housing places in their study within Ile-de-France.

The 'three candidates' presented were consequently an illusion of choice by the allocation commission. If there were greater confidence that mayors were fair in selection, this could allow the personal attendance of their single candidates at the allocation commission and thereby promote transparency. Transparency would also tend to require full inspection of access streams and their application of priorities.

Mayors had strong exclusionary tendencies, but if these could be overcome, they could still ultimately be the best candidates to coordinate local housing allocation, because of their responsibility for public order and public duties for transparency. They have local democratic legitimacy to adapt national criteria to local conditions, as in England, so long as adaptations do not entirely displace national priorities. It is a problem that many *communes* are so small. Mayors' *de facto* power over allocation needed an effective, flexible public framework with responsibilities commensurate to powers, exercised over a larger area within a *communauté*.

This idea almost certainly underestimates the problems: local lack of trust in allocations amongst the public and between actors; how exactly you would impose responsibility on mayors politically; the effect of political divisions emerging in interviews and particularly the insiderness of local loyalties.

7.3.5 Social landlords, allocation and rent

After this initial stage, all processed applications were passed to social landlords. The most important thing in this section is landlords' refusal of applicants unable to pay, but first the organization of their commissions should be explained. Bourgeois (1996) said most social landlords were decentralizing their management to work

The social housing allocation process

closer to estates. This was to meet demands of *communes* better, an implication of collusion, and allowed the abandonment of some sites in favour of others. Today, mayors or *communautés* with more than 2,000 local social homes could insist on a local commission.[619]

Decentralization was now the norm, with many of the larger social landlords managing several local commissions. Large social landlords in head offices stressed the importance of supervising local allocations using centralized regulation and computerization. They had a pyramid structure of decentralized *agences* (agencies) in towns and smaller *antennes* (outposts) on estates, or just had either *agences* or *antennes*. One voluntary worker suggested that occasionally a local employee who had keys to a home might fix an exchange for convenience.

Usually, candidates applying directly to social landlords' local offices were passed to an agent. For SAHLMs, the agent was '*un commercial*' with private service-industry training. Employees or civil servants filled a similar role for public social landlords, often similarly trained. These agents were responsible for the whole application and would commonly remain the contact point for the new tenant. This would tend to make agents aware of existing tenants' concerns. One social landlord's agents did advocacy for candidates before the allocation commission, and were said to get rather overenthusiastic for clients.

Even social landlords who said they had no control over allocations took active steps to process files before the decision stage: receiving them from proposers; checking them; recording them in their database; and preparing files for presentation. They had to ensure statutory requirements concerning the family type for the home and legal residence were correct, and also checked for the correct income to pay the rent, which particularly concerned them. They also ensured third-party guarantees were present, particularly for poor applicants.[620]

It was axiomatic that prospective tenants should afford the rent. Social landlords calculated the candidate's income with housing benefits. Most then calculated rent as a percentage of income, which should not exceed 30 per cent. One said: 'We consider that with allocations the rent must not represent more than 30 per cent of the income of a family or a single person.' In the Nord, some social landlords accepted 35 per cent. One SAHLM instead considered the amount left to live on after rent, because percentages produced different results for a single person and a large family. Another combined these methods.

A social landlord described the risks of subsequent problems: 'Between 30 per cent and 35 per cent, there is a risk. Beyond 35 per cent, it is no longer a risk, it is a certainty. A file beyond 35 per cent [the application] is as good as rejected.' Many social landlords would hold back the files of candidates who were unable afford this, hoping to find a cheaper property,[621] particularly in Lyon and the Nord.

When asked whether they turned down tenants with too low an income, social landlords simply said 'yes' or 'of course'. In the Marseilles judgment,[622] a file should not be rejected only on grounds of income but this was negated by general

The social housing allocation process

practice. Prudence was often seen as benefitting candidates. One social landlord said: 'For us, there is no question of getting a family that is in difficulty more into debt, thus it is necessary to find a home which corresponds to the possibility for the family to pay rent.' Housing people who could not afford rent was not usually possible without extra help.

A majority of social landlords took guarantees against rent arrears from all tenants, including applicants from associations. A landlord in the Hauts de Seine only took guarantees for young people with an insufficient employment record, whilst one in the Nord only took them for people with a high level of effort. One social landlord felt guarantees from relatives made tenants more responsible. Guarantees from the FSL and the CIL have already been discussed in Chapter 5.[623] Requirements for guarantees could thus be a barrier to access for some people.

The effect of all these processing stages was very opaque to the public. In its nature, double processing always excludes more people than single processing. A recent study (Massin *et al.* 2010) found that social landlords would delete applications where anyone made two applications through different streams, something beyond the control of applicants, and which could change their chances of housing according to which application was deleted. This was, however, perfectly lawful during my study.[624]

7.3.6 Lack of transparency

About half the actors interviewed thought the process was transparent. One mayor said it was as transparent as a bottle of ink. The question used in my study[625] did not distinguish between transparency to the public and to the authorities. The latter had increased since Bourgeois's time, but the public often had inadequate information about landlords' priorities.

The public might know neither the best place to apply to, nor the best area to apply for. Many made multiple applications. Nobody communicated with applicants after the application, except on annual renewal, or until their file was to go before an allocation commission. Two social landlords said they would look at applications again, if asked. Much opacity was related to inability to explain or predict outcomes, and consequently the waiting times, to applicants in the multi-stage and multi-actor process. With high demand, this opacity was a recipe for discontent.

Social landlords everywhere faced huge pressure, producing desperation amongst some applicants. A social landlord in Lyon would cancel applications from people who threatened the administrators. Violence by frustrated prefectural applicants has already been mentioned.[626] In the Nord, one applicant drew a gun on a social landlord, saying he would not leave until the keys to a home were handed over. Two actors reported workers sleeping in their cars whilst waiting for housing.

The social housing allocation process

A social landlord said those refused were always discontent and:

> When you call the client, for the person to whom you have allocated the home, you are a god – that will last for the space of some days. Once he is in the home, he will have new demands – this is a bit of a caricature – and for the person to whom you have said no, you are a devil. There is such expectation.

This shows the importance of the process to applicants, but also the change in power when they became tenant-insiders.

Greater transparency to the public concerning local priorities, the process itself and greater predictability could reduce demand levels, because people could apply in the right place, or not apply inappropriately. There might be less discontent if people knew much more specifically how long they might expect to wait. 'Housing for all' led more people to apply where success was unlikely. It might be thought that allocation commissions would increase transparency of process, but this was not necessarily so as proceedings were confidential and in private.

7.4 The allocation commission

The social landlords' allocation commission made the final, and officially the only, decision on allocation, but had little influence over the choice of applications coming before them. It remains to look at this last stage of the procedure – looking at their limited role, then their composition (which meant they would have views similar to reserving actors or the social landlord) and the final decision.

Bourgeois (1996) reported that social landlords sometimes ignored the commission's decisions or housed people without a decision. There was no sign of this in my study, except for special procedures for rare emergencies.[627] Unusually, in the Nord, actors regarded candidates ranked second or third in a commission hearing as approved. These formed a reserve of candidates who could be housed without further decision.

Social landlords administered their own allocation commissions and were closely identified with them. Apart from file processing they provided the commission's room, clerical services and administration. Social landlords presented the dossiers and produced procedural rules.[628] Brouant (2007) said that the C.C.H. allowed social landlords to provide '*orientations*' (guidance) for the commission. He suggested this was illegal because such *orientations* were contrary to *égalité des chances* (equality of opportunity) and caused a lack of equality from place to place.[629] The author saw two such policy documents, but these contained very basic procedures and neither document contained any suggestion affecting the commissions' choices. The social housing inspectors (the MIILOS) could inspect such documents.

The social housing allocation process

7.4.1 The composition of the commission

The composition of the allocation commission did not seem to encourage acceptance of poor or prospectively difficult tenants. All allocation commissions had six members, plus the mayor of the *commune* where the home was located (or their representative), and the latter had a casting vote.

The SAHLM's commission comprised this mayor, five SAHLM representatives and one tenant representative.[630] The SAHLM thus had a controlling majority, usually comprising directors or managers from different departments such as letting, social services and management.

For public organizations, the commission comprised the mayor, two nominees of the local authority *de rattachement*,[631] two nominees of the prefect, one nominee of the family benefits office (the CAF)[632] and one tenant representative.[633] Landlords, tenants and mayors were not disinterested. They could not be expected to welcome potentially disruptive tenants and had an interest in rent being paid. One social landlord said other tenants would effectively end up paying for arrears.

All commission members, except those from the CAF and the social landlord's managers, were part-time volunteers. A social landlord said:

> The real difficulty is that the members of my allocation commission are charming people ... but are people who work, or people who are retired but who also have things to do. If they had to really decide an allocation tomorrow ... I would have to do not just one allocation commission per month, but one per day.'

Members had no powers beyond commission sessions arising from that office.

Who represented disadvantaged outsiders in front of the commissions? The prefect was too busy to attend and prefectural nominees on commissions did not necessarily represent the disadvantaged. The SIAL in Lyon wanted to be able to attend to support the disadvantaged. Associations could be invited consultatively[634] but this very rarely happened.

The law governing the composition of allocation commissions was not constructed to assist outsiders, unless financially supported and with social care provision. The legally prescribed representation on the commissions was very unbalanced, because it promoted the interests of groups of local people already in positions of influence, whilst the most disadvantaged were substantially unrepresented. This raises serious issues about the impartiality of the process.

7.4.2 Commission proceedings

Most local allocation commissions and took place every two weeks. Some mayors and several social landlords interviewed were also commission members.

The social housing allocation process

Proceedings were private, to protect applicants' confidentiality (although there were fair-sized audiences of mayors), and the applicants themselves were not present. Most commission decisions were reported to be by consensus. However, there was increasing disagreement within some commissions, with some members preferring the oldest application – that is, the queue system associated with universal allocations.

Commissions would refuse or adjourn applications for similar reasons to those that mayors and social landlords would have themselves – often behavioural or rent concerns. A mayor said good allocation meant ensuring that a tenant could pay, so they would not have difficulties:

> Eviction is very rarely the consequence of these unhappy times, ... it is very often an error of the allocation commissions, which means that an apartment is allocated with a level of effort from the person which could not be supported in the long term, hence the importance for me of the position of the allocation commission. Allocation commissions should be attentive to the fact that eviction is the worst of social dramas. People are evicted. They find themselves in the road. The children are taken into care by the *département* in hostels, etc. Thus it is really the worst of things but there is a heavy responsibility on the allocation commissions.

This suggested that refusing poor applicants was in their best interests, if they could not afford rent. This was essentially a problem with there being inadequate State financial support for the poorest tenants.

7.5 Conclusion

The evidence in this chapter tends to confirm the necessary conditions and choices for insider–outsider theory:

- the wide choice of tenants
- requirements for tenants likely to pay rent and behave well
- preferences for insiders
- exclusion of stigmatized outsiders
- a process with room to manoeuvre
- lack of transparency
- multiple opportunities to delay or reject outsiders.

The economic orientation of the process and the weakening power of the prefecture with decentralization increased the likelihood that disadvantaged people would not be housed.

Opposing principles and multiple criteria within the law sometimes amounted to a menu from which local actors could choose who they wished to help, a matter for variable individual consciences. There was no legal guidance concerning the relative weight of different principles, apart from the stated priorities, nor any objective or non-stigmatizing way to assess the relative needs of applicants.

Definitions of social mix had particularly large variations in substance and, because of the wide choice this endowed, seemed an odd way to conduct public policy. In practical terms, it allowed exclusion of the disadvantaged from poor areas without providing alternatives and tended to favourably stereotype the stable family or worker.

The conflicting principles and fragmentation of responsibility meant many actors felt it was not their job to house the disadvantaged. This was unsurprising given the inadequate funding, discussed in the last chapter. The system relied on altruism, which was common but not always sufficient to overcome the difficulties of access for the disadvantaged. The disadvantaged might not be housed, not due to lack of goodwill but to someone else being housed instead – usually an insider.

Applicants had to go through a Byzantine, bureaucratic obstacle course, which was discriminatory to the less literate and integrated. There was a peculiar mix of discretionary vagueness and procedural exactitude. The prescriptiveness of the law was unhelpful to the disadvantaged and social reports tended to stigmatize those who needed them. Bourgeois (1996) complained that this complexity and lack of transparency was used by social landlords to protect their interests. The system was still not transparent because of its many entry points, complex local contractualization, variable institutions, multiple influences and fragmented processes.

This was not really a collective process because of serial processing and *ad hoc* bargaining. The public had no reliable information about their prospects or progress of their application. Consequently, the legal process was not trusted to be fair by its users. Despite reform, the old power system described by Bourgeois was still in place, favouring local insiders and respectable people who would pay rent. Serial processing of claims due to reservations could mean just one actor could frustrate general policy by delaying or rejecting cases. Split access points also meant local actors judged against different criteria. Much time and expense was spent negotiating compromises, which increased transaction costs and focussed on local rivalries.

People manning the process were not disinterested, although impartiality is an elusive quality, and balanced formal bargaining was a proxy for this. Unfortunately, the bargaining process did not adequately represent or provide for the disadvantaged. What is worse, these processes were a requirement of the law.

A relative bright spot was that the disadvantaged would have better chances of housing if there were special local institutions to help them. These owed little to the rigid national legal framework, which neither created equality of treatment for applicants from region to region nor permitted formal adaptation to meet local needs. Unique local institutions studied tended to increase transparency and fairness of the process and achieve greater implementation of housing rights, but not invariably so.

Generally, the law governing allocations and its context reinforced tendencies to exclude outsiders. In many places, when local actors succeeded in housing the disadvantaged, this was something of a triumph over an adverse regulatory environment, which was difficult to reform because of its representative nature. The next two chapters explore the inclusion or exclusion of particular groups and take further the analysis of insider–outsider theory.

8 'Insiderness' and local actors

This chapter concerns who obtains access to social housing under the present system, whilst the next concerns those excluded. First, insider–outsider theory is reviewed in the light of evidence from this and other studies before looking at the insiders and entrants who have been likely to obtain access with the current incentive structure. There was favourable reception of insiders in a broad sense by social landlords, mayors, the CIL (see Glossary) and the prefecture, even though, within this, entrants could be preferred. Entrants viewed as desirable tenants generally included existing tenants with a good record, but also the employed and apparently stable families. This was particularly so during the study in poor areas, if entrants could be persuaded to live there.

Apart from the patchy local priorities for the disadvantaged,[635] there were two economic forces at work: favouring insiders and favouring potentially more profitable future tenants (i.e. entrants with a good existing record as tenants).[636] The latter was unexpected because it meant social landlords could behave more like private landlords, where a new tenant offered more rent than an existing tenant's rent plus transaction costs.[637]

Some of the reasons for this were the result of the economic environment, not least reduced public funding and increased need. New construction or new letting permitted higher rents. Many homes needed improvement, but there was also the higher required statutory standards for 'decent homes', in place since 2002,[638] and strong incentives for construction and improvement. Recruiting the better-off into poor areas to produce social mix might be temporary, but cheap homes were likely to be permanently lost. It has been seen how construction changes the intake of social housing by reservation, and could be a strategy to change the tenant population. Here, the vague social mix allowed the better off to be accommodated instead of the disadvantaged.

The insider groups of workers, local people and existing tenants were large, and waiting lists were very long. Outsiders from outside the area were unlikely to obtain a place, except through special schemes, by transfers within larger social

'Insiderness' and local actors

landlords or in unimproved areas. Even people from insider groups could be unsuccessful or wait a long time, and insiders from disadvantaged groups also found access difficult.

The large size of the insider group was to some extent illusory because serial processing meant applicants often had to be an insider in more than one category, such as being local when received by a mayor and then a 'good'[639] tenant when received by the social landlord or, alternatively, being a worker when received by the CIL, plus then being a 'good' tenant. Whether these conditions were relaxed depended on local negotiations and power balances, plus the views of the particular processing agents.

This problem of access was not necessarily because the disadvantaged were not housed, as such, but because of their sheer numbers, a problem which was far from being limited to France. They were more likely to need social housing, but the system formally or informally limited vulnerable population groups – by income, by social mix or the older system of quotas – so there was less housing stock available for the disadvantaged than was apparent.[640] The statutory framework allowed disadvantaged groups to be favoured so far and no further.

8.1 Applying insider–outsider theory

This section revisits insider–outsider theory in the light of more information about the allocation process: the transactions costs and 'insiderness'; the bargaining power of social tenants; the opposition between insiders and entrants, social norms and stigmatization and, finally, the peculiar spatial effects of insiderness in housing markets. Bourgeois's (1996) theoretical framework of thwarted public morality[641] and private greed was not helpful, although the public–private divide was still important as a matter of law. This regulated rights and governed who was responsible or empowered to help.

In my study, it could not be assumed that the State favoured housing the disadvantaged and that this was purely a problem of local obstruction. The right to housing was practically contradicted by national legislation concerning the limitations of the right to housing by social mix, by the limiting procedure and by shortfalls in funding and in supervision of priorities for the disadvantaged. Legislation was also responsible for creating an exclusionary allocation system and imposing strong political constraints in social landlords' governance.

For Bourgeois's profit motivation, there was a striking modern similarity in the regulation of public and private social landlords, both acting in local markets. There was thus greater practical acceptance of business models as useful in the public sector, but also increased need to take account of local politics to get funding for social landlords.[642]

'Insiderness' and local actors

On the evidence, insider–outsider theory provided an alternative explanation for the economic process of exclusion within an administrative process. The theory does not preclude raising new questions about the multiple factors affecting the distribution of social housing, such as divergent local practices, institutions and the extent of the social housing stock. New factors arising in interviews included the effect of divorce and debt,[643] factors which help explain the exclusion of certain groups on account of their perceived social and economic disadvantages as potential tenants, discussed in the next chapter.

An unexpected factor was that the size of both social landlords and local authorities mattered. Rural mayors, with their personal style of governance, were closest to the allocation problems in a small *commune* and seemed most exclusionary to non-locals.[644] For social landlords, the effects were more subtle. Larger private social landlords were permitted a greater detachment from local policies by their rules, more able to choose where they operated, but sometimes more distant from their tenants because they sub-contracted services.[645] The size of organizations is intimately linked to the spatial effects of insider–outsider theory.

8.1.1 Transaction costs and insiderness

Chapter 1[646] explained how rent was social landlords' only profit; thus the irrecoverable transaction costs of removal and recruitment of tenants normally tended to make social landlords reluctant to change their tenant population. This section looks again at transaction costs as a source of tenants' bargaining power.

Transactions costs were also used in Williamson's (1981) analysis of organizations and suggested why the transaction costs of allocation were so high (discussed in section 5.3.3, p. 130). The fragmented organization of actors persisted because it had economic benefits for each. The large efforts actors expended in the allocation process were still less than benefits they received in housing their preferred candidate, because of the contribution of the State and in diminishing cost as the asset matured. The large number of applicants meant the wishes of more than one actor might be met.

To turn to insider–outsider theory, transaction costs in employment markets mean that insider-employees share the 'economic rents' of employment (or letting) with employers (Lindbeck and Snower 2002: 11) because they benefit from insiderness. Transactions costs benefitting tenants included low and falling rents, difficult eviction and requirements for guarantees for new tenants.[647]

This sharing of economic rents did not seem unreasonable where the purpose of social housing to was help those in need, but it was a question of extent. Security of tenure might not have been the problem. French tenancy law under the 1989 statute was a generally agreed social compromise. In fact, private landlords could effectively opt out of this by providing furniture, because the best security

'Insiderness' and local actors

of tenure was linked to unfurnished homes.[648] Less secure furnished tenancies[649] had a role in providing private rented homes for the poor.[650]

Social tenants' formal legal advantages are looked at in the next section but there was also social landlords' concern for their tenants, often warmly expressed. Insiderness is not just an economic advantage but also an information asymmetry, because the landlord knows the insider-tenants. Landlords and tenants have a human relationship and it is desirable that landlord should care about tenants. This still has the downside that this disadvantages outsiders when it comes to access, a tension.

Social landlords were protective of tenants in arrears with rent. Many said they promptly and actively involved the tenant and could generally help tenants who did not ignore their problems. One said: 'Eviction is a procedure of failure, when all other measures have not worked, but in the Hauts de Seine, when evictions are ordered by the judge, they are carried out, unlike in other *départements*.' In contrast, a voluntary worker said that social landlords intending to evict would do so, and assistance was left until late. This illustrates another tension between the professionally benign public duties of social landlords and the economic exigencies of eviction.

Barriers to eviction are typical of insiderness, although this protection must exist to a certain level for reasons protective of essential living conditions and to prevent 'churning' (p. 27). Prefects could unpredictably refuse State permission for eviction after the court eviction order, which happened in about 10 per cent of cases, and then the landlord obtained compensation (Ball 2003). A social landlord called this '*un gâchis*' (a mess), because a poor family had to go through eviction procedures involving the police and social enquiries[651] to obtain this payment.

Transaction costs of eviction include legal expenses, effort and interim rent loss whilst seeking a new tenant. There were a multiplicity of schemes to help and some actors complained of general ignorance of these procedures. It was not easy to evict tenants for antisocial behaviour. One social landlord complained about the reluctance of judges to evict tenants for behavioural issues:

> If there is antisocial behaviour, if they make noise, if they play music all night, if they respect nothing, they break the doors, they spit in the lifts – if they do not pay the rent, one can evict them, but the judge will rarely evict them because they have abnormal behaviour.

There is more about the exclusionary consequences of eviction in section 9.2.1 (p. 206), and about some obstacles to eviction in 10.2.3 (p. 238).

Barriers to access were also a problem for disadvantaged applicants, particularly rent guarantees,[652] together with deposits[653] and compulsory insurance.[654] The CIL and FSL (see Glossary) schemes to assist did not cover everyone in 2005–6.[655] Costs included producing the higher home standards on new lets.

'Insiderness' and local actors

The complexity of social housing allocation of itself produced substantial transaction costs, although allocations are not normally described in these terms. Gatekeepers are needed for rationing because public policy is expected to substitute for the market and clearly not everyone can get in. Nonetheless, it was not clear that the gatekeeper needed to be so expensive, not just in terms of money but in time and effort (discussed above in section 5.3.3, p. 130). Insider–outsider theory could lead to improvement in the procedures of access by attending to the balance of economic interests of the decision-makers.

Barriers to access and eviction seemed to be the symptom of landlords' collective attitudes to protecting their investment and their tenants, rather than the cause. Insiderness, as expressed by transactions for rentals in France, might be 'sticky' – because trying to increase access to tenancies would not necessarily remove the insider practices found outside tenancy law. Once landlords have learned to make more profits from a position of caution, insisting on guarantees or rent receipts from applicants with public policy support, it is difficult for government to restrain landlords' use of such barriers. Landlords who do not require guarantees are disadvantaged because they might get the more unreliable tenants who have been rejected elsewhere.

Excess insiderness can reach a point where it is counter-productive, because landlords start withdrawing from the market. It also means 'good'[656] tenants become more important on account of it being difficult and expensive to evict them. For social landlords, increased tenant security meant they required infusions of public money rather than withdrawing from the market. Perhaps going up-market, or partly up-market for social landlords, where public subsidy permitted this, was a kind of withdrawal from the market.

8.1.2 Social tenants' bargaining power

Elected tenant representatives[657] at local and national level had formal and informal bargaining power, with strong links to other powerful political lobbies for employers, social landlords or unions. There were two types of local tenants' organization, the political organs for negotiation and the *amicale*, a local organization for mutual support and sociability. Tenants had multiple positions of influence. Representatives sat on the mediation commission,[658] and the Commission départementale de conciliation, a dispute resolution body.[659] They also sat on advisory bodies such as the Commission départementale de l'habitat for local planning.[660]

Social tenants had more rights generally than private tenants: sitting on the social landlords' board and the allocation commission; having rights within their apartment block to information, to consultation and to negotiation concerning rent details, deposits, repair and service charges,[661] and future plans. Social landlords and their tenant representatives negotiated within a statutory council.[662] Thus social tenants had collective bargaining power analogous to employees.

Lindbeck and Snower (2002) wrote:

> The greater the union density in an industry, the more leverage unions are able to give insiders in their threats of obstructive activity under bargaining disagreement and thus the greater the bargaining surplus and the higher the resulting insider wages.

It is said that unions are involved variously in harassment, obstruction and cooperation with employers to improve their position relative to outsiders, who might work for less. Similarly, tenants work to improve their position relative to outsiders who might pay more.

On the face of it the 'density' of French tenant unions was not high. The paradoxical situation in France meant low formal support for unions and tenant organizations but unions could still call large numbers of people onto the streets to protest.[663] Tenant representatives, even if elected by a small number, still interacted regularly on behalf of tenants with other housing actors. Even if union power in France had declined, the law changed more slowly.

Tenants were represented nationally and locally in formal bargaining processes,[664] by organizations that advise and support tenants,[665] by a presence on consultative bodies (as already mentioned), on social landlords' boards[666] and on allocation commissions.[667] Representation on landlords' boards has actually increased since 2005.[668]

The job of tenant representatives is to represent tenants, and there were many opportunities to obstruct or assist access for the disadvantaged, primarily on the allocation commission. Tenant representation on allocation commissions was inappropriate because of their interest, by their office, in helping existing tenants.

Insider–outsider theory does not necessarily fully explain the dynamic power of more general, political collective representation in alliance with other strong lobby groups. Tenant security and rent control were the product of legislation, in turn the product of political process, not just private pressure. The status of collective organizations was rooted in French political, cultural and economic movements in history (touched on in Chapter 3) rather than simply transaction costs.

French social housing representation included tenants but not outsiders. Communication between landlords and tenants improved living conditions and fostered community involvement, but at the same time tenants' involvement in allocation could inhibit reception of apparently less desirable outsiders, favouring insiders.

'Insiderness' and local actors

8.1.3 Insiders versus entrants

Insiders do not always have priority over entrants, if the usual economic balances are altered. Chapter 1 suggests that landlords might 'churn' tenants if there are few barriers to recruitment and removal, because entrants will pay more than insiders and so are recruited. This was clearly not so in social housing with high insiderness, but there were some deliberate policies to change the tenant population.[669] Recruitment of the better-off into French social housing had a number of causes, including a mix of planning requirements and financial conditions, and external economic factors that led social landlords to prefer entrants to insiders, particularly in poor areas.

Section 7.3.5 (p. 175) showed how social landlords refused those unable to afford the rent, a common situation. Any retreat in funding would change the profile of the tenant intake towards the better-off and more apparently stable. The stigma associated with outsiders has a role in assessing this. Nonetheless, even people with a higher income could suffer personal disasters and incur debts, thereby becoming undesirable tenants.

It is sometimes assumed that non-profit rental housing will take people excluded by the private sector. Kemeny (2006: 3) said: 'It is something of a paradox that the profit-driven rental market, praised by neo-liberal economists, is supported and preserved thanks to the exclusion from the rental market of non-profit rental housing, which is managed as a centrally planned command economy.'

The French 'centrally planned command economy' often did not effectively command social landlords to house the poor in difficulties. Social landlordism was essentially voluntary and the landlords had to act like profit-maximizing organizations to make ends meet.[670] Consequently they might choose to compete for more apparently attractive tenants, when economic conditions required this.

This preference for entrants and stable families should not be surprising: first, because there was more insiderness in social housing than in private housing and, second, transaction costs are an amendment to economic theory nor a substitute for it, altering existing economic balances (Bergh and Camesasca 2006). Incentives could thus alter the normal preferences for insiders produced by transaction costs, particularly where both disadvantaged insiders and outsiders were insufficiently supported financially.[671]

In social mix policies, there were financial and regulatory incentives to build for the better off in poor areas, and high land prices made it difficult to build anything other than expensive homes in better areas.[672] These required higher income entrants. Existing disadvantaged tenants still had some advantages, such as rehousing on regeneration. Nevertheless, there were just too many broadly defined 'insiders' to be housed, a factor allowing many social landlords to switch to the better-off entrant.

'Insiderness' and local actors

8.1.4 Social norms and stigmatization

Section 1.4.4 (p. 27) explained how social norms affected the competition between insiders and entrants, such as social mix, splitting up ethnic communities for integration, protecting insiders from eviction and risk aversion. Stigmatization interacted with these social norms. Insider–outsider theory predicts the stigmatization of outsiders, where there is a high level of insiderness. In rental markets this has particularly devastating effects on outsiders facing loss of social skills but also physical risks and privations of homelessness or inadequate housing.[673] This stigmatization was supported by social norms and is the subject of the next chapter.

Some social norms support insiders. A strong social norm preventing eviction in preference to promoting access to homes is consistent with the interests of tenant-insiders. Several interviewees thought the applicants' best interests were served by refusing them homes, to avoid the trauma of eviction.[674] In France, there was no sense that people could then pick themselves up and start over again, or that the evicted would easily find social housing. This was again linked to stigmatization for debt and eviction.

Another norm apparent from interviews was that of risk aversion in all actors. Landlords' risk aversion was not just because of insiderness, but due to severe debt law, discussed in the next chapter. Rent and loan guarantees for social landlords reduced their risk but increased the systemic financial interdependence of local housing actors[675] and could exclude applicants without guarantees. Social landlords' financial prudence was reinforced by strong financial regulation.

These social norms tend to lead to housing insiders rather than outsiders or better-off entrants for social mix. The creation of another national legislative norm, the right to housing in favour of the disadvantaged, with implementing legislation, was not sufficient to ensure that disadvantaged outsiders were fairly treated relative to insiders, because it did not change the local balance of economic power. This was because of the existing accumulation of rival rights and privileges for all local insiders.

8.1.5 Spatial effects of insiderness

Intensification of insiderness could help explain the patchy housing provision for the poor. To quote Lindbeck and Snower (2002: 19):

> When hiring and firing is costly, firms' current employment decisions depend positively on their past employment levels. Since insiders and entrants are associated with different turnover costs, the nature of the firm's employment inertia depends on the insider-entrant composition of the firm's workforce.

'Insiderness' and local actors

They suggested that the type of future recruit depended on the current type of workforce.

For tenancies, the type of future recruit depends on the number of entrant newcomers already in estates. Disadvantaged estates had higher tenant turnovers, thus more new tenants, who were still entrants rather than full insiders. This, plus their social insecurity, meant tenants there had less well-established rights. In contrast, estates with lower turnovers experienced inertia in recruitment, reinforced by exclusion of non-locals by mayors. Other reasons for concentrations of poverty might be a local tradition of housing the disadvantaged or the area could have a poor reputation, meaning there were fewer applicants.

In social housing, existing tenants could have a direct effect on tenants recruited, perhaps by rejecting certain types of people. Although existing tenants were not interviewed, some landlords talked about tenants objecting to neighbours or housing conditions, or vigorously pushing complaints. This could happen in any representative forum, including allocation commissions.

If the new tenants recruited reflected the existing tenant population, this could mean that social landlords and *communes* traditionally housing the poor or the rich would tend to continue to do so. If correct, this contributes to geographical patchiness.

8.2 Insiders

This section concerns candidates tending to be preferred by the extended landlord grouping – social landlords, mayors, the CIL and the prefecture. Social landlords housed proportionately more single parents and ethnic minorities than did private landlords,[676] thus some were housed, although they still had difficulty as a group. Insiderness could be a question of choices actors make between disadvantaged people in favour of their own preference.

Bourgeois's contention that particular social landlords were primarily interested in politics or money unjustly omitted the collective goodwill of actors, many of whom were volunteers. A public social landlord explained their concerns:

> We measure the social urgency. For example, we have people who are in hostels or ... women who have been battered by their husbands. For that we go more quickly, depending on the social urgency, but when it is someone, a young girl or a young boy who has just started working and then still lives with his or her mum or dad, you could say that it is not urgent. We have more demand than availability.

Actors often expressed an interest in helping those in housing difficulty and in improving procedures generally, but struggled with a complex and difficult system. Social mix, with the limitations of social stock, meant only a proportion

'Insiderness' and local actors

of entrants in need could be housed. Broadly defined insiders were likely to fill these places, so the rest of this chapter evidences preferences for particular insiders or better-off entrants within a generalized preference for 'good' tenants.

8.2.1 'Good' tenants were preferred

Local actors had common concerns, often wishing to satisfy other actors, when the basic economics of letting and the local politics were united. Mayors and the CIL were all affected by landlords' solvency through financial contribution or guarantees. This was linked to tenant solvency and a concern for the peace of neighbourhoods. To this extent there was always some cooperation.

'Good tenants',[677] people who could pay the rent, were favoured both as insiders and entrants. These included fully funded, local disadvantaged people, with a package of extra local aid, and some outsiders with similar packages, such as through the prefecture or relocation schemes in *communautés*. Better-off entrants might be favoured where actors sought to change tenants in difficult areas or because a social landlord did not specialize in housing the poor. Ability to cover rent was always important.

Commercial HLM companies (SAHLMs) were volunteers in the social housing market, and one private landlord put their position thus:

> The State does not say to us that the most impoverished people are those with a particular level of income. Assessing this is the responsibility of the landlord – to say from what point he will take a risk – and anyway, it [the social landlord] has the majority vote on the allocation commission to decide.

Whether to take the initiative to found public social landlord organizations and make the effort to build was a question of local choice, not obligation.

Social landlords' systematic refusal of those who could not afford rent was seen in the last chapter.[678] Social landlords commonly expressed their position as a risk assessment. Another social landlord thought the greatest problem was: 'defining who is responsible for the households' ability to afford housing. That is the first thing, because today they do not have enough money. Nobody wants to take the risk.' Refusal or delay of someone who could not pay rent according to internal risk assessments was virtually automatic.[679]

Social landlords might need the control mechanism of refusing tenants who could not pay. In France from 1912, the Bonnevay Act meant social landlords, not *communes*, would be indebted.[680] Post-war mass construction could leave public social landlords with large debts,[681] a cautionary memory.

8.2.2 Social landlords' insiders

Social landlords often favoured their tenants on allocation. Tenants were helped to move house within their stock (*mutations*) using the normal allocation processes.

This is useful as an exchange but could reduce available stock. Two landlords volunteered this priority, with *mutations* representing 20 per cent or 40 per cent of allocations respectively. Another large landlord mentioned this in policy documents. This reasoned policy could favour a residential career for tenants, who might otherwise feel social housing was a dead end (Peillon 2005: 327). Another reason to favour tenants was that, with the crisis, tenants not rehoused might have difficulties.

Mutations occurred:

- when tenants moved – for a job or a different home
- where families increased in size
- when adult children formed new households (*décohabitation*)
- on household break-up (causing particular problems for landlords).

In the Nord-Pas-de-Calais 24 per cent of allocations were to social landlords' own tenants, plus 11 per cent more transfers from other local social landlords.[682] Other regions did not seem to keep these figures. A social landlord in the Hauts de Seine said transfers between social landlords did not happen there. Available national figures are older: 33 per cent in the period 1998–2001[683] before shared custody became a common disruptive factor (below).

On divorce and household break-up, allocating two social homes to one existing social tenant household always reduces available spaces for outsiders. This was becoming common. L'Observateur de l'immobilier (2006) described the 'sociological shock'[684] in housing demand caused by ageing populations, smaller households, increased mobility, demand for quality and space, and household instability. During the study, 40 per cent of French marriages ended in divorce, although marriage was of decreasing importance and 47.4 per cent of children were born outside marriage.[685]

When a tenant divorced, all social landlords interviewed tried to house both parties. In deprived areas, this could favour disadvantaged insiders over disadvantaged outsiders. One social landlord said divorce resulted in 30 per cent less income for the new households.

A 2002 divorce law caused further problems by promoting shared custody,[686] whereby parents alternate in residential childcare to advance children's rights.[687] Two family-sized social homes were demanded by social tenants on household break-up and were under-occupied probably one week in two.[688] A social landlord in the Nord confirmed this:

> Today, if a family with two children splits up, well, they no longer have to have a small home for the husband or the lady and a large home for the person who remains with the children. They have to have two large homes.

Social landlords did not welcome having to provide two homes, but often described this as a necessity. One social landlord said it was natural for tenants seek their landlord's help.

'Insiderness' and local actors

This had important distributional consequences, particularly a shortage of family homes. Several social landlords mentioned problems housing 'reconstituted families' – new couples, with each partner having children from previous relationships. Two partners, each with two children, would want a home for six, when large homes were particularly scarce.[689] Here, children with shared custody orders might only be in the home for one week in two. A state actor said divorce was a factor causing civil servants to apply for reserved homes too, which were larger so children could stay.

This advantage was often not extended to young couples. Three social landlords expressed concern that tenants' children forming a new couple might not stay together. One said, 'They both leave their parents, with one ... on a fixed term employment contract. Well today, you unfortunately know this type of couple – they have a great chance of lasting, but also of not lasting.' These candidates had to provide parental guarantees. One social landlord in the Nord ordered social reports for all *mutations*, providing some transparency.

Traditionally, social landlords have provided homes for children of ethnic minority tenants. FASILD (2003: 147) suggested that the renovation of disadvantaged neighbourhoods removed the best chance of housing for these. The concern for the stability of new couples might also adversely affect their chances. Generally, however, insider-tenants had advantages.

8.2.3 Mayors' insiders

Mayors were frequently interested in housing local voters, their insiders in a broader sense. Mayors would have similar concerns to social landlords because they were financially committed through guarantees with other contributions and effort, and sometimes founded and ran groups of public social landlords. They tended to want good tenants, and did not want to suffer a financial burden through social support, provision of schools and facilities for children, policing unruly locals and clearing up vandalism.

The *dotation urbaine de solidarité*, were credits transferred from other *communes* for extra needs, but seemed inadequate. Renard (2003) observed that the infrastructure for development could be expensive for *communes* facing multiple social objectives, something confirmed by my interviewees.

Local mayors had a legitimate concern for voters' welfare, commonly expressed by a preference for locals. Mayors were the first port of call after the prefecture for associations looking for spaces for disadvantaged locals. This reflected mayors' responsibility for public order and other powers.[690] One mayor in a deprived area said that if the prefect proposed an outside candidate: 'I will say to the prefect: "I have certainly received your request, but I have this person locally who clearly fits the criteria and is entitled to have it." It is like that.'

Mayors tended to favour local residents or people with local family connections rather than local workers, even though allocation rules said the distance from work should be considered.[691] Proximity of employment as a factor was only mentioned once in interviews, in the Hauts de Seine, where transport links made considerable travel distance possible.

The Haut comité pour le logement des personnes défavorisées ('le Haut comité')[692] produces very critical annual reports for the prime minister. One mayor said this committee regarded mayors as not wanting to receive disadvantaged populations. He said things were more complicated than that, because mayors of whatever party could only do what voters collectively were capable of accepting, which gave mayors responsibility for leadership.

Some mayors required a certificate of three years' local residence, which was clearly unlawful.[693] Voluntary workers and social landlords everywhere said the majority of mayors preferred local people or excluded non-locals. One mayor said that, if he wanted to survive politically, the system and townspeople's expectations forced him to have no interest in housing outsiders. In Lyon and the Nord, exclusion of non-locals was particularly prominent in rural areas.

A certain defensiveness by mayors in *départements* bordering central Paris was understandable. Since Haussman,[694] people displaced by gentrification within Paris or by successive waves of slum clearance were rehoused here (Carpenter *et al.* 1994). Several million people around Paris could theoretically apply to be housed anywhere, and to get to most places by public transport, so a receptive *commune* there could be swamped.

Bourgeois (1996) argued that mayors favoured voters. During my study, two social landlords in different regions said that *communes* of the left favoured poorer candidates likely to vote for them whilst *communes* of the right favoured richer candidates. A social landlord said: 'You could say that some *communes* are rather electorally minded and try to pull the income profile of applicants higher. Others are also electorally minded and the "most social" income profiles, the poorest people, are the potential voters.' This social landlord tried to correct this to produce social mix, a common landlord response.

Most evidence showed personal electoral concerns for mayors themselves rather than party-political concerns. An actor in the Hauts de Seine reported mayors discussing immigrants: 'Those people are not from the *commune*. They are not people who vote. They do not interest me.' This particularly affected non-EU immigrants without French nationality, who could access social housing but not vote at all.

Mayors could also use their powers for political reasons to assist tenants on eviction. When prefects considered granting State permission for eviction, they consulted the local mayor, who might otherwise object through the administrative courts.[695] Two actors said that prefects worked locally through mayors, paying

'Insiderness' and local actors

more attention to them than to members of the public. Some communist mayors systematically objected to all local evictions on principle, a striking case of unequal treatment between *communes*, also tending to keep voters within the *commune*.

Bourgeois's (1996) proposition that the smaller public HML organizations (OPHLMs), with their political boards, were only concerned with politics was harder to accept. The personal views of individuals interviewed within social landlords did not necessarily reflect the policies of the organization, often being more sympathetic to disadvantaged applicants and occasionally less so. This thus depends on who you mean by 'social landlords'.

During the study, unlawful exclusion of non-local outsiders was very common. For the future, *communautés* could reduce narrow localism if they all allocated homes over their whole area, as happened in Lille and Lyon to a limited extent.[696] Candidates would be less affected by local bottlenecks in demand. Mayors' exclusionary tendencies could also be practically limited by upward delegation of mayors' planning powers to the *communauté*, as in Lyon.[697] Planning permission could then not be so easily used as a bargaining chip or to obstruct new housing construction.

8.2.4 Improper favours

In England 'gerrymandering' is the manipulation of populations for electoral advantage and is heavily penalized. English local councils lay down rules for allocations within the national framework, but legally local councillors should have no personal involvement in administration of individual allocations. In 2001, Shirley Porter, a Westminster councillor, was personally fined £35 million following an audit.[698] The common personal involvement of French mayors in allocation would thus be improper in England.

Although there was a French equivalent to gerrymandering, *charcutage*, the line between activism on individual towns people's behalf and improper manipulation of the electorate was wafer-thin, and impossible to distinguish in the then current system. Large excess demand allowed some mayors to favour candidates who served their personal purposes. This was facilitated by a labyrinthine system, where applicants had little information, where anyone controlling a file could delay it and where priorities for allocation could be multiple, indecipherable and apparently covert, because of the fiction of universal housing provision.

One mayor said the allocation process was 'a poison in the spirit of the nation'. He inherited a *commune* where allocations had been used to grant political favours. A civil servant had asked him to provide a social home for his mistress, which he found outrageous. After a home had been allocated, people would come and complain that it had been understood that they would have this

'Insiderness' and local actors

home. His predecessor used to see townspeople in his surgery and assure them of his personal attention to their applications. He said this generated frustrations amongst townspeople and feelings of illegality and injustice.

This mayor consequently instituted an allocation system based on strict chronological order except for extreme emergency. Weekly surgeries were still embarrassing, when people would demand housing, as if the mayor were guarantor of their right to a home. He would produce the current waiting list, showing there were people ahead in the queue. The mayor suggested the allocation process allowed '*clientélisme*' (illegitimate favours for particular individuals or groups to the advantage of the person granting them).

A social landlord's complicated close commercial relations could also occasionally degenerate into *clientélisme*, involving large sums of construction money and corruption. In 2005–2006, 47 business people were convicted for the improper placing of building contracts in the early 1990s by the OPAC de Paris (*Le Monde* 2006) and the OPAC des Hauts de Seine (Bordenave 2005). Political involvement was not proved and both social landlords have since been overhauled. A much smaller police enquiry was recently opened concerning bribery for homes involving a single employee from Sarcelles (*Le Monde* 2010).

Transparency was difficult within complex local contractualization. Some illegality could arise simply because of the extreme complexity of the rules for planning applications (Renard 2001). Consequently, by analogy and the evidence above, complication in the allocation system did not just allow unfairly favouring insiders but could also conceal corruption.

8.2.5 The CIL's insiders

The CIL also had landlord-type rights but were not interviewed, although other actors commented about them. The CIL only proposed employees who were their insiders, and employees could apply to them through contributing employers. Le Haut Comité (2002, 2003) said that housing employees meant fewer homes for disadvantaged people and most interviewees agreed with this.

The local CIL seemed more influenced by employers' needs than their national organization, UESL,[699] perhaps an effect of localism. A voluntary worker said employers would put forward workers who they wished to retain. SAHLMs controlled by the CIL were not only commercially minded, economizing on services,[700] but also specialized in housing workers, with some particularly providing intermediate housing at higher rents.

Workers housed through the CIL could in fact be disadvantaged. A social landlord explained:

> Most of the time the CIL propose their impoverished people ... It is the cleaning lady, who does the housework for local employees there and does

'Insiderness' and local actors

not work full time. She works 80 per cent of full-time and has 80 per cent of the minimum wage. She is completely impoverished.

Another social landlord said the CIL were likely to propose candidates with credit problems or psychiatric difficulties. Those who mentioned it said the CIL did not discriminate racially.

They had a partial function of housing poor workers. Nowadays employers are interested in the CIL because of the increased difficulty in housing workers. A voluntary worker said: 'Because it is difficult to get a home, … [applicants] have accepted this, even if it does not exactly correspond to what they wanted, because they are really employees in difficulty.'

Around 50 per cent of the intake of landlords interviewed comprised CIL candidates, which excluded the unemployed, the self-employed and non-qualifying workers, but included better-off workers for the better intermediate housing. The scheme was again based around collective agreements between workers and employers. Here, the insiderness of employment markets intruded into the housing market, helping some but not others. Contributing insider-employees received benefits above their contribution in subsidized homes.

8.2.6 The prefectural contingent

The prefect's 'insiders' were those with statutory priority as disadvantaged people.[701] These were not properly insiders, because their status was primarily based on State responsibility, not insider–outsider theory. Despite this responsibility, the difficulty experienced by the prefecture in housing the disadvantaged, or the absence of a contingent in most places, illustrates the insiderness of most local environments and the stigma experienced by these candidates.

Where it existed, the prefectural stream housed some people with cumulative disadvantage. In the Hauts de Seine and the Nord the contingent was vestigially present. Problems included insufficient places and lack of willingness by prefects, faced with other priorities, to force acceptance of the most disadvantaged candidates.

The prefect faced conflicting objectives, needing to negotiate with local actors for many purposes, which included restructuring poor areas to house fewer poor people for social mix, and to raise local contribution to construction funding. The DDE (see Glossary), as part of State financial services, had to also support social mix through PLUS loans (p. 47), facilitating importation of the better-off into poor areas. These other agendas tended to reduce the likelihood of prefectural intervention by regulation and sanction.

In Lyon, the SIAL (see Glosssary) faced acute need, well in excess of available vacancies. Thus the prefectural contingent was failing to house sufficient disadvantaged people anywhere, despite State responsibility. This was a shame, because the SIAL was the most impartial local actor with real concern for disadvantage.

8.3 Entrants' chances of success

Social landlords' inclination to house well-qualified entrants rather than insiders was increased by their pressing need to recover rent, by their need to service loans from rents, by insufficient rent coverage by benefits and by public policy demands for social mix in poor areas accompanied by incentives. Entrants could thus be recruited for various reasons: first as employees, useful for income to pay rent; second as stable families, which were generally well-received but also imported to create social mix in poor areas; or third as disadvantaged families qualifying through special limited-access routes.

8.3.1 Stable families and social mix

The balance favouring insiders was upset in the 'sensitive urban zones', the ZUS. Social mix often meant trying to fill vacancies with employees and stable families. The preference for stable families was due to serious fears about the financial risks of household break-up. A social landlord in a ZUS said:

> The quality of the applications is going down and we have trouble finding very stable candidates – not necessarily with a lot of money, but stable. The thing is that families do not stay together much. Marriages do not last very long. In one of our families there are two small salaries. If one of them goes away the family is in danger ... We have two out of two marriages that break up. [Interviewer: 'What happens then?'] That means that the families are less financially solvent... For us it is dramatic. That means that, before, we needed one apartment for one family and afterwards we need two homes, and in each home the tenant will have little income relative to the rent; that is, they are fragile. Thus for us it is worrying.

A voluntary worker trying to house disadvantaged candidates complained that social landlords had stereotypical views of desirable tenants:

> It is a family profile – a couple with two children, and sometimes we do not have this sort of profile. We have single parent families, etc. ... For them a couple is from a stable family, and a single parent family is in fact an unstable family.

Despite social mix policies favouring stable families, social landlords housed slowly increasing numbers of single parents, as shown in Figure 8.1.[702] 'This was

'Insiderness' and local actors

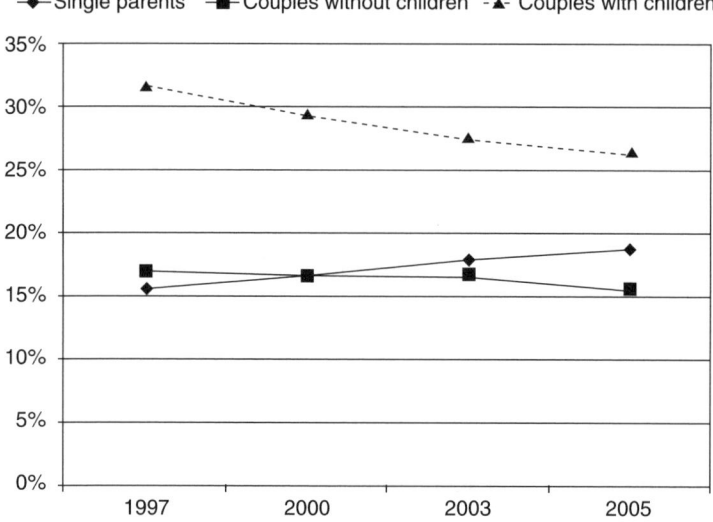

8.1 The structure of households occupying social homes (% of tenants). Source: Ministère du Logement.

still insufficient to meet needs, although it could work in favour of disadvantaged existing tenants who obtained two homes on household break-up, even though this reduced space for outsiders.

The children of immigrant social tenants were particularly affected by preferences for stable families. When applying for their own home, they suffered both their landlords' uncertainties about new couples[703] and discrimination in the private sector, identified by several interviewees. They were insiders whilst living with their parents, but outsiders to employment and to credit. They suffered from not receiving minimum benefits or receiving restricted housing benefits before the age of 25.[704] This inability to move out perhaps caused overcrowding in large families. DEEF (2005) showed the greatest overcrowding in larger homes with middle-aged tenants, which were likely to include the larger ethnic minority families.

Descendants of immigrants often lacked a voice in news reporting and empirical research into their situation,[705] and sometimes had difficulties with the police.[706] Since their schooling included republican ideas of equality, they protested effectively in a recognizably French manner, particularly in the 'red suburbs' such as Seine-St-Denis, traditional socialist or communist strongholds.

As trapped quasi-insiders through their parents' tenancy, they had a strong enough position to protest, but not enough to alter the economic and political balance against them, so this favoured other entrants. Young people suffered

'Insiderness' and local actors

housing difficulties in general (Fondation Abbé Pierre 2005). Children of immigrants outside social housing might protest less but be in a worse position.

8.3.2 People with statutory priority

Many actors expressed concern for disadvantaged people, some of whom would be housed, but this willingness to house the disadvantaged must be qualified. Some disadvantaged people might be insiders in the broader sense, and thus supported by local actors. Mayors might choose a slum-dweller who was also local. A social landlord might choose a battered woman with a good salary or a single mother who was an existing private tenant with a good payment record. The CIL might supply a worker from an ethnic minority. Thus needy people housed could be insiders, but this could limit access for outsiders with greater needs.

Another qualification to access was that social mix legitimized top-down population manipulation, so any needy category would only be admitted to a limited extent. Social landlords no longer had formal quotas for particular population types, but they would not, for example, have too many single mothers housed together, for fear of attracting pimps and drug dealers. One said:

> If a young woman, a single mother in a delicate psychological and financial situation, asks us for a home in a development where we already have 40 per cent of them, then if there is an absolute necessity: because she is in danger, because her children are in danger, because she is living in the open, because she is without a home, we will take her but ... also we know that we increase the risk for that development because the concentration of these young women in the same place will attract a rather particular kind of fauna who will try to exploit this situation.

Accordingly, single mothers, and similarly poor people and ethnic minorities above a certain threshold[707] could be refused.

Some very disadvantaged applicants, such as long-term hostel residents or those whose children had not obtained social skills due to protracted social exclusion, might not be qualified entrants. It has been shown how accumulated disadvantage did not practically give extra priority under the general rules, despite emphasis on disadvantage.

Social landlords would also seek a package of social support from associations or social workers to ensure disadvantaged candidate's needs were met, that they paid rent and were trained to behave correctly, using social reports. Such guarantees for outsiders were useful but expensive. Even then a potentially rowdy tenant risked alienating existing tenants, so more profitable tenants might leave. This limited successful placings.

There was also a shortage of cheap homes or homes available for the disadvantaged. This shortage could be due to other reservations, social mix or social landlord specialization in dearer homes. The means that, overall, there were far fewer homes available for the disadvantaged than apparent from the amount of social stock.

8.4 Conclusion

Insider–outsider theory explains social landlords' inclination to retain existing tenants because transaction costs of allocation and eviction were deducted from their profit. This was reinforced by social tenants' collective bargaining power with other influential groups and by risks presented by more needy applicants. Social landlords favoured people who paid the rent, whether insiders or entrants, although they also favoured existing tenants unless other factors changed their focus to entrants.

Other local actors favoured their insiders. As part of the wider landlord grouping, the mayor had an incentive to favour local people and the CIL to favour employees. Mayors' support for voters was sometimes difficult to distinguish from gerrymandering, because of their personal activism for individual voters. At the same time, the prefecture failed to house all those in need. The disadvantaged people that were excluded because of this are discussed in the next chapter.

People likely to be favoured with social housing as entrants were stable families and prospective good tenants. People in difficulty would be housed up to a limit consistent with social landlords' variable ideas of social mix. This, and a requirement for low rents and social support, made the housing of those with cumulative disadvantage less likely.

9 Stigmatization and outsiders

Which of the disadvantaged tended to be excluded from social housing? This chapter looks at the groups of people most affected – a litany of disadvantage, with the greatest access difficulty being suffered by the homeless possessors of the right to housing – and documents those tending to be excluded, immediately bringing in to consideration the associated problems of debt, eviction, household break-up and race discrimination, and the specific problems affecting young people.

To some extent these outsiders represent people likely to have difficulty in society generally, and their numbers probably exceed the maximum capacity of social landlords. The latter could not be expected to cope with all these problems on behalf of society, but they still seem to handle disadvantage less than their housing capacity would suggest.

The right to housing appears to offer disadvantaged people, in concrete legislative form, both priority access to social housing and a special right to sue the government (the *opposable* right) for failed access. This is early days for this *opposable* right, but the last part of this chapter deals with the failings of both the prefectural stream and the execution of the *opposable* right. Consistently, disadvantaged outsiders, who were the least equipped to negotiate bureaucracy, faced longer and more difficult access processes and lower success rates than insiders. The distributive consequences of this should be considered.

Allocative efficiency in an economic sense was not expected in social housing allocation, because the achievement of its social purposes theoretically removed social housing from the market, which also justified the removal of the need for efficiency. Achievement of these purposes was difficult to measure when various objectives, including construction, housing workers or social mix were in conflict, so there were fewer and more expensive spaces for the disadvantaged. There were also subterranean local objectives, such as providing more allocative power for particular actors for political or even illegal purposes, which are documented in section 8.2.3–4 (p. 194).

Stigmatization and outsiders

The right to housing for the disadvantaged was an important justification for social landlords' special funding regimes. This is only a qualitative study and so it cannot pronounce quantitatively on exclusion, but the widespread rejection of disadvantaged people in this study, and the limitations of homes available to them, raises questions about why social landlords have more favourable fiscal treatment than ordinary ones. This was a matter of degree and proportionality relative to funding.

The disadvantaged have often suffered personal disasters and have an urgent need, but relief through social housing has not been quick and this chapter particularly shows how outside factors contributed to their difficulties. The last part of the chapter shows how outsiders in difficulty paradoxically faced the longest and most difficult access route to social housing, particularly through the *opposable* right to housing, and considers some possible distributional consequences of outsider status.

9.1 Which groups tended to be excluded?

The homeless and hostel occupants were the most common group said by interviewees to have difficulty accessing social housing,[708] often followed by a comment that hostel access was blocked. Hostel applicants and those in squats were particularly stigmatized, even though these were groups to which the right to housing was particularly directed.

Homelessness was frequently the end product of the exclusion of particular groups. People without the right documentation and asylum seekers would have no access to social housing.[709] Other groups of people having difficulty finding any housing were: people in debt, evictees, people suffering divorce or domestic violence, and probably also many young people. Ethnic minorities suffered institutional racism in housing. These problems increased the flows of excluded people away from private renting towards social housing.

A particular group with difficult access was the disabled, but funding for them had recently improved. Predominantly pre-1980s housing was not necessarily adaptable for wheelchairs. In addition, social landlords had difficulties persuading mayors to allow the construction of hostels for the mentally ill or the homeless, something which would engage the mayor's responsibility.

All these groups represented financial risks and were frequently a subset of the poor. Provision for them was variable and reducing, with normal routes through *associations* blocked. For many people there were few local social homes available, either because of the patchy national distribution (seen in Figure 1.3, p. 14) or because they were aimed at the better-off.

The number of cheap vacancies was reducing: by demolition; by the limited number of new homes for the poor; by increased rents or slowing tenant turnover on improvement; by refusals due to inadequate income or lack of sufficient

Stigmatization and outsiders

social support; by insufficient large homes for immigrant families; and by actors' variable understandings of social mix. Informal quotas limited the intake of vulnerable groups, and rural mayors had few housing obligations[710] so allocations to existing tenants and other privileged insiders limited spaces for disadvantaged outsiders.

Insider–outsider theory helped explain the specialized and patchy nature of provision for the disadvantaged, the effects of stigmatization on outsiders and even the general housing shortage. Long waiting lists meant that even insiders had difficulty. Groups described in this chapter would have access difficulties unless they happened to be insiders in the right place.

People in housing difficulty suffered serious stigmatization. Section 1.4.4 (p. 27) introduced Lindbeck and Snower's theory describing the process of deterioration of outsiders in employment markets. Outsiders to housing had similar difficulties and similarly deteriorating conditions, lacking the information and contacts to become insiders. Disadvantaged people can be outsiders to both jobs and homes, and homelessness results in particularly quick personal deterioration and stigmatization. Ex-tenants quickly became undesirable when they were without three months' rent receipts.

There was strong evidence of the deteriorating social and physical status of the disadvantaged. A social landlord explained:

> Someone who lives in a caravan, she has found herself without work again. She has not been able to pay her rent. She has been evicted. ... It is a very difficult life. People lose orientation. People become de-structured. And then an *association* reconnoitres the family. The family or single person must have the will to fight back. Thus there is a work of reconstruction. This can be the management of a budget, but it can also be the education of the children. This can be the rules of hygiene, the maintenance of a home. It is all that.

Stigmatized outsiders found access to any housing difficult without extra financial or social help. The support of social workers was essential for acceptance, so the homeless would not normally obtain immediate or direct access. Social landlords frequently took care to prepare neighbours for a newcomer and applicants should be 'rehabilitated'[711] before entering general housing. Social landlords were expected to fund their own social workers out of rents, but none mentioned having more than two per *département*.

The greatest exclusionary factor in allocation was not being an insider, which was more important than statutory priority need. People qualifying under need criteria were often mentioned in the context of special rehabilitation schemes. Only 1.2 per cent of social stock was let by social landlords to *associations* in order to house the disadvantaged in 2006.[712] Cooperation was wider than this and most social landlords had limited access schemes for particular disadvantaged

Stigmatization and outsiders

groups. Nonetheless, it was not their main job to both house and manage those with social difficulties in normal stock.

9.2 Debt and eviction

Debt and eviction seemed more stigmatized in France than in England (Ball 2010a),[713] affecting almost anyone and exacerbating a general sense of insecurity regarding housing.

9.2.1 Eviction and its disastrous consequences

The evicted were particularly stigmatized. An evicted family might have their children taken into care[714] and people evicted for antisocial behaviour stood little chance of rehousing: A voluntary worker said: 'Once the people are outside, that is it. It is finished.' ANIL (2000: 12) found that, once children were in a hostel, it was not unusual for them to occupy hostels for several years before being rehoused.

A voluntary worker said hostel residents were unjustly stigmatized by stereotypes:

> For the institutions, the fact that they are in a hostel shows that these are people who are fragile. They are afraid. The landlord is also afraid, saying 'Ah! This is someone in a hostel', when in fact, they are people ... who have had social help. They know how to manage. They have been shown how things work.

Someone in difficulty was expected to need rehabilitation, although a voluntary worker during this study said even rehabilitated applicants found little access to social housing.[715]

Difficulties in private letting increased flows towards social landlords. An *association* reported that a private landlord could threaten a tenant who sought repairs with eviction, because disrepair made letting illegal. Another reported problem was that subtenants were squatters, due to an interpretation of Roman law[716] which negated any security of tenure when a landlord let to an associate who sublet. These 'squatters' also had no rehousing rights, causing them problems on urban regeneration (Javaloyès 2003).

9.2.2 Debt and financial difficulties

Debt law seemed to exacerbate the position of poorer people, making them vulnerable, stigmatized and undesirable candidates for housing. Poorer tenants

Stigmatization and outsiders

could not easily borrow to tide themselves over because of a shortage of credit for people like them, including the fact that interest rates were legally limited[717] and that borrowers in difficulty could sue lenders who lent to them unwisely.[718] This produced a lender response of caution.

In contrast, *The Economist* (1999) reported how American people would temporarily borrow at higher rates: 'The ability to borrow $500 significantly lessened the probability that the household would suffer a "spell of hardship", such as not having enough money for food.'[719]

France had a system of low-priced social loans for home purchase, but this might not change problems in obtaining normal credit. High interest rates might cause problems a but total lack of credit might be worse. A social landlord complained that the slightest thing would destabilize tenants: one normally good tenant became unable to pay rent because he needed to replace an ancient car to get to work.

Social landlords might be expected to help those in debt or evictees from the private sector, but the financial caution shown in Chapter 6 limited this. Mortgage borrowers in difficulty also suffered stigmatization. Prospective mortgage evictions were humiliatingly published in the local commercial bulletin so all creditors could claim.[720] French banks generally only gave mortgage loans to existing customers: 'The French banker only agrees to lend if he is almost certain not to have to realize the security.' (Vorms and Taffin 2007b: 19).

Debt relief was accessed via a difficult process. The Commission de surendettement (Commission for Over-indebtedness) negotiated lengthy repayments and could reduce debts.[721] Since 2003, a new procedure for non-businessmen[722] removed all debt, like bankruptcy in England, but the access conditions were severe.[723]

Anyone in rent arrears, or living in an unfit home, could have housing benefit stopped, accelerating their difficulties. Benefit could be temporarily re-instated on application to a departmental committee. In the Hauts de Seine, this committee faced 10,000 files annually.[724]

Lack of credit obliged vulnerable households to turn to State aid, which was not quick and required preparation of application files for several committees, including the Housing Solidarity Fund (the FSL), the Commission de surendettement and the departmental committee restoring housing benefits. A debtor might not qualify for help from the FSL with an income slightly above their ceiling, even though suffering hardship with debt repayments. In Lyon, the capital limit on debt disqualified some people.[725]

This labour-intensive process again favoured those with sufficient literacy to prepare a *dossier* and exposed people to moral scrutiny, such as good faith requirements for the FSL, ramping up demand for social assistance to negotiate bureaucracy. This cumbersome assistance means the position of those in debt could deteriorate quickly.

9.3 Household instability and domestic violence

Disadvantaged individuals suffering household break-up were losing private sector housing in greater numbers than could be rehoused. This section explains some differences from England, concerning the effects of shared custody on outsiders, the financial effects of household break-up and domestic violence. For the last two, this is not at all an in-depth overall assessment of French family law, which has desirable elements such as generous child benefits and good pre-school provision. Its only point is that the empirical evidence highlighted particular aspects of the law, resulting in many single parents being displaced towards social housing, where their access was strongly limited. Different aspects of UK law could be similarly criticized.

9.3.1 Shared custody

Separated and divorced social tenants who occupied two family-sized homes reduced the availability of family homes generally.[726] In private stock too, richer families splitting up could buy or rent two family-sized homes, pushing up private rents and driving poorer families towards social stock. A voluntary worker described a client seeking a larger private rented home:

> This was part of the first approach of a certain gentleman. That is to 'send all the lease documents to my lawyer, to send them to the judge so that I can see my children'. This is not just once. This has happened several times.

In social stock, existing tenants occupied up to 40 per cent of new spaces (Section 8.2.2, p. 192) whilst, simultaneously, social mix limited the density of single mothers. Without detracting from any benefits of shared custody for children, there was a mismatch between public policies promoting shared custody and available housing provision.

Shared custody destabilizes housing policy because generous provision for insiders seriously reduces space for outsiders, particularly disadvantaged outsiders. Social landlords often had humane concern for children, and considered a woman with children on the street as a priority. However, they still lacked any help in prioritizing between two parents with shared custody. Shared custody was also an expensive policy because more rent was payable for two larger homes, and thus more housing benefit.

9.3.2 Financial effects of household instability

Many actors in every region observed high levels of single parent applications, although there were only 8.7 per cent of single parents in France as against 20 per cent in the UK (Taffin 2007: 32). Divorce and household break-up

Stigmatization and outsiders

often means at least one person losing their home who might then apply for social stock.

Seeking an explanation, it seemed the French law on private financial provision on divorce or widowhood for spouses with dependent children exacerbated this housing demand. *The Economist* (2007) described French divorce law as 'stingy' for wives, something which has social consequences in increased need for State provision.[727] Rose (1986) emphasized that the family and the State both had a role in housing provision.

French couples marrying must sign a special contract, basically settling division of assets on divorce or death: a matrimonial régime.[728] Conjugal relations are regulated during the marriage's existence[729] but, for marriages since 2000, on liquidation on divorce there is no continuing obligation to maintain the other spouse. This could affect mortgage or rent payments.[730] Divorcees affected can only obtain child maintenance and financial provision in capital.[731] The courts can intervene to vary divorce arrangements, including for fault. Spouses and regular cohabitants can have tenancies transferred to them (when splitting up) by judges and there is relief through civil partnerships,[732] on the death of a partner.

During my study, women in owned property were often insecure, although divorcees might be allowed to occupy the matrimonial home without paying the other spouse rent.[733] Widows generally[734] only received a life interest in most of their spouses' estate because of children's compulsory inheritance rights (Dyson 2005).[735] Since widows had small entitlements, so divorcing wives were unlikely to receive more[736] and were consequently less likely than women in England to receive a transfer of all or part of the matrimonial home or receive maintenance to pay the mortgage.

It was difficult to refinance loans to buy out a spouse. French lenders preferred the secured contractual promises[737] to the security of the charge on the building.[738] They regarded the loss of one promise seriously, even if property values were adequate. Refinancing of State-assisted loans was almost impossible. If one spouse successfully remained in the home but the other retained a share, forced sale of a home was likely to succeed, if it was co-owned by indivision, the default form of joint ownership (ANIL 2000).[739]

The French 'egoist'[740] concept of property here seemed to support non-custodial spouses, usually men, making it less likely that a single parent with dependent children could continue to occupy the matrimonial home. This probably throws vulnerable single parents and children on to the care of the State. Shared custody also reduces the amount of child maintenance paid by one spouse to the other, either adversely affecting the poorer spouse or limiting the purchasing power of both.[741] Both are also likely to draw heavily on benefits to support two family homes, where this was possible.

Private divorce provision was supplemented by generous State benefits for children, but sufficient access to social housing for displaced single parents was a problem.[742] This conclusion is highly provisional without further research.

Stigmatization and outsiders

9.3.3 Domestic violence

When actors were asked for their most urgent priority, the majority mentioned domestic violence. Were battered women not sufficiently protected? Further legal research indicated heavy reliance on the criminal law.

Since 2004, civil (private law) judges could exclude a violent spouse from the home provided the victim issued divorce proceedings within four months.[743] A voluntary worker reported difficulty in persuading women to divorce. This requirement for a commitment to divorce before injunctive relief was possible could seriously affect women whose religion or community frowned on divorce. This shows insensitivity to such ethnic or religious minority women needing the continuing support of their community.

Startlingly, during the study,[744] unmarried women did not qualify for injunctive protection, an unequal protection from danger. ANIL (2000) reported that usually it was the battered woman who left home. Another problem reported by a voluntary worker was that mayors' local restrictiveness meant a woman could be rehoused in the same *commune* as her violent husband.

Battered women in England are also displaced, but women could arguably more easily return home, having obtained an immediate civil injunction that excluded perpetrators of threats or violence from the home, and have a full hearing some days later. French objections to immediate injunctions include consideration of property rights, privacy and fears of rushing justice (Croze 2004: 69). Preliminary enquiries suggest better protection in other civil jurisdictions – in Austria by immediate police injunction[745] and in Spain without reference to marital status.[746]

It costs more to house a displaced family than a lone person; it is expensive for the State, distressing for children and overburdens social housing. French social housing could not cope with the volumes of women and children from the private sector seeking refuge due to violence or inadequate financial support. These flows were also encouraged by higher income ceilings for access for single parent households.

9.4 Ethnic minorities and young people

Young people and ethnic minorities are dealt with in the same section largely because of statistical difficulties in distinguishing the problems of young people from those of the children of immigrants. 'Large families' was a euphemism for ethnic minorities.[747] In general, young people of any ethnicity had housing difficulties, such as insufficient or non-existent housing benefit and the trend for young people to be employed on fixed-term employment contracts or unemployed (FASILD 2003).

These difficulties were magnified for ethnic minorities facing discrimination. A higher proportion of immigrants tended to buy homes than did French people,

Stigmatization and outsiders

perhaps to avoid discrimination. An exception was for North African and Turkish immigrants, a high percentage of whom lived in social housing (Levy-Vroélant and Tutin 2007: 77).

The 2005 riots in the suburbs were perpetrated by youths (Kokoreff 2006). Because of the statistical problems discussed in 9.4.1 below, it is hard to say how far riots involved disaffected children of social tenants in the worst estates, or dissatisfied ethnic groups. My interviews were shortly after the 2005 riots, so interviewees often commented on this naturally, independently of topic guide questions.

This section deals with why information on ethnicity is so limited, before looking at several effects on social housing. Social mix was linked to *communautarisme*, a term used to express disapproval of concentrations of ethnic minorities, and there was institutional racism. The situation varied in different regions and between local actors. Large families and young people were particularly affected and the law and politics did not seem equal to dealing with discrimination.

9.4.1 Limited information on ethnicity

Research into race discrimination was difficult because of euphemistic expressions, some interviewees' reluctance to discuss this, and insufficient information. Many interviewees conflated ethnicity with other disadvantages. A state actor said: 'We have discrimination against large families, against foreign families, against families who do not have a job. There you are. But very often the large families are at the same time foreigners and do not have a job.'

A few quotes are somewhat sanitized because interviewees restricted the quotations on approval, because these innocently mentioned particular ethnic groups or occasionally because of negative comments. 'Disadvantaged people' or 'large families' were common euphemisms for ethnic minorities, or sometimes 'the poor' or 'the unemployed'.

Caution in discussing this was advisable. A 1978 statute[748] provided: 'It is forbidden to collect or process data of a personal character which directly or indirectly show the racial or ethnic origins, political, philosophical or religious opinion or the union membership of people.' This wide prohibition radically reduced both research and accurate media comment.[749] Available statistics were not fully used. A social landlord suggested these could show discrimination by the percentages of foreigners applying for social housing compared to those accepted.

The colour-blind treatment of minorities arose from the constitutional principle of *laïcité*, closely allied to republican values of equal treatment and impartiality. Collecting statistics was controversial because of wartime misuse of statistics about Jews under the Vichy regime for deportations to Nazi Germany (Blum *et al.* 2007). This important cultural memory shows statistics can be used by the

Stigmatization and outsiders

State against ethnic minorities. Deprived estates were cheap and could be very ethnically mixed (Brouant 2002).

Few statistics on ethnicity and religion were available. The numbers of Muslims were estimated by multiplying the number of mosques by an estimate of their capacity.[750] Only data on 'foreigners'[751] was available. INSEE, the national statistical agency, defined 'foreigners' as people not born in France, even after they obtained French nationality. Consequently, social landlords' statistics showed 11 per cent of social housing tenants as foreign,[752] whilst INSEE showed 27.9 per cent.[753]

There was some research using INSEE statistics or from the many organizations combating discrimination.[754] Simon and Kirszbaum[755] (2001) overcame data difficulties by an anonymous complaints line, and 12 per cent of complaints concerned social housing. The HALDE[756] researches, makes reports and promotes what it considers good practice to combat discrimination. It had recent success in an application to the Constitutional Court to block a statute relaxing the ban on recording ethnicity.[757]

FASILD[758] (2003: 10) said that, in the 1970s, immigrants were reputed to be 'good workers' and to pay rent, but became associated with the deterioration of residential areas. Algerians were the largest immigrant group, concentrated in industrial areas and inferior housing in Ile-de-France (Tchibindat 2005: 57–82). Imported African labour could be accommodated in social housing. This is still an important access route through the CIL today, but there is less such immigration. In the early 1970s, 170,000 work permits were issued annually to immigrants, but during my study only 7,000 were issued (*The Economist* 2006b).

Immigrants were disproportionately affected by various types of disadvantage, shown in Tables 9.1 and 9.2. Immigrants, particularly Africans, were more likely to be poor or unemployed than French people. Only four per cent of immigrants reached university compared to 25 per cent of French people (*The Economist* 2002a). Immigrants took the dirtiest and least desirable jobs. Black and ethnic minority immigrants had not penetrated the establishment during this empirical

Table 9.1 Unemployment for immigrants in 1999

Nationality	Median percentage of unemployment
French people	
Men	10
Women	14
People from north and central Africa and Turkey	
Men	23–33
Women	36–45

Source: GELD (2001).

Stigmatization and outsiders

Table 9.2 Poverty for immigrants in 1996

Nationality	Average percentage below the poverty threshold
French people	11
People from:	
Portugal	17
Sub-Saharan Africa	34
Algeria	45
Morocco	54

Source: GELD (2001).
Note: Poverty measured as 50 per cent of median income with adaptations, GELD (2001: 23).

study, with no black or ethnic minority members of parliament, two prefects and few mayors (*The Economist* 2002a), although the position has improved slightly since then.[759]

Lack of statistics meant only some rather old data available during the study and no precise local information on local communities: An actor in Lyon said: 'When you have, for example, in certain parts of Venissieux, 30–40 per cent foreigners, plus 10 per cent of mixed population, you can have 100 per cent of people of North African origin. You cannot know statistically.' The percentages of various ethnic minorities thus risked being seriously inaccurate, whether too high or too low. French housing actors were aware of local ethnicity: decentralized housing management meant social landlords' agents knew their tenants. In Lyon, an interviewee said State agents were also decentralized and thus knew the ethnic composition of their areas.

Collecting data on ethnicity was impossible for social landlords at that time. Historically, a 1978 circular[760] had encouraged such collection to aid management. A report by Dubedout (1983) noted the poor conditions for immigrant communities and recommended that social landlords record ethnicity so as to be able to discriminate positively to provide homes for immigrants' children or larger homes where needed.

In 1991, a public social landlord was convicted for requiring replacement of a French person by a French person (Brouant 2002). Le Code Pénal (C. pén.), Article 432-7, criminalized discrimination in providing a public service on the basis that a person belongs to a particular ethnicity, nation, race or religion, with similar provisions for private landlords.[761] SOS-Racisme has sought prosecutions by '*le testing*', sending two similar candidates with different racial appearance for a single vacancy.

Brouant (2002) argued that it was still possible to discriminate positively on the basis of social mix, and equality of opportunity, using statistics as proposed

213

Stigmatization and outsiders

by Dubedout in 1983. However, he said the electoral success of the extreme right in the 1980s led successive governments to be discreet about housing policies specifically directed at immigrants. Many interviewees fought any discrimination within their powers.

One mayor was concerned that funding for the poor should be increased, but he said such a policy promoting the right to housing called for a considerable amount of extra housing for black and ethnic minority families. Ethnicity was therefore highly politically charged. The extreme right would thus probably not support housing the disadvantaged because this would help ethnic minorities. These views affect the principle of social mix.

9.4.2 Social mix and communautarisme

Brouant (2002: 159) defined *communautarisme* as the demand by certain inhabitants for a particular identity, whether religious, national or ethnic. Unlike the word community, in France *communautarisme* referred to ethnic concentrations, which nearly everyone who mentioned it thought to be a bad thing.

A state actor said:

> There are people who change, who integrate and all that, but more and more, however, we have this phenomenon of people who, under the social pressure of a neighbourhood which is becoming too ethnic, re-take the veil when they have not worn this for a long time and all that. Thus we have social behaviours which flow, however, from a ... bad initial management of populations, which is not sufficiently diversified.

One landlord associated ethnic densities with rioting: 'When you see how the *banlieues* have exploded you would say that it would have been important not to put all the foreigners which are the product of immigration and vulnerable families in the same neighbourhood.'

In one such area a social landlord objected to *communautarisme* because others could not obtain housing there, owing to exclusionary pressure by local ethnic groups:

> The houses were occupied by people of Tunisian, Algerian, and Moroccan origins etc., thus when a vacated home is suitable ... for large families which are often of foreign origin, ... Either you accept a family which is co-opted by the inhabitants – or you leave the home vacant.

This was, of course, improper, but this is an issue of law enforcement, as for French mayors who refuse outsiders. This was an inversion of exclusion and 'insiderness' by French locals. Similar reinforcing tendencies of segregation in US cities were described as insiderness by Malpezzi (1996).

Stigmatization and outsiders

Everywhere, views of *communautarisme* led actors to split up ethnic concentrations or to prevent them. Two-thirds of actors mentioned this. In private housing in South Lille, where there was a black and Far Eastern community,[762] an actor predicted: 'They will demolish the low priced neighbourhood with dilapidated homes to create different, new homes to create an inevitable social mix, by splitting up people into all parts of the town.' Another said: 'Coming from South Lille, you are marked.' The area had some ethnic restaurants and the potential of these for leisure or as a tourist attraction did not seem to be appreciated.

Stigma in poorer housing was common. Clichy, in the Hauts de Seine, was another stigmatized area of private housing with ethnic minority populations, similarly undergoing regeneration. Two actors thought ethnic communities liked to live together, naturally producing concentrations, although it was not clear why they would pursue this objective in the worst housing.[763] The value of mutual family and community support there was never mentioned.

Breaking up such communities, in conjunction with social mix policies, inevitably meant people were refused a home in particular places because of their ethnicity. A voluntary worker said:

> There are certain areas in a neighbourhood which will be assigned to foreigners, and paradoxically, these areas are sometimes the same areas that will be forbidden for foreigners, although not at the same time. They will say 'I have too many of them.'

Discrimination affected the poor generally:

> We face an inequality of treatment [of ethnic minorities] and we are all aware of it, but in the same way we don't have an equality of treatment with impoverished families. These families say, I want to live in a house in such an area or at such a level of rent and well, we say to them, no, it will not be possible, because you will not manage, even with these housing benefits. This is perhaps also discriminatory.
>
> (Social landlord)

Existing ethnic minority social tenants were rehoused after urban regeneration of social housing, but if they were also poor they could have problems with increased rent like any poor tenant.

The vagueness of social mix, shown in Chapter 7, gave social landlords room to manoeuvre, generally unsupervised by the courts or inspectors, and unrecorded by statistics. This could hide racism within fragmented allocation procedures, for example by mayors excluding non-locals. It is hard to distinguish between a mayor refusing to accept someone because of too much local disadvantage or due to simple prejudice.

Stigmatization and outsiders

Disapproval of *communautarisme* was inherently institutionally racist when taken in conjunction with social mix, the breaking up of areas occupied by ethnic minorities, the refusal of ethnic minority applicants there and insufficient provision of large homes. There was also little provision of housing for young people or ethnic minorities newly in need of housing. *Communautarisme* pervaded the notion of social mix, which was consequently seriously tainted and often applied as an instrument of discrimination.

9.4.3 Institutional racism

The concept of institutional racism emerged in the US in the 1960s (Mason 2000). In England, MacPherson of Cluny (1999) reported on police handling of the murder of a black teenager. He described institutional racism as:

> The collective failure of an organization to provide an appropriate and professional service to people because of their colour, culture, or ethnic origin. It can be seen or detected in processes, attitudes and behaviour which amount to discrimination through unwitting prejudice, ignorance, thoughtlessness and racist stereotyping which disadvantage minority ethnic people.
> (MacPherson of Cluny 1999: para. 6.34)

This includes unintended or indirect discrimination. This approach gained considerable acceptance in England (Holdaway and O'Neill 2006) although the term, if mentioned, was not understood by most French actors.

Given the French restrictions, it is unsurprising that research into ethnicity is more common in England than in France. Because English universities have ethics approval schemes, such academic research is not unregulated. UK census forms allow respondents to self-select an ethnic category. Evidence-based information about ethnicity is thus more normal in the UK, furnishing information for litigation, debate and research. An example is that Mason (2000) described UK urban riots in a way equally applicable in France:

> It is possible to argue that the riots shared certain features. First they challenged and signalled the bankruptcy of colour-blind social policies that relied on continuing assimilationist assumptions ... Second, they were almost always triggered to some degree by community responses to some action of the police ... Thirdly, they all constituted in some measure an attempt by members of local communities to assert a degree of control over the urban space they occupied. This might be in response to what were seen as outside intrusions (such as those by the police or by members of extreme right wing groups), in protest against urban deprivation and unemployment or as a symbolic demonstration of control and resistance.
> (Mason 2000: 90)

Stigmatization and outsiders

No French actor interviewed thought they discriminated racially, except where necessary for social mix. A very few made racist remarks, but most described racism by others or reacted strongly against discrimination.

The social housing allocation process was, nonetheless, institutionally discriminatory, and this is explored in the next sections. The French bureaucratic written process disadvantaged ethnic minorities, particularly by requirements for new birth certificates, with unlawful requirements such as local residence certificates or long residence permits and with refusal of non-locals.[764] A social landlord defending bureaucratic requirements for allocation said: 'It is not a discrimination, it is respect for the Law.[765] The Law envisages a certain number of documents. If you do not supply them, whether you are French or even English, you do not get a home.'

A state actor expressed this view: 'Discrimination is almost a statement made of the handicap of a person who is not completely integrated into the French social system, and there is thus a difficulty in obtaining access to a social home.' A voluntary worker described someone without correct documentation as 'an administrative zero', someone not existing administratively and unable to get public assistance of any kind.

Ethnic minorities faced discrimination in both private housing and in social housing. Many actors pointed to discrimination in private renting. A voluntary worker described a black woman with a good job who was unable to find a flat, and instances where advertised rents doubled when candidates' identities became clear. Such exclusion from private stock made social landlords' attitudes more important. A State actor said non-EU immigrants tended to find private rented property through networks, or *marchands de sommeil* (literally 'sleep merchants'), unscrupulous landlords known for extortionate rents, inferior premises and illegal practices.

Discrimination is a species of stigma for outsiders, predicting their exclusion in French rental markets. Concentrations of stigmatized and poor minorities are found patchily in both public and private sectors, suggesting the same economic processes apply to both, not least because of the cheapness of housing there.

9.4.4 Local variations and different actors

The three regions studied were different. Several provincial actors said Paris had greater problems with *ghéttoisation* or discrimination. One actor suggested that particular ethnic communities in Seine-Saint-Denis could control allocations in their own favour. Insiderness thus tended to reinforce both ethnic minority and white communities' ethnic exclusiveness.

Lyon had strong anti-discrimination policies, but still supported policies against *communautarisme*. A State actor said: 'In the Lyon conurbation, we have an atmosphere of struggle against racism. It is difficult for someone to declare – I

Stigmatization and outsiders

have refused a home to such a gentleman or lady, because they are Arab or black.' Local authorities studied racism, or resisted the exclusion of black candidates.[766] Supervision must be difficult if you cannot legally record individuals' ethnicity, even in anonymized form to prove discrimination, within a culture of public circumlocution.

The Nord was different since it had smaller housing estates. The largest, at Bourgogne-Tourcoing, had around 2,500 homes but estates in old industrial communities were stigmatized. Most actors found no problem with discrimination, and urban troubles were relatively insignificant. There was an ethnic concentration in south Lille, but not so much within social housing. There is no data on whether this was due to discrimination. An actor there said anyone discriminating racially would be sacked and that this was a major problem in Ile-de-France but not in the Nord. A social landlord said they were careful not to create ghettos, because the principle of housing itself meant integration into the Republic.

Different actors approached race differently. A voluntary worker said of discrimination: 'That depends on the actors. For the mayors, it is very important. For the prefecture, that is less so. For a landlord that is not at all important.' Exclusion by mayors of non-locals might not be directed at ethnic minorities, but might as well be. Such policies assist people of local descent rather than workers, probably excluding black service personnel such as cleaners.

Three quarters of 'foreigners' were found in urban areas (Brouant 2002: 162). The rule requiring larger *communes* to have 20 per cent of social housing[767] only applied to 779 predominantly urban *communes* (out of 36,000). Even there, building PLS housing (see p. 149) for the better-off satisfied this duty.[768] Consequently, this limited participation of wealthier *communes* in housing the poor would disproportionately affect poorer ethnic communities. Rural *communes* were exempt from building social homes, yet had cheaper land. Greater decentralization to mayors could lead to more exclusion of outsiders by them in a powerful and unlawful institutional racism.

The CIL still seemed an access route for ethnic minority workers. A social landlord said the CIL were good collaborators, sending good employees, but: 'The CIL and businesses send us, shall we say, foreign workers who are not financially solvent, or polygamous families which present us with problems in life every day because of overcrowding.'

This social landlord had problems with covert polygamy causing overcrowding, also mentioned in other regions. To prevent this he would look for a Muslim surname which might suggest polygamy.[769] He also had problems with applicants from particular countries using the system improperly: 'All methods are good to get a home: false papers, false documents and then the candidate who has a salary etc., takes a home in his name and he gives the keys to a cousin, to a friend, *et cetera*.' This actor responded by examining these applications closely and asking for social reports. This would disadvantage some applicants.

Stigmatization and outsiders

Actors were roughly equally divided about whether social landlords' discriminated. A social landlord said: 'With us, there is no discrimination – none, but I know that it exists.' Several actors thought discrimination existed covertly but was rare and was tackled, if expressed. Certainly, social landlords would negotiate with mayors to place non-local candidates, and some actively supervised staff to avoid discrimination. A state actor thought a committee, such as the allocation commission, diluted discrimination by individuals.[770]

A voluntary worker illustrated subtle discriminations:

> It is not a question of access to housing, but of access to which home. Who are the households which find themselves with offers of homes that are a little too small in relation to the size of the household, in what place?'

Concerning ethnicity and allocations, he added: 'It is rather an aggravating factor which is not a factor which eliminates someone.'

More strongly, a social landlord suggested that some municipal public housing organizations (OPHLMs) discriminated:

> Since mayors do not want to take the risk of saying: 'I am carrying out discrimination there', there are mayors who delegate it to their public organization, and as a result it is the organization which is at the receiving end of the law.

Few actors made explicitly discriminatory remarks, but they still took pride in the rigour of a discriminatory allocation process, including exclusion of people whose income was too low. Another problem was a shortage of large homes for ethnic minority families.

9.4.5 Large families and young people

Large families had particular difficulty finding housing. One social landlord said the problem was few large homes and many large families, which were often of foreign origins, and consequently their difficulties were not related to ethnicity. In Lyon, SIAL (the prefectoral housing unit) had around 300 families waiting for large homes but only around 50 vacancies.

A single, employed person would get an offer in three to four months, but larger families would have difficulty. Local observatories had uncovered the problem. During urban renovation, 12 per cent of large homes were demolished compared to 5 per cent constructed.[771] Also, large homes did not fall vacant frequently.

Large social homes were in short supply in most places, not least because of the shared custody policy. Asked why social landlords did not build more, one social landlord said that statistics suggested greater need for small homes.

Stigmatization and outsiders

However, one state actor said this was: 'Because they do not want to have large families to manage. One of our battles ... is to impose the construction of large homes on HLM organizations and on the *communes* in all the social housing operations that we do.' Public social landlords cooperated better than SAHLMs, which sometimes built two-person bedrooms which were too small for two beds.

Large immigrant families might be common, but large families were encouraged by traditional French natalist family policies. A third or subsequent child attracted extra tax relief and more family benefits with subsidized nurseries (Damon 2006: 19). Allocation criteria specifically favour professional childcare assistants,[772] and single parents enjoyed higher income ceilings for access to social homes.[773]

Many actors talked of problems with children and young people generally, not specifically linked to ethnicity. A social landlord said:

> There is also an educational problem. The children have been brought up solely by their mum. The mum cannot do everything and they are not necessarily kept an eye on at school. A little too often they are at the foot of the block of flats doing stupid things and what you saw on the television happens. That is the crisis and it is also because they bring themselves up. They are in the road rather than in the apartment. Thus, for us, families that separate ... that brings problems at several levels.

Youth social problems were partly caused by overcrowding in insufficiently large homes, which disproportionately affected poor ethnic minorities. A landlord observed that lack of space in an area with many children caused 'a social explosion'. Out-of-town estates with poor transport links made childcare difficult for long-distance commuters.

Live-in *gardiens* might try to keep order. These were employed for cleaning, rubbish collection, commissioning repairs and tenant liaison. Sometimes *gardiens* were victimized by groups of youths, sometimes victimizing *gardiens*' children at school. Many actors stressed the need for the education of children, parents and local professionals.

Young trapped insiders had difficulties in obtaining social housing and few job prospects.[774] These difficulties probably affect young people generally. Fixed-term employment contracts were mentioned as a cause for difficulty in access to social housing for both young people and foreign workers. This account omits young people accessing *foyers*, which is outside this study.

9.4.6 Discrimination law and politics

Discrimination in allocation was primarily policed by the criminal law, apart from the slow and difficult access to administrative courts[775] and the civil claims attached to criminal proceedings. Criminalizing discrimination tends to drive this

Stigmatization and outsiders

underground, particularly without the use of statistics. French *associations* of any kind can act more politically about discrimination than in England: making enquiries, producing recommendations, campaigning and negotiating politically against discrimination.[776] Social landlords thus suffer conflicting political demands about race, involving differing political agendas of left and right.

At the time of this study, there was no obvious systematic attempt by the authorities to check for discrimination in social housing allocation. A state actor said the problem was that, with an extremely limited offer, every time that you made one person happy you made 25 unhappy, and thus you should not seek racist explanations in that situation. Refusal of homes to the poor would disproportionately affect ethnic minorities.

The allocation process was institutionally discriminatory, but patchily so, because of assistance provided through the CIL or the prefecture, by individuals personally objecting to discrimination and because ethnic minority applicants dominate in some areas.

Discrimination was found in:

- pervasive derogatory understandings of *communautarisme* leading to an exclusionary version of social mix
- demolition of large homes
- mayors' attachment to localness
- exclusionary and occasionally pointless bureaucratic requirements, such as for new birth certificates
- the opacity, complexity and fragmentation of the procedure generally.

The latter of these was a particular problem because it allowed discrimination, but there was neither an inspection process to check for this nor any assistance from statistics.

Criminalization was an inadequate response to a complex practical problem and fuelled conflictual political debates. Ethnic minorities were housed up to a point, as were single mothers and other groups experiencing difficulty, but they could similarly be excluded as outsiders or even as insiders due to excess demand.

9.5 Reviewing exclusionary processes

Armed with full information about tendencies to exclude disadvantaged people from social housing, it is now possible to review some exclusionary aspects of access routes. Disadvantaged people faced longer or more difficult processes through the prefecture or the *opposable* right. Some specific and general distributional effects of allocation should be considered, including connections to labour markets. This exclusion is not ubiquitous and many actors do their best to help, but this is a cumulative trend for multi-stage procedures.

Stigmatization and outsiders

9.5.1 Outsiders and the prefecture

Only a small minority of prefectures still used their special contingent for disadvantaged people,[777] so this route was often not available, but when it existed the disadvantaged faced a longer route to social housing and thus more opportunities for refusal. With removal of funding for receptions[778] and with the *opposable* right this method of access could decline further.

Applicants to the prefecture could be referred by mayors, or faced the difficult hurdle for the disadvantaged of applying to the prefecture by post only, if receptions were closed. The prefectural unit still existed in Lyon at the time of writing. If applying to the *commune*, the application passed serially through the hands of: the communal receptionist, *commune*, prefecture, social landlord and allocation commission. Each of the five stages could delay or reject the application. Even receptionists could and did reject incomplete files,[779] although others might help.

Existing social tenants faced three stages,[780] probably all involving their own landlords: their *commercial*, (who managed their application and was also their normal contact point),[781] the landlord and the allocation commission. This was a shorter and easier route. The effect of each procedural stage was to increase the numbers of possibilities of refusal or delay, independent of the will of a majority of processors. The prefectural stream thus carried an inherent significantly lower chance of success, even without its extra procedural difficulty.

The exclusion of disadvantaged people was thus generally facilitated by split housing access points with different criteria, extra chances for delay or refusal and more difficult processes. Since a maximum of three files were ultimately presented to the allocation commission, this process of reduction of files requires explanation, justification and proper regulation. It is not credible to take an official position that there was no reduction in applicant numbers before the allocation commission, with delay and refusal having similar effects. The smallest possible number of procedural stages is desirable for transparency.

9.5.2 The difficult implementation of the opposable right

The *opposable* right to housing[782] seems to impose an even more difficult procedure for social housing access, but it is early days, with few court decisions yet available. Brouant (2011) found reluctance by *associations* to pursue this remedy. There were considerable difficulties in execution of judgments. Some of the procedure's inherent difficulties were set out in section 4.1.7 (p. 96).

This procedure is more difficult than normal allocation procedures and still only exceptionally entitles people to social housing. Those in housing difficulty are not the best litigators. There is now provision allowing for assistance with court claims by social services and specially registered *associations*, and for these representatives to be heard.[783] Applicants without a social home three months after

Stigmatization and outsiders

a favourable mediation decision have been able to appeal to a single judge since 1 December 2008.[784] In a simplified procedure, the judge should assess within two months whether an appropriate home has been offered,[785] but again might redirect applicants to a hostel.

The court cannot itself insist on housing a successful applicant, due to the principle of separation of powers between the administration and judiciary. The successful litigant obtains a judgment ordering the prefect to house the individual in social housing.[786] The new procedure avoids the usual administrative court delays, but all steps to judgment require probably 8 months, or 14 months in larger towns (Brouant 2008).

After judgment, prefects are again obliged to consult local mayors and consider social mix,[787] and social landlords could still contest the allocation, causing placement difficulties. Brouant (2011) found some prefects prioritizing between the applicants they had been ordered to house, rather than housing them in order.

Even with a court order, litigants' applications still went before the social landlords' allocation commission. Some prefects even presented three of these files for allocation commissions to select from, as if for a normal allocation procedure (Brouant 2011).[788] This is not what would be expected by an English reader when a court orders someone to be housed. France has increased the coercive power of the administrative courts in recent years by a process of reform,[789] but there are still evidently serious enforcement problems. If the courts cannot oblige social landlords and *communes* to accept these disadvantaged people, independent-minded social landlords may well not comply with new principles.

An advantage of the court procedure is that fines could be imposed.[790] Additionally, the court could also, exceptionally, award damages against a hostel owner to successful litigants refused a hostel place of up to €10,000 per month for hotel bills.[791] This would have a deterrent effect, but might not help hostels generally.

In the first eight months of 2009, 40,000 applications had been made for the 'friendly' procedure under the *opposable* right, less than the 600,000 that were estimated to be eligible. Around half the cases had been mediated, with 9,000 favourable decisions for social housing or hostel access. After decisions were passed to the prefect, around 2,160 households were offered social housing or a hostel place (Comité de Suivi 2009).

In 23 mainland *départements*, the shortage of housing for this process was critical or overstretched.[792] Nearly two-thirds of applications were in the Paris region, which includes only 18 per cent of the French population. The Comité also found that local mediation commissions limited access to social housing and that the local 'abnormal delay'[793] could be 10 years in parts of the Paris region.

Brouant (2011) also found mediation commissions limiting access, particularly since social landlords were members of the commissions and local authorities did not necessarily choose to sit on them. Some local authorities were resisting

Stigmatization and outsiders

application of the law, even though the right creates an obligation of result and furnishes the prefect with coercive powers.

Lévy-Vroelant (2010) suggested that need categories for the *opposable* right to housing were defined locally, based on the focus of local *associations*. Since a disadvantaged person depends on support by an *association*, those without such assistance are unlikely to be able to apply. A lack of systematic support for cumulative need means that different needs and different *associations* are effectively in competition with each other.

These early reports do not indicate the success of the measure, even though quite large numbers are involved, which is a success of sorts. The long-term success of the right depends on judgments of the courts yet to come, and on effective enforcement. The repeat consultation of local insiders is in evidence in the procedure, which continues its exclusionary force. There is a risk that this difficult and uncertain process will be seen by some as the main route to housing for the disadvantaged.

9.5.3 Some distributional consequences

Insiderness has social and economic effects. The social distributional problems of social housing allocation with multiple objectives were fairly clear. Outsiders, whose situation merited urgent attention, were those who had the slowest access routes to social housing. Hostels run by *associations* were funded to meet urgent need, but were also suffering a slowing and a bureaucratization of access. The consequences of this are measured in human damage and stigmatization. It is still possible to complement this by analysis of the economic consequences of insiderness in housing distribution.

It would be easy to characterize these processes as deliberate exclusion of outsiders perceived to be undesirable. Stigmatization and stereotyping means this may be so, but often this was to do with protecting the rights of particular insiders by particular people in particular places. The variable dominance[794] of different local actors and different levels of housing stock led to variability in intake of outsiders; the allocators' room to manoeuvre was increased rather than reduced by large numbers of eligible people and a choice of which legal principle to apply.

Who then were the outsiders, in the sense of those disadvantaged in the allocation process? An outsider in rental markets is someone who is not an existing tenant and who does not have the necessary connections to become an insider.[795] It follows that the homeless and those in housing difficulties are the outsiders least likely to obtain a home. In this study, this was frequently also true for access to social housing, except where local actors succeeded in overcoming the financial and other local obstacles that caused these problems. This required some very active policies.

Stigmatization and outsiders

Economic incentives had a major role. Insiders normally and properly have some advantages of rental security, but incentives can displace this so that only perceived ability to pay counts. Insider–outsider theory is about economic balances. Social landlords could imperceptibly recruit better-off tenants by choice to balance their books in hard times, and could only obtain funding by construction funding, allowing them to obtain higher rents and change their tenant populations. Such actions, put in place simply so that the landlords could survive economically, allowed displacement of objectives to house the disadvantaged. The extra requirement for local funding also meant raising the importance of particular local commercial, labour and political agendas, according to who contributed, because of the power given to local actors reserving social places.

Insiderness and these distorted agendas were always likely to have distributional effects on the housing market as a whole, with strong linked effects on labour and housing markets; there is an obvious synergy between the labour market and labour relations literature and housing. In a limited qualitative study, obliged to focus on process, the complexities meant this could not be properly explored. Some relevant comments can, however, be made.

'Insiderness' in labour markets causes hysteresis – the delay or inhibition of employment in responding to the market, demands in different economic cycles and conditions (Lindbeck and Snower 2002). Even without insiderness, there is an inherent delay in housing markets meeting demand because of the slowness of construction. Construction is the slowest solution to housing need, so distribution of existing housing is important. Delay in responding to the housing market has the adverse effect not only of unmet housing need, with its human consequences, but also adverse economic results.

Kemeny[796] alludes to the idea that people not housed in the private sector were assumed to find housing in social housing, which was supposed to be a safety net. French social housing often did not work like this because of another delay in meeting demand – the waiting list. People circulate into and out of employment and into and out of marriage. If insiders are seen as inherently preferable to outsiders in a fluid modern society, even insiders will continue to drop out of employment and then out of homes, with no obvious route back to jobs or homes.

Housing the disadvantaged is thus in the interests of insiders. The asymmetrical privileges of existing tenants, 'nimbyism', and the requirements of particular employers can distort public provision in the larger general interest. It would be better to have a housing policy, for example, that did not favour insiders who have shared custody of children over people with no home at all.

Another housing market problem of hysteresis was the lack of mobility of social tenants. This difficulty is well known.[797] Social housing for workers was adapted to times when mobility was less recognized as economically useful or personally desirable. French social housing was not tied to employment, but was constructed close to sites of employment by the CIL in partnership with employers,[798] a

Stigmatization and outsiders

practical geographical tie. If the business moved with redundancies, former social-tenant employees were often stuck where they were, partly because of the nimbyism by mayors elsewhere.

The nimbyism of mayors was driven by concerns for locals within a long tradition of stable local communities, particularly in rural areas. Nevertheless, local people could become unable to leave the security and cheap rents of social housing, or perhaps even move out of the areas where they were awaiting social housing. The disadvantaged would be the least able to move out. This spatial insiderness probably contributed to a lack of qualified workers for new industries and a need to build yet more social housing. Home exchange was not easily possible.

Fitoussi *et al.* (2004) observed that social housing was relegated to hard-to-reach sites away from economic centres of activity, creating an economic hysteresis on the lives of tenants, reducing access to work and increasing travel.[799] Social tenants' economic creativity was thus suppressed, as they were unable to easily move for employment or set up business at home. A French social tenant could not take risks to fund a business or move from the narrow track of paying rent. Housing benefit was assessed annually in arrears,[800] so that a short run of success could disqualify someone from benefits later.

Insiderness meant that social housing was not responsive to the needs either of trapped insiders or disadvantaged outsiders. Delays in allocation meant they needed interim accommodation, and the market efficiency of their housing choices was heavily dampened. The choice of home and its location might have changed since applying (sometimes after years of waiting). Insiderness across the whole housing market, with bureaucratization of access to both social housing and hostels, hampered responsiveness.

Some hysteresis was inevitable, but there were greater barriers to accessing social housing than other types of housing. This had an effect on the whole market, which should be justified in a cost–benefit analysis of the virtues of social housing, given the effects of this hysteresis and failures in housing provision. Social landlords provided decent housing and well-managed estates for ordinary people, which were of better quality than in the private sector: the result of subsidy. Nonetheless, the distortions of local insiderness meant there was a discrepancy between the policy and the actual response towards the disadvantaged.

9.6 Conclusion

The social effects of distribution of social housing in tending to exclude the disadvantaged could be disastrous. If access to both social housing and hostels were the solutions to disadvantage, the bureaucratization of access and exclusionary nature made them increasingly unsuitable to meet urgent or chronic need. The public policy response to such need was thus clouded by insiderness and by complex bureaucracy.

Stigmatization and outsiders

The legal procedure was the instrument of exclusion of disadvantaged people. Any legal mechanism could be used for this, and it happened to some extent everywhere in my study. Allocation gave ample room to manoeuvre to very local actors who had a voice at every stage of the process. The law imposed procedural complexities that had the practical effect of tending to hide what was happening and to frustrate those seeking to use the legislation for its stated purpose. Local actors' rights have to be protected, but this is a question of balance.

The roll-call of those excluded was long and consisted of people who would tend to be excluded by their inferior economic bargaining position in any event, rather than simply because they were outsiders. It is difficult not to conclude that social landlords did not act so very differently to ordinary landlords with no social mission to house the disadvantaged. The available spaces for outsiders were often only in deprived areas or represented a small percentage of vacancies.

This situation cannot entirely be remedied by legal reform. There were powerful and understandable political and economic drivers behind this exclusion. Anyone suffering from accidents in life could become an outsider, particularly if they had strayed from their home *commune*. Disadvantaged people, when they lost their existing home, did not easily obtain housing because they become part of generically stigmatized groups.

A regular cost–benefit analysis of social housing relative to its stated objectives, and objectives actually achieved, would be useful. The effect of social housing on the housing market in general could be benign: Kemeny (2006) proposed unitary markets, designed to work in step with the market to provide affordable good quality housing. Alternatively, if social housing continues to follow primarily political objectives that are out of step with demand, responding instead to pressure from insiders, this is a disbenefit. Many countries have used insider–outsider theory to restructure the regulation of employment markets (OECD 1993, 1998) and this might also facilitate the implementation of housing policy by improved functioning of the market to provide appropriate homes to meet general demand, not just for insiders.

10 Housing some of the disadvantaged

Are social landlords at least a partial solution to housing disadvantaged people? French social landlords only housed limited numbers of the disadvantaged, and it is unclear that their subsidy was justified on that basis. There may be other justifications, but the housing objectives should be more apparent and their performance made clear. Social landlords may be helping to fulfil these objectives but it is necessary to review the evidence.

A social landlord said that the worst housing problems did not happen with social landlords:

> It is the *marchands de sommeil*. They receive isolated women with young children. They house them in lamentable conditions with rents which are three times what we could offer them. Quite evidently ... these young women immediately have difficulty in paying the rents asked of them and they will see two or three hefty, well-muscled individuals arrive, armed even with razors and bottles of acid, for example, and who propose prostitution or things of that nature to her. She cannot pay and then ... they rape her and throw her out of the window, also the furniture, her goods, the children. The young woman is lost.

This suggests a dysfunctional housing market, because these '*marchands de sommeil*', black-market 'sleep sellers', could not exist without unsatisfied demand at the bottom end of the market. French social housing has not solved the problem of housing the disadvantaged.

This quotation also illustrates the dilemmas of social landlords. They worked to provide decent, secure and affordable housing for different populations, but there was a housing shortage, the cost of housing was high and they could not help everyone. Amzallag and Taffin (2003) were right about the difficulty in housing the very poor.[801] The exclusionary economic processes described by insider–outsider theory could frustrate the best intentions.

Housing some of the disadvantaged

Access to social housing for the disadvantaged under the right to housing proved to be variable and patchy. Some social landlords struggled to house disadvantaged people, despite inappropriate funding for this purpose, while others excluded them or only housed a few. The European Committee of Social Rights (ECSR) decision in *FEANTSA v France*[802] confirmed that France was failing in its obligations towards the disadvantaged, including in the allocation process, and the *opposable* right[803] has changed things surprisingly little.

This book has shown the procedural and economic mechanisms for how and why disadvantaged people could be excluded. The 'how?' in the first section of this chapter concerns the legal mechanisms that permit exclusion. The 'why?' is then considered, reviewing insider–outsider theory and its spatial effects. Next, consideration is given to opacity, a dysfunction by itself that has serious effects. The following section shows how the different allocation models and recent European developments can be reformed. Finally, insider–outsider theory suggests routes to reform.

The author unsurprisingly tends to have English attitudes towards reform, including favouring housing need, preferring impartial decision-makers, the creation of detailed case-law to regulate discretion, and local authority responsibility.[804] Much of the history and many difficulties with social housing are common to England and France, a similarity likely to increase with European influence.

Because of the commonality of many dilemmas, a few comments from English authors are included in this chapter (Davis 1977; Nelken 1983; Galligan 1986). This is not to imply any general English superiority. Usually, features complained about in this book were also a breach of French principles, such as equal treatment and *neutralité*, so English law does not need to intrude.

10.1 An exclusionary legal process

French housing allocation processes allowed the exclusion of disadvantaged people from access to social housing. Any legal mechanism might potentially be exploited by those wishing to reject particular applicants, a kind of opaque local freedom. There were particular problems with the vagueness of the right to housing, conflicts in rights[805] and procedural problems.[806] This complex process almost had an obstructive personality of its own, not mastered by any of the actors.

10.1.1 The vague right to housing

The right to housing benefitted both disadvantaged people and tenants, whilst also providing a general qualitative principle in spatial planning.[807] Broad principles and conflicts between beneficiaries caused difficulties. The vague definition of both the right to housing and social mix allowed decisions favouring

Housing some of the disadvantaged

people in lesser need.[808] There was a lack of practical acceptance of cumulative need, with competition between priority needs and other categories.[809]

The many procedural difficulties are not repeated here but require the attention of reformers. The *opposable* right to housing has not structurally altered the access difficulties of disadvantaged people from my earlier field study. This difficult route had many of the faults of the normal allocation procedure, including involvement of insider representatives. This is still a hope for its future despite limited and variable local results.[810]

10.1.2 Conflicts with other rights

Even if the *opposable* right generated more court decisions supporting the disadvantaged, refusal of access would still be possible because of conflicting rights and principles, property, solidarity, equality and social mix. These could not be excluded because anyone can apply to the administrative courts for breach of their rights. These courts had not delivered an effective recourse to disadvantaged applicants – there was still a lack of correspondence between their statutory priority for allocation and the reality.[811]

There was no consensus about the current balance between these principles. Political disagreements about who social housing should house were played out at national level, then again in local politics within contractualization and re-opened yet again in the allocation process itself. Different principles supported different decisions.

The right to property permitted all landlords to refuse disadvantaged applicants, if desired. Public prudence similarly empowered public social landlords,[812] a difficulty causing refusal of the disadvantaged when combined with the important funding problems described in Chapter 6.

A secondary effect of the right to property arose from the nineteenth-century disputes, when property was used to oppose social and health regulation. Collective negotiation between employers and employees or landlords and tenants had resolved disputes in the beginnings of the French welfare state. Private-law solidarity within these agreements was the mechanism for mutual social insurance and welfare.[813]

Solidarity was still explicitly referred to in the statutory right to housing for the disadvantaged,[814] even though the 1994 Conseil constitutionnel decision based this in human dignity instead. Collective representation of insider representatives still affected governance of social housing, protecting the interests of financial contributors and stakeholders,[815] the social partners acting in solidarity. In a similar vein, the allocation process privileged insider representatives. As for outsiders, social housing allocation neither protected them by representation within the process nor by the State acting effectively in the general interest.

The idea of solidarity, as conceived by Bourgeois, linked together contractual solidarity with older philosophies of mutual help within groups. This ethos later allowed the co-opting of the middle classes to contribute to national insurance and welfare to provide universal benefits (Esping-Andersen 1990). Unfortunately, in its French implementation, universal social housing allocation meant lack of effective clarity about who exactly was being helped. This vagueness, apparently offering all applicants access, probably helped raise funding.

The modern basis of French solidarity in private contract, social and public law turns around agreement, harnessing the contractual 'interdependence and community of interest' of private-contractual solidarity.[816] This *association* with agreement is unavoidable and very useful for bonding any community or group with common interests. Local community interest is necessary for successful social housing construction and local integration of tenants. Local reservation contracts ensured financial contribution for local insider groups, but that funding might be reduced if visibly providing only for stigmatized and underfunded groups without any concrete benefits for contributors.

Solidarity as a value, twinned with contractual devices, seemed to have three adverse consequences for the disadvantaged in French social housing allocation. The first and most important was the presence in the allocation procedure of people with loyalties to insiders, who were in competition for places with outsiders. This conflict of interest was exacerbated by spatial 'insiderness': nimbyism, local economic and political interests and limited housing stock. The second problem relates to the first – the 'community of interest' between the social partners might include not allowing outsiders into the *commune* who might have expensive needs or be seen as a risk for social problems. The smaller the *commune*, the greater the impact on local decision-makers of this risk.

The third problem is whether the basis of solidarity in mutual insurance meant an expectation of some kind of contractual financial or political return for their contribution. An example is that actors in the Nord referred to housing applicants from the CIL (see Glossary) as 'subscribers' and the difference between a solidary contractual entitlement and solidarity in a wider sense could be unclear. Solidarity as a value often presupposes family or social bonds of support between larger or smaller groups, and philanthropy towards everyone might not be the real common objective of social housing at local level.

National solidarity does not have to act like this, because those housed could be more closely defined and this policy enforced. Local actors had formal loyalties to insiders competing with disadvantaged people for social housing places. This would suggest excluding them from the allocation process, if intended to house outsiders. Local opinion could be expressed instead at the political level for this particular purpose. However, more balanced representation to support the disadvantaged in the allocation process would probably be a more politically acceptable solution in France to the problem of creating more access for the disadvantaged.

The principle of equality was also problematic in social housing allocation. Homes differ in their size, position, rent and other ways. People cannot all have the same thing. It was difficult to reconcile equality with fitting dissimilar people into a limited number of dissimilar homes. The adoption of universal housing allocation was understandably popular because of its association with equality. Nevertheless, Nelken (1983: 72) said: 'The application of universal standards to unequal parties necessarily produces unequal results.'

Once social tenants were housed, inherent problems with equality persisted. Social tenants with reduced rents and better quality homes were better-off than people on the same income in private rented housing, which was difficult to justify for equality, but useful for tenant welfare. Social housing is an all-or-nothing solution, because of limited supply. Those helped into a home have an advantage over those not helped.

Race discrimination is also a breach of equality. Ethnic minorities and young people in the *banlieues* have been worst affected by social mix policies.[817] Stigmatization of ethnic minorities has not improved since 2006, with hard-line government policies, the ban on the wearing of the veil in public and continuing tension in the suburbs. In 2009 there were 39,887 arson attacks on vehicles or property, only 3,000 fewer than during the 2005 riots (*The Economist* 2010a, 2010b).

Alesina and Glaeser (2005) suggested that where poverty became identified with ethnic minorities in the US, the general public lost interest in helping them. There is a danger of this becoming true in France.

A final principle, social mix, should never have been allowed to be a motive for refusal of social housing, unless another place was provided elsewhere. Its implementation was a major cause for reduction in cheap vacancies and for refusal of disadvantaged people. Whatever the benefits of existing mixed communities, anyone proposing social mix should be aware of difficulties in creating this. The principle risks being used as a local tool for politically or economically profitable building and redevelopment, with consequences excluding and displacing the disadvantaged.

The right to housing was consequently not a simple statement of entitlement. It frequently stood in opposition to principles supporting property, equality and social mix, and was weakened by all of these. It was a campaigning banner and negotiating position, asking for more than could be attained, such as no eviction without rehousing[818] or a sacred right to property without social constraints.[819] In a such a political system, the taking of these extreme traditional positions was necessary to ensure that any ultimate agreement was balanced between the extremes.[820]

Law changes only slowly. To look at these principles is to see the scars of the nineteenth-century struggles between capital and labour. The riots by youths in the suburbs show some real grievances expressed in adaptations of traditional French methods of protest. The challenge is to how to defuse these tensions in a peaceful way to meet modern needs, without reviving these oppositions or creating new forms of complaint such as terrorism.

10.1.3 Exclusion by process

Social housing allocation presented many opportunities to refuse disadvantaged people. Many of Bourgeois's comments (1996) still had resonance, despite copious legislative changes. Nelken (1983) argued in *The Limits of the Legal Process* that legislation had to fit within existing institutions, thus:

> Any particular piece of legislation can be seen as an exercise in 'controlled social change', which presupposes and tends to reproduce all those features of a society's institutions and practices it does not specifically set out to alter.
> (Nelken 1983: 210)[821]

Bourgeois's findings included opacity, fragmentation of procedure and improper local influences. Reform since then had not addressed structurally privileged interests or this difficult procedure for the disadvantaged.

The allocation was still fragmented and opaque with split access streams, each with different unclear priorities and at least three serial decisions. Decision-makers had *de facto* individual opportunities to interfere to favour their preferred candidates. The allocation commission, created to see fair play, again represented insiders. The commission had little independence, or capacity for enquiry, and few powers to act other than simply by saying 'no'.[822]

The detailed difficulties with the procedure cannot easily be summarized in this book: the large choice of applicants, vague principles, serial and parallel processing with different criteria, inadequate funding and local agendas all contributed to exclusion. These all require rethinking in a process of simplification.

As a matter of law, the proper loyalties of local actors to their insiders becomes improper if not effectively balanced by someone to represent outsiders. This conflict of interest means decision-makers were not disinterested. As a matter of economics, the loyalties and mutual financial interests of insiders to build social housing are often useful, but not yet adapted to housing disadvantaged people. Both the procedure and the incentives could be adjusted appropriately. Local economic interests particularly affect decentralization.

10.1.4 Local institutions and decentralization

Bourgeois (1996: 32) argued that fragmented local environments did not change social landlords' basic strategies and that local underlying interests tended to resurface following reform. Nonetheless, locally invented innovations in my study might still help the disadvantaged to some extent.

The local organizational inventiveness and experimental approaches[823] found in this study could be facilitated more. The analysis in section 5.3.3 (p. 130) suggests that if these are local collective-choice rules, they would be more efficient. These arrangements were suitable for local conditions and addressed lack of coherence

Housing some of the disadvantaged

in national policies, but were fragile without national support. The government instead preferred detailed compulsory local contracts, a contradiction in terms. This analysis also suggests that a reduction in classes of people allowed to access social housing would encourage simplification of allocation processes, because the waste of time and effort of negotiations would have less point.

Contractual decentralization pulled together some of the fragmented finance[824] but increased bureaucratic expense in negotiation without diminishing the volume of national regulation. Some arrangements succeeded despite national rules, such as common file processing by social landlords in the Nord,[825] probably reducing processing costs, improving fairness and easing bottlenecks. National policies sometimes obstructed innovation, such as the removal of funding from the active prefectural unit in Lyon.

If the effects of spatial insiderness discussed below are correct, size or organization and level of decision-making mattered. *Communautés* might ultimately reduce mayors' tendencies to defend their patch against incomers by organizing policy over a larger area, but such policies were limited in 2005.[826] The *communautés* of Lyon and Lille could help the disadvantaged to an extent.

The greatest risk of decentralization for the disadvantaged was the reinforcement of mayors' exclusionary tendencies. There was still obvious unfairness and inequality in very local practices, such as refusal to house non-locals in one *commune* and not in the next, or objections to eviction in one *commune* and not the next.[827] These local differences and patchy provision made central regulation difficult, because mayors were politically powerful as a group. Local funding might increase local taxpayers' concerns that their money should house locals and not difficult incomers, which increased nimbyism.

It is as yet unclear how decentralization will affect social housing for the disadvantaged. Delegation of the prefectural contingent to local authorities was possible but not common. Brouant (2011) suggested local unwillingness to take on the responsibility for the right to housing. This does not bode well.

10.1.5 Politics and money

Much had changed since Bourgeois's comments about the profit motivation of private social landlords and the political motivation of public social landlords. During my study, public and private approaches were not easy to separate and social landlords had similar regulation, practices and budgets. Any budget-limited organization can fail to achieve its mission if not appropriately funded and effectively run.

All social landlords worried about politics, finance and much more besides. They were more tightly run financially than in Bourgeois's time, but also more affected by funding limitations.[828] All social landlords were concerned with politics, with the involvement of all sorts of insider representatives, who were collectively armed with not only a range of powers in allocation and management

Housing some of the disadvantaged

but also influence through planning powers, reservations, and the need for local finance.[829] Modern budgetary constraints increased the importance of both finance and local influence.

Size mattered for social landlords, something not mentioned by Bourgeois. SAHLMs (private social landlords) enjoyed independence from local authorities, usually due to their larger size, and due to their greater control over allocations. This governance gave greater choice concerning where they operated and the types of tenants sought, which in turn gave rise to different institutional cultures.[830] Perhaps there is generally a right size for both social landlords and local government, if it is desired to create both local responsibility and sufficient effectiveness, without too much nimbyism. This is linked to the spatial effects of 'insiderness'.

10.2 'Insiderness' in social housing

It is now possible to pull together the threads of this book to review insiderness: its effects, the importance of rent, the interaction with debt and construction law, and its important spatial consequences. None of this is inevitable or invariable in France and can be altered by reform.

Insiderness raises questions of legitimacy beyond its economics, about whether this is excessive when one group has more advantages than another anywhere, particularly when due to public policy. Advantages could be justified as the product of work, social need or contribution, as for social security. Despite these justifications, slightly surprisingly, the adverse effects of insiderness in housing means that housing more outsiders can help create a better functioning housing market, quite apart from its social benefits.

Lindbeck and Snower (2002) suggested that union pressure increased insiderness, but French insider representation and privileges were embedded in employment and rental law, the accumulated product of past pressure. Political power reinforced the economic power of insiders. French unions could be very philanthropic, as co-founders of the French welfare system, but in social housing, insider pressure had meant that landlords were legally obliged to use this fragmented and exclusionary allocation procedure.

It is a mistake to think that the interests of outsiders and insiders, particularly local insiders, always lie together for housing welfare (see also p.109). Transaction costs providing socially useful benefits for insiders can, for example, make it difficult to remove tenants. This is useful for insiders, but has also resulted in landlords ratcheting up their requirements for hypothetically 'good' tenants, making access less easy for outsiders. Such stasis also reduces vacancies, however socially useful. The study showed there was also competition for social housing places between insiders and outsiders,[831] and that insiders were better represented.

The spatial effects of insiderness meant that despite the benefits of local voices, it was not ideal to have tenants or mayors on small allocation commissions

Housing some of the disadvantaged

in small *communes*, because of their very localised interests. To repeat a social landlord: 'Everyone agrees we should house people with behavioural problems ... but in the *commune* next door, not in my home.'[832]

10.2.1 Insiderness in French social housing

Insiderness was prominent in social housing, in fact in rented housing generally. Social landlords constantly faced tenants in governance and allocation and tried to avoid disturbing them. Insider-tenants took up to 40 per cent of all allocations, including two family homes on divorce.[833] Social tenants enjoyed good security of tenure, extra space and cheaper rents, gradually becoming effectively cheaper.[834] There were barriers to eviction (through difficult eviction processes) and barriers to access to housing (including through requirements for guarantees).[835] This is generally good for insiders but demonstrably caused access problems for outsiders under current incentives.

The high transaction costs of renting generally were not simply security of tenure. You could not say definitively that French security of tenure in rented property was too high, when most non-social landlords could avoid this by providing furnished accommodation.[836] Low historic-cost rents were important, but there were outside factors; for example, the law did not require guarantees, but simply supported them.[837]

For social landlords, the highest transaction costs were in the allocation process itself: managing the administration of allocation: multiple access points, serial stages, negotiations, allocation commissions and the many compulsory local agreements. Transaction costs are generally barriers to access, so you have to ask who this barrier is protecting. The allocation decision is public law, reflecting its public funding and regulation. If this works to help insiders, regardless of need, contribution or other purposes, then it is a barrier to access for disadvantaged people, as in the private sector. It can even be a covert diversion of taxpayers' money for political or, occasionally, personal gain.

Unionization was said by Lindbeck and Snower to produce increased insiderness, but France had a profusion of representative bodies, each pushing for their own funding. Any reform could produce a new public body and there were support costs even for volunteers. This hive of industry was a credit to the many volunteers, but must come at a considerable financial support cost. This was supported by up to five layers of local government, negotiating with other layers and other bodies. Getting everyone concerned around a table was an attractive French trait, but it could create immobilism,[838] high costs and risk aversion.

It does not take much economic theory to suggest that simplifying the process and enforcing priorities for the disadvantaged would reduce the cost and exclusionary nature of the process. The organizational arguments in section 5.3.3

Housing some of the disadvantaged

(p. 130) support this, suggesting narrowing criteria and increasing local informal contracting, but it needs further research. This has to be weighed against loss of interest by local actors no longer obtaining benefits.

Insiderness does not always benefit insiders, as is apparent from the disadvantaged insiders trapped in deprived estates, unable to move elsewhere without state sponsorship under the current incentive structure. This illustrates another possible disadvantage of insiderness in the indirect effect of general housing shortage. Rigid housing markets run parallel to rigid employment markets, a double drag on the economy. Renard (2003: 7) observed several reasons for the slowness of house prices to respond to an economic downturn, such as lack of statistics and reluctance of vendors to lower prices. Insider–outsider theory could provide another reason for this hysteresis.[839]

10.2.2 More about rent

Rent has primordial importance for the application of insider–outsider theory, and the effects of increased focus on rent due to funding can be seen: social landlords relied heavily on funding by loans, which had to be serviced from rents. Consequently, landlords had to seek tenants able to pay rent and unlikely to disturb neighbours. Stephens *et al.* (2002) suggested that shortfalls in housing benefits to pay rent in Europe were often compensated by other benefits. This view was probably always an overgeneralization for France.

Rent was not covered by benefits, which slipped, and tenants still had to pay the excess rent. Contributory benefits could mean no problem with rents, but they had limits and were threatened by budgetary constraints. Non-contributory benefits did not prevent rent shortfalls, and some people did not receive them. Poor or part-time workers and young people had particular difficulty.[840]

In contrast, low rents could sometimes provide the best hope of a home for poorer people, because historic-cost rents reduced over time without burdening government income streams, and without political intervention. The public burden in paying housing benefit is also lower and landlords do not necessarily make a loss.[841] However, low rents also benefitted the better-off. They also resulted in social housing attracting poor applicants from the private sector. Low rents might not cover repair and poor tenants might be unable to afford to move to other housing. This study cannot explore either the large literature on this[842] or resolve which is the better subsidy, although both are probably needed. The point here is the effects of rent on disadvantaged people.

French social landlords routinely refused or delayed applicants who could not pay. Social landlords received nothing for social disadvantage after construction with expensive and fragmentary public aid (Deschamps 1998). A sole focus on rent is useful for fiscal prudence, but not for access by the disadvantaged.

10.2.3 Debt, eviction and stigma

There seemed to be strong links between the severe French credit environment and insiderness in rental markets. Restrictive lending practices by banks can exclude individuals from home purchase, and financially cautious landlords can be reluctant to let to poorer tenants. Eviction is an issue in both debt recovery and tenant insiderness.

Very cautious attitudes by lenders and landlords were enforced by regulation or rewarded with subsidy; for example, landlord caution was rewarded by supported guarantee schemes, increasing transaction costs. Prudence and severity towards home-seekers are different sides of the same coin. Stigma has a role to play in both insiderness and a severe credit environment. Lack of credit for poorer people makes them vulnerable to short-term crises, and debt and eviction are seriously stigmatizing.[843]

Insider–outsider theory means that the choice between protection from eviction and creating access is not neutral, the one requiring increased insiderness and the other reducing it. Protection from eviction tends to make things worse beyond a certain point, causing difficulties of access. Nonetheless, too little tenant protection causes 'churning', a similarly undesirable and unstable position[844] profiting the landlord and probably increasing land values based on rents.

The high risks of eviction favoured insiders who would not or could not move, also increasing landlords' financial risks of investment. This risk and a general fear of the irreversibly stigmatizing effects of eviction can lead to the refusal of a social home, in order to spare the impecunious from eviction,[845] which is not the best kind of help. Outsiders, particularly evictees, consequently suffered exclusion from all housing.

Particular French protection-from-eviction measures discouraged landlordism because of large or unpredictable transaction costs. When the State refused eviction for social reasons,[846] landlords obtained compensation equal to rent. However, this could prompt a social landlord to push through eviction to obtain this finance.[847] There was also an uncompensated ban on winter evictions. A voluntary worker described a rush of precautionary evictions before the winter moratorium.[848] Effective public response would be easier to manage when emergencies arose, although winter evictions would be unacceptable to French public opinion.[849]

Fear of eviction was an effect of the longstanding housing crisis, and long-term change requires consistent and effective access to emergency care for the evicted and the slow reduction in the insiderness that blocks access to more permanent housing. French evictees could not easily pick themselves up and start all over again, because nobody would house them.

The rescue function of hostels was also stigmatized, with the homeless the least likely to find a social place in 2005–6. The *opposable* right to housing could not grant immediate access to accommodation in an emergency, perhaps the most

Housing some of the disadvantaged

important thing, when hostel access was blocked.[850] It encumbered *associations* providing hostels with the prospect of legal action.[851]

All social landlords were risk averse and took pride in prudence,[852] so reduced funding meant fewer disadvantaged people accepted. This severe debt environment is thus closely associated with insiderness. Perhaps insiderness is the extent of the turning inwards of society against the perceived risk presented by outsiders.

10.2.4 Insiderness and construction

French insiderness in rental markets interacted with construction funding. When social landlords' incomes declined with reducing rents, they could seek higher rents by improving homes. Their funding was for construction and they faced tax disincentives for inaction.[853] They could use construction to reorganize tenants spatially,[854] including redeveloping poor areas to bring higher rents. Higher quality requirements for new lets from 2002 also required removal or improvement of homes that were cheap but did not meet new standards.[855]

The role of capital expenditure in rental markets differs from that in employment markets. Insiderness in employment might mean employers investing in technology to reduce the number of necessary employees. In contrast, tenants are also the customers, so reducing their numbers is not profitable. Houses, when built, have to be occupied by paying tenants to recoup construction costs. For French social landlords, going upmarket by assisted construction could enable them to break even by receiving higher rents.

Social landlords thus had an interest in promoting the desirability of construction to solve housing problems, within a construction lobby seeking capital for this and public works. Perverse effects of construction incentives included: increased rents; price-competition for land; temporarily blocked access to social housing while rehousing existing tenants; sometimes failure to rehouse all tenants on regeneration of private land (Javaloyès 2003); demolition of large and cheap homes in the ZUS; higher rents not fully compensated by benefits; and occasional building corruption cases.[856]

Housing construction should help housing problems, but two things tended to defeat this. First, disadvantaged outsiders had difficulty accessing expensive new homes, whilst cheaper older stock was removed. Second, better-off insiders could have extra space, larger homes, second homes for their children and under-occupied homes.[857] The capacity for insider households to expand to fill the space available was underestimated. On household break-up, state-supported access to two family homes reduced available housing stock in both public and private sectors,[858] probably faster than it could be built and resulting in a radical reduction in housing availability for outsiders.

Despite these difficulties, walking around social housing estates for this study, there was much to impress in new construction. There were attractive new social

Housing some of the disadvantaged

homes and system-built blocks were adapted in ingenious ways. Transport links were improving and businesses and voluntary bodies were encouraged. Those able to afford suitable new housing might be well satisfied. Leisure facilities for young people could be good, even in private areas scheduled for improvement.

It was difficult to discern when there was excess construction; for example, in South Lille, it was to be wondered why this slightly scruffy area needed large-scale regeneration, and why the ethnic minority population should be split up. Social housing was in considerable need of improvement, but there were also political and financial reasons to build.

Construction finance benefits primarily the builders, including social landlords. France does not have the empty incomplete estates of the Spanish and Irish construction booms, but there are still perverse effects of construction incentives, particularly for affordability.[859] The French government was often effectively the paymaster or instigator for construction, not individuals more limited by their income. Fewer large-scale works could allow more to be spent on social care, benefits, or small repairs.

10.2.5 Spatial adaptations to theory for housing

Landlords sell the use of space, not products, so insider–outsider theory has spatial effects, which are more obvious for the locally connected social landlords. First, there was the effect of nimbyism, depending on the size of the area or the organization, already described. Then, there was a stratified housing market. Linbeck and Snower (2002) described how insiderness produces stratified employment markets with good, bad, and black market jobs. Similarly, there were good and bad French housing areas with a black market, run by *marchands de sommeil*.

Since insiders are also customers, they may be favoured more than employees, as long as they pay. Social landlords can be very protective of tenants but they cannot withdraw from the market, so replacing low income tenants with higher income tenants is a logical use of the space. This is particularly so if subsidy favours this replacement, altering the usual economic preferences for insiders.

Low rent areas tended to concentrate disadvantage for affordability reasons, but insider–outsider theory also predicts such patchiness. Such areas constantly recruit the same kind of deprived tenant, in the absence of special incentives, partly because of the high turnover of disadvantaged entrants without much bargaining power.[860] Local political insiderness or nimbyism by mayors elsewhere exacerbates this concatenation of circumstances.[861]

Lindbeck and Snower (2002) described how deprived areas are occupied by the unemployed, living on social transfers, which is in fact a spatial rental market effect rather than automatically being a labour market effect.[862] Rental markets always produce such local effects, because houses cannot be moved like businesses. A chain of local people are affected by employment dismissals.

In employment markets, firing employees only concerned employers within the limits of legal obligations, but social landlords then dealt with the consequences of this dismissal. If tenants then suffered a double dismissal from job and home, mayors were then concerned with this third stage. These events impose local social costs, which explain some very local strategies to cope, such as exclusion of non-locals and outsiders by alliances of mayors and social landlords. This is both spatial insiderness and a link between housing and labour markets.

Insiderness in housing markets thus has strongly spatial effects. The economic risks of disadvantage were clear but also affected political choices, by localism of local voters and *a priori* stigma attached to disadvantaged outsiders. Nimbyism is a kind of insiderness, whether for political or economic reasons, so the territorial organization of allocation at a higher territorial level is important for correcting this.

10.3 Transparency

Opacity was another important feature of allocation. Bourgeois's comments were still true and opacity obfuscated what happened, disguising messy compromises. This also had economic effects on the whole housing market.

10.3.1 The uses of opacity

Bourgeois (1996: 223) said that opacity facilitated the autonomy and profitability of social landlords. Local actors might still have reason to conceal their processes. The acute political sensitivity of allocation was such that almost any allocation decision could be criticised by rival lobbies.

On top of political conflicts, social landlords suffered conflict between their social duties and budgetary requirements. Mayors faced conflicts between assisting local people and concern for the needy generally. The prefectures suffered conflict between obligations to the disadvantaged and necessity for negotiation with actors. The CIL might have a conflict between pleasing employers and concerns for fairness. Two interviewees suggested employers used the scheme to favour preferred workers.

Contractualization promoted self-interested conflict between actors, in a culture of negotiation. Messy compromises might be difficult to explain publicly. Actors must fall back on what Nelken (1983: 23) called 'impression-management' where non-specific legislation dealt in ideals and was symbolic rather than instrumental:

> Although a perfectly managed account of legislative outcomes would provide a patina of consistency over the conflicting activities of different agencies and reconcile claims and actual achievements, in practice no such level of success is either possible or necessary because the need to account for the

appropriateness of actions taken is so highly specific to the context and audience concerned.

Local audiences would hear of long waiting lists and support more construction. Legislators appeared to have helped the needy by extending disadvantaged categories. National statistics only partially revealed considerable local variability between *communes* and between social landlords. This was apparent social progress.

Opacity included inadequate statistics. Social landlords complained about this for planning and about the misleading nature of long waiting lists.[863] There was disagreement about the extent of need at national level (Renard 2006, 2007: 4),[864] and a general shortage of locally produced statistics. In Lyon, local observatories were based mainly in difficult areas. This increased impressions of difficulty, and did not disclose spare capacity elsewhere.[865] Rural and better-off areas were under-studied.

10.3.2 Transparency and discretion

Opacity and fragmentation increased local actors' already generous room to manoeuvre in allocation, a discretion in the UK. Davis (1977: 27) said: 'discretionary power is a necessary governmental tool but excessive discretionary power is dangerous and harmful. What is obviously needed is balance.' He added that discretion could be constrained by legal rules, rules made by those involved or by principles from cases.

There were not enough specific, transparent and effective French rules to guide difficult decisions between priorities. Galligan (1986: 20) said: 'Any exercise of official power should be capable of being explained in terms of its purposes and within a framework of constraining principles.' French difficulties in explaining the system to the public were linked to complexity, fragmented power, unclear objectives and failure to insist on priorities for the disadvantaged, linked to inappropriate or insufficient funding.

This excessive discretion should be constrained, even allowing for the greater French room for manoeuvre described by Whittaker (2008). This would necessarily involve reduction of the practical freedom in allocation now enjoyed, in favour of clearer national and local public priorities (Galligan 1986: 69). This would require effective enforcement, so far as possible, but also sufficient flexibility to permit transparent local innovation, perhaps through cases under the *opposable* right to housing,[866] or a code of deontology[867] to provide guidance.

Light judicial supervision of French social landlords' allocations was partly due to their perceived expertise,[868] but their constraints in allocation make this inappropriate. Social landlords did not see the files retained by proposers. Rejection could be a decision of the mayor or allocation commission, not social

Housing some of the disadvantaged

landlords themselves. Social landlords might be unable to prevent concentrations of poverty. Historic income ceilings had been very low at times (Lefèbvre *et al.* 1991: 64). Even today, placing poor tenants in ZUS meant they could afford rents.

Social landlords should be particularly supervised in applying social mix, because their structural interest in rents and peaceful estates could lead to overshoot in excluding the disadvantaged so as to obtain higher rents. Because rent has always been social landlords' most important economic concern, social mix could derail obligations to house the disadvantaged, creating a discretion incapable of supervision because of exceptional vagueness.

Applying social mix in allocation seemed to limit access in highly variable ways. Suggesting there could be too many poor people or black people necessarily involves discrimination against them. Lack of statistics and opacity of process could hide such discrimination.[869] Social mix might oblige better-off *communes* to construct social housing, but the right to housing for the disadvantaged could do the same.

10.3.3 Transparency and the housing market

The MIILOS (2006: 28) reported lack of transparency towards applicants about their chances, probably also a breach of EU competition law for subsidizing public services.[870] Transparency for competition relates to a market model of efficiency to produce optimum pricing and sufficient supply. Akerlof (1970) exposed problems caused by insufficient information and transparency within the market, and Stiglitz (2002) proposes the interdependency of public and private markets.

Transparency within a market means transparency towards individuals making their choice of home, not simply towards the authorities. The beneficial effect of competition in producing price efficiency depends on these individual choices, but, the longer the housing waiting lists, the less this constitutes a real choice. A transparent allocation framework would help the public plan their housing in real knowledge of their chances, based on realistic criteria and predictions of waiting times.

Lack of transparency about allocation and inadequate statistics on need probably caused insufficient provision of cheap housing by the market. Both public and private sector rented housing were trying to serve the same market for 'good' tenants. If these tenants are taken by social housing, this increases the pool of risky tenants applying to the army of two million French small landlords,[871] who are less equipped to handle risk and who receive a lower subsidy than social landlords.[872] This could increase their prices, causing acute problems to the disadvantaged.

The *associations* were effective campaigners[873] and raised the alarm about this by campaigning politically. This sense of crisis had drawbacks because people might stay put in their homes for fear of difficulty, contributing to the freezing up

Housing some of the disadvantaged

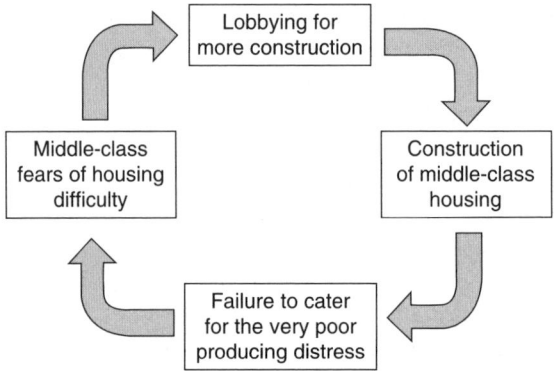

10.1 The perpetuation of the housing crisis.

of housing markets and entrenching the positions of existing tenants. In fact, more general housing was built in response to the crisis, although this was not directed to the poor or disadvantaged, because of a political consensus favouring 'housing for all'[874] and a ubiquitous conviction that construction would solve the crisis.[875] Middle class insecurity[876] and the lobbying power of insiders exacerbated this tendency to construct for the better-off.

The alarm was then raised by the *associations* again because of continuing problems for the disadvantaged. The cycle continued as shown in Figure 10.1. Distributional problems in French housing could mean that the advantages of construction for the disadvantaged were not in sight. More transparency within a simpler allocation procedure would mean housing provision could be incentivized to follow demand. As it was, political drives to assist were diverted into construction funding for any housing.

Generating outrage to help outsiders had limits as a strategy. French *associations* were past masters at collecting evidence and bringing this to the attention to the public.[877] This proper activity unfortunately generated a sense of housing insecurity, encouraging people to batten down the hatches to protect their own position, in a country with a history of housing difficulty and stigmatization of the evicted.

10.4 Social housing and Europe

The EU Commission (2009) identified groups excluded from housing in eight countries, which were similar to groups having difficulty in France, probably due to their general social and economic difficulties. However, the EU Commission found that this situation was exacerbated by a lack of priority for the disadvantaged in social housing, a strong tendency in France.

Housing some of the disadvantaged

France was a test case for the several competing models for housing allocation,[878] which might produce similar results elsewhere. Insiderness can occur in any model, but some models make insiderness more probable. These approaches are affected by recent European developments, limiting available housing policies.

10.4.1 Which model of allocation?

The main allocation models were 'housing for all', housing workers, housing the poor and housing those in need, in variable combinations. The first three models might permit social landlords to act prudently to seek 'good' tenants to satisfy budgetary requirements. This can lead to exclusion of the most disadvantaged with preference for those with good career prospects or closest to income ceilings, as found by Bourgeois (1996). This can be a culture of 'the deserving poor', including employees, married couples, 'stable' families and people on a rising income, based on stereotypes.

Since people within these first three models are theoretically equal, these rely heavily on the mechanism of the queue for fairness. This has to be both rigorously and generously applied to prevent exclusion of less advantaged queue members. Nielsen (2010), for example, reported legislation allowing people on benefits associated with poverty to be excluded from deprived areas in Denmark.

The queue might prevent the disadvantaged being passed over, but is not necessarily fair by itself. Stiglitz (2000: 140) argued that people needing medical care would wait longer, but questioned whether this rationing was fair. Social housing queues are different because of spatial effects. Bottoms *et al.* (1989) studied two similar estates, but one had higher crimes levels. People who could afford to wait for homes in the better estate did so; consequently, desperation limited housing choices. Opacity also favours insiders who could wait for particular areas and with knowledge of when and where to apply.

The French 'housing for all' model did not produce equality in treatment or result, shown by the variability of provision, often particularly excluding the disadvantaged.[879] This approach represented a settlement between the left and right notionally based on equality rather than any realistic or coherent social housing allocation model. The left obtained continuing privileges for workers and increased State intervention. The right promised more new homes, including homes for purchase and middle-class access to social housing to ease insecurity. It was a high funding model in a political context where every government promised reduced spending. This illusion of equality disguised rather than settled local housing priorities.

Probably 'housing for all' can result in housing those not catered for elsewhere, giving the disadvantaged implicit priority by funding their housing. This seems to require either that the rest of the housing market is reasonably accessible, or

Housing some of the disadvantaged

that some social housing should be slightly undesirable to limit social housing applications. This is probably also true of 'housing the disadvantaged'.

As for 'housing the poor', where there is excess demand and lack of access for the disadvantaged, some limitation of universal access is required. Income ceilings are not sufficiently descriptive of need by themselves without additional need criteria dominating and limiting consideration. Without this limitation, the disadvantaged might find no home. This model can exclude outsiders who are in difficulty for reasons other than poverty, either by outright discrimination or where the applicant has social difficulties thought unattractive by landlords.

Housing 'workers' provides additional State subsidy for people who already have advantages, creating insiderness. The CIL scheme was unfair to many disadvantaged people, to non-qualifying workers and even to qualifying workers who could not get access. French employers can pay selected employees less and be more competitive abroad, possibly distorting the EU internal market. This might adversely affect competing private landlords. Despite this, the CIL could provide an access route for disadvantaged workers and ethnic minorities, alongside better-off employees. This approach could also be useful where there is a temporary local scarcity of suitable housing.

None of these outcomes are universal and all depend on the particular implementation in the particular situation. In large cities, such as London and Paris, allocation creates large responsibilities and dilemmas for policy-makers. High prices mimic the effects of housing shortage for lower income groups in cities. Many more people suffer difficulty, particularly workers within a range of modest incomes. More people are forced to either live in inferior conditions in towns or trek large distances to work on expensive transport.

This economic hysteresis, a drag on the life chances of people in out-of-town estates, was identified by Fitoussi *et al.* (2004). Commuters might clean offices, nurse in hospitals, teach children, serve in shops, guard buildings or provide myriad services. Housing workers in priority in these extreme circumstances is understandable, but how exactly can government prioritize the right workers for current economic needs? How can it avoid disproportionately favouring insider lobby groups or distorting the market? In big cities, is difficult to work out who are the wrong people living in a given place.

French-style social mix provides no easy answer to this dilemma. The seriously adverse effects of that process there have been described. The perceived advantages of social mix could be the product of people choosing to remain living next to a quite different type of person. This openness could be the real cause of advantages of social mix, and trying to create social mix by exclusionary spatial insiderness is the antithesis of this.

Perhaps the question should not be, 'Who should benefit from social housing?' but 'What is the purpose of having a social housing allocation process at all?' If the same insiders and better-off people will obtain social housing in the

Housing some of the disadvantaged

public and private sectors anyway, it would be cheaper to allow a normal waiting list, of the sort kept by private developers for those who can afford it. Social housing allocation, to be social, needs to do something different from the market to justify its extra subsidy for this, such as demonstrably housing disadvantaged people.

The insights of insider–outsider theory mean policy-makers should ask themselves whether legal instruments are being used to favour primarily insiders. A similar point was made by Rueda (2005) for labour markets. It is important to stand aside from the influence of popular social norms and the voices of insiders dictating that, really, these workers, existing tenants and local people are the ones who must be helped.[880]

Amongst allocation models, housing the disadvantaged in decent conditions most actively defeats insiderness. This combines alleviating the normal disadvantages of poverty and reducing societal tendencies to subsidize better-off or apparently more attractive groups. Housing the disadvantaged as a real priority tends to lead to dualist housing markets, but not inevitably, where there is enough local spare social housing. This kind of redistribution is more uncertain in other allocation models.

In systems combining models, it matters whether the disadvantaged have priority and other applicants are infill, as often in the UK and the Netherlands, or whether, in real terms, ordinary people have priority and disadvantaged people are infill for rejected spaces, as often in France. The former makes a difference to disadvantage (EU Commission 2009). It is easy to slip from the first to the second.

The care of disadvantaged outsiders requires queue-jumping into some kind of accommodation to meet urgent needs. This conflicts with the interests of others in the queue, but if people have housing emergencies or long-term housing needs there are good reasons to provide social housing to prevent stigmatization, allowing people to recover from misfortunes which could happen to anyone. In France, this would mean real priority consideration for the disadvantaged in every application stream in every *commune*.

Allocation schemes that prioritize those with the greatest need can make it easier to objectively[881] and transparently maximize the use of available social housing to relieve disadvantage. This would reduce the French competition between *associations* supporting different priorities. This has been described as a 'manageable domain' (Cowan and Marsh 2005: 27). This means defining different needs and insisting on housing those who objectively cumulate those needs, within an internally consistent ethical model such as that of Fitzpatrick (1999) who provided a basis for comparing urgent and persistent need.

10.4.2 EU policies

EU Competition policies restrict the possible beneficiaries of State-aided housing. The 2010 decision concerning the Netherlands required a very high level of

Housing some of the disadvantaged

allocation to people below the poverty threshold.[882] The latter could improve French allocation because, after all, allocation involves the distribution of subsidy.

The EU Commission policy might perhaps increase subsidy for housing the disadvantaged, and it is broadly in line with insider–outsider theory in compensating for outsiders' disadvantages. It would be hoped that enforcement would penalize an apparent but ineffective priority for the disadvantaged in allocation in subsidized homes. However, this limitation of subsidy could be too simple in a multifactorial situation.

Competition policy does not and could not require that States should subsidize the disadvantaged. Public funding can allow volunteer social landlords to be effectively commanded to house the disadvantaged, but they cannot easily be commanded to build for them. There was already limited willingness to build very social housing in France and the bad reputation of the ZUS risked stigmatizing the whole sector.

In France, England, the Netherlands and Austria most social housing was not originally built for the disadvantaged but for the working classes. The disadvantaged have tended historically to colonize middle class social housing as it ages, through oversupply or through public policy redefinitions of social housing purposes. Normally within cities, whole areas can become successively improved and deteriorate, in ways originally identified by Park *et al.* (1925). Will this still happen if the disadvantaged are isolated within stigmatized special housing? Will this happen if constant redevelopment means there are no cheap areas at all?

An important question is: what now happens to workers needing just some housing assistance to bridge the increasing affordability gap between stigmatized renting and ownership? What now fills the former function of social landlords, all unwillingly and compulsorily assigned to housing the disadvantaged? This is not the purpose of this book but housing difficulty in poorer workers was also a problem in the evidence of my study. Such intermediate housing, including shared ownership, requires both some lesser subsidy and usually the intervention of some facilitating organization such as social landlords (Monk and Whitehead 2010).

To the English lawyer, renting and ownership are both the same kind of thing and there is a continuum of security from one to the other. A popular perception that ownership and renting are the only options is socially divisive and shared ownership falls in this divide. The most useful follow-up research would be to compare European tenures, to look at detailed principles and the comparative effects of rental security in order to produce the necessary understanding before, not after, European regulation, also seeking intermediate tenures between stigmatized residualization and absolute ownership.

The Commission decision favours holding housing for the disadvantaged in a separate company (Von Danwitz 2009) but this specialization could mimic the stigmatization of the French prefectural contingent. Scattering homes for the disadvantaged amongst other homes might combat stigmatization[883] but is

Housing some of the disadvantaged

expensive to administer. It could be difficult to persuade established communities to accept this for new housing, particularly where homes for the disadvantaged can be immediately identified.

Another issue is that EU policy threatens the model of unitary housing markets,[884] and with it the idea that rental market effects can be mitigated by strategic public construction investment. This should lower rents and improve quality across the market, which is particularly important to keep States' budgets under control to pay benefits to support that rent.

Affordable rent is central to any housing policy. In a unitary market, social or other below-market-rent housing is subsidized upfront in sufficient quantities to affect market rents. It follows that more people, including the better-off, access this subsidy, contrary to EU rules, and that competition to reduce private landlords' profits is deliberate. This is part of a well-established and diverse European tool-kit of policies, which is threatened by forced harmonization.

The issue is how far the State can use its economic power to invest and compete, like other actors, provided private landlords obtain enough return to retain their interest. When upfront loans are repaid, increasing social rents could later produce profits to be ploughed back into new homes. This policy of competition with private landlords is arguably in the common interest, costing less in the longer term, both in lower average rents and lower land prices based on rents.

To argue for unitary markets is to some extent to play devils' advocate, because unitary markets tend to result in increasing regulation to control the market (Kemeny 2006). Historically this has produced high security of tenure and thus insiderness, which can disadvantage outsiders. Also, if social rents are maintained just below market rents, there could be an affordability problem.

A controlled market has adverse consequences. French low-rent homes were a refuge for poverty, and even slowly increasing rents could cause difficulty, particularly where prosperity did not increase too, as in parts of the Nord. Insiderness should consequently not be reduced by sudden crude policy changes to reduce tenant security or increase rents, because of its human consequences, and particularly where strong social norms stigmatize evictees. This requires a long-term strategy based on the characteristics of the particular locality.

It will also be difficult to enforce EU limitations on public subsidy for housing. Any possibly illegal French State assistance by tax relief, historic-cost rents and local aids by cheap land are difficult to discover and enforce in a very complex system. General avoidance of control could include tax reliefs and aids favouring home purchase instead. The latter does not obviously compete with private landlords but continues advantages for the better-off and reduces rental housing stock for outsiders.

The EU Commission opted for an income ceiling for allocations in the Netherlands. This is easy to measure objectively, but could still lead to landlords

Housing some of the disadvantaged

seeking the 'deserving poor' as described above. Where there is insiderness, this policy may still favour locals, workers and existing tenants, excluding disadvantaged outsiders.

EU competition policy seems not yet sufficiently flexible, particularly given large regional variations in circumstances, complex issues and multi-factorial problems. Assessment of competition law subsidy should consider the extent of subsidy relative to objectives, in a very long-term cost–benefit analysis considering a wide range of factors in the particular national context, something which might be possible under the new 2010 Protocol to the TFEU.[885]

10.4.3 Problems with European rights

The ECtHR and the ECSR are increasingly acting as constitutional courts for Europe. This is a large topic and these developments post-date the empirical study. However, the tribunals raise important relevant issues in welfare and property law.

The first problem is that principles in the ECtHR and the ECSR decisions reported in section 2.1.6 (p. 42) conflict. The ECtHR strongly supports landlords in *Hutten Czapka* whilst the ECSR strongly supports tenants in a similar situation, partly because of differing treaty provisions. *Hutten-Czapka* proposes guaranteeing landlords' rents at a level which pays repair costs. This rent to cover repair in *FEANTSA* was ruled a breach of the right to housing, because it was not affordable.

This inconsistency could make policy choices difficult in low rent areas of France. It also tends to revive opposition between landlords and tenants, an opposition that was historically dangerous for social peace in France, a social peace already strained by riots in social housing estates.

The second problem is that both cases imposed improbably heavy financial responsibilities on States to pay out to both landlords and tenants. *Hutten Czapka* echoes French *jurisprudence*[886] in suggesting that the welfare of tenants is the responsibility of the State not the landlord. Thus powerful rent control was disapproved and eviction supported. There was also a large amount of compensation to be paid to both landlords and tenants in the different courts, who should assist the disadvantaged by benefits, always unlikely in those countries at present.

A third problem is that these ECtHR and ECSR decisions together limit housing policy tools for States and all increase the possibilities of landowner profiteering at the expense of the State, whether by guaranteed profit or by benefits for tenants. Sometimes the interests of landlords and tenants in practical terms run together in extracting State support for insiders.[887]

These decisions do not support balance between landlords and tenants, nor between insiders and outsiders. It is too soon for such European invention, even if this could cater for local conditions. The limiting of subsidy for social housing by the EU and these inconsistent rulings by the ECtHR and ESCR on rent levels restric housing policy in ways that are incoherent when taken together.

10.5 Reform

Lindbeck and Snower (2002) suggested reforms to increase the voice of outsiders. This section concerns such reform, including adapting existing institutions, although simplification of French procedure is still essential. Reducing social landlords' focus on rent, and increasing transparency would also help, as would reforms outside housing.

10.5.1 More reform for social housing

Lindbeck and Snower (2002: 79) said: 'Insofar as insiders have more favourable opportunities than outsiders, policies that create a more level playing field in the labour market can improve both efficiency and equity. This is so regardless of what form the insider–outsider distinction takes.' They did not suggest reducing insiders' advantages because this was not Pareto improving, here meaning it would reduce welfare. There would be no point in turning poor insider-tenants into outsiders by trying to help outsiders.

Snower and Lindbeck argued for helping outsiders by reducing insiders' power or giving outsiders a greater voice. Consequently, tenant representatives in allocation commissions and social landlords' governance should be balanced by people representing the disadvantaged, perhaps from the *associations*. Since outsiders would still be a minority and still suffer stigma, they need access to effective sanction for housing failures, through some effective champion.

Any reform of allocation would have to be a simplification of the process, to reduce its impossible and compulsory complexity, fragmentation and opacity that frustrated most of the actors interviewed. This would necessarily involve an enforced tightening-up of allocation criteria, so that agreed national and local decisions about who should be housed were not constantly being re-opened by any housing actor.

Allocation could alternatively be delegated to any person or body that could be locally trusted to carry it out, without fear or favour, within any existing and effective local arrangements that could be explained to the public. The MIILOS had proved effective and could perhaps help more with enforcement of allocation principles at earlier allocation stages.

The prefecture had consistently failed to sufficiently help the disadvantaged by unambiguously policing provision for them. It had been weakened by having the most needy candidates and was also unable to penalize local actors; obliged to make concessions whilst negotiating multiple agreements; excessively busy; distracted by social mix; ceding the instruments of social assistance to the

Housing some of the disadvantaged

underfunded *département*; facing enormous coordination problems; and processing mind-numbing amounts of detailed documentation. The State had not yet found a balance between supervision and delegation of powers in decentralization.

At the time of this study, social landlords had similar upfront construction funding, whether taking disadvantaged tenants or not. This did not cover social tenants' subsequent problems and increased focus on rent. It encouraged selecting the minimum level of disadvantage after construction that still qualified for subsidy. Czischke, (2005: 10) said:

> Some costs are linked to lower income and are easy to estimate, whereas other costs arise from a smaller capacity to control tenant's risks in terms, for example, of non-payment, damage, lack of satisfaction of sitting tenants, increased administrative costs and social assistance which can only be assessed from a dynamic point of view after the event, and not from a static point of view beforehand.

Many social landlords would do more if appropriately funded 'after the event', addressing real social problems, thus reducing focus on rent and insiderness.

This same problem of upfront construction funding also affected mayors, who in my sample were concerned about disadvantage and often had the dynamism to help their community. Mayors' inclination to help would be assisted by a properly funded increase in mayors' public order obligations[888] for housing need as it arose, not primarily for construction. French people can apply for housing anywhere, so that social landlords and mayors who allowed generous access to the disadvantaged were punished with large numbers of potentially expensive residents. A fear of this can discourage generosity or encourage exclusive, high-priced enclaves.

Larger groups of mayors in *communautés* were less narrowly exclusionary and could be empowered collectively for all local government allocations across a larger area than currently. Mayors might have to be persuaded to accept this, with appropriate funding. Some local insiderness might be unavoidable, because allowing people to apply nationwide in all circumstances seemed unworkable and was effectively unregulated.

Housing the disadvantaged might often encounter local resistance. The UK has had priorities for disadvantaged groups for social housing since the 1930s and it took a long time for this to be effective. For public allocation decisions, tenants, social landlords and employees are not allowed any personal influence in the allocation process, with detailed criteria settled by the local council within a national framework.[889] There are some problems even now (Cowan *et al.* 2008).

10.5.2 Reform outside social housing

Social housing was strongly affected, not just by insiderness but by other problems in the housing market as a whole. Chapter 9 suggests that the homeless, people in hostels, people in debt, victims of domestic violence, single parents, young people and ethnic minorities could be stigmatized and excluded from both social and private rental markets. Poverty exacerbated these difficulties.[890] The effects of ethnicity, debt and household instability showed the multi-factorial nature of housing problems generally.

The law could take a less severe approach to debt than that described in section 9.2 (p. 206) or help single parents, mainly women and children, stay in their homes more than it does. There are, of course, already many and substantial moves in that direction, including some ideas the UK could copy,[891] but particular applications of French law can cause extra pressure on social housing stock.[892] This is because they had policy purposes other than keeping these families in their homes. An example of this problem is the gaps in injunctive protection for battered women and their children,[893] which could force these towards social housing. Shared custody also caused a shortage of family homes, because of double provision for insiders' children, despite some outsiders being homeless.[894]

Institutional racism was an unexpectedly large factor in exclusion from social housing. Official colour-blindness hid discrimination rather than promoting impartiality. The absence of systematic, effective mechanisms to trace and avoid indirect or hidden race discrimination in allocations was extremely serious, particularly when taken with the redevelopment and breaking up of ethnic minority areas.[895]

Discrimination, poverty, and often larger family size, meant inadequacy of housing available to ethnic minorities. Recently, Brouant (2011) found that one in two applications under the *opposable* right to housing were foreign, as against 13.54 per cent for the population as a whole, suggesting the seriousness of this housing exclusion.

10.6 Conclusion

This book began by asking whether social housing could provide the solution to housing the disadvantaged. In France, social landlords did not provide this solution to the extent expected. The author may have had cultural expectations that social landlords would cater for need, but this perception was shared by many French interviewees in the study. This priority is now also effectively found in EU competition law subsidy limitations.

The French priority for the disadvantaged created an obligation of result bedevilled by enforcement problems and the promotion of other local interests.

Housing some of the disadvantaged

The right to housing was vague and limited by other principles, by the allocation procedure and by the necessity for tenants to pay the rent. Those in difficulty 'by reason of insufficiency of financial resources or their conditions of existence'[896] under the right to housing were those least likely to find social housing in general.

Solidarity was the indispensible basis for the French welfare system, permitting both regulatory coercion and beneficence,[897] but with historically created institutions which represented insiders, as contracting parties to a common fund, but not outsiders. Perhaps these origins in contract law and in consent have diffuse effects on housing actors: a culture of negotiation, an independent-mindedness, a creativity of action, and mutual respect in the midst of disputes, but also a tendency to treat as optional national policies viewed as unreasonable and as subjected to their personal consent, backed up by their constitutional rights.

There was no lack of effort by local actors to help different groups. Social landlords could not meet their conflicting objectives and built mainly for general purposes. Managing those with special needs was not the normal function of social landlords except in partnership with others, or with scarce packages of support. Social landlords were also limited by other factors including mayors' powers, the funding regime, different local institutions, local land prices and tight budgets.

Most local actors interviewed were concerned about the blockage of housing for the disadvantaged – a sclerosis of the housing market. This system provided subsidy for many not needing it, was expensive to run and not transparent to the public, distorting their housing choices. Construction funding helped the disadvantaged to a very limited extent. Social housing allocation has an important role in diverting the purposes of social housing to the myriad preoccupations of particular actors.

Satisfying very local demands provided a strong spatial and political dimension to insiderness. This helped produce patchiness of provision between with poor and rich *communes*. Because this localism was unlawful, it could not be reasonably controlled. Size mattered, both at the level of local government and for social landlords, with larger organizations being more detached from local policies.

Insider–outsider theory helped explain many things. Long-term institutionalized bargaining procedures produced strong advantages for existing tenants, locals and employees. An effect of this insiderness was that outsiders were stigmatized, based on stereotyping. Social norms supporting this included: concerns for eviction rather than access; the favouring of workers and stable families; debt aversion, social mix and objections to *communautarisme* by ethnic minorities.

How does such a policy failure help with the problem of how to house disadvantaged people? Certainly the potential for French social housing to house disadvantaged people was realized in places and this residualization is increasing,[898] within broader or different purposes for social housing. This book hopes to help, with ideas for ways to reform which increase the capacity of social housing to receive the disadvantaged, thus contributing to French efforts towards this aim.

This study concerns housing disadvantaged people, but does not rule out other uses for social housing or models of allocation, in a Europe of great diversity and varied local conditions. Social landlords simply represent a collection of useful characteristics, which vary everywhere. They might construct in ways and in places where the private sector will not, support intermediate housing or contribute to neighbourhood renewal or general housing where there is shortage. Many of these uses are temporary.

Not-for-profit status is a major social advantage for any landlord, not just social landlords, reducing the cost of housing and not always pressing for high rents, provided tenants can pay. Most of us value landlords who care for tenants in pragmatic ways and do not collectively exclude the needy. Unfortunately, social landlords can absorb public aids without housing the disadvantaged, with consequent inadequate provision elsewhere. This is part of the mischief of insiderness, targeted by the Competition Commission, although this policy could be less of a blunt instrument.

The interdependence of public and private housing markets means that the high level of insiderness in social housing can adversely affect the market as a whole. Social housing can be a solution, but also part of the problem, varying with current market conditions. This means a cost benefit analysis weighing the purposes of social housing against the effect on the whole market of the particular types of insiderness on the market, detail by detail, law by law. If extra public subsidy for social landlords was justified because of their mission to house the disadvantaged, it should be paid to social landlords who actually did house the disadvantaged, including when need arose after construction.

The theory might explain the mechanisms of the French housing crisis. This sense of crisis normalized continually trying to rescue insiders, exacerbating the insiderness and distributional problems causing these difficulties. This was not simply a general shortage of homes. For a lawyer, insiderness must be a matter of the detail of policies, processes and practices to mitigate but not displace economic processes – a question of what is possible.

Unitary housing markets and their wholesale manipulation of housing markets may be destined to fade, even without Competition Commission regulation, as a highly regulated and funded market model in a Europe of restricted budgets. Nonetheless its insight remains into the possible uses of interdependence between public and private sectors to keep rents reasonable and encourage landlordism. EU policy risks loss of valuable local experience of regulating housing markets. More information is needed before regulation.

The element of housing policy that is slowest to change, is the law of property and tenures, which is even slower than housing construction. It is knotted in with varied historic national conflictual experiences. Knowledge of culturally entrenched European tenures and related institutions is in its infancy, and requires more research. This probably means a primacy of subsidiarity for housing to ensure efficient local response to problems. This means slow change, respecting local historic settlements of social conflicts between landlords and tenants, and between insiders and outsiders, for fear of reopening those conflicts in different modern form in social unrest, riots or even terrorism.

Without reform the French outlook for the disadvantaged was looking bleak. The law could be applied in such a way as to displace priorities to help. Social mix was intended to improve the life chances of the disadvantaged but was implemented to reduce the available housing. The *opposable* right to housing was intended to ensure housing. It helped some, but ensnared the *associations* in bureaucratic procedures and litigation which probably reduced their ability to react quickly in an emergency. The army of French volunteers were unable to help the disadvantaged as much as they would have liked.

It might seem odd, initially, to use economic theory to suggest that welcoming disadvantaged outsiders into any housing would improve the functioning of the housing market. But excess insiderness can mean that even insiders have a difficult time by a freezing up of the market. To reform French social housing, people have to be convinced that disadvantaged outsiders could improve the position for everyone and therefore be in the general interest, an insight into market dysfunction. The way social mix was applied to benefit insiders showed a lack of such conviction. It is a bad situation when social housing apparently houses the disadvantaged more than it actually does.

Appendix 1: methodological detail

This appendix contains supplementary information about some of the legal considerations and about survey design: the method, the selection of interviewees, factors taken into account and the topic guides. Please note that all translations from the French are by the author, unless in an English text or cited translation.

A1.1 Legal considerations

Comparative law theory helped formulate the original research question for this study: 'How do you house people on a low income?' Zweigert and Kötz (1998: 34) suggested that comparative questions should be formulated as a function like this. This cuts across the boundaries of different legal disciplines, which actually made this study more difficult. Early on, describing both English and French law became impossible because of extensive non-equivalence of many kinds of law in this subject area.

Foster (2006: 7) argued that single-country studies could still be implicitly comparative. Comparative law: 'consists of the study of phenomena within single systems, conducted from, or bearing in mind, the viewpoint of a lawyer trained in another system, a view from the outside, with a consequent comparative slant.' As an English lawyer, qualifying as a solicitor in 1978, the author has a 'view from the outside'.

Zweigert and Kötz (1998: 35)[899] strongly advocated a finding of similarity between legal systems, even going so far as to imply that the researchers are likely to be incorrect if they cannot find this similarity of function. This conventional approach to post-war consensus has diplomatic advantages in allowing lawyers to communicate without quarrels and to find what they have in common, a European common core. Not every comparative lawyer agrees (Legrand 1996).[900] Some areas, particularly property, are more different than others. Now, harmonization is so far developed that differences are becoming more important, as highlighted by neglected areas of detailed comparison such as this.

Some economists feel less constrained in seeking difference. La Porta *et al.* (2008) summarized a decade of economic studies finding persistent and pervasive differences between common-law and civil-law countries, including a different style of social control of economic life and different economic outcomes. This relied on both statistical data and a limited account of law.

La Porta *et al.* also found that nineteenth-century common law property rights were more strongly protected in common law countries than in civil law countries. French property rights are strongly expressed (above, p. 64), but not necessarily better protected. Perhaps the strong French expression of the right to property was then necessary to push against difficulties in realizing those rights.

La Porta *et al.* identified other civil law system characteristics including controlled labour markets, more State intervention and formalism. The first two could also be linked to property rights, because they relate directly to implementation of French 'insiderness' in property markets and the reaction to that in labour and tenant movements (see Chapter 3). The third factor, formalism, could have a role in rejecting disadvantaged social housing candidates who have difficulty with process.

Despite extensive similarities in the social histories of social housing in England and France, it is reasonable to look for reasons for the lower proportion of disadvantaged people housed in France than England (see Table 2.2, p. 49) in institutional and procedural differences.[901] The legal problem lies in historically rooted differences in principles, but there are many other factors.

Lawyers, when explaining current issues to a foreign audience, can take for granted their own basic system history, features and assumptions, in the same way that occupants of a home move around the furniture, barely noticing it.[902] The different legal taxonomy around property and welfare might explain some of the differences between civil law and common law systems uncovered by La Porta *et al.* (2008).

La Porta *et al.* might be criticised for a lack of depth of legal study. What then, is rigour for a study like this book? Rigour consists in making available the maximum amount of primary data, preferably in a form understandable to the particular audience, in this case a general audience including lawyers. Law is a species of data and correctly cited in detail in this book where needed, but an applied account must focus on effects not legal philosophy. Happily, practical French legal work in this area also extensively cites sociological and economic work and official reports.[903]

The twin requirements of accessibility of data and generalization in this book often mean using sociological data rather than legal data. An example is that the author read all through provisions on land taxation in the four volumes of the C.G.I. (the General Tax Code), to find extensive tax reliefs benefitting social landlords, but then mainly cited statistics to show this briefly. The English general legal reader should be aware French legal conventions are different, with different distinctions between 'primary' and 'secondary' legal sources[904] and greater generalization,[905] which cannot be fully explained here.

This book also makes brief allusion to the English law, necessarily without legally sufficient detail or exposition, in a book about France. There are special sociological reasons for this here. The English lawyers' attitudes should be as explicit as possible. A general sociological insight is that objectivity is conditioned by the background of the observer (Gilbert 2001). That conditioning should be exposed, as it casts light on the results. It also helps an international audience unfamiliar with English law and can suggest future comparisons or assist reform.

Both Zweigert and Kötz (1998) and Watson (1974) urged tolerance for comparative law because of its technical difficulty and the increased chance of error in trying to understand another legal system. This is increasingly necessary today for anyone seeking an overview of modern legal systems in a climate of specialization. This is an important task for the comparative lawyer, to counter the fragmentary processes of legal specialization.

Appendix 1: methodological detail

A1.2 Survey method and questions

A qualitative study was used here as particularly suitable for 'how' questions (Arber 2001), such as how social housing allocation works, particularly since Bourgeois's study (1996) was also qualitative. Insider–outsider theory was normally examined by quantitative rather than qualitative evidence, but the qualitative option helped when considering local variations and complexity in an area with inadequate statistics.

ANIL (the National Agency for Information for Housing) helped trace interviewees through the Departmental Housing Information Offices (ADILs) in the areas chosen and these supplied local information. My English identity might have affected interviewees, either through caution with a foreign visitor, or a risk of being seen as 'official' because of the help from ANIL and the ADILs. In fact, interviewees were frank about problems and friendly. Being English meant the process could be fully explained to someone not expected to understand.

Interviewees were found using a 'network' method (Arber 2001: 63), because interviews were sought with senior people, who might require some verification or introduction of the interviewer. These interviewees were chosen because they could understand and explain complexities, including local contractualization. This meso-sample generally dealt with the middle range of policy between the national level and local implementation by street-level bureaucrats.

Broad questions were asked across many subject areas to investigate what factors local actors thought problematic. This approach was supported by Strauss and Corbin (1998), who proposed that theory emerges from the data (grounded theory). Yin (2002: 29) suggested that this typically avoided specifying theoretical propositions at the outset, but a sufficient blueprint for the study should already exist to provide a structure for enquiry. There were already theoretical ideas behind this study, but this approach facilitated discovery of new factors, such as divorce. Interviews were taped and transcribed, producing around 163,000 words, which were manually coded.

Grounded theory also allowed the application of insider–outsider theory after the interviews, because of its good fit for the evidence. Insider–outsider theory describes a wider range of effects than Bourgeois's explanation of public and private motivation on similar evidence.

Insider–outsider theory also tends to be morally more neutral, and as much a description of human behaviour as economic theory. It does not assume either altruism or lack of altruism in actors driven by their economic circumstances. French exploration of failure to house the disadvantaged in social housing is not new, but insider–outsider theory additionally shows what sort of distortion of the law is to be expected and how to compensate for it, in order to achieve policy objectives.

A1.3 Factors taken into account

After seeking a balanced representation of actors in the allocation process, my sample was designed so far as possible to balance regional differences, party politics, land prices and demand for social housing. Survey questions included financial, political and local policy issues but there were other possible factors as well.

Land prices were high in the Ile-de-France area,[906] which could have affected Bourgeois's study (1996). The sample sought a mix of land prices because this might affect

Housing Disadvantaged People

whether social landlords could afford to house lower income tenants, either because they had to charge higher rents or because poor tenants were financially risky. Central Paris had the highest land prices in France, but it was impractical to study this area because of the distortions of government and heritage buildings. The Hauts de Seine had the second highest land prices, whilst the other two areas had a mix of medium and low land prices.[907]

Both long waiting lists for social housing or insufficient demand could affect the nature or quality of candidates. In England there was difficulty in letting in some parts of the North of England during the study (Cole *et al*,. 1999). The Nord seemed similar to the North of England with historic coal, steel and textile industries with difficulties of transition. It was unexpected that all regions studied had long waiting lists, and the reasons for this would reward future study. Areas with low demand for social housing might produce different results and were not studied.

These groups were interviewed:

- Senior managers or directors of **social landlords** involved in allocation in every kind of public and private social landlord across the regions. Private social landlords interviewed were of varied sizes and had varied shareholders.
- **Elected representatives** (particularly **mayors**) and **civil serv**ants from every level of local government, except the region, and from the prefecture and their technical services (all referred to as 'state actors').
- Extra comment came from *associations*, voluntary bodies assisting disadvantaged people, as outside the allocation process but seeing its effects.

Interviews could not be arranged with the CIL on the available timescale and those contacted did not seem interested.

Obtaining political balance between left and the right in the elected representatives interviewed was not easy. This should be explicit provided it did not threaten anonymity. Only three mayors were interviewed, two of the political right and one of the left. There was a political balance of sorts, because the overall political control of the Hauts de Seine was of the right, the control of the Nord was of the left, and Lyon was mixed. Le Grand Lyon was controlled by the left whilst the *département* was of the right.

Civil servants in the DDE and the Prefecture were interviewed, but not in the DDASS.[908] Thus, regrettably, no social workers could be interviewed, although other actors commented about them.

Anonymity means mentioning either the approximate political orientation of politicians or their region, but not both. A 'state actor' in this book refers to both civil servants and elected local representatives, excluding mayors, to better protect their anonymity, given their small numbers. Anonymity also often means mentioning the region of the interviewee or their position, but not both. Finally, the gender of the interviewees cited in this book is not necessarily their real gender.

A1.4 The questions asked

Topic guides were intended to invite explanations of policy with descriptions and comment on the allocation process. Actors were also asked their views on legal principles (particularly rights), about the effect of local policies to support tenants and those excluded from housing and about changes since Bourgeois's (1996) study. A short preliminary questionnaire provided basic information in advance, for example, the size and location of

Appendix 1: methodological detail

social housing stock and extent of reservations. The different involvement in allocation of actors meant six slightly different topic guides.

The final topic guides prepared for the Nord are below, the last area studied. Alterations were slight, for example, inserting a question on divorce when raised by the very first interview. Actors with less involvement in allocation could be asked more contextual and local questions about disadvantage and local policies. Numbering discontinuities in the question lists below relate to the master questionnaire controlling the consistency of all the questions.

A. A civil servant or employee within in a social landlord

A1 The role of the actor

1.a   What is your role concerning the allocation of social housing?

A2 The allocation of social housing

A2.1 Questions concerning homes reserved for the respective proposers

2.1.a   I know that there are reservations of social homes, but in what proportion are the homes in fact allocated to the candidates of the different proposers?
2.1.b   How do you get on with the proposers?

A2.2 Questions on the allocation criteria

2.2.a   Are the acceptance criteria for a candidate for the prefectural contingent different to those for the communal contingent?
2.2.b   In what way?
2.2.c   To what extent do allocation actors insist that the housing candidate should be local?
2.2.d   Do you personally agree with the social housing allocation criteria for social homes imposed on your organization?
2.2.e   Why? (or why not?)

A2.3 Questions concerning the allocation process

2.3.a   (If a SAHLM) – What are the characteristics of the allocation commission?
2.3.b   I would like you to describe to me the allocation process from the reception of an application.

Prompts:
2.3.c   Who receives the candidates at your organization and where are they received?
2.3.d   What happens between the reception of the application and when it goes before the allocation commission?
2.3.e   What enquiries are made of all candidates?
2.3.f   In what circumstances will a *dossier* be rejected before the allocation commission?

2.3.g By whom?
2.3.h Are there allocations which do not pass before the allocation commission, that are made by a direct decision of the social landlord?
2.3.i In what circumstances?
2.3.j How many?
2.3.k Approximately what proportion of applications are rejected by the commission and why?
2.3.l How does the allocation commission decide between candidates who all have need of a home?
2.3.m In these cases, which of the criteria is the most important?
2.3.n In your opinion, is there race discrimination by the process of allocation of social homes?
2.3.o In what way?
2.3.p Does your organization reject candidates who have been accepted by the allocation commission?
2.3.q What sort of candidate?
2.3.r Does this happen often?[909]
2.3.s Is an insufficiency of financial resources a reason to reject an application at any stage?
2.3.t What is the effect of divorces on allocations?
2.3.u Do you take candidates proposed by *associations*?
2.3.v Do you insist on a guarantee for this or for the candidates in general?
2.3.w Are you aware of any irregularities concerning the implementation of the law of the allocation of social homes?
2.3.x Do you think that the system is sufficiently egalitarian and transparent?
2.3.y Why? (or why not)?
2.3.z How would you evaluate the process of allocation of social homes in the department?

A3 The right to housing and social mix

A3.1 Questions concerning the right to housing and social mix

3.1.a. What do you understand by the right to housing?
3.1.b How do you implement this right?
3.1.c The High Committee for the Housing of Disadvantaged People proposes an enforceable right to housing. What do you think of this idea?
3.1.d How does your organization implement the principle of social mix?
3.1.e Do you find that there might be a conflict between your objectives concerning disadvantaged people and your obligations for social mix?
3.1.f How can you reconcile them?
3.1.g The principle of social mix and the reservations in favour of the CIL (for employees) seem to reduce the housing available for the most disadvantaged. To what extent is this true?

A3.2 Questions concerning the populating of geographical sites

3.2.a Do you have housing estates which are stigmatized?

Appendix 1: methodological detail

Prompt: Does this have an effect on employers?[910]
3.2.b (If yes) What changes would you like to see to improve this?
3.2.c How do you manage the populating of sites in general?

A3.3 Questions concerning the support for tenants in difficulty

3.3.a What measures internal to your organization exist to support tenants in difficulty?
3.3.b What measures external to the organization are the most efficient to help these people?
3.3.c To what extent do these measures succeed?
3.3.d Are eviction procedures pursued promptly within normal timescales by your organization?
3.3.e What do you think of these procedures?
3.3.f Can they be improved?
3.3.g To what extent are eviction procedures respected by all landlords?

A3.4 Questions on the usefulness of local partnerships to give access to a home or to support people in difficulty

3.4.a I will give you a list of the legal instruments in the Nord. Please tell me to what extent these arrangements improve the position of disadvantaged people locally.

- The PDLPD
- The Programmes Locaux de L'Habitat
- The Chârtes Intercommunales de Logement
- The Collective Departmental Agreements with the social landlords who engage themselves to take a certain number of people in difficulty (the replacement for the POPs[280])
- Any other agreement?[911]

3.4.b How has the FSL improved the position of people in difficulty in the Nord?
3.4.c Is the financing of the FSL satisfactory?
3.4.d What evaluation would you make concerning the effect of local contractualization to help people on a low income?

A4 Financing

4.a Is the financing for a deprived tenant sufficient?
4.b How would you reform this?
4.c What incentive exists for social landlords to take deprived people?
4.d What action by the public authorities would incentivize you to take a larger proportion of deprived people?
4.e Does your organization have problems with solvency?
4.f (If yes) Why?
4.g If your organization makes a profit, who receives it (SAHLM only)?
4.h Why do social landlords not take loans from private banks?
4.i What reforms would you like to see for the financing of social landlords on general?

A5 The reforms and decentralization

5.a Please describe the local changes in the administration of social housing brought about by the decentralization in recent years.
5.b What is the effect of this on the allocation of social homes?
5.c What is the effect of the transfers of the personnel of the prefectures or the DDE to the local authorities?
5.d What changes were contemplated in the Nord with the recent reforms?
5.e What effect will this have on the allocation of social homes to the most disadvantaged in the Nord?

A6 The problems or the advantages of the EPCI[912]

6.a (If it is the case) What is the effect of the administration of housing by the EPCI in the Nord on the policy of housing the poorest people?

A7 General questions

7.a What are the principal problems of the allocation of social housing?
7.b What reforms would you like to see which would contribute to the housing of people on a low income?

B. A mayor of local councillor concerned with social housing

B1 The role of the actor

1.a What positions do you occupy as a mayor to do with social housing?
1.b Of what political party are you a member?

B2 The allocation of social housing

B2.1 Questions concerning homes reserved for the respective proposers

2.1.a Do you think that the *commune* ought to have a larger proportion of the available places in social housing?
2.1.b Why?
2.1.c Does your *commune* reserve places in return for finance?
2.1.d How many places?
2.1.e How do you get on with the other proposers?

B2.2 Questions on the allocation criteria

2.2a
2.2b
2.2c } As A2.2 a–e
2.2d
2.2.e

2.2.f Do you think that your powers concerning the allocation of social homes are sufficient?

Prompt: (If yes), what powers should be added?

Appendix 1: methodological detail

B2.3 Questions concerning the allocation process

2.3.a I would like you to describe to me the allocation process from the reception of an application.

Prompts:
2.3.b Who receives the applicants to the *commune* and where?
2.3.c What happens between the reception of the application and when it goes before the allocation commission?
2.3.d What enquiries are made of all candidates?
2.3.e In what circumstances will a *dossier* be rejected before the allocation commission?
2.3.f By whom?
2.3.g Are there allocations which do not pass before the allocation commission, that are made by a direct decision of the social landlords?
2.3.h In what circumstances?
2.3.i How many?
2.3.j How many candidates do you present per available home in the social stock?
2.3.k Approximately what proportion of applications are rejected by the commission and why?
2.3.l How does the allocation commission decide between candidates who all have need of a home?
2.3.m In these cases, which of the criteria is the most important?
2.3.n In your opinion, is there race discrimination in the process of allocation of social homes?
2.3.o In what way?
2.3.p Is an insufficiency of financial resources a reason to reject an application at any stage?
2.3.q What is the effect of divorce on allocations?
2.3.r What sanctions are there to be feared for an irregular allocation process?
2.3.s Do you think that the system is sufficiently egalitarian and transparent?
2.3.t Why? (or why not)?
2.3.u How would you evaluate the process of allocation of social homes in the department?

B3. The right to housing and social mix

B3.1 Questions concerning the right to housing and social mix

3.1.a What do you understand by the right to housing?
3.1.b The High Committee for the Housing of Disadvantaged People proposes an enforceable right to housing. What do you think of this idea?
3.1.c How does your organization implement the principle of social mix?

3.1.d
3.1.e
3.1.f } As for A3.1.e–g.
3.1.g

Housing Disadvantaged People

B3.2 Questions concerning the populating of geographical sites

3.2.a
3.2.b } As 3.2.a–c.
3.2.c

B3.3 Questions concerning the support for tenants in difficulty

3.3.a What measures that exist in the *commune* are the most effective in supporting tenants in difficulty?
3.3.b To what extent do these measures succeed?
3.3.c Are eviction procedures pursued promptly within normal timescales in your *commune*?
3.3.d What do you think of these procedures?
3.3.e Can they be improved?
3.3.f To what extent are eviction procedures respected by all landlords?

B3.4 Questions on the usefulness of partnerships to give access to a home or to support people in difficulty

3.4.a
3.4.b
3.4.c } As for A3.4.a–d.
3.4.d

B3.5 Questions concerning people excluded from social housing

3.5.a What part do you take in local action concerning people excluded from social housing (apart from allocation)?
3.5.b The report of the High Committee for the Housing of Disadvantaged People (2004) judges that the access to a permanent home works badly, with the privileged access routes (reservations) and a blockage if this is delegated to the mayors. Do you agree with this analysis?
3.5.c Why (or why not)?
3.5.d To what extent do the services for the homeless result in the provision of a decent home?
3.5.e What sort of reform would result in an improvement of the situation?

B4 Financing

4.a } As for A.4.a, b.
4.b
4.c What action by the public authorities would incentivize the social landlords to take a larger proportion of deprived people?
4.d Why do social landlords not take loans from private banks?
4.e What reforms would you like to see for the financing of social landlords in general?

Appendix 1: methodological detail

B5 The reforms and decentralization

5.a
5.b
5.c
5.d } As for A5.a–d.

B6 The problems or the advantages of the EPCI

6.a   What is (generally) the division of powers between *communes* and the *communauté* concerning housing?
6.b   Does this work well?

B7 General questions

7.a
7.b } As for A7.a, b.

C. A member of the administrative board or high grade civil servant in an EPCI (*Communauté*)

(*Communauté* board members are councillors or mayors of the constituent communes.)

C1 The role of the actor

1.a   What is your role concerning the allocation of social housing
1.b   What political party are you a member of? (if a counsellor)

C2 The allocation of social housing

C2.1 Questions concerning homes reserved for the respective proposers

2.1.a   Do you think that the *commune* or *communauté* ought to have a larger proportion of the available places in social housing?
2.1.b   Why?
2.1.c   Does your *commune* (or *communauté*) reserve places in return for finance?
2.1.d   How many places?
2.1.e   How do you get on with the other proposers?

C2.2 Questions on the allocation criteria

2.2.a
2.2.b
2.2.c
2.2.d
2.2.e } As A2.2.a–e

2.2.f   Do you think that your powers concerning the allocation of social homes are sufficient?

267

C2.3 Questions concerning the allocation process

2.3.a I would like you to descrbe to me the allocation process from the reception of an application.

Prompts:

2.3.b Who receives the applicants and where?
2.3.c What happens between the reception of the application and when it goes before the allocation commission?
2.3.d What enquiries are made of all candidates?
2.3.e In what circumstances will a *dossier* be rejected before the allocation commission?
2.3.f By whom?
2.3.g Are there allocations which do not pass before the allocation commission, that are made by a direct decision of the social landlords?
2.3.h In what circumstances?
2.3.i How many?
2.3.j Approximately what proportion of applications are rejected by the commission and why?
2.3.k How does the allocation commission decide between candidates who all have need of a home?
2.3.l In these cases, which of the criteria is the most important?
2.3.m In your opinion, is there race discrimination by the process of allocation of social homes?
2.3.n In what way?
2.3.o Is an insufficiency of financial resources a reason to reject an application at any stage?
2.3.p What is the effect of divorce on allocations?
2.3.q Are you aware of any irregularities concerning the application of social housing allocation?
2.3.r What sanctions are there to be feared for an irregular allocation process?
2.3.s Do you think that the system is sufficiently egalitarian and transparent?
2.3.t Why or why not?
2.3.u How would you evaluate the process of allocation of social homes in the department?

C3. The right to housing and social mix

C3.1 Questions concerning the right to housing and social mix

3.1.a What do you understand by the right to housing?
3.1.b The High Committee for the Housing of Disadvantaged People proposes an enforceable right to housing. What do you think of this idea?
3.1.c How do you implement the principle of social mix in your *communauté*?
3.1.d ⎫
3.1.e ⎬ As for A3.1.e–g.
3.1.f ⎭

Appendix 1: methodological detail

C3.2 Questions concerning populating of geographical sites

3.2.a
3.2.b } As A3.2.a–c.
3.3.c

C3.3 Questions concerning the support for tenants in difficulty

3.3.a What measures existing in the *communauté* are the most efficient at supporting tenants in difficulty?
3.3.b To what extent do these measures succeed?
3.3.c Are the eviction procedures pursued promptly within normal timescales in your *commune*?
3.3.d What do you think of these procedures?
3.3.e Can they be improved?
3.3.f To what extent are allocation procedures respected by all landlords?

C3.4 Questions on the usefulness of partnerships to give access to a home or to support people in difficulty

3.4.a
3.4.b
3.4.c } As for A3.4.a–d.
3.4.d

C3.5 Questions concerning people excluded from social housing

3.5.a What part do you take in local action concerning people excluded from social housing (apart from allocation)?
3.5.b } As for B3.5.b, c.
3.5.c
3.5.d To what extent do the services for the homeless result in the provision of a decent home?
3.5.e What sort of reform would result in an improvement of the situation?

C4 Financing

4.a } As A.4.a, b
4.b
4.c As B.4.c
4.d Why do social landlords not take loans from private banks?
4.e What reform would you like to see for the financing of social landlords in general?

C5 The reforms and decentralization

5.a
5.b
5.c } As for A5.a, b, d and e.
5.d

C6 The problems or the advantages of the EPCI

6.a   As A.6.a
6.b   What is, generally, the division of powers between the *communes* and your EPCI?
6.c   Does this work well?

C7 General questions

7.a } As for A7.a, b.
7.b }

D. A civil servant from the DDE who advises on housing

D1 The role of the actor

1.a   What is your personal role concerning social housing?
1.b   And that of the housing service?
1.c   What are the difficulties in the *département* in this respect?

D2 The allocation of social housing

D2.2 Questions on the allocation criteria

2.2.a   Do you personally agree with the allocation criteria for social housing in general?
2.2.b   Why? (or why not)?
2.2.c   To what extent to the allocation actors insist that the candidate for a social home should be local?
2.2.d   When the DDE advises on social housing (for example for financing) does it take into account the allocation criteria by the social landlords and local authorities?
2.2.e   If allocations are not in conformity with the criteria in Articles R. 441 to R. 441–2-6 of the C.C.H. and exclude particular populations, what sanctions would you advise the prefect to take?

Prompts: In what context? How does this happen?
2.2.f   Who else is in a position to insist on conformity with these criteria?
2.2.g   To what extent is it probable that such an action will be followed?

D2.3 Questions concerning the allocation process

2.3.a   Are you conscious of irregularities concerning the application of the law of social housing allocation?
2.3.b   In your opinion, is there race discrimination by the process of allocation of social homes?
2.3.c   What is the effect of divorce on allocations?
2.3.d   What sanctions are there to fear concerning the allocation process?
2.3.e   Do you think that the system is sufficiently egalitarian and transparent?

Appendix 1: methodological detail

2.3.f Why or why not?
2.3.g How would you evaluate the process of allocation of social homes in the department?

D3 The right to housing and social mix

D3.1 Questions concerning the right to housing and social mix

3.1.a What do you understand by the right to housing?
3.1.b The High Committee for the Housing of Disadvantaged People proposes an enforceable right to housing. What do you think of this idea?
3.1.c What is your role for the implementation of social mix?
3.1.d It is obligatory under Article L. 305–2, C.C.H., for certain *communes* to have 20% social housing. How many *communes* in the *department* have attained this objective?
3.1.e What progress is there for *communes* which have not attained this proportion?
3.1.f
3.1.g } As for A3.1.e–g.
3.1.h

D3.2 Questions concerning the populating of geographical sites

3.2.a Do you have housing estates in the *department* which are stigmatized?
3.2.b What changes would you like to see to improve this?

D3.3 Questions concerning the support for tenants in difficulty

3.3.a What do you think of the eviction procedures?
3.3.b Can they be improved?
3.3.c To what extent are eviction procedures respected by all landlords?

D3.4 Questions on the usefulness of local partnerships to give access to a home or to support people in difficulty

3.4.a
3.4.b
3.4.c } As for A3.4.a–d.
3.4.d

D3.5 Questions concerning people excluded from social stock

3.5.a What part do you take in local action concerning people excluded from social housing?
3.5.b Please describe the possibilities of shelter for people in difficulty.
3.5.c Is this sufficient?
3.5.d Please describe the major strategies of the prefecture in this matter.

3.5.e How are the prefectural services concerning housing coordinated between the different sections (social services, housing service, DDE)?
3.5.f What public services exist in the *départment* for those who find themselves in an urgent situation?
3.5.g Does this work well?
3.5.h To what extent do these services result in the provision of a decent home?

D4 Financing

4.a What action by the public authorities would incentivise the social landlords to take a larger proportion of disadvantaged people?
4.b Do social landlords have problems with insolvency?
4.c Why?
4.d Please describe briefly the policy of the prefecture to support the construction of social homes (for example zoning, finance or by sanctions for nonconformity).
4.e Why do social landlords not take loans from private banks?
4.f What reforms would you like to see for the financing of social landlords in general?

D5 The reforms and decentralization

5.a
5.b
5.c As A5.a–e.
5.d
5.e

D6 The problems or the advantages of the EPCI

6.a As A6.a

D7 General questions

7.a
     As A7.a, b.
7.b

7.c What reforms would you like to see which would contribute to the housing of people on a low income?

E. A civil servant from the prefectural housing service

E1 The role of the actor

1.a What are the roles of the housing service for housing and social housing services?

E2 The allocation of social homes

E2.1 Questions concerning homes reserved for the respective proposers

2.1.a I know that there are reservations of social homes but in what proportion are the homes in fact allocated to the candidates of the different proposers?

Appendix 1: methodological detail

2.1.b How do you get on with the proposers?
2.1.c Do you believe that the prefectural contingent should represent a higher proportion of available places in social housing?
2.1.d Why?

E2.2 Questions on the allocation criteria

2.2.a ⎫
2.2.b ⎪
2.2.c ⎬ As A2.2a–e.
2.2.d ⎪
2.2.e ⎭

2.2.f Do you think that the powers of the prefecture concerning allocations are adequate?

Prompt: What powers should be added to them?

2.2.g If local authorities are not in conformity with the national criteria and exclude particular populations, what sanctions would you advise the prefect to use?
2.2.h Who else was in a position to insist on conformity with these criteria?

E2.3 Questions concerning the allocation process

2.3.a The housing service manages the departmental unique number for allocation.[913] Does this improve the allocation process?

Prompt: How?

2.3.b Please describe the part of the housing service in the allocation process and how this works form receipt of the application.

Prompts:

2.3.c Who receives candidates who will end up being part of the prefectural contingent and where are they received?
2.3.d What happens between the reception of the application and when it goes before the allocation commission?
2.3.e What enquiries are made of all candidates?
2.3.f In what circumstances will a *dossier* be rejected before the allocation commission?
2.3.g By whom?
2.3.h Are there allocations which do not pass before the allocation commission, that are made by a direct decision of the social landlord?
2.3.i In what circumstances?
2.3.j How many?
2.3.k How many candidates do you present per home available in social stock?
2.3.l Approximately what proportion of applications are rejected by the commission and why?
2.3.m How does the allocation commission decide between candidates who all have need of a home?
2.3.n In these cases, which of the criteria is the most important?

Housing Disadvantaged People

2.3.o In your opinion, is there race discrimination by the process of allocation of social homes?
2.3.p In what way?
2.3.q Is an insufficiency of financial resources a reason to reject an application at any stage?
2.3.r Are you aware of any irregularities concerning the implementation of the law of the allocation of social homes?
2.3.s What sanctions are there to fear for an irregular allocation process?
2.3.t Do you think that the system is sufficiently egalitarian and transparent?
2.3.u Why? (or why not)?
2.3.v How would you evaluate the process of allocation of social homes in the department?

E3 The right to housing and social mix

E3.1 Questions concerning the right to housing and social mix

3.1.a What do you understand by the right to housing?
3.1.b How do you implement this right locally?
3.1.c ⎫
3.1.d ⎬ As for B3.1.b, c.

3.1.e ⎫
3.1.f ⎬ As for A3.1.e–g.
3.1.g ⎭

E3.2 Questions concerning the populating of geographical sites

3.2.a Are there estates of social homes in the Nord which are stigmatized?
3.2.b (If yes) What changes would you like to see to improve this?

E3.3 Questions concerning the support for tenants in difficulty

3.3.a What measures existing in the prefecture are the most efficient to support tenants in difficulty?
3.3.b To what extent do these measures succeed?
3.3.c Please describe the action of the housing service in general to prevent eviction.
3.3.d What do you think of the eviction procedures?
3.3.e Can they be improved?
3.3.f To what extent are eviction procedures respected by all landlords?

E3.4 Questions on the usefulness of local partnerships to give access to a home or to support people in difficulty

3.4.a ⎫
3.4.b ⎬ As for A3.4.a–d
3.4.c ⎪
3.4.d ⎭

Appendix 1: methodological detail

E3.5 Questions concerning people excluded from social stock

3.5.a   What does the housing service do to improve the situation of people excluded from social stock?
3.5.b   Does this work well?
3.5.c   To what extent do the services for the homeless result in the provision of a decent home?
3.5.d   What sort of reform would result in an improvement of the situation?
3.5.e ⎱
3.5.f   ⎰ As for B3.5.b, c

E4 Financing

4.a ⎱
4.b ⎰ As for A4.a, b.

4.c   As for B4.c
4.d   What reforms would you like to see for the financing of social landlords in general?

E5 The reforms and decentralization

5.a ⎱
5.b ⎰ As for A5.a and b.

5.c   What is the effect of transfers of personnel from the prefectures or DDE to the local authorities?

5.d ⎱
5.e ⎰ As for A5.d and e.

E6 The problems or the advantages of the EPCI

6.a   As A6.a

E7 General questions?

7.a ⎱
7.b ⎰ As for A7.a, b.

H. Someone from an *association* which receives disadvantaged people (not CHRS)[914]

H1 The role of the actor

1.a   What is the role of your *association* concerning social housing?

Prompt: For what sort of client?
1.b   Does this *association* form part of one or several networks of *associations*? Describe this briefly please.
1.c   What are the major difficulties in the Nord concerning housing?

H2 The allocation of social housing

H2.1 Questions concerning homes reserved for the respective proposers

2.1.a Can your clients obtain access to a social home without a reservation or through the process of intermediation?[915]
2.1.b Has your *association* had some success in participating in intermediation? To what extent?
2.1.c Do you think that your clients should obtain access to a social home by another route?

H2.2 Questions on the allocation criteria

2.2.a Do you personally agree in general with the allocation criteria in the Nord?
2.2.b Why? (or why not)?
2.2.c To what extent do the allocation actors insist that the candidate for a social home should be local?
2.2.d Do you think that the application of the allocation criteria are sufficiently controlled by the State?
2.2.e In what way could this be improved?

H2.3 Questions concerning the allocation process

2.3.a Please describe your experiences with the allocation process from receipt of the demand

Prompts:
2.3.b What happens to the candidate when he or she makes his or her application?
2.3.c What enquiries are made of all candidates?
2.3.d In what circumstances will a *dossier* be rejected before the allocation commission?
2.3.e By whom?
2.3.f Are there allocations which do not pass before the allocation commission, that are made by a direct decision of the social landlord?
2.3.g In what circumstances?
2.3.h How many?
2.3.i Approximately what proportion of applications are rejected by the commission and why?
2.3.j How does the allocation commission decide between candidates who all have need of a home?
2.3.k In these cases, which of the criteria is the most important?
2.3.l In your opinion, is there race discrimination by the process of allocation of social homes?
2.3.m In what way?
2.3.n Is an insufficiency of financial resources a reason to reject an application at any stage?
2.3.o What is the effect of divorce on allocations?

Appendix 1: methodological detail

2.3.p Do social landlords insist on a guarantee for your candidates in general?
2.3.q Are you aware of any irregularities concerning the implementation of the law of social housing allocation in the Nord?
2.3.r What sanctions are there to be feared for an irregular allocation process?
2.3.s Do you think that the system is sufficiently egalitarian and transparent?
2.3.t Why or why not?
2.3.u How would you evaluate the process of allocation of social homes in the department?

H3 The right to housing and social mix

H3.1 Questions concerning the right to housing and social mix

3.1.a What do you understand by the right to housing?
3.1.b How do you see your role in the implementation of the right to housing?
3.1.c The High Committee for the Housing of Disadvantaged People proposes an enforceable right to housing. What do you think of this idea?
3.1.d
3.1.e } As for A3.1.e–g.
3.1.f

H3.2 Questions concerning populating geographical sites

3.2.a Do you tend to work rather with the public social landlords or the SAHLM?
3.2.b If you find a social home for a client, Where is it probable that he or she will be housed?
3.2.c What do you think of the quality of the homes where your clients are housed?
3.2.d Do you have clients who are badly housed in the social housing stock?
3.2.e How do you manage to help them?
3.2.f Once a person has a social home, do the tenants have difficulty leaving HLM housing?
3.2.g Why? (or why not ?)

H3.3 Questions concerning the support for tenants in difficulty

3.3.a What is your judgment of the value of the support for tenants in difficulty provided by social landlords and their partners?
3.3.b To what extent do these measures succeed?
3.3 c Is there is difference between the support supplied by public social landlords and the SAHLM?

Prompt: (If yes) What is the difference?

3.3.d Are the eviction procedures followed promptly within the normal time periods by social landlords?
3.3.e What do you think of these procedures?
3.3.f Can they be improved?
3.3.g To what extent are allocation procedures respected by all landlords?

Housing Disadvantaged People

H3.4 Questions on the usefulness of partnerships to give access to a home or to support people in difficulty

3.4.a
3.4.b
3.4.c
3.4.d
} As for A3.4.a–d.

H3.5 Questions concerning people excluded from social housing

3.5.a Please describe the possibilities for shelter and for services for the people in difficulty in the Nord.
3.5.b Is this sufficient?
3.5.c To what extent do the services for the homeless result in the provision of a decent home?
3.5.d What sort of people are excluded from social rented housing?
3.5.e What sort of reform would result in an improvement of the situation?

H4 Financing

4.a
4.b
} As A4.a–b.

4.c As B4.c
4.d What reforms would you like to see in the financing of social landlords generally?

H5 The reforms and decentralization

5.a
5.b
5.c
5.d
} As for A5 a–d.

H6 The problems or the advantages of the EPCI

6.a As for A6.a

H7 General questions

7.a
7.b
} As for A7.a–b.

Appendix 2: allocation principles

This is the version from the Code de la construction et de l'habitation (C.C.H.) as at 28 November 2005, the beginning of interviews, taken from the public database, Legifrance (République de France, undated). Past codes can be accessed but were sometimes only amended every few months and there could be missing articles. Apart from Article L. 441, which defines responsibilities, this section contains the main principles.

The sections refer to various local agreements (*conférences*, charters, *réglements*) described above in section 5.3 (p. 127).

Article L. 441

The allocation of social homes participates in the implementation of the right to housing, to satisfy the needs of people of modest financial resources and disadvantaged people.

The allocation of social homes must notably take into account the diversity of demand established locally; it must favour equality of opportunity of applicants and the social mix of towns and neighbourhoods.

Local authorities, depending on their powers, work towards the realization of the objectives mentioned in the previous paragraphs, notably in the framework of *conférences* [*intercommunales du logement*] and intercommunal charters.

Social landlords allocate rented social homes in the framework of the provisions of the present section.

The State supervises the respect for the allocation rules in the allocation of social homes.

Article L. 441-1

The Conseil d'Etat decree envisaged by Article L. 441-2-6 determines the conditions under which homes built, improved or acquired and improved with the financial assistance of the State or giving right to APL, and belonging to HLM organizations or managed by these, are allocated by those organisations. For the allocation of the homes, this decree envisages that account is taken notably of the composition, of the level of resources and the current housing conditions of the household, of the distance from the places of work and the proximity of facilities responding to the needs of the candidates. For the allocation of a home, the professional activity of a household is taken into account if this is a mother's assistant or registered family assistance. It fixes the general criteria for priority for the allocation of homes, notably in favour of disabled people or families having a dependent in a situation of disability, in favour of people who are poorly housed, disadvantaged or suffering particular housing difficulties for financial reasons or relating to their conditions of existence, as well as people in hostels or temporarily housed in transitional establishments and homes. It also fixes the conditions in which the mayor in the *commune d'implantation*[916] of the homes is consulted on the principles governing these allocations and the result of their application. ...

The income ceilings for the allocation of rented social homes are fixed in application of the provisions of the present article are revised annually following the evolution of the minimum wage[917] envisaged by Article L. 141–2 of the Code de travail (labour code).

(Articles preceded by 'R.' indicate decrees of the Conseil d'État, here in its role as advisor and assistant to government rather than its judicial role.)

Article R*.441-3

The allocation commission provided for in Article L. 441-2 proceeds to examine applications, taking account notably of the composition, of the level of financial resources and of the present housing conditions of the household. They also take account of the distance of the place of work and of the proximity of facilities corresponding to the needs of applicants.

Whilst supervising the social mix of towns and neighbourhoods, they allocate the available homes in priority to people deprived of homes or whose application presents an urgent character by reason of the insecurity or unfitness of the home which they occupy, as well as people accumulating economic and social difficulties mentioned in the collective departmental agreement provided for in Article L. 441-1-2 and those sheltered or housed temporarily in transitional establishments or homes.

The other housing applications are dealt with in priority for the benefit of persons defined by the *règlement départementale* provided for in Article L. 441-1-1 and respecting the guidance defined by the *conférences intercommunales* envisaged by Article L. 441-1-5, when they exist.

Notes

Introduction

1 Loi no 90-449 du 31 mai 1990, Art. 1.
2 *La collectivité* indicates the people acting together, in local or national government.
3 Discussed in sections 2.1.2 and 10.4.1 (pp. 37 and 245).
4 Adopted on the 10 December 1948 by the United Nations General Assembly.
5 Author's emphasis.
6 The European Convention for the protection of Human Rights and Fundamental Freedoms (ECHR), Rome, 4 November 1950.
7 Rome, 3 May 1996.
8 Protocol 1 to the ECHR, Rome, 20 March 1952.
9 ECHR, Art. 14, prohibits discrimination. In contrast, consider the motto of the French Republic 'liberty, equality and brotherhood', Article 2 of the '1958 constitution', of 4 October 1958.
10 Directive 2006/123/EC of the European Parliament and of the Council of 12 December 2006 on services in the internal market [2006] OJ L376/36.
11 Section 2.1.4 and 2.1.5 (pp. 39 and 40).
12 Thirty-two texts stating the right to housing or implementing this were listed in the ECSR decision of the *FEANTSA v France,* Complaint No. 39/2006, (ECSR decision, 5 December 2007), paras. 19–52.
13 C.C.H., Art. L. 441.
14 Particularly C.C.H., Art. L. 441-1.
15 See note 12.
16 Fédération européenne des associations travaillant avec les sans-abri.
17 See Kenna (2005) for an account of housing rights across the treaties here.
18 Loi n° 2007-290 du 5 mars 2007. The legislative process took less than a month.
19 See particularly sections 4.1 and 9.5.2 (pp. 85 and 222 for remedies).
20 Section 6.4.2 (p. 151).
21 Art. 17 of the Déclaration des droits de l'homme et du citoyen du 26 août 1789, incorporated into the 1958 Constitution.
22 See note 9.
23 C.C.H., Arts. L. 441 al. 2, L. 441-1-1 al. 1 and R. 441-3 al. 2., see sections 4.2.2 and 7.1.3. (pp. 100 and 163).
24 For access rules see from section 7.1 (p. 159).
25 The ceilings are in Table 2.1 (p. 47).
26 Ch. 7.
27 Particularly section 3.3 (p. 72).

Endnotes

28 Literally, banned place.
29 See section 1.3.1. below (p. 19).
30 See particularly sections 8.1 and 10.2.5 (pp. 184 and 240).
31 See section 7.2 (p. 166) for regional diversity in practice and Chs 7–9 generally for some very local practices.

1 Social landlords and insider–outsider theory

32 All rules are from this period unless otherwise clear from the text.
33 See p. 1.
34 Section 3.2 (p. 63) for conflicts with constitutional rights historically and 4.2 (p. 98) for conflicts with social mix.
35 See Ch.7.
36 See p. 74.
37 Ibid.
38 'Habitat' has wider environmental implications than 'housing'.
39 See pp. 81 and 104.
40 In 2009, HLM organizations started work on 12,300 homes for sale and sold 4,600 existing homes to tenants (USH 2010).
41 Section 3.3.4 (p. 78).
42 Section 6.3 (p. 145).
43 Section 6.1 (p. 137).
44 Non-HLM social landlords are described p. 137ff.
45 Book IV of the C.C.H., particularly Titles I–II.
46 The government could effectively determine model company rules, under Art. R. *423-85, C.C.H.
47 See section 6.1 (p. 137) for their organization and Book IV, Arts. L. 441 to L. 441-15 for common allocation rules (also section 7.1.2, p. 160).
48 C.C.H., Art. L. 411 (statutory mission). Government publications: Ministère de l'Equipement des Transports et du Logement (1998) and government-sponsored research such as Benguigui (1995, 1997); Ballain and Benguigi (2004); Pichon (2005) and Lelévrier (2008), although there are other concerns, particularly the environment, social mix, housing sociology and the effects of construction.
49 By décret (decree) du 27 mars 1954.
50 C.C.H., Art. L. 411.
51 C.C.H., Art. L. 441-1. See Table 2.1 (p. 47) for income ceilings.
52 From ANIL in 2004.
53 Section 3.3.2 (p. 74).
54 Regions can no longer control social landlords.
54 C.C.H., Arts. L. 441 for responsibility for allocation and L. 441-1 for reservations. Civil servants were exempt from income ceilings.
56 This survived piecemeal around Paris, and in the Rhône, including Lyon.
57 Sections 4.1.7 and 9.5.2 (pp. 96 and 222).
58 Loi n° 82-256 du 22 juin 1982.
59 See p. 259.
60 Section 5.1.4 (p. 117).
61 The region, *département*, *communauté*, *commune* and *arrondissement*.
62 The framework for this is elaborated under C.C.H., Art. L. 441-1.
63 C.C.H., Arts., L. 313-1 to L. 313-19-7, with implementing regulations, described there as '*la participation des employers à l'effort de construction*'.

Endnotes

64 UESL (undated). €1.5 billion collected from employees and €2.2 billion from loan repayments in 2007. This was recently renamed 'Action logement'.
65 For the commissions' composition see section 7.4.1 (p. 179).
66 See the special arrangements in section 7.2 (p. 166) and social reports p. 173.
67 Ch. 3 has a short history of this.
68 Ch. 7.
69 Section 2.2.1 (p. 47).
70 Section 1.4.5 (p. 28).
71 For example, Repentin (2005).
72 La Fondation Abbé Pierre pour le logement des défavorisées ('La Fondation Abbé Pierre').
73 See p. 75ff.
74 Section 3.2 (p. 63).
75 Their website usually carries the slogan '*Pas d'expulsion sans relogement*' (no eviction without rehousing), for example, DAL (2007).
76 For example, Mulholland (2005).
77 Not all in Table 1.1 but from the same statistics and that series generally.
78 See list of acknowledgements for some of those consulted.
79 See p. 91.
80 See p. 176.
81 Most-agreements in Section 5.2 (p. 123) required wide consultation.
82 Lindbeck and Snower's (2002) usual terminology.
83 See section 3.3.3 (p. 76) for landlords 'and tenants' organizations.
84 See from ibid. for representative organizations and their privileges.
85 C.C.H., Art. L. 613-3, from 1 November to 15 March.
86 Government (State) permission is needed for physical eviction, *le concours de la force publique.*
87 For an account of French rental law see Ball (2003) and pp. 77ff, 89ff and 152ff.
88 Clear on interview evidence, see p. 180.
89 See section 6.4.2 (p. 151) for how rent is set.
90 From interview evidence.
91 More fully described in section 6.4.2 (p. 151).
92 Loi n° 89-462 du 6 juillet 1989.
93 For incentives to private renting, see note 580, and social landlords' finance, Ch. 6.
94 C.C.H., Art. R. 441-3 for commission responsibility and see section 7.4.1 (p. 179).
95 The 1989 statute, Art. 1, e. See section 4.1.3 (p. 87) for discussion of this balance and state intervention.
96 Section 10.2.5 (p. 240).
97 Section 9.4.2 (p. 214).
98 See also section 8.1.1 and 9.2 (pp. 185 and 206).
99 Section 5.3.3 (p. 130).
100 Private social landlords could distribute a very limited profit.
101 Prescribed clause no.13.
102 Closer inspection contributed, p. 139.
103 Section 7.1.1 (p. 159).
104 Particularly illustrated by Chs 7, 8 and 9.
105 Explained at p. 259.
106 Such as local chambers of commerce, but employers themselves could collect.
107 From UESL.
108 The CIL administer several national housing products, including: housing loans, small grants and guarantees.
109 See 'Acknowledgements'.

Endnotes

2 Exploring the function of social housing

110 See p. 4.
111 Varied non-HLM social housing, providing subsidized holidays for disadvantaged people and affordable holidays generally (Etienne 2004).
112 Lévy-Vroelant *et al.* (2008: 33).
113 Paris had 27 per cent social housing (INSEE 2002).
114 Including debates in the ENHR social housing project, producing Whitehead and Scanlon (2007) and Scanlon and Whitehead (2008).
115 This was work in progress in the above project, leading indirectly to Ghékière (2008).
116 Cowan and Marsh (2005) explain the history of this.
117 Lévy-Vroelant and Tutin (2007: 74).
118 See p. 115.
119 See p. 16ff.
120 The 1989 statute, Arts. 17 and 19, determines rents, with exemption for HLM organizations by Art. 40, al. 1. Private rents clearly out of line with local rents can be increased (Art. 17, c).
121 Thanks to Jean Bosvieux for this information.
122 From interview evidence, and Massin *et al.* (2010), showing refusal of more expensive homes in Paris, suggesting competition.
123 See Fig 1.3 (p. 14).
124 Section 2.1.4 (p. 39).
125 Section 2.1.5 (p. 40).
126 [2010] OJ C83/389.
127 [2008] OJ C115/52.
128 Council Directive 2000/43/EC of 29 June 2000 implementing the principle of equal treatment between persons irrespective of racial or ethnic origin [2000] OJ L180/22.
129 Council Directive 2000/78/EC of 27 November 2000 establishing a general framework for equal treatment in employment and occupation [2000] OJ L303/16, useful for international working.
130 Art. 26 (2) of the TFEU (formerly Art. 14 TEU).
131 Tenants can be consumers under Council Directive 93/13/EC of 5 April 1993 on Unfair Terms in Consumer Contracts [1993] OJ L95/29, although not important in many countries (Schmid, undated).
132 Consolidated version of the Treaty on European Union [2008] OJ C115/13.
133 See note 127.
134 Competition control does not in principle distinguish public and private undertakings, although the test for these is slightly different (Fehling 2009).
135 The TFEU now refers to the common interest rather than the general interest, Art. 107 (3) (c) and (d).
136 The Protocol (No. 26) on Services of General Interest (SGI) [2010] C83/308, Art. 1.
137 Kenna (2011) explains this distinction for housing organizations and its importance. SGI are state or para-state organizations whilst SSIG, are narrowly defined by particular social activities. The European definitions of public services here bear marked resemblance to French law, not directly relevant to this book.
138 This distinction is debated and not clear at the time of the study in France.
139 Decision of the Commission of 28 November 2005 no. 2005/842/CE, O.J. 29 November 2005, Point 16 of the preamble [2005] L312/67.
140 Exempt from notification requirements does not necessarily mean exempt from review.
141 Directive of the European Parliament and of the Council 2006/123/EC of 12 December 2006 on services in the internal market [2006] L376/36.
142 Only one of these actions resulted in a decision, see note 144.
143 Thanks to Laurent Ghékière, for this information.
144 The Commission of the EU, Note of Agreed decision no. C (2009) 9963 of 4 December 2009, OJ document no. 1899, not yet reported at time of writing.

Endnotes

145 Ibid, para. 36.
146 See the discussion in section 10.4.2 (p. 247).
147 Case C-226/1 *Altmark Trans and Regierungspräsidium Magdeburg* [2003] ECR I-7747. [2003] ECR I-7747, see also Touvenin (2009).
148 Ibid., para. 88.
149 See p. 21 for Bourgeois' view and throughout this account of process.
150 See p. 42.
151 Ibid.
152 The UK Parliament is subjected to the ECHR, for example, by certificates of compliance of bills by ministers under s.19, Human Rights Act 1998, and by actions in the Administrative Court under sections 2–4 and 6–8.
153 Read and construed together, particularly between Arts. 1, 2 and 6 of the *Grundgesetz*.
154 *R (on the application of Limbuela, Tesema and Adam) v Secretary of State for the Home Department* [2005] UKHL 66, [2006] 1 AC 396, following closely after a medically important decision on Art. 3, ECHR on human dignity, *Pretty v UK* (2002) 35 EHRR 1.
155 Décision no. 94-359D, 19 janvier 1995C, as above, based on a preceding medical decision: no. 94-343/344DC, 27 juillet 1994, concerning respect for the human body.
156 There are also differences in legislation in Wales and N. Ireland.
157 Tenancies are not part of the French *numerus clausus* (the limited permitted property rights) in Book II of the Code Civil (C. civ.), except for the emphyteusis, a long lease of 18–99 years: C. civ., Arts. 529, 1968, and Code rural (C. rur.), Arts. 1974–1977 and 1979 (and related devices) which give the tenant-holder real property rights.
158 The basis of this was the subject of historic debate between the great jurists, Savigny and Ihéring.
159 Section 3.2 (p. 63).
160 Particularly Hume (1758) Ch.2. For French law, see, for example, Carbonnier (1973). This field is too large to reference here. For an explanation of this difficulty, see Appendix 1.
161 Under s.1(1)(b) or 1(3) of the Law of Property Act 1925.
162 Freeholders, technically owning a 'fee simple absolute in possession' under s.1(1)(a) of the Law of Property Act 1925 or long leaseholders owning a 'term of years absolute' under s.(1)(b) of that act. Absolute here does not have the same sense or extent as in French law.
163 Grey and Grey (2009) particularly pp. 86ff.
164 See the strong statement at p. 64.
165 *Bien* translates as 'a good', as in 'goods', although this word applies to all property including land, C. civ., Arts. 516–34.
166 For example in *Iatridis v Greece* (2000) 30 EHRR 97, concerning a business lease. The ECtHR can also provide procedural protection against eviction, as in *Connors v the UK* Series Ap. no 66746/01 (ECtHR, 14 November 2002), particularly under Arts. 6 and 8.
167 (2007) 45 EHRR 4.
168 Ibid,. para. 208.
169 It is arguable whether these were tenants in the normal sense. See Ball (2010b).
170 In *Mellacher v Austria* (1990) 12 EHRR CD97.
171 *Hutten-Czapska* above note 167, para. 82.
172 See p. 64 and discussion in section 4.1.2. (p. 86).
173 See the dissenting judgement of Judge Zupančič in *Hutten Czapska*.
174 Ibid., para. 17.
175 Central Statistical Office (2007).
176 *FEANTSA v Slovenia*, (2010) 51 EHRR. SE10. Slovenia differed as Polish landlords remained on the land registers in a compulsory letting scheme.
177 From talking to representatives of the respective organizations.
178 *Hutten-Czapka*, para. 150. See Ball (2010c) for benefits in Slovenia.
179 Another similar application is pending at the time of writing, *Stežovatel and the Civic Association of Owners of Houses, Flats and Other Real Estate v Czech Republic*.
180 See p. 92.

Endnotes

181 See p. 1.
182 For example, see from p. 89.
183 C.C.H., Art R. 331-12 and an *arrêté* (order) du 29 juillet 1987, as amended.
184 Thanks to ANIL for that information.
185 This does not preclude this being taken into account elsewhere.
186 Not all tax deductions are allowed for calculating eligibility below income ceilings. There were different deductions in different national datasets: Occupation du patrimoine sociale or OPS (such as Ministère du Logement 2007); Fichier du logement communale or FILOCOM (such as Ministère d'Equipement 2005); the Enquête logement, (such as INSEE 2002, 2005) and the National Census. FILOCOM is a combination of data from other sources.
187 People within the lowest three income deciles, p. 12.
188 See section 9.4 (p. 210) for this vulnerability for ethnic minorities.
189 From USH (2009), not changing greatly since 2006.
190 Discussed in section 9.4.1 (p. 211).
191 Ministère de l'Equipement (undated).
192 From local interviews.
193 Ministère de l'Equipement (undated).
194 See pp. 48ff.
195 Section 5.3 (p. 127) for the current situation.
196 Arts. L. 421-8 to L. 421-14 of the C.C.H. The size and composition of the board is from Art. R. 421–4.
197 She uses the word *rentabilité*, which can mean what pays, as well as what is profitable.
198 Specifically the UMP party, the Union pour un mouvement populaire.
199 Results from *Le Monde* (2007a, 2007b).
200 Under s. 188–9 of the Housing Act 1996 local housing athorities have an interim duty to accommodate individuals in priority need, homeless (a broad definition under s. 175) and not intentionally homeless (s. 192), pending investigation. Cowan (1997) gives a dated but still useful critical account of this process. All people in statutory priority need should have 'reasonable preference', s. 167(2) for social housing allocation, within local allocation schemes determined under Part VI of the Act. This is not a book on English law but see, for example, Arden (2003), Morgan (2007).
201 This may be changing, for example, Brouant (2011) draws on interviews to illustrate practice.
202 See p. 258 for an aspect of the different 'primary sources' in French law.
203 Particularly Legifrance (République de France, undated) the large and constantly updated French legal database with links to major courts and their decisions, English translations and historic versions of codes.
204 See p. 260.
205 See p. 49.
206 At a meeting of the ENHR special project on social housing, Paris, 12 March 2006. Jean-Pierre Schaeffer is a director of the CDC.
207 Other exceptions to control of State aid in Art. 107 TFEU, include depressed areas, or in emergencies.
208 See p. 19.

3 The historical context: from revolution to rights

209 Relative to stronger duties of good faith existing in more limited circumstances in English law (Zimmerman and Whittaker 2000).
210 See section 2.3.3 (p. 53 and p. 257).
211 Roman (2001) sugggested this was uncommon.
212 Loi du 16–24 août 1790, Art. 20.
213 After the decision in *Blanco* (TC 8 février 1873).

Endnotes

214 The Tribunal of Conflicts decides the unusual cases where this status is unclear.
215 Except, for example, particular plenary formations of the Cour de cassation.
216 For private law. The administration has some extra discretionary powers, such as *actes de gouvernement,* for example, allowing normal tax increases without suffering administrative compensation claims from individuals. There are other much more limited administrative discretions.
217 Not an accurate translation because French judges do not make law, p. 61.
218 Separate from other judicial institutions and so not shown in Fig. 3.1 (p. 62).
219 The 1958 Constitution, Art. 61-1.
220 Formerly parishes, fortified towns, communes and other local arrangements.
221 Substantially in the night of 4–5 August, during antifeudal riots in the countryside (Bart 2009; Doyle 1989).
222 Tenants or 'takers' of, the emphyteusis, (long lease, note 157) have real property rights, but only because the holder of the reversion (*nu-propriétaire*) then has no real property rights. Other fragmented property rights also survived the Revolution or were created by statute (Ball 2010d).
223 Quoting Patault (1989).
224 Also, by 1810, a commercial code, a criminal code, and codes for criminal and civil procedure.
225 Robert-Joseph Pothier wrote a series of treatises on the law of obligations from 1761. Domat (1691) was particularly noted for *Lois Civiles dans Leur Ordre Naturel.*
226 Turpin (1994) Ch. 1, particularly pp. 13 and 23. The sexist term reflects the climate of the times.
227 Art. 3 of the 1958 Constitution.
228 Loi du 13 avril 1850. There were problems in expropriating unhealthy property, because of high compensation, determined by committees of property owners (Shapiro 1985).
229 As an anarchist, Proudhon was as much attacking large-scale State ownership as private ownership.
230 This is a rather shorthand description for a different movement.
231 Tenants should provide enough furniture to cover rent if sold. Apartment-blocks often had posts in the front of the entrance door to prevent furniture removal.
232 Session of the 5th messidor year III, *Moniteur* du 12 messidor.
233 From his journal, quoted in Guerrand (1967: 263).
234 For its basic contractual uses see p. 68. The distinction between solidarism and solidarity is less frequently made today.
235 See p. 68.
236 France did not have income tax until roughly a century later than England.
237 C. civ. Art. 1200, imposing responsibilities, with Art. 1197, C. civ. governing benefits.
238 C. civ., Art.1220.
239 An archaic word (for English usage) revived for the European harmonization research project, known as the Draft Common Frame of Reference (a potential European Civil Code). The inclusion of solidarity is of immense importance, but particularly affects the UK, not the subject of this book. See Ball (2010b, 2010c, 2010d).
240 See sections 3.2.3–4 (p. 67ff).
241 *La prestation,* or obligation.
242 Because of the French equivalent of privity, an English principle limiting claims to contracting parties: C. civ., Art. 1165, although there are exceptions, particularly Art. 1135. See p. 78.
243 C. civ., Art. 220 for spouses PACS or Civil Solidarity Pact, Art. 515-1ff., C. civ., with responsibility in Art. 515-4, al.2.
244 In *concubinage,* described as a *de facto* union in Art. 515-8, C. civ.
245 Arising from art 220 C. civ., for parents, although care of a child is a public responsibilty for parents Art. 394, C. civ.
246 Dyson (2005).
247 Art. 1202, C civ. Solidarity is not presumed but easily implied in commercial contracts (Terré *et al.*, 1996: 922).
248 P. 68.

Endnotes

249 For divorce this covers both maintenance obligations between spouses and for children, from Art. 208, C. civ. For spouses this obligation terminates on divorce, see section 9.3.2 (p. 208).
250 C. civ., Arts. 206–209, and for housing, Arts. 210–11.
251 Section 3.2 (p. 63ff) traces this development generally.
252 C. civ., Art. 1120.
253 Art. 2 of the 1958 Constitution.
254 From Proudhon (1994), quoted in Courvoisier (2005: 8).
255 Arts. 544 and 545, C. civ. See p. 92ff for public utility.
256 Ibid.
257 Particularly in Art. 1382, C. civ., but also affecting property in Art. 544, through *jurisprudence*.
258 For the double meaning of *jurisprudence* see p. 62.
259 Ibid.
260 Section 4.1.3 (p. 87).
261 In the founding statute of 1901 see p. 76.
262 Based on Art. 1832, C. civ., but modified to become more like institutions by European harmonizatuon (Cozian *et al.* 2008).
263 See p. 219 for an example of this view, that a committee diluted discrimination.
264 See the quotation from Le Play on p. 66.
265 Some French social landlords still have 'garden cities' in their title.
266 Exempted from window and door taxes and from land tax for three years.
267 See p. 80. The CDC could lend a fifth of particular reserves.
268 *Sociétés de crédit immobilier* belong within the family of HLM organizations mainly lending to individuals, and recently considerably reorganized.
269 See p. 67.
270 P. 73ff.
271 Allowed mainly on reversion of long leases, a loophole.
272 Regions could propose public social landlords until recently.
273 P. 141.
274 Ibid.
275 The programme was never entirely completed.
276 See note 262, for the legal source of its status.
277 Art. 3 of the loi du 1 juillet 1901.
278 Long-established charitable purposes were redefined in the Charities Act 2006, ss.1–3, and political campaigning would be outside those exclusive purposes.
279 Following an earlier 1912 organization.
280 The CNL, UNAF, CLCV, CSF and Association force ouvrière consommateurs. The latter is that strange creature, a Marxist consumers' association.
281 Class actions under the Code de la consommation (Consumer code, or C. consom.), Book IV.
282 Their website usually recorded the most recent negotiations.
283 Loi no° 48-1360 du 1 septembre 1948.
284 Ibid., under Art. 10, with a quantity of exceptions decontrolling the private sector. Since 2007, some better-off social tenants were excluded.
285 Loi n° 82-256 du 22 juin 1982.
286 Loi n° 86-1290 du 24 juillet 1986.
287 By Art. 10 of the 1989 statute, with exceptions in Arts. 12–15 and s.40 of the 1989 statute for social landlords.
288 Ibid.
289 There is a French report in the EU tenancy project (European University Institute, undated) but it omits important pre-1982 legislation.
290 Agreements between employers and unions in the UK are not even binding contracts.
291 C. civ, Art. 1134.
292 Governed by décret n° 88-274 du 18 mars 1988.

Endnotes

293 The 1986 statute, Art. 41 ter.
294 For all the representations rights in the 1986 statute, cheaper rents over time and on balance, better security of tenure.
295 The communist party was the largest party in the ruling coalition immediately after the war (Duclaud-Williams 1978).
296 By a décret du 9 septembre 1953.
297 By the ZUP or Zones à urbaniser en priorité.
298 In 1958, some new special zones required a minimum construction of 500 homes, paving the way for much larger zoned developments (Deschamps 1998).
299 Deschamps (1998) provides a sourced history of this with its predecessors and related other zone types, implicated in urban segregation. A primary reference here would mislead, because of a proliferation of zones and plans in constant mutation.
300 Ibid. pp. 44ff.
301 Including Nora and Eveno (1975) and UNFOHLM (1975).
302 Section 2.1.5 (p. 40).

4 The right to housing in context

303 See p. 1.
304 Arts. 52–53 of the 1958 Constitution.
305 Under Arts. 54 and from 61 of the 1958 Constitution.
306 Subject to compliance by the other party.
307 For example, Conseil consitutionnel (C. cons.) 15 janvier 1975, no. 74-54, loi relative à l'interruption volontaire de la grossesse.
308 See Conseil d'Etat, (CE) 30 octobre 1998, *M. Saran, Levacher et autres*.
309 CE 20 octobre 1989, *M. Nicolo*.
310 Ibid.
311 Sections 4.1.7 and 9.5.2. (pp. 96 and 222).
312 See p. 4.
313 See above note 18.
314 For problems see sections 4.1.6-7 and 9.5.2 (pp. 95ff and 222).
315 Discussed on p. 91.
316 Now in the preamble to the 1958 Constitution. This was not a question in topic guides.
317 See note 155, but for similar German and UK approaches see notes 154 and 153.
318 Implied since the 1789 Declaration, Art. 1.
319 For example, Art. L. 1-1111 of the Code général des collectivités territoriales (C.G.C.T.).
320 See note 155.
321 Because of its established use in the German constitution, see note 153.
322 For example the right to property, in ECHR, Art. 1 of Protocol 1.
323 See, for example, the medical cases in notes 154 and 155 (see note below).
234 It has been applied to areas such as privacy, the integrity of the human body and labour law.
325 See note 242.
326 Before promulgation of statutes, referred by political leaders or groups of parliamentarians, Art. 61 of the 1958 Constitution recently extended, see note 328.
327 Currently under the 1989 statute.
328 By a new Art. 61-1 of the 1958 Constitution, particularly reformed by a loiorganique n° 2009-1523 du de 10 Décembre 2009 as part of wider reform.
329 Quoted on p. 1.
330 See note 255, in the form of public utility, see p. 92.
331 See p. 44.
332 See pp. 40ff.
333 See note 155.

Endnotes

334 C. cons. 7 décembre 2000, no. 2000-436DC.
335 CA Paris, 15 septembre 1995, unpublished, described in Radigon and Horvath (2002: 17).
336 Argued on p. 76, ibid.
337 The 1958 Constitution, Art. 5.
338 Code de l'urbanisme (C. urb.), Art. L. 110. For its origins, see Flamand (2001: 291–3). This is less explicit today.
339 See note 469.
340 See Deschamps (2005: 173) for his reasoning.
341 French bases for claim for *un recours pour excès de pouvoir* were different to *ultra vires* in English law, but the *recours* could also lead to quashing of an adminsitrative decision (Brown and Bell 1998).
342 Sections; 4.1.4–5 (pp. 91ff).
343 For the public function for English social landlords: *R (On the Application of Heather) v Leonard Cheshire Foundation* [2002] EWCA Civ 366, [2002] 2 All ER 936 and *R (On the Application of Weaver) v London and Quadrant Housing Trust*, [2009] EWCA Civ 587, [2009] 4 All ER 865 (CA) and *Poplar Housing and Regeeration Community Association Ltd v Donohgue* [2002] EWCA Civ 595, [2002] 4 All ER 604.
344 TC, 8 February 1873.
345 CE, 13 mai 1938, *Caisse Primaire 'Aide et Protection'*.
346 Section 2.1.5 (p. 40).
347 See the commentary by Brouant (2007: 346).
348 C.C.H., Art. L. 442-2-2.
349 See p. 171.
350 23 avril 2001, *Droit au Logement* (DAL) (reported in *Le Monde,* 3 May 2001).
351 C.C.H., Art. L. 411.
352 6 août 2001, *Taga Fosso*, (reported in *le Monde*, 15 August 2001).
353 CE, 3 mai 2002, décision no. 245697.
354 From *FEANTSA V France*, p. 4 and note 12.
355 For example, Prosser (2005) describes its use in English competition policy.
356 Art. L. 441-2-3 of the C.C.H.
357 Decreed then under Art. L. 441-1-4 or L. 441-2-6 of the C.C.H.
358 Under ibid. and C.C.H., L. 441-2-3.
359 Loi no. 2006-872 du 13 juillet 2006, and la loi DALO.
360 A service provided by the ADIL in the Nord.
361 See note 12, (para.112 of the decision).
362 For a minimum period of residence, p. 160.
363 Under C.C.H., L. 441-2-3 and L. 441-2-3-1, and by decree under C.C.H., Art. L. 300-1.
364 From C.C.H., Art. L. 441-2-3, II, slightly limited by Art. R. *441-14-1, at the time of writing. Unfit here means dangerous or threatening health. Urgency and good faith are also to be considered under the latter.
365 Or other temporary accommodation for 18 months.
366 This includes the disabled and people with a disabled dependent whose housing is a health of safety risk.
367 C.C.H., Art. L. 441-2-3, II al. 2. Good faith was not defined.
368 C.C.H., Arts. L. 441-2-3, III and R. *441-18-2 for failure to do so for temporary accomodation.
369 C.C.H., Art. R. 441-2-3, II, al. 10.
370 In la loi contre les exclusions, Art. 56 (note 425).
371 From interviews with *associations*.
372 Such as those run by the CHRS (the Centres d'hébergement et de réinsertion sociale or Centres for Shelter and Social Reinsertion), a nationwide network.
373 Elected representative or civil servant, see p. 260, for reasons for this terminology.
374 Two social landlords, one mayor and one state actor.
375 One public and one private in these quotes.

Endnotes

376 Literally 'construct himself'.
377 See p. 162.
378 *La collectivité,* as explained above in note 2.
379 See also section 7.1.3 (p. 163).
380 See p. 104.
381 Circulaire du 21 mars 1973, J.O., 5 avril 1973, p. 3864.
382 Loi no. 91-662 du 13 juillet 1991.
383 Discussed in sections 2.1.2–3 and 10.4.2 (pp. 37 and 247).
384 See also p. 81.
385 CE, 22 novembre 2002, *Commune de Gennevilliers. ADJA* note Brouant.
386 Sections 3.2.3–4 (pp. 67ff).
387 See note 385 above, in the note Brouant.
388 Ibid.
389 See pp. 106 and 242 for the consequences of this.
390 Art. 1. The translation is from the website of the Conseil constitutionnel.
391 See p. 81.
392 Widely reported, also suggesting cleaning out the *banlieux* with a hosepipe (De Montvallon 2005).
393 Recording individuals' ethnicity was illegal (section 9.4.1, p. 211).
394 Section 9.4 (p. 210).
395 By judicial review for allocation generally, and for homelessness by s. 202, Housing Act 1996, with an internal review first. There are general duties of information and advice in sections 168 and 172. See note 200 for the homelessness legislation.
396 This is for private law, but rules can apply by osmosis or assumption between the two sectors, sometimes with different labels.
397 The term 'quasi-judicial decision' is effectively redundant for access to judicial review, with wider bases for judicial review under the Human Rights Act 1998.
398 For an introduction to the English allocation process see Hughes (2000), Arden (2003) and Morgan (2007) and for empirical socio-legal studies criticising this see Cowan (1997) and Cowan *et al.* (2008).
399 Art. 1 of the 1958 Constitution (as related to equality).
400 Respectively, the Tribunal paritaire des baux ruraux and the Tribunal de la sécurité sociale.
401 These include some remaining discretions, see note 216.
402 The courts' discretion is often described as sovereign, tending to demote administrators' margin of appreciation.
403 My thanks to Hubert Légal of the Conseil d'État for this explanation (at the World Congress of Comparative Law in 2006).
404 See above, pp. 103 and 242.
405 For example, considering materiality and weight.
406 For example, for *la compétence liée*, the administrator has no room to manoeuvre. Administrative judges are civil servants, thus part of the administration themselves.
407 Some administrative review situations to not require this.
408 See p. 179.
409 Definitions in the Code de commerce (C. com.), Arts. L. 110-1 to L. 110-4 and L. 121-1 C. consom. excluded farmers, artisans, company employees, anyone in the public sector and others. Generally, the present of furniture or of ownership of more than four homes meant a landlord was a businessman.
410 From the time of Cochon, p. 76.
411 See p. 77.
412 See p. 21.
413 From a faction in the 1789 Revolution.
414 See p. 137.
415 See p. 64.

Endnotes

416 The version proposed by DAL, p. 20.
417 Besson Act, Art 1.

5 Complex institutions in the grip of change

418 Such as described on pp. 162 and 178.
419 Section 8.2.2 (p. 192).
420 For a summary of tenant representation in different roles, see p. 187.
421 Section 7.4.1 (p. 179).
422 Section 8.2.2 (p. 192).
423 See C. urb., Art. L. 422-3 for continuing state planning powers, delegating power in Art. L. 422-1.
424 Section 5.2 (p. 123).
425 Loi no. 98-657 du 29 juillet 1998.
426 Texte no. 89 (2004–5) introduced by Michelle Deresss and No. 38 (2005–6) introduced by Tiérry Repentin.
427 Loi no. 2006-872 du 13 juillet 2006.
428 In 2000, the Housing Ministry was within the Ministry of Infrastructure, Construction, Transport and the Sea, but after multiple changes, including attachment to the Ministry of Employment and Solidarity, housing was now within the Ministry of Ecology, Development and Sustainable Regional Development. For an example of ministerial conflict, see Chevallereau (2008).
429 Initial objectives in Art. 6 of loi no. 2003-710 du 1 août 2003.
430 Without income ceilings, places obtained under C.C.H., Art. R. 441-5.
431 C.C.H., Art. L. 441-1-1, al. 3.
432 From interviews.
433 Other national agencies helping to fund development were: ANAH for home improvement and ANRU, which was created for the Borloo plan (p. 115) and is not directly relevant to allocation, except by promoting construction.
434 Before decentralization, community services for things like pregnancy care, lead poisoning, homelessness, drug addiction. social services and unfit housing (with the DDE for the latter).
435 Departmental Plan for the Housing of Disadvantaged People. See also section 5.3.1 (p. 127).
436 See pp. 129ff.
437 See p. 117.
438 By decree under C.C.H., L. 441-1 and L. 441-6. By Art. R. 441-1, people could apply anywhere. A Conseil d'État decision, CE 10 juillet 1996, *Ville d'Epinay-sur-Seine,* reinforced this, avoiding the idea that people could apply but did not have to be accepted.
439 C.C.H., Art. L. 441-1, al. 1.
440 C.C.H., Art. L. 441-2.
441 Such guarantees generally were limited to 50 per cent of a commune's budgetary receipts.
442 A long lease, *un bail emphtéotique* (Ball 2010b).
443 Governance generally was in C.C.H., from Art. R. 421.
444 By the DDE and the Minister of Construction and Housing (through the prefect): See, for example, Art. L. 431-4, C.C.H.
445 C.C.H., from Arts. R. 331-13 and R. 331-13-1.
446 By loi n° 66-1068 du 31 décembre 1966. Now Book V 1st Title of the C.G.C.T.
447 Regret was expressed at his departure by the Ministry of the Interior, with thanks for service.
448 Villeneuve-la-Garenne, Colombes, Asnières and Boulogne-Billancourt (which had more than 100,000 inhabitants).
449 Cœur-de-Seine, Sud–de-Seine, Hauts-de-Seine, Hauts-de-Bièvres and Sèvres-Boulogne-Billancourt. (The interviewee was unable to identify the sixth).
450 Booth (1992) described this arrangement in Lyon before the reforms.

Endnotes

451 Cinquième Partie of the C.G.C.T. The EPCI is finally created by decree in the Conseil d'État.
452 C.C.H., Art. L. 441ff. allows for this.
453 An interviewee suggested one tenth of posts were unfilled, producing a shortage.
454 See section 5.3.1 for context (p. 127).
455 National Housing Information Agency.
456 Not illegal but because of different rules for intermediate housing.
457 Regulated under C.C.H., Art. R. 411-1.
458 See note 108 for the aids provided.
459 See p. 76.
460 Such as SOS Racisme and Force Ouvrière.
461 See p. 76.
462 Through an agreement with the prefect, paid for people not qualifying for other housing benefits, from Art. L. 851-1 of the C.S.S.
463 See Figure 3.2 (p. 82).
464 Particularly sections 4.2.3, 7.1.3 and 9.4.2 (pp. 103, 163 and 214) for this policy and its results.
465 La loi sur la solidarité et le renouvellement urbain, n° 2000-1208 du 13 décembre 2000, as amended.
466 See note 567.
467 Zone of Concerted Development.
468 See p. 81.
469 Existing since 1991 now under C.C.H. from Art. L. 302-5, imposed on communes of 3,500 more inhabitants (1,500 in Ile-de-France) in an urban area (*agglomération*) of more than 50,000 inhabitants and possessing at least one commune with 15,000 inhabitants, slightly extended in 2008. This thus catches towns but not groups of villages or unconnected commuter areas.
470 Now C.C.H., Art L. 302-5.
471 C.C.H., Arts. L. 441-1-4, als. 3 and 5-8 and L. 441-1-5, abolished in July 2006.
472 C.C.H., Art. L. 441-1-6. Also compulsory where the prefect designated a *bassin d'habitat* on local proposition and on advice, C.C.H., Art. L. 441-1-4-, al. 3.
473 This and general intercommunal charters were elaborated by intercommunal conferences above, C.C.H., Art. L. 441-2.
474 Still mentioned in C.C.H. Art. L. 441-1-2, al. 1° during the study but moribund.
475 *Accompagnement social lié au logement.*
476 From a state actor.
477 DGHUC.
478 This implies that tenants can lose their deposit.
479 The region, the Grand Lyon area and Lyon town.
480 The Departmental Agreement for the Housing of Disadvantaged People under C.C.H., Art. R. 441-1-2.
481 Information from the local CAF in 2005.
482 Originally created by the loi d'orientation pour la ville.
483 Completed in 2007.
484 See p. 120 for some reasons for this.
485 See note 345 for the source, and p. 187 for a rationale for this.
486 For example, see p. 120.
487 Other aspects are uncertainty and frequency of transactions.
488 See p. 131.
489 See quote from Williamson p. 132.
490 Section 8.2.3–4 (p. 201ff).
491 Evident in the process in Ch. 7, but also in execution of judgments. See sections 4.1.4-7 (pp. 91ff) and 9.5.2 (p. 222).
492 See p. 122.

Endnotes

6 Social landlords and their financing problems

493 For example, by increased political representation in the new public social landlord, p. 141.
494 Icade, then in process of transferring most stock to the private sector.
495 Amzallag and Taffin (2003: 3).
496 Ibid. (2003: 1).
497 Ibid.
498 Art. L. 441-2.
499 Art. R. *422-29.
500 A small percentage above the rate for the Livret A savings account, p. 80.
501 See note 197 for meanings of *rentabilité*.
502 See section 5.1.7 (p. 121).
503 A question of agency costs for people not acting on their own account.
504 See p. 30.
505 By décret n° 93-236 du 22 février 1993.
506 There was a list of institutions inspected by name.
507 For more details of actual nos. of dossiers submitted see p. 175.
508 See p. 79.
509 *Etablissements publics à caractère administratif.*
510 *Etablissements publics à caractère industriel et commercial.*
511 A process involving approval by the Conseil d'Etat, C.C.H., Arts. L. 421-2 and L. 421-4, after local advice.
512 And neighbouring communes, C.C.H., Art. R. 421-52.
513 C.C.H., Art. R. *421-6 for OPACs.
514 Their regional base was their registered office and permission was needed from communes where homes where to operate elsewhere, Art. R. *422-3.
515 For example, by a special statutory scheme the OPAC or Programmed Operation for the Improvement of Housing with special funding and planning arrangements.
516 Décret n° 93-852 du 17 juin 1993 for new staff as employees, but Art. 13 of décret n° 86-518 du 14 mars 1986 for existing staff as civil servants on conversion from OPHLM.
517 C.C.H., Art. L. 421-1-1, abolished in 2007.
518 See p. 140.
519 Section 8.2.3 (p. 194).
520 See p. 66.
521 For the board make-up, C.C.H., Arts. L. 421-8 to L. 421-14, and Arts. R. *421-4 to R. *421-18.
522 C.C.H., Art. L. 421-8.
523 C.C.H., Arts. R. *421-4 to R. *421-6.
524 C.C.H., Art. R. *421-12.
525 C.C.H., Art. R. *421-18.
526 C.C.H., Arts. R. *421-5 and R.*421-6.
527 Loi n° 66-539 du 24 juillet 1966 as amended, but now codified within the C. com. since 2000.
528 C.C.H., Art. R. *422-1.
529 Plus one vote., C.C.H., Art. L. 422-2-1, 1 *v* and Art R*, 422-1-1, III.
530 C.C.H., Arts. L. 422-2-1 and R. *422-2-1.
531 The author sometimes met a team, not just the one person interviewed.
532 See p. 170.
533 Employment and tenancies are both classified together as hire contracts in adjacent sections of the C. civ. The revolutionary idea was that the individual owned their own body, which they hired out (Bart 2009), although today the body is not capable of being owned. See, for example, C. civ., Art. 16 for bodily products.
534 See p. 77.

Endnotes

535 See, for example, the reports by the Fondation Abbé Pierre, and the various squats and demonstrations reported in this book.
536 C.C.H., Arts. L. 421-17.
537 Thanks to ANIL for updating this.
538 From €26.1 billion recorded housing aids (INSEE 2004).
539 ALF was found in C.S.S. Arts. L. 511 to L. 513-1, L. 542 to L. 542-7 and ALS in C.S.S., Arts. L. 831-1 to L. 835-2. APL was in C.C.H. Arts. 351-1 to 353-20.
540 See note above.
541 Despite this dated source, basic principles were still correct during the study.
542 The 1989 statute, Art. 7.
543 Ministry of Infrastructure of the Italian Republic and Federcasa (2006).
544 Three years earlier than this article.
545 Section 2.1.5 (p. 40).
546 Lefèbvre *et al.* (1991) give a 50-year history of these loans. See p. 148, for a brief history.
547 C.C.H., Book III, Title III for government housing loans.
548 Section 6.4.3 (p. 154).
549 Social mix requirements are only found in loans after 1990.
550 ANRU constructed more, supporting the Borloo regeneration plans, p. 115.
551 Fig. 1.1 (p. 12).
552 Poverty can be documented but much less so disadvantage (section 2.2.1, p. 47).
553 See also p. 170.
554 See p. 176.
555 See p. 73 and Carpenter *et al.* (1994). Marseilles seemed different with town-centre slums (Javaloyès 2003).
556 From UESL.
557 By regulation under C.C.H., Art. L. 441-1.
558 From interviews.
559 This was threatened, p. 122.
560 By order under C.C.H., Art. R. 441-1.
561 *Le supplement de loyer de solidarité* (a smallish supplementary rent) was to encourage better off tenants to move: C.C.H., Arts. L. 441-3 to L. 441-15.
562 The 1989 statute, Arts. 17 and 19.
563 Ibid., Art. 17, d.
564 Ibid.
565 See p. 183 and note 638.
566 An early action by the Sarkozy government was to remove budgets for unused construction loans.
567 The controversial film *La Haîne* (Kassovitz 1995), was reputedly based on 1990 riots in Vaulx-en-Velin in Grand Lyon.
568 See p. 38.
569 The number of refusals by better-off applicants in Paris city suggests they have a choice, see p. 31.
570 C.C.H., Art. R. 331-15.
571 Ibid., around 20 per cent in 2006.
572 C.C.H., Art. R. 331-15-1.
573 See p. 79.
574 Up to 35 per cent, C.C.H., Art. R. 331-15 (This is variable).
575 C.C.H., Arts. R. 323-1ff.
576 See p. 115.
577 At the ENHR seminar, see note 206.
578 Tax exemptions included: C.G.I., art 207, 4° (from corporation tax); Art. 232, II (from tax on empty homes); Art. 795, 7° (from transfer taxes for gifts); Art. 261, e, 2° (from VAT on

Endnotes

transfers); Arts. 257, 7° and 284 (for certain capital taxes on transfers). All HLM organizations enjoyed exemptons on transfers (C.G.I. Arts 1049-1051) and OPHLMs obtained exemptions as *établissements publics* (C.G.I., Arts. 206-1 and 206-5).

579 *Taxe foncière sur la propriété bâtie*, and with relief from other land transaction taxes: then C.G.I., Arts. 1384 and 1284A.
580 La Banque de France (2001). Initially these schemes had generous capital allowances for first lets homes under the 1989 statute, becoming less generous by 2001 (C.G.I., Art. 200-0).
581 Section 1.4, particularly p. 24.

7 The social housing allocation process

582 The Besson Act, Art. 4, g.
583 Figure 1.3 (p. 14).
584 An approximation, due to recording changes in Legifrance, the government legal database (République de France, undated).
585 Thanks to Jean-Philippe Brouant for this explanation.
586 From pp. 47 and 160ff.
587 Under C.C.H., Art. R. 441-1 for requirement but note 615 for the residence period and p. 172.
588 C.C.H., L. 441-1, al. 1.
589 Section 5.3 (p. 127).
590 C.C.H., Art. R. 441-1-1.
591 But see p. 178.
592 C.C.H., Art. L. 441-1, al. 1.
593 See p. 161.
594 Section 4.1.6 (p. 95), for its composition.
595 See note 357 for this power.
596 Up to 10 years, p. 223.
597 Section 4.1.6 (p. 95).
598 Some systems give 'reasonable preference' (see note 200) by crediting individuals with time, not points (below), to obtain a home earlier.
599 By awarding local priority points, within a scheme conforming national requirements, the Housing Act 1996, Parts VI and VII (see note 200).
600 Except in the Hauts de Seine.
601 Particularly C.C.H., Art. R. *441-3.
602 C.C.H., Art. L. 441, al. 2.
603 See the quotation on p. 201.
604 From section 8.3.1 (p. 199), and p. 215.
605 Under an agreement to accept nominations between local authorities and registered social landlords under Part VI of the Housing Act 1996.
606 Both through their commission and its administration, C.C.H., Art. R. *441-3.
607 See p. 179.
608 DREIF, AORIF and ARSEM, as well as OLAP and the regional organisation of notaries.
609 See p. 130, for mayors failure to honour agreements.
610 Similar to the intercommunal housing conference (section 5.3.1, p. 127), which was compulsory everywhere from 1996–99 (Houard 2009), but still possible in Ile-de-France under C.C.H., L. 441-1-4, al. 8.
611 An interviewee said this was calculated as a percentage not pertaining to particular houses. They thus lost fractions of homes in any development.
612 See p. 170 for difficulties. Social landlords should report reservations to prefects (C.C.H., Art. R. 441-5, al. 2) but figures were not generally available.
613 See note 469.

614 My thanks to Christiane Thouzellier and Marie-Christine Jaillet from le Mirail University, Toulouse, for answering my questions following a 2009 visit there.
615 Code de l'Entrée et du Séjour des Etrangers et du Droit d'Asile, Arts. L. 313-1 to L. 313-13 and décret n° 46-1574 du 30 juin 1946.
616 Cass. crim. arrêt n° 3603 du 30 mai 2000.
617 See pp. 22ff.
618 A local government study described by a Lyon actor but not traced.
619 Art. L. 441-2, al. 2.
620 See p. 177.
621 See p. 94.
622 Ibid.
623 See pp. 122 and 128.
624 C.C.H., Art. R. 441-2-6 (a).
625 Section 2.3 of the questionnaires in section A1.4 (p. 260). (Numbering varies between questionnaires.)
626 See p. 167.
627 For example, a fire in a social home meant emergency allocation could be retrospectively approved.
628 C.C.H., Art. R. 441-9, II.
629 In a comment in, TA Marseille, 23 avril 2001, *Association Droit au Logement Marseille-Provence*.
630 C.C.H., Art. R. 441-9.
631 For the privileges of local control, see section 6.1.2 (p. 139) on governance.
632 See p. 140.
633 C.C.H., Art. R. 441-9.
634 From interviews.

8 'Insiderness' and local actors

635 Section 8.1.5 (p. 190).
636 Defined on p. 24.
637 Section 1.4.3 (p. 26).
638 Art. 6 of the 1989 statute (unfurnished homes) and Art. 1719, al.1° of the C. civ. (*inter alia* furnished homes), since 2002 elaborated by decree.
639 See pp. 156 and 162.
640 Particularly section 9.4.2-3 (pp. 214ff).
641 See p. 21.
642 See p. 33.
643 Sections 9.2–3 (pp. 206ff).
644 See pp. 119ff.
645 See p. 138.
646 Section 1.4.1 (p. 23).
647 Introduced at pp. 26ff and summarized in section 10.2 (p. 235).
648 The 1989 statute.
649 Regulated by C. civ, mainly Arts. 1713-62. Insecurity could also be created by subletting, since subtenants became squatters, as tenants had no property rights to grant.
650 Described in Amzallag and Taffin (2003: 8) as *de facto* social housing.
651 Only the police can physically evict, after enquiry and notifying the *département*.
652 See p. 177.
653 Two months' rent, the 1989 Statute, Art. 22, now one month's rent.
654 Against tenant's risks such as fire, ibid., Art. 7, g.

Endnotes

655 But see the new universal guarantee, p. 122.
656 See pp. 156 and 162.
657 Elected quadrennially, C.C.H., Art. R. *421-8 to R. 421-15 for OPHLM, for example, also sections 6.1.2–3 (pp. 139ff).
658 See p. 96.
659 Established under Art. 20 of the 1989 statute.
660 Particularly in the SCOT.
661 The 1989 statute, Art. 17.
662 The 1986 statute, Arts. 41 and 44 ter. There were direct negotiations, if no elected tenant representatives.
663 See p. 137.
664 See p. 78.
665 See p. 77.
666 Section 6.1.2-3 (pp. 139ff).
667 Section 7.4.1 (p. 179).
668 See p. 141.
669 See p. 126.
670 Section 1.4.6 (p. 30).
671 See section 6.3 (p. 145).
672 See the quotation on p. 152.
673 Section 1.4.4 (p. 27) for stigmatization.
674 Section 9.2.2 (p. 206).
675 For limits to guarantees, note 441.
676 Section 2.2.1 (p. 47) for poverty, and p. 49, for ethnicity and single parents.
677 See pp. 156 and 162.
678 Section 7.3.5 (p. 175).
679 See pp. 176ff.
680 See p. 75.
681 For example, Bourgeois's (1996) account of indebted social landlords in communist communes.
682 2006 figures supplied by interviewees from Observatoire Régional de la Demande.
683 INSEE (2002).
684 The title of the article.
685 From INSEE (2006).
686 Loi n° 2002-305 du 4 mars 2002. In both France and England, the term 'custody' was replaced by residence orders, but interviewees used the older term.
687 Art. 4, ibid., amending Art. 371-4 of the C. civ.
688 One voluntary worker disagreed.
689 See pp. 168 and 219.
690 See p. 119.
691 C.C.H., L. 441-1, para. 1.
692 The High Committee for the Housing of Disadvantaged People.
693 See note 438.
694 See p. 73.
695 From interviews.
696 Sections 7.2.2-3 (pp. 167ff).
697 See p. 168.
698 See *Magill v Porter* [2001] UKHL 67, [2002] 2 AC 357.
699 The CIL only housed employees and see p. 241.
700 See p. 138.
701 See p. 14 for extent of the prefect's rights.
702 Figures include SEM homes.
703 See p. 194.

704 See p. 146.
705 Section 9.4.1 (p. 211).
706 See p. 104. The deaths of two young people in Clichy-sous-Bois triggered the the 2005 riots (de Montvallon 2005).
707 See p. 163.

9 Stigmatization and outsiders

708 Interviewees frequently volunteered who was excluded, whether or not asked specifically.
709 From interviews.
710 For example no obligation to construct 20 per cent social housing under C.C.H., Art. L. 302-5.
711 The usual word for this, as translated.
712 Ministère du Logement (2006).
713 For mortgage eviction but rental eviction has many commonalities.
714 See the quotation, p. 180.
715 Also evidenced in blockage of access generally, pp. 124 and 204.
716 A tenant without any property cannot normally grant a subtenancy.
717 *Le taux de l'usure,* C. consom., Arts. L. 313-4 to L. 313-6.
718 Civ. (1) n° 1263-6 du 12 juillet 2005 and Com. arrêts n° 638-9 du 3 mai.
719 See also *The Economist* (2005a).
720 BODACC (Official Bulletin of Civil and Commercial Announcements). Unsecured creditors can make claims for payment in French mortgage possession actions.
721 C. consom. Arts. L. 331-1 to L. 332-4.
722 *Ré-établissement personnel:* C. consom, Arts. L. 332-5 to L. 332-12, for non-commercial insolvency.
723 By recommendation of the Commission de surendettement or by disputing their decision (C. consom., Art. L. 332-6). the judge must find their situation 'irredeemably compromised' in a hearing with the creditors.
724 From interviewees.
725 See p. 129.
726 Section 8.2.2 (p. 192) explains how housing existing tenants exacerbates this.
727 The same article found the UK the most generous county in Europe to wives.
728 A default regime applies in the absence of other agreement, C. civ., Art. 1393. Various regimes are listed in Title V of Book III.
729 See also Renault-Brahinsky (2005).
730 Existing older arrangements will continue. The *prestation compensentoire,* could oblige spouses' children to continue maintenance.
731 Paid in no more than eight capital instalments (Renault-Brahinsky 2005: 70–73).
732 Created under Art. 515-1, C. civ. Financial relief is available under Art. 515-3-1.
733 Residence for a cohabitant was not so strongly protected as a spouse, although with some provision for a *concubin notoire* (a known established sexual partner) or under the civil partnership, *le pacte civil de solidarité* (ANIL 2000: 12).
734 Depending on the regime adopted, ranging from the survivor taking all to neither automatically being entitled. See note 728, for regimes generally.
735 Widows commonly automatically receive a life interest in the part of the estate compulsorily left to the children or other blood relatives, between half and three-quarters of the estate, Dyson (2005). Later reforms were slightly more favourable to spouses.
736 Ferrial Drosso kindly confirmed this view exists.
737 *Le gage* (C. civ., then, Arts. 2073-84). This security contract has no English equivalent since the similar English contractual obligation alone is unsecured.
738 'Mortgage' only approximately translates *hypothèque.*

Endnotes

739 C. civ, from Art. 815-2, also as suggested in two interviews.
740 See the quotation from Pauliat (1998); p. 64 and effects of this concept on p. 209.
741 See the social landlord's comment on p. 199.
742 From ibid.
743 C. civ., Art. 220-1.
744 A new offence of mental torture in domestic violence was recently created.
745 A civil injunction could be obtained there some days later. A police injunction may be possible in France but preliminary enquiries did now show use of this.
746 My thanks to Julio Ponce and Wolfgang Amann.
747 See also p. 211 for other euptemisms.
748 Loi n° 78-17 du 6 janvier 1978, Art. 8, very similar now and during the study.
749 Limited areas of research were exempted on approval usually by the Commission national d'informatique et des libertés, in ibid.
750 Thanks to Jean-Philippe Brouant for this information.
751 *Etrangers.*
752 From USH in 2005.
753 From 1996. The 1999 Census and INSEE (2002) showed where foreigners lived.
754 Including HALDE, GELD, and FASILD, with *associations*, monitoring bodies, university studies and those sponsored by local actors.
755 Groupe d'etudes et de lutte contre les discriminations
756 La Haute autorité de lutte contre les discriminations et pour l'égalite.
757 C. Cons., 2000-557 DC. This did not disapprove statistics collection in principle, but mainly the context within an immigration statute.
758 Fonds d'action et de soutien pour l'integration et la lutte contre les discriminations.
759 Ibid. The Sarkozy government initially appointed two ethnic minority cabinet ministers.
760 B.O. Ministère du Travail, n° 35, 22 août 1976.
761 C. pén., Arts. 225-1 and 225-2.
762 From interviewees and from a number of foreign restaurants there.
763 An idea from Smith (1989: 36).
764 See p. 172.
765 Capital inserted by interviewee.
766 Such as p. 174 in Lyon.
767 See p. 125.
768 From 2008, 250 more communes were included.
769 Names could not be easily changed. See C. civ., Arts. 61 to 61-4.
770 For a brief discussion of group behaviour see p. 29 and pp. 72ff. Also for possible reasons for why people work together, section 5.3.3 (p. 130).
771 From a local actor.
772 C.C.H., Art. L. 441-1, para. 1.
773 See Table 2.1 (p. 47).
774 From p. 200.
775 Section 4.1.5–6 (pp. 93ff).
776 See their class action rights, p. 77.
777 From interviews.
778 See p. 167.
779 See p. 171. Incomplete files could properly be rejected.
780 The exact route of these applications was uncertain if there were reservations.
781 See p. 176 for their training.
782 Under the DALO Act, see section 4.1.7 (p. 96).
783 For example, C.C.H., Art. L. 441-2-3, I, al. 3° new legislation, not 2005.
784 C.C.H., Art. L. 441-2-3, I, or three months after the prefect failed to find a home, in the public or private courts, Arts. L. 441-2-3 to L. 441-2-6, and R. *441-14 to R. *441-18-5.

785   C.C.H., Art. L. 441-2-3, I, al. 5. Delays for hostel access were shorter.
786   After a series of steps, the prefect can allocate. Art. L. 441-2-3, II, al. 10.
787   C.C.H., Art. L. 441-2-3.
788   This requires a series of consultative and information procedures before the prefect allocated personally. Such a coercive decision could be judicially reviewed anyway.
789   For example, by injunction since 2007, and by damages in addition to quashing an order on *recours pour excès de pouvoir* (similar to judicial review).
790   C.C.H., Art. L. 441-2-3-1, I, al. 7. Fines were paid towards the construction funds under Art. L. 302-5, C.C.H. see note 469.
791   Under C.C.H., Art. L. 441-3-1. This emerged during discussion at a meeting of the Paris Bar and the GRIDAUH in November 2009.
792   Particularly bad in the four overseas *départements*
793   Now under C.C.H., Art. L. 441-2-3-1.
794   An analysis of process using game theory might be possible, since dominance and transparency are important (Kreps 1990; Schelling 1956).
795   See p. 6 and section 1.4.4 (p. 27).
796   See p. 189.
797   For example, Coolos and Taffin (1998) and cycle of life studies, such as Jousselin (1998).
798   For example, for car factories in the Hauts de Seine.
799   See p. 246.
800   Based on tax returns or declaration.

10 Housing some of the disadvantaged

801   See p. 12.
802   See note 12.
803   Under the DALO Act, see sections 4.1.7 and 9.5.2 (pp. 96 and 222).
804   See p. 106.
805   Particularly sections 3.2 and 3.3.3 (the right to property; pp. 63ff), 4.2.3 and 7.1.3 (social mix; pp. 103 and 163), 4.1.3 and 4.2.1 (the right to housing; pp. 87 and 98) and Ch. 7.
806   Particularly Ch. 7 and section 9.5 (p. 221).
807   See p. 91.
808   A theme of Ch. 7 generally.
809   For example, p. 162.
810   See actors' views on p. 99.
811   See the ECSR decision, p. 229, and section 9.5.2 (p. 222).
812   See p. 144 for the duty of prudence.
813   A theme of sections 3.2-3 (pp. 63ff).
814   See p. 1.
815   Both by reservations, section 7.1.4 (p. 165), and on the allocation commission section, 7.4.2 (p. 179).
816   From p. 68.
817   Section 9.4.2 (pp. 214ff).
818   See p. 20.
819   See p. 64.
820   See Schelling (1956) for bargaining effects.
821   Nelken was describing the application of the Rent Acts 1957 and 1965 by private landlords.
822   See section 7.4.2 (p. 179).
823   Section 7.2 (p. 166).
824   Section 5.3 (p. 127).
825   See pp. 169ff.

Endnotes

826 The *communauté* of Lyon returned spaces obtained through reservation to mayors. See p. 168.
827 See p. 196.
828 Ch. 6 generally.
829 Section 5.1.4 (p. 117).
830 See p. 142.
831 But public policy can be successful. See the SIAL, p. 168.
832 See section 8.1.5 (p. 190) for a discussion of nimbyism and spatial insiderness.
833 Sections 8.1.2 and 8.2.2 (pp. 187 and 192).
834 For rent, see section 6.4.2 (p. 151).
835 Sections 1.4 and 8.1.1 (pp. 22 and 185) for a discussion of transaction costs.
836 The 1989 Act only concerned unfurnished premises. Furnished letting fell with C. civ. Arts. 1708–1762.
837 By guarantee schemes, for example, p. 128.
838 See p. 167 (for Lyon), and for contractualization, sections 5.2 and 5.3 (pp. 123 and 127).
839 See p. 225 for hysteresis in labour markets.
840 Section 6.3 (p. 145).
841 In modern fair value accounting, low rent might appear as a loss in the landlord's balance sheet, if showing the current expected return on asset value.
842 Such as Kemp (2007).
843 Section 9.2 (p. 206).
844 See p. 27.
845 From p. 180.
846 See p. 26 and note 86.
847 From interviews.
848 See note 85 for sorce of ban.
849 Partly because of the iconic historical response to death on the streets, p. 80.
850 See pp. 19 and 124.
851 From pp. 98 and 223.
852 From p. 176 and p. 192.
853 Section 6.5 (p. 155).
854 On urban regeneration. See p. 126.
855 See note 638.
856 See p. 197.
857 Section 8.2.2 (p. 192).
858 Ibid.
859 Chapter 6 generally.
860 Section 8.1.5 (p. 190).
861 Section 8.2.3 (p. 194).
862 See p. 28.
863 See p. 159.
864 The CFF had estimated need as above 500,000, to general approval.
865 See p. 169.
866 This is likely to arise, see section. 9.5.2 (p. 222).
867 See p. 139.
868 See pp. 103 and 106. Cowan and Marsh (2005) also suggested that regulation of English social housing allocation was affected by valorization of expertise in management.
869 Section 9.4.1 (p. 211) for lack of statistics.
870 Section 2.1.5 (p. 40) above.
871 Estimated by ANIL.
872 Table 6.5 (p. 155).
873 See pp. 19ff.
874 See p. 115.

Endnotes

875 Section 5.2.1 (p. 123).
876 See p. 28.
877 See p. 19 and the activities of tenants' *associations* (pp. 77ff).
878 Section 2.1.1 (p. 36).
879 Section 8.3.1 (p. 199).
880 See p. 33.
881 See the brief description of the UK system, p. 37 and note 200.
882 From p. 42.
883 Seen, for example, in housing estates of the Bourneville Trust, near Birmingham.
884 Section 2.1.3 (p. 38).
885 Above p. 41 and note 136.
886 Section 4.1.3 (p. 87) particularly p. 90 for State responsibility.
887 See p. 235.
888 See p. 119. Public order in this sense can be a basis for homelessness assistance elsewhere, such as in Germany.
889 Under the Housing Act 1996, Parts VI and VII.
890 Ch. 9.
891 The French cohabitation contract, the PACS, has much to offer.
892 Shared custody, sections 8.2.2 and 9.3.1 (pp. 192 and 208ff), and insecurity in sections 9.2–3 (pp. 206ff).
893 Some policy reasons here are protection of the rights of the person accused of violence (section 9.3.3, p. 210) and expected greater responsibility on police (who enforce injunctions anyway).
894 Section 8.2.2 (p. 192).
895 Section 9.4.2 (p. 214).
896 Besson Act, Art. 1.
897 Sections 3.2.3–5 (pp. 67ff).
898 See the incomes in Fig. 1.1 (p. 12).

Appendix 1: methodological detail

899 See also below Appendix 1, section A1.1 (p. 257).
900 See p. 72.
901 The role of function in comparative law is discussed at pp. 257ff.
902 This observation comes from 10 years organizing international workshops, as co-coordinator of the ENHR working group on housing land and planning.
903 This is widespread but includes Deschamps (1998) and Jégouzo-Vienot (2002).
904 For example, legal doctrine, *la doctrine*, means the writings and opinions of doctors of law and learned authors, which are not secondary sources.
905 Inherent in the widespread use of principle, but also a Napoleonic tradition of explanation to the public.
906 See p. 152.
907 Information from ANIL.
908 See p. 117 for their work.
909 Omitted from topic guides in Lyon and the Nord. Other questions cover the point.
910 Omitted for Lyon and the Nord (not within direct knowledge of actors).
911 Added for the Nord to cover other local arrangements.
912 See Glossary.
913 See p. 172.
914 See note 372, due to a then fear they were too close to government.
915 Whereby an *association* acts as an intermediary between a landlord and a risky tenant.

Endnotes

Appendix 2: allocation principles

916 Or *commune de rattachement*, in which the public social landlord was based.
917 Known as SMIC.

Bibliography

Acosta, R. and Renard, V. (1993), *Urban Land and Property Markets in France,* London: UCL Press Ltd.
Adams, J.N. and Brownsword, R. (2000) *Understanding Contract Law,* 3rd edn, London: Sweet and Maxwell.
Ahlfinger, N.R. and Esser, J.K. (2001) 'Testing the groupthink model: Effects of promotional leadership and conformity predisposition', *Social Behavior and Personality,* 29(1): 31–41.
Akerlof, G.A. (1970) 'The market for "lemons": Quality, uncertainty and the market mechanism', *Quarterly Journal of Economics,* 84 (August): 488–500.
Alesina, A. and Glaeser, E.L. (2005) *Fighting Poverty in the US and Europe,* Oxford: Oxford University Press.
Amzallag, M. and Taffin, C. (2003) *Le Logement Social,* Paris: L.C.D.J.
ANIL (2000) *Etude: Logement et Instabilité Familiale,* January 2000, Paris: ANIL. Available online at http://www.anil.org/fr/publications-et-etudes/etudes-et-eclairages/2000/logement-et-instabilite-familiale/index.html (accessed 25 May 2011).
—— (2005) *La Politique du Logement des Départements: Etat des Lieux et Perspectives. Bilan de l'Enquete auprès des Présidents de Conseils Généraux,* April 2005, Paris: ANIL.
Arber, S. (2001) 'Designing samples', in Gilbert N. (ed.) *Researching Social Life,* 2nd edn, London: Sage Publications, pp. 58–82.
Arden, A. (2003) *Manual of Housing Law,* London: Sweet & Maxwell.
Audier, S. (2007) *Léon Bourgeois. Fonder la Solidarité,* Paris: Michalon.
Ball, (A.)J. (2008) 'The limitations to the right to housing for the poor and disadvantaged in France: Insiders and outsiders in social housing allocation', unpublished thesis, University of Sheffield.
Ball, J. (2003) 'Renting homes: Status and security in the UK and France. A comparison in the light of the Law Commission's proposals', *The Conveyancer and Property Lawyer,* 67 (January/February): 36–58.
—— (2006) 'The boundaries of property rights in English law', *Electronic Journal of Comparative Law,* 10.3 (December). Available online at http://www.ejcl.org/103/art103-1.pdf (accessed 25 May 2011).
—— (2010a) 'Using banks: The effect of national attitudes to public intervention in mortgage lending and eviction in French and English law', *The International Journal of the Law of the Built Environment,* 2(2): 118–37.

Bibliography

—— (2010b) 'Towards a deeper understanding of property, tenancies and land occupancy in the face of legal doctrinal divergence', paper presented at ENHR annual conference, Istanbul, June 2010.

—— (2010c) 'Where will European property law go next? Tenancies and property after *Hutten-Czapska v Poland* and *FEANTSA v Slovenia*', paper presented at COBRA annual conference, Paris, July 2010.

—— (2010d) 'Fragmenting property for affordability: Shared ownership or "new" tenures in England and France', paper presented at the seminar, Accèss a l'Habitage en el Context del Crisi, Tarragona, May, 2010.

Ballain, R. (2005) *Pauvreté, Exclusion et Logement, Bilan des Etudes et Recherches,* Grenoble: Iep-Grenoble-Cerat.

Ballain, R. and Benguigi, F. (2004) *L'Accès au Logement: Des Evolutions en Débat,* Paris: PUCA.

Banque de France (2001) *Bulletin No. 92, August 2001,* Paris: La Banque de France. Available online at http://www.banque-france.fr/archipel/publications/bdf_bm/bdf_bm_2001/bdf_bm_92.pdf (accessed 25 May 2011).

Barker, K. (2004) *Delivering Stability: Securing our Future Housing Needs,* final report of 12 March 2004, London: HM Treasury.

Barre, R. (1976) *Rapport de la Commission d'Etude d'une Réforme du Financement du Logement, Présidée par Raymond Barre (Décembre 1975),* Paris: La Documentation française.

Barré-Pépin, M. and Coutant-Lapalus, C. (2005) *Logement et Famille: Des Droits en Question,* Paris: Dalloz.

Bart, J. (2009) *Histoire du Droit Privé, de la Chute de l'Empire Romain au XIXe Siècle,* Paris: Monchrestien.

Batiactu (2002) 'Robien veut relancer le vote des représentants des locataires', *Batiactu,* 7 November. Available online at http://www.batiactu.com/data/05112002/05112002-160808.html (accessed 25 May 2011).

—— (2005) 'Le Conseil Economique et Social à Paris occupé par des mal-logés', *Batiactu,* 14 September. Available online at http://www.batiactu.com/data/14092005/14092005-155830.html (accessed 25 May 2011).

—— (2006a) 'Sondage: Les logements sociaux en ligne de mire', *Batiactu,* 22 February. Available online at http://www.batiactu.com/data/22022006/22022006-113633.html (accessed 25 May 2011).

—— (2006b) 'L'OPAC de St. Etienne attaqué en justice par SOS Racisme', *Batiactu,* 22 February. Available online at http://www.batiactu.com/data/22022006/22022006-154538.html (accessed 25 May 2011).

—— (2006c) 'Plus d'un millier de manifestants à Paris contre les expulsions', *Batiactu,* 3 March. Available online at http://www.batiactu.com/data/13032006/13032006-101334.html (accessed 25 May 2011).

—— (2010) 'Plus de 50,000 foyers aisés dans les HLM', *Batiactu,* 29 November. Available online at http://www.batiactu.com/edito/plus-de-50000-foyers-aises-dans-les-hlm-27472.php (accessed 11 February 2011).

Baudrillard, J. (1990, originally written in 1970) *The Consumer Society, Myths and Structures,* trans. 'C.T.', London: Sage Publications.

Bégassat, L. (1997) 'Les aides personnelles au logement à la lumière des expériences européennes', *L'Observateur de i'immobilier,* 35 (March): 6.

Beguin, J-C., Charlot, P. and Ladié, Y. (2005) *Soldarité en Droit Public Français,* Paris: l'Harmattan.
Bell, D.S. (2003) 'The French Communist Party, from revolution to reform', in Evans, J. (ed.) *The French Party System,* Manchester: Manchester University Press, pp. 29–41.
Bell, J. (2001) *French Legal Cultures,* London: Butterworths.
Bell, J., Boyron, S. and Whittaker, S. (1996) *Principles of French Law,* Oxford: Oxford University Press.
Bell, M. (2010) 'Irregular migrants: Beyond the limits of solidarity?' in Ross, M. and Borgmann-Prebil, Y. (eds) *Promoting Solidarity in the European Union,* Oxford: Oxford University Press, p. 151.
Benguigui, F. (dir.) (1995) *La Politique du Logement à l'Epreuve de la Précarité,* Paris: Plan, construction et architecture.
—— (dir.) (1997) *Loger les Personnes Défavorisées*, Paris, La Documentation française.
Bergh, R.J. van den and Camesasca, P.D. (2006) *European Competition Law and Economics: A Comparative Perspective,* 2nd edn, London: Thompson Sweet & Maxwell.
Bernard-Gélabert, M-C. (2004) *L'Intercommunalité,* 5th edn, Paris: L.G.D.J.
Berry, M. and Hall, J. (2005) 'Institutional investment in rental housing in Australia: A policy framework and two models', *Urban Studies,* 42(1): 91–111.
Bissuel, B. (2002) 'Un nouveau motif de refus pour les offices HLM', *Le Monde,* 27 April. Available online at http://abonnes.lemonde.fr/cgibin/ACHATS/ARCHIVES/archives.cgi?ID=0ad6059936e34fd4993263eec2bd9ca8b798600444f18942//www.lemonde.fr (accessed 7 February 2011).
—— (2005) 'Les allocations-logement pourraient jouer un rôle dans la hausse des loyers des familles à bas revenues', *Le Monde,* 2 November. Available online at http://www.lemonde.fr (accessed 25 May 2011).
—— (2010) 'La pérennité du financement du «1% Logement»' n'est plus assurée.' *Le Monde,* 30 March. Available online at http://abonnes.lemonde.fr/cgi-bin/ACHATS/ARCHIVES/archives.cgi?ID=74715cefcd4ec16f7755398619b7539e2136a0b2c567b369 (accessed 7 Feburary 2011).
Blanc, M. (2010) 'The impact of social mix policies in France', *Housing Studies,* 25(2): 257–72.
Blandy, S. and Goodchild, B. (1999) 'From tenure to rights: Conceptualizing the changing focus of housing law in England', *Housing, Theory and Society,* 16(1): 31–42.
Blum, A., Guérin-Pace, F. and Le Bras, H. (2007) 'La statistique, piège éthnique', *Le Monde,* 10 November. Available online at http://abonnes.lemonde.fr/cgi-bin/ACHATS/ARCHIVES/archives.cgi?ID=5c7a1a173637c61bb688839493602ecaa54fa0bbdda08fe4 (accessed 1 February 2011).
Bobasch, M. (2003) 'Tribunal administratif, mode d'emploi', *Le Monde,* 21 May. Available online at http://abonnes.lemonde.fr/cgi-bin/ACHATS/acheter.cgi?offre=ARCHIVES&type_item=ART_ARCH_30J&objet_id=804856 (accessed 25 May 2011).
Boccadoro, N. (2007) 'Le droit au logement', unpublished thesis, University of Paris X-Nanterre.
Bolt, G., Phillips, D. and Van Kempen, R.(2010) 'Housing policy, (de)segregation and social mixing: An international perspective', *Housing Studies,* 25(2): 129–35.
Booth, P. (1992) *TRP 106, Undertaking Comparative Research: The Experience of Working on French Development Control,* Sheffield: The University of Sheffield.

Bibliography

Bordenave, Y. (2005), 'Un an de prison ferme requis contre M. Schuller', *Le Monde*, 17 August. Available online at http://abonnes.lemonde.fr/cgi-bin/ACHATS/acheter.cgi?offre=ARCHIVES&type_item=ART_ARCH_30J&objet_id=909570 (accessed 18 February 2011).

Bosvieux, J. (1998) 'Besoins et demande de logements', in Segaud M., Bonvalet, C. and Brun, J. (eds) *Logement et habitat, L'etat des savoirs,* Paris: Éditions la découverte, pp. 86–93.

Bottoms, A., Mawlby, R.I. and Xanthos P. (1989) *A Tale of Two Estates. Crime and the City,* Basingstoke: Macmillan.

Bourgeois, C. (1993) *Le Logement Social: Un Enjeu Local, les Mécanismes de Gestion des Organismes HLM,* Paris: Institut d'études politiques de Paris.

—— (1996) *L'Attribution des Logements Sociaux, Politique Publique et Jeux des Acteurs Locaux,* Paris: L'Harmattan.

Brouant, J-P. (2002) 'Mixité sociale, droit au logement et communautarisme', in le GRIDAUH, *Droit de l'Aménagement, de l'Urbanisme et de l'Habitat 2002,* Paris: le GRIDAUH, pp. 159–181.

—— (ed.) (2007) *Code de la Construction et de l'Habitation Commenté,* Paris: Dalloz.

—— (2008) 'Un droit au logement ... variablement opposable', *AJDI,* 64(10), 506–10.

—— (2011) 'La mise en œuvre du DALO à l'épreuve des territoires', in Noémie Hourd (dir) *Loger l'Europe, le Logement Social dans Tous ses Etats,* La Documentation française.

Brouant, J-P., and Jégouzo, Y. (1998) *La Territorialisation des Politiques du Droit de l'Habitat Social, Les Cahiers du GRIDAUH No.2,* Paris: GRIDAUH.

Brousse, P. [1883] (1910) *La Propriété Collective et les Services Publics,* Paris: Bureaux du 'Prolétaire'.

Brown, L.N. and Bell, J. (1998) *French Administrative Law,* 5th edn, Oxford: Clarendon Press.

Brunelli, P. (1998) *Le Contrôle de Légalité,* Paris: L.G.D.J.

Buttin, V. (2006) 'Le débat politique sur l'avenir du logement social s'ouvre au congrès du mouvement HLM', *Batiactu,* 18 September. Available online at http://www.batiactu.com/edito/le-debat-politique-sur-l-avenir-du-logement-social-4020.php (accessed 20 January 2011).

Carbonnier, J. (1973) *Droit Civil. 3. Les Biens,* Paris, Presses universitaires de France.

Carpenter, J., Chauviré, Y. and White, P. (1994) 'Marginalization, polarization and planning in Paris', *Journal of the Built Environment,* 20(3): 218–30.

Castells, M. (1977) *The Urban Question: a Marxist Approach,* London: Matthew Arnold.

CECODHAS (2006), *Colloquium Proceedings: Current Developments in Housing Policies and Housing Markets in Europe: Implications for the Social Housing Sector, 13 September 2006,* CECODHAS: Brussels.

Central Statistical Office (2007) *Housing Economy in 2007,* Warsaw: Central Statistical Office.

Charlet, P. and Laurent, M. (AORIF) (2006) *Les Attributions dans le Parc Social Francilien en 2005,* Paris: Observatoire du logement social en Ile-de-France.

Chevallereau, E. (2008) 'Christine Boutin ne croit pas au plan banlieue de Fadela Amara', *Le Monde,* 15 January. Available online at http://abonnes.lemonde.fr/societe/article/2008/01/14/christine-boutin-ne-croit-pas-au-plan-banlieue-de-fadela-amara_998981_3224.html (accessed 17 March 2010).

Bibliography

Coase, R. (1960) 'The Problem of Social Cost', *Journal of Law and Economics,* 3: 1–44.
COHRE (2000) *Sources Four: Legal Resources for Housing Right,* 2nd edn, Geneva: COHRE. Available online at http://www.cohre.org/view_page.php?page_id=4 (accessed 15 July 2010).
Cole, I., Kane, S. and Robinson, D. (1999) *Changing Demand, Changing Neighbourhoods: The Response of Social Landlords,* Sheffield: CRESR, Sheffield Hallam University.
Comité de suivi de la mise en oeuvre de droit opposable au logement (2009) *Assumer l'Obligation de Résultat du Droit au Logement sur l'Ensemble du Territoire, Deuxième Rapport,* Paris: Comité de Suivi.
Coolos, B. and Taffin, C. (1998) 'Mobilité résidentielle et statuts d'occupation', in Segaud M., Bonvalet, C. and Brun, J. (eds) in *Logement et Habitat, L'Etat des Savoirs,* Paris: Éditions la découverte, 110–19.
Costa, A. (2007) 'L'application de la loi LRL de 2004 – Politiques, de l'habitat et décentralisation', *l'Observateur de l'immobilier,* 69 (March): 34–36.
Courvoisier, C. (2005) 'Introduction' in Béguin, J-C., Charlot, P. and Laidié, Y. (eds) *La Solidarité en Droit Public,* Paris: l'Harmattan, pp. 7–10.
Cowan, D. (1997) *Homelessness,* Aldershot: Ashgate.
Cowan, D. and Marsh, A. (2005) 'From need to choice, Welfarism to advanced liberalism? Problematics of social housing allocation', *Legal Studies,* 25(1) 22–48.
Cowan, D., McDermont, M. and Morgan, K. (2008). *Problematic Allocations. Final Report to the ESRC.* Available online at http://www.bris.ac.uk/law/research/centres-themes/nominations/nominationsreport.pdf (accessed 23 May 2011).
Cozian, M., Viandier, A. and Deboissy, F. (2008) *Droit des Sociétés,* 21st edn, Paris: Litec.
Croze, H. (2004) *Le Procès Civil,* 2nd edn, Paris: Dalloz.
Czischke, D. (2005) *Social Housing in the EU. Time for Legal Certainty for Local Authorities, Social Housing Providers and Millions of European Households,* Report to the European Commission, March 2005, Brussels, CECODHAS European Social Housing Observatory.
—— (2009) 'Managing social housing in the EU: A comparative study', *European Journal of Housing Policy,* 9(2): 121–51.
DAL (1996) *Le Logement un Droit pour Tous,* Paris: le Cherche midi éditeur.
—— (2007) *Droit au Logement.* Available online at http://www.globenet.org/dal/(accessed 26 May 2011).
Damon, J. (2006) *Les Politiques Familiales, Que Sais-Je?* series, Paris: PUF.
DARES (2008) 'Le paradoxe du syndicalisme français: Un faible nombre d'adhérents, Mais des syndicats bien implantés', *Première,* April 2008, No. 16(1).
David, M. (2005) 'Soldarité et fraternité en droit public français', in Beguin, J-C., Charlot, P. and Ladié, Y. (eds) *Soldarité en Droit Public Français,* Paris: l'Harmattan.
Davis, K.C. (1977) *Discretionary Justice, A Preliminary Inquiry,* Chicago and London: University of Illinois Press.
De Búrca, G. (2005) 'The future of social rights protection in Europe', in De Búrca, G. and De Witte, B. (eds) *Social Rights in Europe,* Oxford: Oxford University Press, pp. 3–13.
De Búrca, G. and De Witte, B. (eds) (2005) *Social Rights in Europe,* Oxford: Oxford University Press.
Decocq, A. and Decocq, G. (2004) *Droit de la Concurrence Interne et Communautaire,* 2nd edn, Paris: L.G.D.J.
DEEF (2005) *Le Parc HLM au 1 Janvier 2004,* Paris: l'Union sociale de l'habitat.

Bibliography

De Montvallon, J-B. (2005) 'Emeutes de Clichy-sous-Bous: Les interventons de Nicolas Sarkozy sont contestées, même à droite', *le Monde*. Available online at http://www.lemonde.fr/web/ep/password_envoyer/1,27-0,1-0,0.html?param=B66BA5722BC4D818C537E7B8051981AB-CFCF5835934B6EDA1B317FAE103F0D2B (2 January 2011).

Deschamps, E. (1998) *Le Droit Public et la Ségrégation Urbaine (1943–1997)*, Paris: L.G.D.J.

Deschamps, E. (2005) 'Solidarité et politique de la ville: L'example du logement social' in Béguin, J-C., Charlot, P. and Laidié, Y. (eds) *La Solidarité en Droit Public*, Paris: l'Harmattan, pp. 185–240.

DGCL (Direction Générale des Collectivités Locales) (2009) *Bilan Statistique 2009*, Paris: DGCL. Available online at http://www.dgcl.interieur.gouv.fr/sections/a_votre_service/statistiques/intercommunalite/bilan_statistique/bilan_statistique_20/view (accessed 11 February 2011)

Dogge, P.J.C. and Smeets, J.J.A.M. (2007) *Freedom of Choice on the Housing Market: The Case of Eindhoven*, paper given at the ENHR conference, Rotterdam, June 2007.

Doling, J. (1997) *Comparative Housing Policy. Government and Housing in Advanced Industrial Countries*, Basingstoke: Macmillan.

—— (1999) 'De-commodification and welfare: Evaluating housing systems', *Housing, Theory and Society*, 16(4): 156–76.

Domat, J. (1691) *Lois Civiles dans leur Ordre Naturel, Le Droit Public et Legum Delectus*, reproduced online by L'Université Paul Cézanne-Aix-Marseille 3. Available online at http://flora.univ-cezanne.fr/flora/pub_aix/fr/document/droit/Domat/DOMAT.pdf (accessed 6 January 2010).

Donner, C. (2000) *Housing Policies in the European Union*, Vienna: Christian Donner.

Donnison, D. (1967) *The Government of Housing*, Harmondsworth: Penguin.

Doyle, W. (1989) *The Oxford Book of the French Revolution*, Oxford: Oxford University Press.

Dreyfus, M. (2009) 'France', in Krajewski, M., Neergaard, U. and Gronden, J. van de (eds) *The Changing Legal Framework for Services of General Interest in Europe. Between Competition and Solidarity*, The Hague: Asser Press.

Driant J-C. (2002) 'Vers l'éclatement du système HLM', *Etudes foncières*, 100 (November-December): 16–17.

—— (2004) 'La géographie complexe de la délégation des aides à la pierre', *Etudes Foncières*, 111 (September-October): 16–19.

Dubedout, H. (1983) *Ensemble Refaire la Ville, Commission Présidée par H. Dubedout*, Paris: La Documentation française.

Dubois, J-P. (2005) 'Rapport de Synthèse' in Béguin, J-C., Charlot, P. and Laidié, Y. (eds) *La Solidarité en Droit Français*, Paris: l'Harmattan, pp. 329–347.

Duclaud-Williams, R.H. (1978) *The Politics of Housing in Britain and France*, London: Heinemann Educational.

Duguit, L. (1912) *Les Transformations Générales du Droit Privé depuis le Code Napoléon*, Paris: LeBon.

Dupeyroux, J-J. (1998) *Droit de la Sécurité Sociale*, 13th edn, Paris: Dalloz.

Dupuis, G., Guédon M-J. and Chrétien, P. (2000) *Droit Administratif*, 7th edn, Paris: Armand Colin.

Durkheim, E. (1986) *De la Division du Travail Sociale*, Paris: PUF.

Dutton, P.V. (2002) *The Origins of the French Welfare State,* Cambridge: Cambridge University Press.

Dyson, H. (2005) *French Property and Inheritance Law,* Oxford: Oxford University Press.

The Economist (1999), 'Consumer finance: Pay dirt. Creative financial products for America's poor', *The Economist,* 3 June. Available online at http://www.economist.com/world/unitedstates/displaystory.cfm?story_id=E1_NDJRNQ (accessed 4 January 2010).

—— (2002a) 'France, race and immigration. Who gains?', *The Economist,* 28 February. Available online at http://www.economist.com/node/1011490 (accessed 5 February 2010).

—— (2002b) 'A question of colour, a matter of faith. France must face up to its immigration problem', *The Economist,* 14 November. Available online at http://www.economist.com/node/1428558 (accessed 25 May 2011).

—— (2005a) 'Credit cards: Sub-prime time – The risky business of lending to people with poor credit records', *The Economist,* February 17. Available online at http://www.economist.com/node/3672805 (accessed 25 May 2011).

—— (2005b)'France's riots –An underclass rebellion', *The Economist,* 14 November. Available online at http://www.economist.com/world/displaystory.cfm?story_id=E1_VTPVSJV (accessed 25 May 2011).

—— (2006a) 'France and Immigration. Let the skilled come'. *The Economist,* 4 May. Available online at http://www.economist.com/world/europe/displaystory.cfm?story_id=E1_GRRRSDT (accessed 25 May 2011).

—— (2006b) 'Survey: France – Reforming the unreformable'. *The Economist,* 28 October, p. 9.

—— (2006c) 'Survey: France. Insiders and Outsiders', *The Economist,* 28 October. Available online at http://www.economist.com/surveys/displaystory.cfm?story_id=E1_RDQRPRR (accessed 25 May 2011).

—— (2007)'.For richer or for poorer', *The Economist,* 1 March. Available online at http://www.economist.com/world/international/displaystory.cfm?story_id=E1_RSRDTSP (accessed 25 May 2011).

—— (2010a) 'French politics resumes. Tough-guy Sarko' *The Economist,* 26 August. Available online at http//www.economist.com/node/16889547?story_id=16889547 (accessed 25 May 2011).

—— (2010b) 'Violent crime in France. Burn, baby, burn', *The Economist,* 15 April. Available online at http//www.economist.com/node/15913046 (accessed 25 May 2011).

Elsinga M., Haffner M., Heijden, H. van der and Oxley M. (2009) 'How can competition in social rental housing in England and the Netherlands be measured?' *International Journal of Housing Policy,* 9(2): 153–176.

Erp, S. van (2003) 'A *numerus quasi-clausus* of property rights as a constitutive element of a future European property law?', *Electronic Journal of Comparative Law,* vol. 7(2). Available online at http://www.ejcl.org/72/art72-2.html (accessed 6 January 2011).

Esping-Andersen, G. (1990) *The Three Worlds of Welfare Capitalism,* Princeton: Princeton University Press.

Etienne, J. (2004) *L'Hébergement Touristique,* Nantes: Conseil économique et social des pays de Loire. Available online at http://cesr.paysdelaloire.fr/index.php?id=55&tx_ttnews%5Btt_news%5D=41&tx_ttnews%5BbackPid%5D=2419&cHash=7bef977a1c (accessed 5 January 2011).

Bibliography

EU Commission (2009) *Study of Housing Exclusion, Welfare Policies, Housing Provision and Labour Markets,* 10 April, Brussels: EU Commission, Directorate-General for Employment, Social Affairs and Equal Opportunities.

European University Institute (undated) *Tenancy Law and Procedure in the EU.* Available online at http://www.eui.eu/DepartmentsAndCentres/Law/ResearchAndTeaching/ResearchThemes/ProjectTenancyLaw.aspx (accessed 11 February 2011).

Euvrard, M. (1992) 'Le financement des acquéreurs de logements en France', in Institut d'Etudes Bancaires et Financières (ed.) *Logement et son Financement en France et dans les Principaux Pays Industrialisés,* Paris: Berger Levrault, 91–138.

Evans, J. (2003) *The French Party System,* Manchester: Manchester University Press.

FASILD (2003) *Les Discriminations des Jeunes d'Origine Etrangrère dans l'Accès à l'Emploi et l'Accès au Logement,* Paris: la Documentation française.

Fehling, M. (2009) 'Problems of cross-subsidisation', in Krajewski, M., Neergaard, U. and Gronden, J. van de (eds) *The Changing Legal Framework for Services of General Interest in Europe. Between Competition and Solidarity,* The Hague: Asser Press.

Le Figaro (2009) 'Le 1% Logement maintient le cap de sa réforme' *Le Figaro,* 12 November: p. 22.

Filippi, B. and Tutin, C. (2006) *Social Housing, Housing Markets and Urban Structures: The French Case,* paper presented at a seminar of the ENHR special project on social landlords, Brussels, 17 March 2006.

Fitoussi, J-P., Laurent, E. and Maurice, J. (2004) *Ségrégation Urbaine et Intégration Sociale,* Paris: Conseil d'analyse economique.

Fitzpatrick, S. (1999) 'Homelessness, need and desert in the allocation of council housing', *Housing Studies,* 14(4): 412–31.

Fitzpatrick, S. and Stephens, M. (2007) *An International Review of Homelessness and Social Housing Policy,* York: Centre for Housing Policy, University of York.

Flamand, J-P. (2001) *Loger Le Peuple: Essai sur l'Histoire du Logement Social,* Paris: Editions la découverte et Syros.

Fondation Abbé Pierre (2005) *L'Etat du Mal Logement en France, Rapport Annuel 2005,* Paris: L'Artésienne.

—— (2006) *L'Etat du Mal Logement en France, Rapport Annuel 2006,* Paris: L'Artésienne.

—— (2008) *L'Etat du Mal Logement en France, Rapport Annuel 2008,* Paris: L'Artésienne.

Forsyth, D.R. (2006). *Group Dynamics,* 4th edn, Belmont, CA: Thomson Wadsworth.

Foster, N.H.D. (2006) 'The Journal of Comparative Law: A new scholarly resource', *The Journal of Comparative Law,* 1(1): 1–7.

Foster, N.H.D. and Ball, J. (2006) 'Imperialism and accountability in corporate law: The limitations of incorporation law as a regulatory mechanism', in MacLeod, S. and Parkinson, J. (eds) *Global Governance and the Quest for Justice: Volume II, Corporate Governance,* Oxford: Hart, pp. 103–9.

Fourrier, C. (1829) *Le Nouveau Monde Industriel et Sociétaire ou Invention du Procédé d'Industrie Attrayante et Naturelle Distribuée en Séries Passionnées,* Paris: Bossange père.

FR avec AFP (*sic*)(2006) 'Cachan: Les deux grévistes de la faim hospitalisés sont déterminés à continuer', *Le Monde,* 2 October. Available online at http://www.lemonde.fr/societe/article/2006/10/02/cachan-les-deux-grevistes-de-la-faim-hospitalises-sont-determines-a-continuer_819271_3224.html (accessed 26 May 2011).

Friggit, J. (2006) 'Sur le coût de la mixité sociale', *Etudes foncières,* 123: 6–8.

Bibliography

Galano, M. (2002) *Une Lutte Exemplaire,* Paris: GISTI. Available online at http://www.gisti.org (accessed 25 May 2011).
Galligan, D.J. (1986) *Discretionary Powers,* Oxford: Oxford University Press.
Galster, G. (2007) 'Neighborhood social mix as a goal of housing policy, a theoretical analysis'. *European Journal of Housing Policy,* 7(1): 19–43.
Geindre, F. (1990) *L'Attribution des Logements Sociaux,* Paris: Ministère de l'équipement, de logement, des transports et de la mer.
Ghékière, L. (2008) 'Social housing as a Service of General Interest', in Scanlon, K. and Whitehead, C. (eds) *Social Housing in Europe II,* London: LSE, 271–86.
Gilbert N. (ed.) (2001) *Researching Social Life,* 2nd edn, London: Sage Publications.
Gill, J-P., Hubert, C. and Lanversin, J. de (eds) (1996) *Les Grands Arrêts du Droit de l'Urbanisme,* Paris: Dalloz.
Glaser, B.G.L. and Straus A.L. (1967) *The Discovery of Grounded Theory, Strategies for Qualitative Research*, Chicago: Aldinea.
Goetz, E.G. (2010) 'Desegregation in 3D: Displacement, dispersal and development in American public housing', *Housing Studies*, 25(2): 137–58.
Gonnard, R. (1943) *La Propriété dans la Doctrine et dans l'Histoire,* Paris: Librairie générale de droit et de jurisprudence.
Goodchild, B. (2003) 'Implementing the right to housing in France: Strengthening or fragmenting the welfare state?', *Housing, Theory and Society,* 20(2): 86–97.
Gordley, J. (2006) *Foundations of Private Law. Property, Tort, Contract, Unjust Enrichment,* Oxford: Oxford University Press.
Goze, M. (2005) 'Intercommunalité et décentralisation', *Etudes foncières,* 116 (July-August): 7–12.
Grear, A. (2003) 'A tale of the insider, the outsider and human rights. An exploration of some problems and possibilities in the relationship between the English common law property concept, human rights law and discourses of exclusion and inclusion', *Legal Studies,* 23(1): 33–65.
Grey, K. and Grey, S.F. (2009) *Elements of Land Law,* 5th edn, Oxford: Oxford University Press.
Guerrand, R-H. (1967) *Les Origines du Logement Social en France,* Paris: Quintette.
Guesde, J. (1992) 'Un acompte', *L'Egalité,* 18 June 1882.
Harloe, M. (1981) 'The re-commodification of housing', in Harloe, M. and E. Lebas (eds) *City, Class and Capital: New Developments in the Political Economy of Cities and Regions,* London: Edward Arnold, 17–50.
Harloe, M. (1995) *The People's Home: Social Rented Housing in Europe and America,* Oxford: Blackwell.
Haut Comité (2002) *8ème Rapport du Haut Comité pour le Logement des Personnes Défavorisées*, Paris: La Documentation française.
—— (2003) *9ème Rapport du Haut Comité pour le Logement des Personnes Défavorisées*, Paris: La Documentation française.
Hayek, F.A. (1960) *On the Constitution of Liberty,* London: Routledge and Kegan Paul.
Heller, M.A. (1998) 'The tragedy of the anticommons: Property in the transition from Marx to markets', *Harvard Law Review,* 111: 621–88.
Henry, L. (1949) 'Structure de la population et besoins en logement', *Population,* no. 3, Paris: INED.

Bibliography

Holdaway, S. and O'Neill, M. (2006) 'Institutional racism after Macpherson: An analysis of police views', *Policing and Society*, 16(4): 349–69.
Holmans, A.E. (1987) *Housing Policy in Britain*, London: Croom Helm.
Houard, N. (2009) *Droit au Logement et Mixité, les Contradictions du Logement Social*, Paris: l'Harmattan.
Hughes, D. (2000) *Public Sector Housing Law*, London: Butterworths.
Hume, D. (1758) re-published in Miller, E.A. (ed.) (1985) *Essays, Moral, Political and Literary*, Indianapolis: Liberty Classics.
Hunter, C. and Nixon J. (1998) *Tenure Preference, Housing Policy Discourse and Debt: The Role of Language in Creating and Transmitting Tenure Stigmatisation*, paper presented at the ENHR annual conference, Cardiff, September 1998.
INSEE (2002) *Enquête Logement*, Paris: INSEE.
—— (2004) *Enquête Logement*, Paris: INSEE.
—— (2005) *Enquête Logement Provisoire 2005*, Paris: INSEE.
—— (2006) *France, Portrait Social*, Paris: INSEE.
Janis, I.L. (1972) *Victims of Groupthink*, Boston, MA: Houghton Mifflin.
Javaloyès, S. (2003) *L'Obligation de Relogement des Occupants dans les Actions ou Opérations d'Aménagement*, Memoire de DESS, Aix/Marseille III. Available online at http://www.gridauh.fr/fr/285.htm (accessed 5 January 2010).
Jégouzo, Y. (1995) *L'Emergence d'une Mission de Service Public Local de l'Habitat*, Paris: Fédération nationale des offices d'HLM.
Jégouzo-Viénot, L. (2002) *Etablissement Public et Logement Social*, Paris: L.G.D.J.
Jousselin, B. (1998) 'La mobilité résidentielle des ménages en 1994', in Segaud, M., Bonvalet, C. and Brun, J. (eds) *Logement et Habitat, L'Etat des Savoirs*, Paris: Éditions la découverte, 120–7.
Kassovitz, M. (1995) *La Haîne* (film).
Keck, J.-L. (1995) *Les Organismes HLM, Statuts, Réglementation, Activités*, Paris: Masson.
Kemeny, J. (1995) *From Public Renting to Social Housing: Rental Policy Strategies in Comparative Perspective*, London: Routledge.
—— (2006) 'Corporatism and housing regimes', *Housing, Theory and Society*, 23(1): 1–8.
Kemp, P. (2007) *Housing Allowances in Comparative Perspective*, Bristol: Policy Press.
Kenna, P. (2005) *Housing Rights and Human Rights*, Brussels: FEANTSA.
—— (2011) *Housing Law, Rights and Policy*, Dublin: Clarus Press.
Kettering, S. (2001) *French Society, 1589–1715*, Harlow: Pearson Educational.
Kokoreff, M. (2006) 'Comprendre le sens des émeutes de l'automne 2005', in Masquet, B., Flahault, I. and Denis, B. (eds) *Regards sur l'Actualité, Comprendre les Violences Urbaines, no. 319,* Paris: La Documentation française, pp. 15–27.
Krajewski, M., Neergaard, U. and Gronden, J. van de (2009) *The Changing Legal Framework for Services of General Interest in Europe Between Competition and Solidarity*, The Hague: Asser Press.
Kreps, D.M. (1990) *Game Theory and Economic Modelling*, Oxford: Clarendon Press.
Kullberg, J. (1997) 'From waiting lists to adverts: the allocation of social rental dwellings in the Netherlands', *Housing Studies,* 12 (3): 393–403.
Laë, J.-F. (2002) *Du Côté Droit du Louage des Choses,* Paris: PUCA.
Lafore, R. (2004) Comment in a debate in Ballain, R., and Benguigi, F. (2004) *L'Accès au Logement: Des Evolutions en Débat,* Paris: PUCA, pp. 42–3.
La Porta, R., Lopez-de-Silanes, F. and Shleifer, A. (2008) 'The economic consequences of legal origins', *Journal of Economic Literature*, 46(2): 285–332.

Bibliography

Laval-Reviglio, M-C. (2005) 'L'objectif de mixité social et les disciminations familiales', in Barré-Pépin, M. and Coutant-Lapalus, C. (eds) *Logement et Famille: des Droits en Question*, Paris: Dalloz, 319–30.

Lavrijssen, S. and Vries, S. de (2009) 'The Netherlands', in Krajewski, M., Neergaard, U. and Gronden, J. van de (eds) *The Changing Legal Framework for Services of General Interest in Europe. Between Competition and Solidarity,* The Hague: Asser Press.

Lechevalier, A. (2002) 'La protection sociale en Europe: La convergence par le marché', *L'Economie Politique*, 2002/1 (no. 13). Available online at http://www.cairn.info (accessed 25 May 2011).

Lefèbvre, B., Mouillart, M. and Occhipinti, S. (1991) *Politique du Logement, 50 Ans Pour un Echec,* Paris: L'Harmattan.

Legrand, P. (1996) 'European legal systems are not converging', *The International and Comparative Law Quarterly*, 45(1): 52–81.

Lelévrier, C. (2008) *Mobilité Résidentielle et Trajectoires Résidentielles des Ménages Relogés lors d'Opérations de Renouvellement Urbain,* Paris: PUCA. Available online at http://rp.urbanisme.equipement.gouv.fr/puca/arguments/trajectoires_lelevrier_fev 2009.pdf (accessed 1 February 2011).

Lévy-Vroelant, C. (2010) 'Housing vulnerable groups: The development of a new public action sector', *International Journal of Housing Policy,* 10(4): 443–56.

Lévy-Vroelant, C. and Tutin, C. (2007) 'Social housing in France', in C. Whitehead and K. Scanlon (eds) *Social Housing in Europe,* London: LSE, pp. 70–89.

Lind, H. (2007) *The Municipal Housing Companies in Sweden: Current Situation and Future Prospects,* paper presented at the ENHR annual conference, Rotterdam, June 2007. Available online at http://www.enhr2007rotterdam.nl/pages/papersdownload.htm (accessed 25 May 2011).

Lindbeck, A. and Snower, D.J. (1988) *The Insider–outsider Theory of Employment and Unemployment*, Cambridge, MA.: MIT Press.

—— and —— (2002) *The Insider–outsider Theory: A Survey*, Discussion Paper no. 524, July 2002, Germany: IZA. Available online at http://ssrn.com/abstract_id=325323 (accessed 25 May 2011)

Llewellyn, K. (1931) 'What price contract? An essay', *Yale Law Journal,* 40(5): 704–51.

—— (1940) 'The normative, the legal and the law job: The problem of juristic method', *Yale Law Journal*, June 1940, 49(8): 1355–400.

Low, K.F.K. (2009) 'The use and abuse of taxonomy', *Legal Studies,* 29(3): 355–75.

Lowe, S. (2004) *Housing Policy Analysis, British Housing in Cultural and Comparative Context,* Basingstoke: Palgrave Macmillan.

Lux, M. (2006) 'Housing systems: Change on the way to the EU. Similarities and differences, integration or convergence', paper presented at the ENHR conference, Ljubljana, 2–5 July 2006.

Macpherson of Cluny, W. (1999) *The Stephen Lawrence Inquiry: Report of an Inquiry by Sir William Macpherson of Cluny,* London: HMSO.

Madell, T. (2009) 'Sweden' in Krajewski, M., Neergaard, U. and Gronden, J. van de (eds) *The Changing Legal Framework for Services of General Interest in Europe. Between Competition and Solidarity,* The Hague: Asser Press.

Magri, S. (1995) *Les Laboratoires de la Réforme de l'Habitation Populaire en France, de la Société Française des Habitations à Bon Marché à la Section d'Hygiène Urbaine et Rurale du Musée Social 1889–1909,* Paris: Ministère de l'équipement, du logement des transports et du tourisme.

Bibliography

Malpezzi, S. (1996) 'Housing prices, externalities and regulation in US metropolitan areas', *Journal of Housing Research*, 7(2): 209–41.
Martin, C. and Le Jouan, E. (2006) 'Une enquête dans le Val de Marne. Qui sont les locataires menacés d'expulsion?' *Etudes foncières,* 124 (November-December): 8–9.
Mason, D. (2000) *Race and Ethnicity in Modern Britain,* Oxford: Oxford University Press.
Massin, I., Prévoit, M. and Laporte, P. (2010) *Mission d'Analyse de Conditions d'Accès par de Publics Prioritaires, Rapport No. 007070-01,* Paris: Conseil général de l'environnement et du développement durable.
Matznetter, W. (2006) '*Quo vadis,* comparative housing research?', paper presented at the ENHR annual conference, July 2006, Lljubjana.
Maurel, E. and Ballain, R. (2000) *Le Logement Très Social. Extension ou Fragilisaton du Droit au Logement?* Paris: PUCA.
McFarlane, B. (2008) *The Structure of Property Law,* Oxford and Portland: Hart.
MIILOS (2002) *Rapport Annuel d'Activité 2001,* Paris: MIILOS. Available online at http://www.developpement-durable.gouv.fr/IMG/pdf/Miilos2001.pdf (accessed 25 May 2011).
—— (2003) *Rapport Annuel d'Activité 2002,* Paris: MIILOS. Available online at http://www.developpement-durable.gouv.fr/IMG/pdf/Extraits_MIILOS_2002.pdf (accessed 25 May 2011).
—— (2004) *Rapport Annuel d'Activité 2003,* Paris: MIILOS. Available online at http://www.developpement-durable.gouv.fr/IMG/pdf/MIILOS_2003.pdf (accessed 25 May 2011).
——(2005) *Rapport Annuel d'Activité 2004,* Paris: la MIILOS. Available online at http://www.developpement-durable.gouv.fr/IMG/pdf/Miilos2004.pdf (accessed 25 May 2011).
—— (2006) *Rapport Annuel d'Activité 2005,* Paris: la MIILOS. Available online at http://www.developpement-durable.gouv.fr/IMG/pdf/rapport_public_2005.pdf (accessed 25 May 2011).
Ministère de l'équipement (undated) *L'Occupation du Parc Social: Une Caracterisation avec le Fichier FILOCOM*, Paris: Ministère de l'équipement. Available online at http://www.statistiques.equipement.gouv.fr/rubrique.php3?id_rubrique=315 (accessed 25 May 2011).
Ministère de l'équipement des transports et du logement (1998) *Lutte Contre les Exclusions, Loi d'Orientation. Le Volet Logement,* Paris: Ministère de l'équipement des transports et du logement.
Ministère du logement (2007) *Occupation du Patrimoine Social*, Paris: Ministère du logement.
Ministry of Infrastructure of the Italian Republic and Federcasa (eds)(2006) *Housing Statistics in the EU 2005/6.* Available online at http://www.federcasa.it/news/housing_statistics/Report_housing_statistics_2005_2006.pdf (accessed 25 May 2011).
Le Monde (2006) 'Dernier jour du procès des HLM de Paris, en l'absence des politiques', *Le Monde,* 5 April. Available online at http://lemonde.fr (accessed 25 May 2011).
—— (2007a) 'Présidentielle résultats, second tour, Seine-Saint-Denis', *le Monde*, 8 May.
—— (2007b) 'Présidentielle résultats, second Tour, Seine-Saint-Denis', *le Monde*, 8 May.
—— (2010) 'L'informatique pour limiter les passe-droits' *Le Monde,* 8 September. Available online at http://www.lemonde.fr/cgi-bin/ACHATS/acheter.cgi?offre=ARCHIVES&type_item=ART_ARCH_30J&objet_id=1134207 (accessed 25 May 2011).

Bibliography

Monk, S. and Whitehead, C. (2010) *Making Housing More Affordable, The Role of Intermediate Tenures,* Chichester: Wiley Blackwell.
Moret, F. (1998) 'Le logement et la question sociale', in Segaud, M., Bonvalet, C. and Brun, J. (eds) *Logement et habitat, L'état des savoirs,* Paris: Éditions la découverte, pp. 19–26.
Morgan, J. (2007) *Aspects of Housing Law,* London: Routledge-Cavendish.
Morlet, O. (1999) 'La gestion de l'urbanisme dans les communes', *Etudes foncières,* 77.
Mulholland, H. (2005) 'Older people fuelling housing crisis, charity warns', *The Guardian,* 27 September. Available online at http://www.guardian.co.uk/uk_news/story/0,,1579301,00.html (accessed 25 May 2011).
N. C-M avec AFP *(sic)* (2005) 'Drame du Paris-Opéra: Des leçons à tirer', *Batiactu,* 18 April. Available online at http://www.batiactu.com/edito/drame-du-paris-opera—des-lecons-a-tirer-19283.php (accessed 23 May 2011).
Nelken, D. (1983) *The Limits of the Legal Process. A Study of Landlords, Law and Crime,* London: Academic Press.
Nicholls, W.J. (2006) 'Associationalism from above: Explaining failure through France's politique de la ville', *Urban Studies,* 43(1): 1779–802.
Nickell, S.J., and Wadhwani, S. (1990) 'Insider forces and wage determination', *Economic Journal,* 100(401): 496–509.
Nielsen (2010) 'When the cold wind blows: Legal strategies against ghettoisation in Denmark' *The Journal of Legal Affairs and Dispute Resolution in Engineering,* 2010 (Feb.): 42–9.
Nora, S. and Eveno, B. (1975) *L'Amélioration de l'Habitat Ancien,* Paris: La Documentation française.
L'Observateur de L'immobilier (2006) 'Famille instable cherche logement', *L'Observateur de l'Immobilier, Numéro Hors Série, Demande de Logement: La Réalité du Choc Sociologique,* November 2006: 22–29.
OECD (1993) *The OECD Job Study,* Vols 1 and 2, Paris: OECD.
—— (1998) *The OECD Jobs Strategy: Progress Report on Implementation of Country Specific Recommendations,* Economics Department Working Paper no. 196. Paris: OECD.
—— (2009) *OECD Economic Surveys, France, 2009,* vol. 2009/5, Paris: OECD.
ONPES (2006) *Rapport Annuel de l'Observatoire National de la Pauvreté et de l'Exlusion Sociale 2005–6,* Paris: La Documentation française.
Oswald, A. (1986) 'Unemployment insurance and labor contracts under asymmetric information: Theory and facts,' *American Economic Review,* 76: 365–377.
Oxley, M. (2000) *The Future of Social Housing; Learning from Europe,* London: IPPR.
Paris, R. (2006) 'Les petites misères du production du logement social', *Etudes foncières,* 118 (January-February): 22–6.
Park, R.E., Burgess, E.W. and McKenzie, R.D. (1925) *The City,* Chicago: University of Chicago.
Patault, A.-M. (1989) *Introduction Historique au Droit des Biens,* Paris: PUF.
Paugam, S. (2002) *La Société Française et Ses Pauvres, Essai,* 2nd edn, Paris: Quadrige/PUF.
Pauliat, H. (1998) 'Logement et propriété: Un aperçu historique', in Segaud M., Bonvalet, C. and Brun, J. (eds) *Logement et Habitat, L'Etat des Savoirs,* Paris: Éditions la découverte, pp. 11–19.

Bibliography

Pawson, H., Jones, C., Donohoe, T., Netto, G., Fancy, C., Clegg. S. and Thomas, A. (2006) *Monitoring the Longer Term Impact of Choice-Based Lettings,* London: Department for Communities and Local Government.

Pébereau M. (2005) *Rompre Avec la Facilité de la Dette Publique au Service de Notre Croissance Economique et de Notre Cohésion Sociale,* Paris: La Documentation française.

Peillon, P. (2005) 'La mixité sociale et les discriminations familiales', in Barré-Pépin and Coutant-Lapalus (eds) *Logement et Famille: des Droits en Question,* Paris: Dalloz, 319–30.

Perrot, R. (1995) *Institutions Judiciaires,* 7th edn, Paris: Monchrestien.

Pichon, P. (2005) *Les SDF: Sortir de la Rue. Discontinuités Biographiques et Travail de la Reconversion,* Paris: PUCA.

Price, R. (1997) *A Concise History of France,* Cambridge: Cambridge University Press.

Prosser, T. (2005) *The Limits of Competition Law, Markets and Public Services,* Oxford: Oxford University Press.

—— (2006) 'Regulation and social solidarity' *Journal of Law and Society,* 33(1): 364–87.

Proudhon, P.J. (1994, first printed 1840) *What is Property? An Inquiry into the Principles of Right and of Government,* trans. Kelly, D.R. and Smith, B.G., Cambridge: Cambridge University Press.

Radigon, J-L. and Horvath, S. (2002), *Expulsion et Droit au Logement,* Paris: Delmas.

Reinprecht, C., Lévy-Vroelant, C. and Wassenberg, F. (2008) 'Learning from history: changes and path-dependency in the social housing sector in Austria, France and the Netherlands (1889–2008)', in Scanlon, K. and Whitehead, C. (eds) *Social Housing in Europe II,* London: LSE, pp. 47–62.

Renard, V. (2001) 'Les nouvelles frontières de l'illégalité', *Urbanisme,* 318 (May-June): 70–73.

—— (2003) 'Les enjeux urbains des prix fonciers et immobiliers', in Prager, J.C. (dir.) *Ville et Economie,* Paris: la Documentation française, pp. 95–108.

—— (2006) 'L'obscure clarté des marchés immobiliers ou pourquoi l'économie immobilière n'est pas encore une science', *FNAIM,* 97 (April): 19–24.

—— (2007) 'La question du logement en France en 2007. Crise du logement et perspectives politiques', *Frankreich Analysen.* Available online at http://ceco.polytechnique.fr/fichiers/ceco/publications/pdf/2007-02-22-1576.pdfm (accessed 25 May 2011).

Renault-Brahinsky, C. (2005) *L'Essentiel du Droit des Régimes Matrimoniaux,* Paris: Gualino éditeur–EJA.

Repentin T. (2005) *Rapport d'Information Fait au Nom de la Commission des Affaires Economiques et du PLAN, par le Groupe de Travail sur les Facteurs Fonciers et Immobiliers de la Crise du Logement,* Rapport au Sénat No. 442 2004/5 Session, Paris: le Sénat.

République de France (undated) *Legifrance.gouv.fr. Le Service Public de Diffusion du Droit,* Available online at http://legifrance.gouv.fr (accessed 12 February 2011).

Richier, L. (2002) 'Préface', in Jégouzo-Viénot, L., *Etablissement Public et Logement Social,* Paris: L.G.D.J., V-VI.

Roman, D. (2001) *Le Droit Public Face à la Pauvreté,* Paris: L.G.D.J.

Rose, R. (1986) 'Common goals but different roles: the State's contribution to the welfare mix' in Rose, R. and Shiratori, R. (eds) *The Welfare State East and West,* Oxford: Oxford University Press, pp. 13–39.

Bibliography

Ross, M. and Borgmann-Prebil, Y. (eds) *Promoting Solidarity in the European Union*, Oxford: OUP.

Rueda, D. (2005) 'Insider-outsider politics in industrialized democracies: The challenge to social democratic parties', *American Political Science Review*, 99(1): 61–74.

Sanfey, P.J. (1993) 'On the interaction between efficiency wages and union-firm bargaining models.' *Economics-Letters*; 41(3), 319–24.

Sauvez, M. (2006) 'Le maire, le président et les enjeux territoriaux de demain', *Etudes foncières,* 123 (September-October): 13–15.

Scanlon, K. and Whitehead, C. (eds) (2008) *Social Housing in Europe II, A Review of Policies and Outcomes*, London: LSE.

Schelling, T. (1956) 'An essay on bargaining', *American Economic Review,* 46(3): 231–306.

Schlager, E. and Ostrom, E. (1992) 'Property-rights regimes and natural resources: A conceptual analysis', *Land Economics,* 68(3): 249–62.

Schmid, C.U. (undated) *General Report, Tenancy Law and Procedure in the EU,* Florence: European University Institute. Available online at <http://www.eui.eu/Documents/DepartmentsCentres/Law/ResearchTeaching/ResearchThemes/EuropeanPrivateLaw/TenancyLawProject/TenancyLawGeneralReport.pdf (accessed 25 May 2011).

Shapiro, A.-L. (1985) *Housing the Poor of Paris, 1850–1902*, Madison: University of Wisconsin Press.

Sharland, J. (1979) *A Practical Approach to Local Government Law*, London: Blackstone.

Shiller, R. (2005) *Irrational Exuberance*, Woodstock, Oxfordshire: Princeton University Press.

SIAL (2006) *Le Service Inter-administratif du Logement,* Lyon: La Préfecture du Rhône. Available online at http://www.rhone.gouv.fr/web/325-le-service-inter-administratif-du-logement.php (accessed 23 May 2011).

Simon, C. (2007) 'Jean-Luc Richard, sociologue, docteur en démographie économique (université Rennes I) 'Désormais, le vote à droite n'est plus tabou', *Le Monde,* 27 January. Available online at http://www.lemonde.fr/cgi-bin/ACHATS/acheter.cgi?offre=ARCHIVES&type_item=ART_ARCH_30J&objet_id=974599.

Simon, P. and Kirszbaum, T. (eds) (2001) *Les Discriminations Raciales et Ethniques dans l'Accès au Logement Social, Note de Sythèse du GIP GELD,* Paris: La Documentation francaise.

Smith, J. and Oxley, M. (1997) 'Housing investment and social housing. European comparisons', *Housing Studies*, 12(4): 489–507.

Smith, S. (1989) *The Politics of 'Race' and Residence,* Cambridge: Polity.

Sowerwine, C. (2001) *France Since 1870. Culture, Politics and Society,* London: Palgrave.

Stébé, J.-M. (1998) *Le Logement Social en France,* Collection *Que Sais-Je?,* Paris: PUF.

Steiner, E. (2010) *French Law – A Comparative Approach,* Oxford, Oxford University Press.

Stephens, M., Burns, N. and MacKay, L. (2002) *Social Market or Safety Net,* Bristol: Policy Press.

Stewart, A. (1997) *Rethinking Housing Law,* London: Sweet and Maxwell.

Stiglitz, J.E. (2000) *The Economics of the Public Sector,* 3rd edn, London: W.W. Norton.

—— (2002) 'Information change and the change in the paradigm in economics', *American Economic Review*, 92(3): 460–501.

Strauss, A. and Corbin, J. (1998) *Basics of Qualitative Research. Techniques and Procedures of Developing Grounded Theory,* 2nd edn, Thousand Oaks, CA: Sage.

Bibliography

Taffin, C. (2007) 'La crise du logement de Patrick Grépinet', *l'Observateur de l'immobilier*, 69: 31–3.
Tchibindat, S. (2005) *Le Logement des Algériens en France. Historique et Inventaire des Problématiques Actuelles*, Paris: l'Harmattan.
Terré, F., Simler, P. and Lequette, Y. (1996) *Droit Civil, Les Obligations*, 6th edn, Paris: Dalloz.
Topalov, C. (1987) *Le Logement en France. Histoire d'une Marchandise Impossible*, Paris: Presses de la Fondation nationale des sciences politiques.
Torgersen, U (1987) 'Housing, the wobbly pillar under the welfare state', in Turner, B., Kemeny, J. and Lundqvist, L.J. (eds) *Between State and Market, Housing in the Post-industrial Era*, Stockholm: Almqvist and Wiksell.
Touvenin, J.-M. (2009) 'The *Altmark* case and its consequences' in Krajewski, M., Neergaard, U. and Gronden, J. van de (eds) *The Changing Legal Framework for Services of General Interest in Europe. Between Competition and Solidarity*, The Hague: Asser Press, pp. 103–16.
Tunstall, R. (2003) '"Mixed tenure" Policy in the UK: Privatisation, pluralism or euphemism?' *Housing, Theory and Society*, 20: 153–9.
Turkington, R. and Sangster, K. (2006) 'From housing mix to social mix – housing's contribution to social sustainability', Town and Country Planning, June 184–5.
Turpin, D. (1994) *Droit Constitutionnel*, Paris: Presses universitaires de France.
UESL (undated) *Qu'Est-ce que le 1% Logement?* Paris: UESL. Available online at http://www.actionlogement.fr/qui-sommes-nous/faits-marquants.
Uhry, M. (2007) 'Les effets secondaires de l'amélioration de l'habitat et de la sécurisation locative sur le logement des pauvres', in Laflamme, V., Lévy-Vroelant, C., Robertson, D. and Smyth, J. (eds) *Le Logement Précaire en Europe, aux Marges du Palais*, Paris: l'Harmattan, pp. 391–402.
UNFOHLM (1975) *Livre Blanc. Propositions pour l'Habitat. Rapport des Groupes de Travail de l'UNFOHLM*, Paris: UNFOHLM.
—— (1999) 'Social. Recommendations sur l'application de la loi d'orientation rélative à la lutte contre les exclusions, concernant le refus d'attribution (Art. L.441-2-2- du C.C.H.)', *Actualité HLM*, 59 (November):1–3.
USH (2009) *Chffres Clefs*, Paris: USH. Available online at http://www.union-habitat.org/chiffres (accessed 25 May 2011).
——(2010) *Chiffres Clefs*, Paris: USH. Available online at http://www.union-habitat.org/Web/Ushgp.nsf/PW/200?opendocument (accessed 25 May 2011).
Van Lang, A. (1996) *Le Juge Judicaire et Droit Administratif*, Paris: L.G.D.J.
Von Danwitz, T. (2009) 'State aid control over public services: a view from the court' in Krajewski, M., Neergaard, U. and Gronden, J. van de (eds) *The Changing Legal Framework for Services of General Interest in Europe – Between Competition and Solidarity*, The Hague, Asser Press.
Vorms, B. (2007) 'Développement de l'accession sociale, Elargissement de l'accès au crédit et maîtrise des risques', series *ANIL Habitat actualité*, October 2007, Paris: ANIL.
Vorms, B. and Taffin, C. (2007a) 'Etude – Le subprime, d'abord une crise de la protection du consommateur', series: *ANIL Habitat actualité*, Paris: ANIL.
—— (2007b) *Elargir l'Accès au Crédit au Logement des Emprunteurs Atypiques. Le Prêt Sécurisé à l'Accession à la Propriété et le Prêt Hypothécaire Cautionné*, Paris: L'ANIL.

Bibliography

Wachsmann, P. (2005) *Libertés Publiques,* 9th edn, Paris: Dalloz.
Watson, A. (1974) *Legal Transplants, an Approach to Comparative Law,* Edinburgh: Scottish Academic Press.
Weis, H. (1995) *Beck-Rechtsberater, Meine Grundrechte,* Munich: DTV.
Whitehead, C. and Scanlon, K. (eds) (2007) *Social Housing in Europe,* London: LSE.
Whittaker, S. (2008) 'Burden of proof in the consumer *acquis* and in the DCFR', *ERCL,* 4(3): 411–44.
Wieacker, F. (2003) *A History of Private Law in Europe,* Oxford: Clarendon Press.
Williamson, O.E. (1979) 'Transaction cost economics: The governance of contractual relations', *The Journal of Law and Economics,* 22(2): 233–62.
Williamson, O.E. (1981) 'The Economics of Organization: The Transaction Cost Approach', *American Journal of Sociology,* 87(3): 548–77.
Yin, R.K. (2002) *Case Study Research, Design and Methods,* 3rd edn, London: Sage.
Zimmermann, R. and Whittaker, S. (eds.) (2000) *Good Faith in European Contract Law: The Common Core of European Private Law*, Cambridge: Cambridge University Press.
Zweigert, K. and Kötz, H. (1998) trans. T. Weir, *An Introduction to Comparative Law*, 3rd edn, Oxford: Clarendon Press.

Index

1789 Declaration 61, 64

abnormal delay 161–2
access
   barriers to 186, 187
   fragmentation of 16–17
   to social housing 2
accommodation deposits 128
actes discrétionnaires 106
actors
   and decentralization 113–23
   economic analysis of 130–4
   local 8, 51, 112
   in social housing 10–16
Adams, J.N. & Brownsword, R. 107
ADIL 145
administrative courts 62, 223
administrative involvement, increased 72
administrative judges, and prefects 116
administrative law 61–3, 92, 106
administrative power 63
Administrative Tribunal of Marseilles/
   Versailles 94
African workers 116, 212 *see also*
   Algerians; ethnic minorities;
   foreigners; immigrants
aid, by lower rents 153
Aide personalisée au logement *see* APL
aids to the person, and rents 145–8
Algerians *see also* African workers; ethnic
   minorities; foreigners; immigrants,
   104, 212
alliances, campaigning groups 109

allocation 134 *see also* allocation process
   and bargaining 51
   economics explanation 108
   efficiency of 133
   local government involvement 13–16
   and MIILOS 139
   models of 37–8, 245–7
   political dimension 52–3
   and prefects 116
   principles 279–80
   race discrimination in 105
   reform of 251
   refusal to allocate 93–5
   regional institutions 166–71
   remedies for delayed 95–6
   rights 32
   social distributional problems 224–6
   social housing 4, 8, 9, 16–18
   and social mix 243
   and social norms 29
allocation commission 17, 165, 178–80,
   233
allocation process *see also* allocation
   allocation criteria 134, 160–6
   *clientélisme*197
   complexity of 158
   criticisms of 21
   and disadvantaged people 7, 9, 17–18,
      181
   and discrimination 221
   enquiries/social reports 173–4
   as exclusionary legal process 229–35
   exclusionary tendencies 8

323

Index

allocation process *(Continued)*
  and mayors 15, 32, 112, 115, 119, 175
  and opacity 21, 42, 241–2
  procedure 171–8
  proposing candidates 174–5
  registration/file transfer 172–3
  and risk 31
  room to manoeuvre 105–7
  and social housing 17–18
  and social landlords 32
  social landlords/allocation/rent 175–7
  tenant representation 27, 113
  transaction costs 23–5
  transparency 177–8
'all property is theft' 66
Altmark judgement 42
altruism 72
America *see* United States
amicale 187
Amsterdam 36
Amzallag, M. & Taffin, C. 12
ANAH 79, 155, 292n.433
anarchy/anarchists 66
d'Anglas, Boissy 66
ANIL 206, 210
ANRU 155, 292n.433
l'Anti concièrge 66
APL 146, 147, 148
applicants, classes of 97
arrears 129
arrondissements 15
asset specificity 133
associations
  as campaigners 243, 244
  consumers 77
  representing outsiders 122–3
  role of 98, 113, 172
  and social housing 144
  voluntary work 76
asylum seekers 160, 204
Aubry, Martine 115
Australia 22–3
Austria 36, 38, 248

banlieux 6, 100
bargaining
  and allocation 51
  landlords/tenants 29
  levers of groups 29
  power of disadvantaged people 227
  power of social tenants 187–8
Barker Report 20
Barre, Raymond 115
Barre Report (1976) 81, 146

barres 81, 100, 101
barriers to access housing 186, 187
Baudrillard, J. 107
Bell *et al.* 91
benefits
  and construction 81–3
  housing 144
  and rent 237
  system 145
Bergh, R.J. van den & Camesasca, P.D. 133
Berry, M. & Hall, J. 22–3
Besson Act 1, 12, 46, 84, 87, 110, 172
  Article 1 89, 96
  Article 4 128
  Article 28 102 and social exclusion 91
Blanc, M. 102–3
Blanco 92
Bonnevay Act 75, 192
Borloo, Jean-Louis 115
Borloo plan 115, 155
borrowing, and poor people 207
Bourgeois, C. 8, 21, 22, 32, 50–3, 122, 136, 140, 163, 173, 178, 233
Bourgeois, Léon 67, 68
Brouant, J-P. 160, 178, 213–14, 223
Brousse, P. 67
Brown, L.N. & Bell, J. 61
building and housing code 160
bureau 141

cahiers de doléances 60
Caisse des dépôts et de consignations *see* CDC
Caisses d'épargne 80
campaigning groups, alliances 109
capital expenditure, and rental markets 239
C.C.H.
  Article L. 300-1 96

Index

Article L. 302-5 91
Article L. 441 160, 161, 162, 279, 282n.54
Article L. 441-1 9, 279–80, 282n.54
Article L. 441 - L. 441-2-6 160
Article R. *441-3 162, 280
Book VI 138
and *orientations* 178
CDC 75, 80, 148–9
Cellule interface offre-demande *see* CIOD
central control, v. decentralization 109
centralization, historic 63
centrally planned command economy 189
certificate of three years residence 195
C.G.I. 155
charcutage 52, 196
charges, cost of 147
charity 65
chârte de prévention de l'expulsion 128
Charter of Fundamental Rights 40
charter to prevent eviction 128
cheap housing
  and reconstruction 126, 239
  reduction in/shortage of 183, 201–2, 204–5, 243
Cheysson, Emile 66, 74
child maintenance 209
children
  of ethnic minority tenants 194
  in hostels 206
  of immigrant social tenants 200
  as priority applicants 161
  shared custody of 193, 208, 209, 253
  stigmatization of 220
choice-based lettings 37
choisi (re voluntary solidarity) 69
churning 27, 189, 238
CIL 31, 138
  and allocation process 32
  and collected funds 17, 80
  and ethnic minority workers 218
  and housing policy 121–2
  and immigrant workers 212
  insiders of 197–8
  and loans 151
  Loca-pass scheme 128
  and reservations 169

schemes guaranteeing rent 122, 126.
  and UESL 165
CIOD 168
Cité Napoleon 74
cité ouvrière 66, 74
civil law countries, tenants in 45
civil servants 116, 135, 194
Claudius-Petit, E. 80
clientélism, allocations process 197
Cochon, G. 76–7
Code civil (C. civ.) 68, 69, 77
  Article 1135 78
  Articles 544;545 64
Code de la construction et l'habitation *see* C.C.H.
Code de l'action sociale et des familles (C.A.S.F.), Article L. 115-2 114
Code de la sécurité sociale (C.S.S.), Article 111-1 145
Code des communes (C. communes), Article L. 131-2 119
Code général des impôts (C.G.I.) 155
Code Pénal (C. pén), Article 432-7 213
collective action, tenants 76–7
collective advantages, and social movements 76–8
collective bargaining
  insider-outsider theory 25–6
  social tenants power 202
collective contracts 72, 77
collective organizations 25
collective protest 107
collective representation 188
collective rights, tenants 107
collectivism 76
comercialization, organization of social landlords 22
Comités interprofessionnels du logement *see* CIL
command economy, centrally planned 189
commission d'attribution 17
Commission de surendettement 207
commission d'ultime recours 128
Commission for Over-indebtedness 207
Commission nationale de la concertation 78
Commission of Last Resort 128

Index

commodification of housing 21
common-law/civil-law countries 257–8
common law property rights 258
communautarisme, and social mix 214–16
communautés 15–16
    construction/allocation powers 130
    and decentralization 120
    delegated planning powers 168
    and exclusionary practices 234, 252
    role of 119–21
    Toulouse 170
communautés d'agglomeration 120
communautés de communes 120
communauté urbaine 120
    Lyon 16
    Nord 169
communes 15, 63, 117–18
    and decentralization 112–13, 114
    and delegation of construction powers 167
    and disadvantaged people 102
    and localised interests 236
    and OPHBMs 75
community of interest, matrimonial special contracts 69
companies for good value housing 10
comparative law 257, 258
competition
    in construction 151–4
    control 41
    EU policy 40, 108
    law 243, 250
    policy 57, 108, 247–8, 250
    between social landlords 39
    and transparency 243
    unfair 39
Competition Commission 39, 41, 42, 93
compulsory contracts 114
Confédération général du travail 77
Confédération nationale du logement (CNL) 77
conférence intercommunale de logement 127–8
conjointe liability 68
Conseil constitutionnel 62, 85–6, 87, 89
Conseil d'État 61, 86, 94, 103
Conseil général 114, 116–17, 121
Considérant, Victor 73

Constitutional Council 62
constitutional rights 89
constitutional value 88
Constitution, the 3, 85
    1946 78
    1958 104, 129
    1958 Article 55 86
    1958 Article 72-2 129
construction
    and allocation process 123
    and benefits 81–3
    and DDE 117
    decentralization and funding 134
    delegation of powers to *communes* 167
    facilitating 80
    funding 120, 121, 125, 129, 240, 252, 254
    grants/gap funding 154–5
    HLM organizations 11
    and housing problems 123–4
    incentives 11, 155, 239
    and insiderness 239–40
    loans for 148–51, 150, 156
    and mayors 118
    post-war 75–6, 82
    and the prefecture 116
    rents and funding 148–55
    rent setting/competition 151–4
consultation, local 133
consumer law 107
consumer protection, English tenancies 107
consumers
    tenants as 107, 284n.131
    and welfare 108
consumers' associations 77
consumer-welfarists 107
contingents 165
contracting
    for diversity 127–34
    transaction costs 131
contract law 67, 68
contracts
    compulsory 114
    legislative effect of 77–8
    and public morality 78
    time-limited local 114
contract, the 64

Index

contractualization
  construction/planning 113
  and decentralization 32–3, 64, 233–4
  and opacity 241
contrôle de légalité 115
cooperatives, private tenant 36
corporatism, in social housing 107–8
corruption 51, 52, 197
Cour De Cassation 61
courts 62
Courvoisier, C. 68
Crédit foncier de France *see* CDC
credit, poor peoples lack of 207
le Cri du peuple, l'Egalité, le Révolté 66
crisis of 1789 60
cumulative disadvantage 198, 201, 202
Czechoslovakia 23, 154

DAL 19, 20, 65, 87
DALO Act 4, 86–7, 96, 115
data, confidentiality of 172, 173
DDE 117, 198
debt
  disastrous consequences of 206–7
  Lyon 129
  national/European restriction 40
  and stigmatization 190, 238
De Búrca, G. 3
decentralization
  and *communautés* 120
  and *communes* 112–13
  and construction funding 134
  and contractualization 32–3, 64
  and housing actors 113–23
  housing-related powers 63
  and local institutions 233–4
  and local policy 16
  and the prefecture 180
  and social landlords 176
  and unfairness 234
  v. central control 109
Declaration of the Rights of Man and the Citizen 61
  Article 17 64
decommodification
  of housing 109
  and public sector 21
DEEF 200

deficits, and social landlords 139
delay, abnormal 161–2
Delebarre, Michel 102
delegation, of housing powers 129–30
demand
  for social housing 159
  and sociological shock 193
Denmark 38, 245
départements 63
  and OPHBMs 75
departmental regulation of allocation 128
deprivation 5
deprived areas
  planning/regeneration 124–5
  and stigmatization 101
deprived neighbourhoods, segregation of 28
Deschamps, E. 101, 102
deserving poor, the 245, 250
dignity, human 43
Direction départementale d'action sociale et sanitaire (DDASS) 117
Direction départementale d'équipement *see* DDE
dirigisme 39, 42, 109
disabled people 204
disadvantaged outsiders 256
disadvantaged people
  accessing social housing 10, 26, 33
  and allocation process 7, 9, 17–18, 181
  and commissions 179
  and *communes* 102
  deteriorating status of 205
  European social housing 37, 48–9
  exclusion of 226
  housing of 3–5
  as insiders 201
  legal category 2
  and local working arrangements 134
  and mayors 157
  obligations to 11–12, 162
  and prefectural contingent 198–9
  priority of 247
  and rent 237
  representation of 144
  right to housing 203–4
  and social housing 5
  and social landlords 157
  United Kingdom 252

Index

disadvantage, social housing 46–50
discretionary power 242
discretion/*discrétion* 105, 242–3
discrimination
   and allocations process 221
   of ethnic minorities 118, 217
   Nord 218
   race 253
   and social mix 243
discrimination law, and politics 220–1
distributional effects, insiderness 225
diversity, contracting for 127–34
divorce 193, 194, 208–9, 210, 236
divorce law 209
documentation, importance of 217
Dogge, P.J.C. & Smeets, J.J.A.M. 23, 28
Dolfus, Jean 74
Doling, J. 109
domestic violence 210, 253, 300n.744
Donnison, D. 37
dossier 171, 173
   for State aid 207
dotation urbaine de solidarité 194
Dreyfus, M. 108
droit au logement see DAL
le droit au logement opposable 4
droit opposable 93
droit social 76
dualist system 38–9, 41, 154, 247
Dubedout, H. 213
Dupuis *et al.* 63
duty of financial prudence 144

Eastern Europe, rented property 39
ECHR 3
   Article 1; Protocol 1 44–5
   Article 3 88
   Article 14 281 n.9
   in France 86
   and national constitutional rights 42–6
   support for landlords 46
economic analysis, of organization of local actors 130–4
economic hysteresis 226, 246
economic power, employee-insiders 163
economics explanation, allocation 108
economic theory 23, 54
   insider-outsider theory 30–1

Economist, The 104
ECSR 4, 250–1
   FEANTSA v. *France* 229
   profitability of private landlords 39
   and Slovenia 45–6
ECtHR 250–1
   and landlords 39, 45
   property rights 43
electoral concerns, of mayors 195
Elsinga *et al.* 30
employee-insiders 163
employees, and social housing 16–17
employment
   barriers to entering/exiting 26
   insiderness in 239
enforcement
   and the prefecture 98
   problems 223
England *see also* United Kingdom
   allocations process 105, 106
   and housing crisis 20
   and human dignity 43
   property law 44
   social housing 248
Enlightenment, the 43, 59, 64
entrants 24
   chances of success 199–202
   v. insiders 189
equality 3
   and Conseil constitutionnel 87
   of opportunity 161
   principle of 5, 84, 231–2
equity, in law 58
Erp, S. van 45
Esping-Andersen, G. 21
Esping-Anderson classification 107
Estates General 60–1
ethnic communities 103
ethnicity
   and allocations 219
   information on 104, 211–14
   and social mix 103–5, 164
ethnic minorities *see also* African workers; Algerians; foreigners; immigrants
   children 194, 200
   and CIL 218
   discrimination of 118, 217, 232
   euphemisms for 210, 211

Index

and exclusion 204, 253
integration of 124
and social landlords 49, 191
EU Commission 244, 249
EU Competition Commission 39, 41, 42, 93
EU competition directive 2006 3
EU competition law 243, 250
EU competition policy 57, 108, 247–8, 250
EU policies 247–50, 255
EU regulation 40–2, 54
European Committee of Social Rights *see* ECSR
European Convention on Human Rights *see* ECHR
European Court of Justice 41
European Network for Housing Research (ENHR) 55
European rights, problems with 250–1
European Social Charter (Revised) 1996 *see* RESC
European social housing 2–3, 35–46, 244–51
  diversity/commonality 36–7
  models of 37–8
  national constitutional rights/ECHR/RESC 42–6
  and regulation 39–40
  social housing/rental markets 38–9
eviction
  barriers to 26, 187
  disastrous consequences of 206
  Hauts de Seine 186
  and mayors/prefects 195–6
  procedures 146
  protection from 238
  and stigmatization 190
exclusion 7–8
  allocation process 8, 229–35
  and Besson Act 91
  of disadvantaged people 50, 226
  groups liable to 204–6
  and housing practices 23, 185
  by mayors 169, 170, 194, 195, 196, 234
  by process 233
  and right to housing 114
  social 6, 21–2

exclusionary processes, reviewing 221–6
excuses bâteaux 94

fairness, allocation process 181
families, large 172
family allowances 76
FASILD 194, 212
FEANTSA 250
FEANTSA v. *France* 4, 229, 281n.12
FEANTSA v. *Slovenia* 45, 46, 57, 96, 285n.176
Federation of European Organizations Working with the Homeless 4
feudalism 60, 63
file processing, common 234
Filippi, B. & Tutin, C. 125, 149
filtering down 151
financial difficulties, disastrous consequences of 206–7
financial tensions
  rental markets 30
  right to housing 100
Finland 38
fisheries, collectively managed 131
Flamand, J-P 73
fonction publique 92
Fondation Abbé Pierre 19, 147, 149
Fonds de solidarité logement (FSL) 128, 207
foreigners *see also* African workers; Algerians; ethnic minorities; immigrants
  data on 104, 212
  and urban areas 218
formalism 258
Fourrier, C. 74
foyers 109, 137
free market 39–40, 108
French Revolution 58, 59
  leading up to 60–1
FSL 128, 207
funding
  construction *see* construction: funding
  housing 81, 120
  social landlords 136–7
furnished accommodation, and security of tenure 236

329

Index

Galligan, D.J. 242
Galster, G. 102
garden cities, UK 10, 74
gardiens 220
gatekeepers 187
Geindre report 12, 162
general economic interest 93
general interest 41
General Tax Code 155
geography, and insider-outsider theory 27–8
Germany 36, 38, 43, 44, 76
gerrymandering 52
Ghékière, L. 37
ghéttoisation 100, 102, 217
Glorious Revolution 1688 59
Goetz, E.G. 102
good tenants 192, 235
governance
   local 14–15
   of mayors 119
   and SAHLMs 141
   of social housing 108
   social landlords 137, 143
   state regulated 75
Grand Lyon 168
grands ensembles 80, 81, 100
grants, construction 154–5
Grear, A. 23
great confinement, the 60
Grenevilliers 103
groupthink 29
guarantees
   for construction 64
   loan 118
   non-contributing young people 122, 177
   for outsiders 201
   parental 194
   rent arrears 122, 177

habitations à bon marché see HBM organizations
habitations à loyer modéré see HLM organizations
HALDE 212
Harloe, M. 37
Haussmann, Baron 73
Haussmannization 75
Haut Comité, le 195, 197

Hauts de Seine
   allocation powers 130
   allocations process 166–7
   construction funding 120
   contractualization 128
   eviction 186
   housing stock 127
   mediation commission 96
   refusals in 94
   rent arrears 207
   transfers 193
HBM organizations 76
heirarchy, in France 105
historic-cost rents 153, 237, 249
history, and law 59–60
HLM housing 81, 154
HLM organizations 10–11, 80, 92, 137–43, 151, 288n.268
HMB organizations 10, 67, 74–5, 76
homelessness
   and associations 122–3
   and exclusion 204
   and mayors 119
   and stigmatization 7, 205
   Toulouse 170
home ownership, and dualist system 38
hostels 19, 98
   children in 206
   construction of 204
   occupants of 7, 204, 206
   rescue function of 238–9
Houard, N. 120, 167
household instability 208–9, 239
housing *see also* social housing
   cheap 124
   government intervention 79
   large 219–20
   post-war 16, 80–1
   shortage 28
housing benefit 81, 146
   and rent 144, 147, 237
   and rent arrears 207
   social tenants receiving 148
housing conditions, nineteenth-century 73–4
housing crisis 19–20, 28, 244
housing expenditure, by tenure 156
housing for all model 5, 37, 115, 245–6

Index

housing insecurity 244
housing markets 241, 255
   insider-outsider theory 6–7, 22–33
housing need
   post-war 79
   and social housing 36
housing officers, English 106
housing policy *see also* policies
   and CIL 121–2
   Hauts de Seine 166–7
   and rent 249
   and shared custody of children 208
housing powers, contractual delegation of 129–30
housing problems, and construction 123–4
housing quality standards 154
housing rights, and human dignity 43, 88
housing service 79
Housing Solidarity Fund *see* FSL
housing statistics, France/UK 20
housing stock
   for disadvantaged people 184
   private rental 26
   reduction in 12, 127, 192–3, 239
   and shared custody 208
   shortage of 13, 124
   social 82
housing studies 55
housing the poor model 246
housing workers model 246
human dignity 230
   and housing rights 43, 88
Human Rights Act 1998 92
Hutten-Czapska v. *Poland* 45, 46, 57, 90, 250
hysteresis
   economic 226, 246
   and insiderness 225

Ile-de-France 103, 116, 119
immigrants *see also* African workers; Algerians; ethnic minorities; foreigners
   childrens voting patterns 53
   and housing applications 181
   and mayors 195
   non-EU 217
   and poverty 213
   and social landlords 172
   and social mix 103
   stigmatization of 212–13
immigration 104
impartiality, housing allocations 106
impression-management 241
improper favours, mayors 196–7
incentives
   and behaviour 130
   construction 11, 155, 239
   and contracts 127
   economic 225
   favouring better-off 27
   to form *communautés* 119
   social landlords 9, 26, 30
inclusion 7–8
income
   and PLUS loans 47
   of tenants 12, 48, 49
income ceiling, allocations 249
industrialisation 65
inequality
   and decentralization 234
   prior to French Revolution 60
   regional benefits 128
information, on ethnicity 211–14, 216 *see also* statistics
inheritance rights 209, 299n.735
injustice, perceived 104
insecurity, middle class 244
INSEE 212
insider advantage *see also* insiderness; insiders
   social housing 183–4
   and trade unions 25
insiderness *see also* insider advantage; insiders
   allocation process 29, 158
   and construction 239–40
   and disadvantaged people 133
   distributional effects 225
   and employment 198, 239
   and eviction 81
   housing markets/unemployment 28
   and hysteresis 225
   in social housing 235–41
   spatial 190–1, 226
   for tenancies 26
   and transaction costs 185–7

Index

insider-outsider theory 18–19
  and access 109
  allocation process 33, 158, 180
  applying 184–91
  and choice of tenant 157
  collective bargaining 25–6
  economic theory 30–1
  housing markets 6–7, 22–33
  insider privileges 25–6
  labour markets 6–7
  market effects/social norms 28–30
  and rent 143–5
  social housing 34
  spatial aspects 112, 240–1
  stigmatization/geography 27–8
  transaction costs 23–6, 185–7
insiders 191–9 *see also* insider advantage; insiderness
  of CIL 197–8
  disadvantaged 236
  disadvantaged people as 201
  employee 26, 163
  local 112
  market power of 143
  of mayors 194–6
  of prefects 198–9
  of social landlords 192–4
  and stigmatization 224
  types of 18, 31–3
  v. entrants 189
  young people 220
insider-tenants 113, 236
institutional racism 204, 216–17, 253
institution, term 59
inter-communality 121
International Union of Tenants 46
Ireland 36, 38
iron triangle 19, 57

Jacobins 109
Janis, I.L. 29
Jégouzo-Viénot, L. 139
joint and several liability 68
judges 61, 106, 116
jurisprudence 62, 86, 88, 250

Kemeny, J. 19, 38, 39–40, 107
Kemp, P. 146, 148

labour market effect 240
labour markets 6–7, 23–4, 241
laïcité 104
landlords *see also* social landlords
  as businessmen 107
  not-for-profit status 255
  organizations 77
  support for 46
  unfair competition 39
land prices 151, 152, 155
land reform, Europe 59
La Porta et al. 257–8
large families, stigmatization of 219–20
law
  and allocation process 182
  competition 243, 250
  consumer 107
  contract 67, 68
  development of administrative law 61–3
  discrimination 220–1
  divorce 209
  English 43, 58
  English housing 53–4
  private 287n.216
  private company 138
  of property and tenures 255–6
  public/private 61
  and rights 86–7
  Roman 43–4, 206
  social housing 1, 2, 34
  social welfare 69
  tenancy 27
League against Property Owners 66
Lechevalier, A. 42
légalité 95
Lelévrier, C. 103
le Play, Frédéric 66, 74
Leroy-Beaulieu, Paul 67
level of effort 146, 147, 180
Lévy-Vroelant, C. 224
Lévy-Vroelant, C. & Tutin, C. 48
Lindbeck, A. & Snower, D.J. 24, 25, 26, 27–8, 72, 190, 235, 240, 251
literacy
  and housing applications 172, 181
  and State aid 207

Index

Livret A 80
loan guarantees 118
loans
 for construction 148–51, 156 *see also* construction funding
 and rent 237
 social 207
local authorities, guarantees for construction 64
local councils, democratic 15
local government, and allocation process 13–16
local housing plan 117
local institutions, and decentralization 233–4
Loca-pass scheme 128
logements intermédiares 125
loi Besson *see* Besson Act
Loi contre les exclusions 114, 115
Loi d'orientation pour la ville 91, 102
lois organiques 86
Loucheur Act 1928 76
Lowe, S. 59
low income applicants 176
low rent areas 240
loyer d'équilibre 152
l'Union d'economie sociale pour le logement *see* UESL
L'Union sociale de l'habitat (USH) 11
Lux, M. 23, 154
Lyon
 allocations process 167–9
 communauté urbaine of 16
 construction funding 120–1
 and contractualization 127, 128
 and debt 129, 207
 housing policy 126
 mediation commission 96
 older property 153
 prefectural contingent 97, 116
 race discrimination in 172
 refusals in 94
 and reservations 302n.826
 SIAL 198–9
 stigmatization in 217–18

MacPherson of Cluny 1999 216
maintainance, of spouse/children 209

maintien dans les lieux, le 77
Malpezzi, S. 23
manageable domain 247
marchands de sommeil 228, 240
market effects, insider-outsider theory 28–30
market-individualists 107
markets
 housing/labour 241
 and social housing 21
 unitary 38
Marseilles judgement 176
Mason, D. 216
Massin *et al.* 31, 95
matrimonial régime 209
matrimonial special contracts, community of interest 69
mayors
 and allocation process 15, 32, 112, 115, 119, 175
 Czechoslovakia 23
 and disadvantaged people 157
 exclusionary housing practices 169, 170, 194, 195, 196, 234
 funding of 252
 improper favours 196–7
 insiders 194–6
 nimbyism 226, 240
 role of 117–18
 and social landlords 143
 Sweden 38
mediation commission 95–6, 97–8
mentally ill people 204
middle class insecurity 244
middle class social housing 248
MIILOS 139, 174, 240, 243, 251
Minister for Reconstruction and Urban Planning 80
mobility, lack of 225
Morlet, O. 119
mortgage evictions 207
mortgage funding, private 80
motivation
 of actors 131
 of landlords 21, 52, 234
 political/economic 33
mouvement social 104
Mulhouse 74

333

Index

municipal housing services 79
mutations 192–3, 194

Napoleon I 61, 64
Napoleon III 73, 74
natalist family policies 220
National Agency for the Improvement of Housing *see* ANAH
National Front 53
national tenants union 77
national welfare funds 17
need
   cumulative 162
   extent of 242
   lack of information on 243
   prioritization of 247
negotiating power, of tenants 77 *see also* bargaining
Nelken, D. 233, 241
Netherlands 36, 37, 38, 39, 41–2, 248, 249
Neuilly-sur-Seine 127
Nicolo 86
nimbyism 112, 118, 141, 225, 226, 240, 241
non-contributory benefits 145
non-profit rental housing 189
Nord
   allocations process 169–71
   common file processing 234
   contractualization 128
   mediation commission 96
   and northern England 159
   prefectural contingent 166
   refusals in 94
   stigmatization/discrimination 218
   and subscribers 122
   transport links 124–5
   voting patterns 53
Nord-pas-de-Calais 53, 193
norms
   hierarchy of 85–6
   social 163
Norway 38
not-for-profit status, landlords 255

obligations alimentaires 69
Observateur de l'immobilier, L' 193

observatory of housing demand 159
   Hauts de Seine 167
Office public d'aménagement concerté *see* OPACs
Office public de l'habitat (OPH) 141
Office public d'HBM (OPHBM) 10, 75
Office public d'HLM *see* OPHLMs
older property, and poor people 153
opacity
   of allocation process 21, 42, 241–2
   and insiders 245
OPACs 11, 52, 75, 118, 139, 140, 142
OPH 141
OPHBMs 10, 75
OPHLMs 11, 118, 139, 140, 142, 219
opportunism 133, 134
opposable right
   and Besson Act 91
   difficulty in implementing 222–4
   and disadvantaged people 230
   effectiveness of 256
   and imposition of tenants 95
   and priority applicants 161
   procedure for 96–8
   and public law 92, 93
   right to sue 203
   Sarkozy government 115
opposition
   landlords/tenants 250
   and social housing 108–10
Ordo-liberal movement 38, 39, 154
organismes de l'habitat social 11
out-of-town estates 246
outsiders
   disadvantage of 33, 239
   and prefecture 222
   stigmatization of 205, 254
   who are they? 224
overcrowding 200, 218
owner occupancy 13
ownership
   rights, social housing 32
   social function of 70–1

PALULOS 155
parental guarantees 194
Pareto efficiency 108

Index

Paris
  and *départements* 128
  ghéttoisation 217
  housing market 31
  nineteenth century 73
  Paris Commune 65
  riots 104
  social housing 36
passive contractual solidary responsibility 68
pauperization, social tenants 82
pay, of employees and CIL 246
PDLPD 117, 128, 129
Pébereau, M. 40
Peillon, P. 101
Phalansterie, the 74
Pierre, Abbé 80
PLA-1 loans 149, 154
Plan Borloo, le 115, 155
Plan départemental pour le logement de personnes défavorisées *see* PDLPD
planning
  consent 118, 119
  delegation of powers 168
  deprived areas 124–5
  and housing shortages 123
  local effects of 125–7
  and right to housing 91
PLH 117
PLS loans 149, 151
PLUS loans 47, 149, 151, 154, 170, 198
points system 162
Poland 39, 45
police administrative, la 119
policies
  EU 247–50, 255
  and innovation 234
  national 220, 254
policy *see also* housing policy
  failure 254
  of renovation 159
  and social housing 34
  and social mix 102
political right 109
politics
  dirigiste 109
  and discrimination law 220–1

local/national 115
  and money 234–5
  problems with national 114–15
politique de la ville 153
polygamous families 116, 218
poor people
  and commissions 180
  as 'dangerous class' 65
  housing of 12, 52
  and older property 153
  the very poor 228
population
  manipulation, and social mix 201
  post-war 79
Porter, Shirley 196
post-war
  social provision 19, 78–81
  tenants rights 44
pouvoir d'appréciation 106
poverty
  assessing 48
  for immigrants 213
  prior to French Revolution 60
  regional variation 49–50
power
  administrative 63
  economic 163
  state 64–5
power of appreciation 106
power relations
  France 19
  rural 64
prefects/prefecture
  and allocation process 16, 32
  and disadvantaged people 251
  and eviction 186
  insiders of 198–9
  local 14–15
  and outsiders 222
  prefects insiders 198–9
  role of 98, 115–17
  weakening power of 180
prefectural contingent 15
  delegation of 167
  Lyon 116
  Nord 166, 169

335

Index

prefectural contingent *(Continued)*
   and *opposable* right 97
   prefects insiders 198–9
prefectural housing office
   Hauts de Seine 167
   Rhône-Alpes 168
principles affecting social housing 90
principles of law 91
priority groups 161
Priority Urban Development Zones 81
privacy, and housing applications 172
private company law 138
private-contractual solidarity 231
private law 287n.216
   community of interest 69
private law disputes 90
private-law judges 106
private-law solidarity 230
private tenant cooperatives, Scandinavia 36
profit and loss, HLM organizations 138–9
profit, and tenants/workers 143
profits, landlord 26
Programme local de l'habitat (PLH) 117
property
   absolute approach to 64
   egoist concept of 209
   law England 44
   older 153
   ownership 20, 64, 66
   rights *see* property rights
   social basis of 71
   and solidarity 70–1
property rights
   common law 258
   England 44
   Europe 43
   France 43
   national 43
   and property owners 20
   and social rights 63–72
protest, collective 107
Proudhon, P.J. 66, 287n.229
public function 92
public health 67
public law
   family obligations 69
   levels of centrality 93
   and welfare 71–2

public loans 149
public morality, and contracts 78
public organizations, commissions 179
public-private divide 21
public/private law, and social landlords 92
public service 92
public social landlord companies 13

quality, and social homes 154
quasi-rents 132, 133, 134
queue-jumping 38
queue, the 245
Quillot Act 77, 87

race discrimination 105, 172, 232, 253
racial segregation 23
racism, institutional 204, 216–17, 253
Radigon, J-L. & Horvath, S. 89
reconstituted families 194
reconstruction, and cheap housing 126
redistributive question 3
re-education of tenants 126
refinancing 209
reform 251–3, 256
refusal to allocate 93–5
regeneration
   deprived areas 124–5
   and tenant turnover 126
regional development planning 80
regional institutions
   and allocations 166–71
   and regulation 134–5
region, role of 121
réglement départemental d'attribution 128
regulation 54, 134, 138–9, 255
rehabilitation
   of stigmatized outsiders 205
   of those in difficulty 206
Reinprecht et al. 36, 37
religion, statistics on 212
remedy 86
Renard, V. 194
renovation, policy of 159
rent
   and aids to the person 145–8
   arrears 122, 207
   average social 152
   freeze 77

Index

historic-cost rents 153
and housing benefits 144
and housing policy 249
increases for low income families 147
and insider-outsider theory 143–5, 237
setting 151–4
sharing of economic rents 185
social 5
and social landlords 143
and social mix 243
strikes 77, 109, 144
and tax relief 144
urban/rural 152
varying 156
rental markets 7
and capital expenditure 239
financial tensions 30
insider-outsider theory 22–3, 24
renting, private 12–13
representatives, elected tenant 187
requisition of homes 79
RER line A 124
RESC 3, 40, 46, 85
Article 1 45
Article 31 4, 45
reservation contracts 231
reservations 132, 151, 165, 168, 170, 173
and CIL 169
Responsabilité solidaire 68
revised European Social Charter *see* RESC
revolution, and opposition 65–7
rights *see also* individual rights
1789 Declaration 61
of children 193
conflicting 230
and law 86–7
local 33
national constitutional rights 42–6
social/economic 3, 63–72
and social/private tenants 187
of tenants 78, 187
to the town 91
right to housing 2, 4, 72, 87–91
actors' view of 99–100
Besson Act 110
delayed allocation 95–6
disadvantaged people 10, 14, 84, 203–4
effectiveness of 33

FEANTSA v. *Slovenia* 45
hierarchy of norms/treaties 85–6
legal effects of 85–98
opposable right 96–8
political support for 114–15
problems caused by 232
refusal to allocate 93–5
regulation of rights by courts 91–3
rights and laws 86–7
and right to property 89, 90
and social exclusion 114
and social mix 98–9, 161, 164
vague nature of 229–30, 254
right to insurrection 65
right to property 5, 64, 89, 90, 230
right to sue 4, 91
right to the town 91
right to work 45
riots
and ethnic densities 214
Paris 53, 104
and Sarkozy government 144
social housing estates 250
United Kingdom 216
and young people 211, 232
risk
and allocation process 31
and social landlords 192, 239
RMI 50, 145, 146, 172
Roman law 206
Rousseau, Jean Jacques 64
Rueda, D. 33
rural areas
and exclusion 195, 218
nimbyism 226

SAHLMs 11
and CIL 122, 142, 197
commissions 166, 179
construction by 82
governance of 235
housing poor people 52
operation of 140
preferred tenants 51
private 141–3
and profit 138
size of 137
sanctions, social landlords 30

337

Index

Sarkozy, Nicolas 53, 104, 115, 120, 127, 144
Scandinavia 36, 38
Schlager, E. & Ostrom, E. 131
SCOT 124
Second Empire 104
Section d'hygiène urbaine et rurale du Musée social 74
security of tenure 26, 77, 78, 91, 185–6, 236
segregation
　removing 102
　urban 100, 104
Seine-Saint-Denis 53, 217
service charges 147
Service inter-administratif du logement *see* SIAL
service public 92, 108
services of general economic interest (SGEI) 41
services of general interest (SGI) 41, 284n.137
Shapiro, A.-L. 67
shared custody of children 193, 208, 209, 253
shared ownership 248
shelters 168
SIAL 168, 198–9
sickness insurance 76
Siegfried Act 1894 74
Siegfried, Jules 74
Simon, P. & Kirszbaum, T. 212
single parents 49, 191, 199–200, 253
　and divorce 209
Slovenia 39
social cohesion, and social mix 102, 103
social contract, and state power 64–5
social democratic governments 33
social distributional problems, allocation 224–6
social exclusion *see* exclusion
social housing *see also* housing
　and allocation process 17–18, 129–30
　availability of 50
　context 72–82
　corporatism/consumerism 107–8
　disadvantage 46–50

distribution of 13, 14
England/France 54
Europe 2–3, 35–46, 244–51
French law 1
heirarchy of principles affecting 90
history 5–6
insiderness in 235–41
and insider-ousider theory 19
and law/policy 34
and opposition/transaction costs 108–10
organizations 11
ownership/allocation rights 32
poorer people in 149–50
and poverty 48
representation 188
rules 4
standard agreements 151
state intervention in 75
stock *see* housing stock
structure of households occupying 200
socialism, small-scale 66, 109
le Socialiste 66
socialists 66
social landlords
　allocation commission 178
　and allocation process 5, 32, 176
　background 72–3
　and competition 39, 41
　concern for tenants 186, 240
　and decentralization 176
　and disadvantaged people 150, 157
　European model 3
　funding 10, 136, 136–7, 252
　incentives/sanctions 9, 26, 30
　insiders of 192–4
　and less literate/immigrants 172
　loans to 79–80
　and mayors 143
　motivation of 21
　Nord 170
　organization of 11, 22, 75
　origins of 73–6
　and politics 234
　and population management 165–6
　and prefects 116
　public 138–9, 139–41
　and public/private law 92

Index

and rent 143
and risk 192, 239
size of 235, 254
social mission 11–13
transaction costs of 236
types of 137–8
and unemployment 241
social loans 207
social mission, social landlords 11–13
social mix 100–3
  actors' application of 163–4
  and allocation 243
  and *communautarisme* 214–16
  definitions of 181
  and discrimination 243
  and ethnicity 103–5
  and insiders 256
  local effects of 125–7
  policies 5, 53, 189
  and population manipulation 201
  problems caused by 232, 246
  and rent 243
  and right to housing 98–9, 161, 164
  and stable families 199–201
social movements 25, 76–8
social norms 28–30, 163, 190
social objectives, and corporatism 107
social obligation 71
social organizations, beginnings of 65
social reports, and *mutations* 194
social rights 3, 63–72
social security system 69, 78–81, 145
social services of general interest (SSGI) 41
social tenants
  collective bargaining power 202
  income of 48
social urgency 191
social welfare law 69
social workers 117, 174, 201, 205
Société française des HBM *see* HBM organizations
Sociétés anonyme d'HLM (SAHLMs) *see* SAHLMs
Sociétés d'habitations à bon marché 10
Sociétés d'HBM *see* HBM organizations
Society for Social Economy 66

sociological shock, housing demand 193
solidarism 67–8
solidarity
  advantages/disadvantages of 88
  duty of 90
  English understanding of 72
  historical context 68–70
  juridification of 70
  and right to housing 230–1
  role of 91
  and social basis of property 70–1
  and social mix 100
  and social rights 71
  as a value 231
  and welfare system 254
solidary obligations 68, 69–70
solvency, and landlords/tenants 192
SOS-Racisme 213
Spain 36, 44
spatial effects, insider-outsider theory 240–1
spatial insiderness 226, 235–6
spatial rented market effect 240
special housing subsidy 108
special planning zones 81
squatting 116, 204, 206
SRU Act 125
stable families, and social mix 199–201
standard agreements, social housing 151
State aid 207
state funding, post war construction 80
state power, and social contract 64–5
State, the
  and evictions 238
  and social housing 75, 114
statistics *see also* information
  on ethnicity 104
  housing 20
  inadequate 243
  suspicion of 211–12
statute of 16-24 August 1790 61
statute of 1 September 1948 77
statute of 6 August 1953 80
Statute of 1986 (see Glossary) 77
Statute of 1989 (see Glossary) 26, 77
  Article 1 89

339

Index

statute n° 91-662 of 13 July of 1991, Article 1 102
statutory priority 201–2
Steiner, E. 101
Stephens *et al.* 237
stigmatization
  of children/young people 220
  and debt 206–7, 238
  and deprived areas 101
  and dualist system 38
  of ethnic minorities 232
  and eviction 206, 238
  and *grands ensembles* 81
  the homeless/hostel dwellers 7
  of immigrants 212–13
  and insider-outsider theory 6, 27–8
  and insiders 224
  local variations/different actors 217–19
  and mortgage evictions 207
  Nord 218
  of outsiders 205, 254
  people in housing difficulty 205
  in poorer housing 215
  and social norms 190
stratified housing market 240
subi (re compulsory solidarity) 69
subsidies
  for the disadvantaged 248
  for housing 249
  and housing allocation 133
  to landlords 26, 39, 40
  social housing 41
  special housing 108
  supply-side 148
supervision of legality 115
Sweden 36, 38, 39, 41
Switzerland 38

Taga Fosso 94, 95
tax deductions 286n.186
tax disincentives 239
tax incentives, social landlords 155–6
taxonomy 54
tax relief 144, 249
tenancies, consumer protection 107
tenancy law 27
tenancy terms, and collective action 77
tenant-insiders, bargaining power of 143–4
tenant representation 113, 187, 188
tenants
  better-off 189
  collective rights 107
  as consumers 107, 284n.131
  French social 47–9
  good 192, 235
  lack of mobility 225
  local organizations 187
  negotiating power of 77
  re-education of 126
  rights of 78, 187
  security/insecurity 27
  support for 46
  unions 188
  welfare of 250
tenant turnover, and regeneration 126
Terré *et al.* 68, 69
le testing 213
TFEU 86, 250, 284n.135
  Article 151 40
third sector 21
time-limited local contracts 114
Toulouse 170
Touvenin, J.-M 42, 93
tower blocks 81
trade unions 25, 76, 77, 137 *see also* unions
transaction costs
  and allocation process 132, 236
  of eviction 186
  and insiderness 185–7, 235
  insider-outsider theory 23–5, 29, 30
  local actors 130–1
  and rent/renting 143, 236
  and social housing 109–10
transfers 193
transparency
  allocations process 175, 177–8, 181
  Altmark judgement 42
  and contractualization 197
  and housing market 241–4
transport links, deprived areas 124–5, 239
treaties, hierarchy of 85–6

Index

Treaty of Lisbon 2007 40
  2010 Protocol 41
Treaty on the European Union (TEU)
  Article 16 41
  Article 136 40
Treaty on the Functioning of the European Union *see* TFEU
tri en amont, le 165
Turpin, D. 108
tutelle 115

UESL 17, 122, 165
Uhry, M. 123
un pourcent logement 16–17, 80
unemployment
  benefit 145
  disastrous consequences of 241
  and immigrants 212
  and stigmatization 27–8
Union nationale des propriétaires immobiliers 77
union, national tenants 77
unions 188, 235, 236 *see also* trade unions
unitary concept, property 65–6
unitary markets 38, 39, 249, 255
unitary rental systems 38, 154
United Kingdom *see also* England
  disadvantaged people 252
  dualist system 38
  housing poor people 48–9
  information on ethnicity 216
  post war construction 76
  social housing 37
  social mix 102
United States
  availability of credit 207
  public housing 102
Universal Declaration of Human Rights (1948) 70
  Article 25 3
universal housing allocation 37, 38
urban areas, and foreigners 218
urban design and planning 10

urban development, and social landlords 75
urban segregation 100, 104

vacancy rates 159
Val-de-Marne 145–6
valeur constitutionnel, de 88
very disadvantaged people 201
very social housing 48, 50, 149
Vienna 36
violence, by housing applicants 177
voluntary bodies 76
voluntary work, and associations 76, 122
voting patterns, poor people 53

waiting lists 38, 225, 242
welfare
  and consumers 108
  and public law 71–2
welfare state
  legal structures 25–6
  start of 76
welfare system, and solidarity 254
Whittaker, S. 106
widows, and inheritance rights 209, 299n.735
Williamson, O.E. 23, 132
winter evictions 26, 238
women, and property ownership 209
workers' housing 74
workers, housing of 11, 36, 38, 122, 151, 195, 197, 248
working-class housing, construction of 80
World War II, housing problems 19

young people
  housing difficulties of 200–1
  and riots 211
  stigmatization of 220

ZUP 81
ZUS (*zones urbaines sensibles*) 81, 103, 125, 150